Book release

The federal Bureau of Investigation before Hoover

Volume I:
The fBI and Mexican Revolutionists, 1908-1914

by

Heribert von Feilitzsch and Charles H. Harris III

Copyright ©2023 by Heribert von Feilitzsch and Charles H. Harris III

All rights reserved. No part of this book may be reproduced or transmitted in any form or by any means, electronic or mechanical, including photography, recording, or by any other information storage and retrieval system, without permission in writing from the author.

First published in the United States of America in 2023 by Henselstone Verlag LLC

First Edition

Every effort has been made to locate and contact all holders of copyright to material reproduced in this book. For information about permission to reproduce selections from this book, contact info@henselstoneverlag.com or send mail to Henselstone Verlag, P.O. Box 201, Amissville, VA 20106

Library of Congress Control Number: 2023946047

Keyword Data

Harris, Charles Houston, 1937-
von Feilitzsch, Heribert, 1965-

The federal Bureau of Investigation before Hoover: Volume I: The fBI and Mexican Revolutionists, 1908-1914 / Heribert von Feilitzsch, Charles Houston Harris
p. cm
Includes biographical references and index.

ISBN 978-1-7349324-4-7 (hardcover) | 978-1-7349324-5-4 (paperback) | 978-1-7349324-6-1 (e-book)

1. United States – History – Law Enforcement
2. United States – History – 20th Century
3. United States – History – Bureau of Investigation
4. United States – History – Foreign Policy - Mexico
5. Mexico – History – Revolution, 1910-1920 – Diplomatic History
6. United States – Foreign Relations – Mexico
7. Mexico – Foreign Relations – United States
8. United States - Intelligence History – 20th Century
9. Mexico – History – Revolution, 1910-1920 – Diplomatic History
10. Mexico – Foreign Relations – United States
11. Mexico – Intelligence History – 20th Century
12. Germany – Intelligence History – 20th Century
I. von Feilitzsch, Heribert; Harris, Charles Houston. Title.

www.fbibeforehoover.com
www.fbihistoryblog.com

Printed in the United States of America

"At present the members of the staff of the department are simply watching the border. We have no special instructions save to prevent infractions of the neutrality laws. The orders we are following strictly."

Agent in Charge Hy A. Thompson to a reporter of the *Bisbee Daily Review*, March 18, 1911

PRAISE FOR

The authors' meticulous research fills in longstanding gaps in our understanding of the history of counter-intelligence in this critical period. It's a valuable complement to their earlier works and a must-read for anyone interested in the intelligence war during the Mexican Revolution.

Mark E. Benbow,
Marymount University

Deftly researched and written, The fBI and Mexican Revolutionists, 1908-1914 digs into national and military archives by way of cross-disciplinary approaches and through a web of political conflicts in foreign lands, both distant and near. A major achievement in the study of U.S. international intelligence and national security, told lucidly, with keen insight, and in full command of its manifold sources.

Roberto Cantú,
California State University, Los Angeles

Instant Classic is the only description for The FBI and the Mexican Revolutionists, 1908-1914. Heribert von Feilitzsch and Charles H. Harris III have written this first volume of a multi-book series that provides analysis of the only aspect of the Revolution that has never been investigated. In every sense of classic, the authors have done extensive, thorough research that others have found impossible in the FBI archives, and collections, such as military intelligence, in several countries; they have written with clarity and sophistication about the issues of US-revolutionary relations, outlined foreign, e.g. German, intrigue along the border, and given interpretative depth to historical accounts of the revolution. Ray Sadler, before his untimely death, had searched out materials for decades on this topic, so the book is a marvelous salute to him. As for classroom professors and textbook authors of the Mexican revolution this book must be incorporated in their narrative of the world's first social revolution.

William H. Beezley,
University of Arizona

To Louis R. Sadler

Table of Contents

List of Figures iii

Acknowledgments v

Preface vii

Chapter 1: Beginnings 1

Chapter 2: Challenge To The Dictator 13

Chapter 3: A Foreign Policy U-Turn 37

Chapter 4: Thwarted Ambition 71

Chapter 5: Aftermath 91

Chapter 6: Youthful Leadership 101

Chapter 7: Unprecedented Intelligence Cooperation 141

Chapter 8: Chasing Schooners 171

Chapter 9: Federals vs Locals on The Border 199

Chapter 10: California Intrigues 237

Chapter 11: Clash of The Titans 295

Conclusion 347

Endnotes 351

Bibliography 393

Index 405

List of Figures

Figure 1 George W. Wickersham viii

Figure 2 Charles Joseph Bonaparte 2

Figure 3 Stanley Wellington Finch 3

Figure 4 Harry John Jentzer 5

Figure 5 Charles Wyman Morse 7

Figure 6 General Porfirio Díaz 13

Figure 7 Ricardo Flores Magón (left) and his brother Enrique 15

Figure 8 Librado Rivera and Enrique Flores Magón 16

Figure 9 Luther T. Ellsworth 20

Figure 10 Jay Herbert Cole 24

Figure 11 Samuel L. Geck 26

Figure 12 John W. Vann 27

Figure 13 Guy Hamilton Scull 28

Figure 14 Marshall Eberstein 29

Figure 15 Francisco I. Madero 37

Figure 16 Porfirio Díaz Mori 38

Figure 17 Francisco I. Madero 39

Figure 18 Manuel A. Esteva 40

Figure 19 José Ives Limantour 41

Figure 20 The Hotel Astor 42

Figure 21 Sherburne Gillette Hopkins 44

Figure 22 C. F. Z. Caracristi 54

Figure 23 General Bernardo Reyes 68

Figure 24 Francisco A. Chapa 69
Figure 25 Bernardo Reyes.. 71
Figure 26 Oscar B. Colquitt 75
Figure 27 Waller T. Burns.. 92
Figure 28 A. Bruce Bielaski 102
Figure 29 Emilio Vázquez Gómez... 105
Figure 30 Fred Hill Lancaster 160
Figure 31 William Offley.. 161
Figure 32 Harry Berliner in Mexico City 172
Figure 33 Venustiano Carranza 175
Figure 34 Keystone View Company.. 176
Figure 35 Sonora, Yaqui Indians 177
Figure 36 Forrest Currier Pendleton 195
Figure 37 John Killian Wren 221
Figure 38 Colonel Emilio Kosterlitzky 224
Figure 39 Baltazar Avilés... 238
Figure 40 Colonel Esteban Cantú Jiménez....................................... 239
Figure 41 Stephen Lee Pinckney.. 307
Figure 42 Harry Berliner... 338
Figure 43 Alexander Bruce Bielaski 347

Acknowledgments

The idea for this book started many years ago when Charles Harris and Louis Sadler received and analyzed the microfilm reels containing the Case Files of the Bureau of Investigation, 1908-1922, "Old Mexican Files" from the National Archives. Sadly, before the first word could be committed to paper, Louis Sadler, best friend and 50-year research and writing partner of Charles Harris, passed away. Heribert von Feilitzsch and Charles Harris continued the project. The book, The FBI and Mexican Revolutionists, took shape over a period of two years, and expanded into a four-volume study about the FBI before J. Edgar Hoover. This momentous task did not come to fruition in a vacuum. First and foremost, Betty Harris deserves heartfelt thanks for hosting the writing team in her living room, sunroom, and kitchen, navigating ever-increasing piles of papers and books. Betty also coached and patiently assisted in virtual meetings twice-a-week, which are still on-going. Berkley von Feilitzsch supported and joined in cross-country drives and several research trips within the US and Great Britain, including uprooting to New Mexico for a few months to give the writing team a mighty, creative push.

Several scholars, researchers, and descendants of federal agents have supported our insatiable thirst for details and information. We would like to give special thanks to John Fox, the historian of the FBI, who forwarded to us valuable files and information. To a large measure, John helped us bring A. Bruce Bielaski to life in our story. Friedrich Schuler supported our efforts with sharing cases from the FBI's "Old German Files," and other valuable information. Thank you both! John Harris, Mark Benbow and Roberto Cantú read the manuscript early on and provided valuable insights. Kristin Rounds not only provided us with an important diary of her grandfather, Special Agent Harry Berliner, but she also recounted family stories and important personal details. One of the stories made both of us laugh so hard that we had tears streaming down our cheeks. Thank you for everything, especially adding to the fun in this project.

We also want to thank the archivists in the US National Archives in Maryland and St. Louis for their dedication and assistance, especially in the face of challenging COVID-19 restrictions. The friendly staff in the British National Archives helped us search for several needles in massive haystacks. Thank you!

Lastly, we would like to thank Rosa DeBerry King for her patience and challenging questions. Rosa edited this manuscript and prepared the publishable document you hold in your hands (or on your e-reader) today.

Preface

THE FBI IS ARGUABLY THE MOST famous law enforcement organization in the world, ranking ahead of Scotland Yard, the Royal Canadian Mounted Police, and the Texas Rangers. The prevailing view is that the federal Bureau of Investigation was of little account prior to J. Edgar Hoover becoming Director in 1924. A prime example is Athan G. Theoharis with Tony G. Poveda, Susan Rosenfeld and Richard Gid Powers, *The FBI: A Comprehensive Reference Guide from J. Edgar Hoover to the X-Files*.[1] This view is also found in more recent works, such as Rhodri Jeffreys-Jones, *The FBI: A History*[2], 61; and Garrett M. Graff, *Watergate: A New History*, 43.[3]

Hoover deliberately downplayed the pre-Hoover history of the FBI. Writing the Introduction to *The Story of the FBI: The Official Picture History of the Federal Bureau of Investigation* in 1947, Hoover recounted the Bureau's inception in 1908 and touched upon the agency's enforcement of the Mann Act and the neutrality laws.[4] While he mentioned the efforts of the Bureau during the neutrality years of World War I in a single paragraph, Hoover devoted more space to the Bureau's activities in World War I and its raids on radicals in the immediate postwar years, stressing that "I had no responsibility for them."[5] This publication includes charts tracing the growth of the FBI — the charts begin in 1924, when Hoover became Director.

Hoover remained as Director for 48 years until his death in 1972.[6] He was a master of public relations, drawing a stark picture of how terrible conditions were until he took over. Using techniques such as commissioning the official history of the FBI, Don Whitehead, *The FBI Story: A Report to the People*, Hoover adroitly built the image of the Bureau as an organization composed of highly trained professionals who were unswervingly committed to enforcing the law.[7] In reality, as a law enforcement arm of the Executive, the FBI, by its very nature, has always operated within a political framework.⁸ The timing, sources, and subjects of investigations have frequently led to political controversies to this day.⁹

Because of the Hoover emphasis, the preceding era 1908-1924 has been largely overlooked by historians. To date, no comprehensive history of the FBI before Hoover exists. Nevertheless, this is a significant part of FBI history. The origins of the FBI date back to July 26, 1908, when Attorney General Charles J. Bonaparte created an investigative and law enforcement arm in the Department of Justice. Attorney General George

Figure 1 George W. Wickersham. Courtesy Library of Congress Prints and Photographs Division.

W. Wickersham officially named the new agency the federal Bureau of Investigation, the BI, in 1909. It was not until July 1, 1935, that the BI received the capital "F" in its name, the Federal Bureau of Investigation, the FBI. The Hoover myth has been so ingrained in the Bureau's historiography that one reads things such as, "No one remembers the force's first chief, Stanley W. Finch, or his successor, A. Bruce Bielaski, who had worked for him. Until J. Edgar Hoover became director in 1924, the Bureau was faceless."¹⁰ As we shall see, Finch, and especially Bielaski, merit a much more prominent place in the history of the FBI.

The nascent Bureau devoted much of its energies to matters such as enforcing the Mann Act against white slavery and combatting other varieties of white-collar and interstate crime. The organization did reach its low point in the early 1920s, before Hoover's time, but during the preceding decade some of its enduring features and characteristics developed. Prominent among these was the emergence of the Bureau as a national law enforcement agency oriented around investigative techniques, intelligence gathering, and tradecraft as core doctrines.

Historian Raymond J. Batvinis in his book, *The Origins of FBI Counterintelligence*, stated that the FBI's counterintelligence capability developed "in the critical years before the Second World War."[11] However, counterintelligence became a critical part of the BI's mission much earlier. Historian Ronald Kessler in *The Bureau: The Secret History of the FBI* postulated that when the United States entered World War I on the side of the Allies in 1917, "Overnight, the Bureau had been transformed from an agency that merely investigated violations of criminal law to one that investigated spying and was responsible for the internal security of the country."[12] There was nothing "overnight" about it; from its inception, the Bureau worked on neutrality law enforcement investigations against Mexican revolutionists. This important but neglected aspect of the Bureau's activities involved enforcing the neutrality laws in the Federal Penal Code: Section 10 prohibited anyone being hired or retained or entering or enlisting himself in the service of any foreign prince, state, colony, district or people; and, Section 13 prohibited any military expedition against the territory or dominion of any foreign prince or state or of any colony, district, or people with whom the United States was at peace.[13] While enforcing the law, mainly concerning revolutions in Mexico, the BI developed investigative techniques that would subsequently provide the agency with a counterintelligence capability.

Revolutionary activities along the southern border continued to parallel and intersect with the challenges the US faced during the Neutrality Period of World War I (1914-1917), especially starting in 1915 as a result of German activities: counterintelligence, espionage, and sabotage. By the time the US entered the war, the Bureau was this country's premier intelligence agency. The Bureau was not merely enforcing the laws of the United States, but was now heavily engaged in counterintelligence.

The United States helped shape the Mexican Revolution (1910-1920) by extending or withholding diplomatic recognition of a Mexican regime. No Mexican government could feel secure unless it had been recognized by the United States; otherwise the United States had the option of supporting that regime's enemies. Recognition also dictated the enforcement of the neutrality laws. By the selective enforcement of these laws, the Bureau was implementing United States foreign policy. The State Department decides who is, or is not, a "friendly" foreign government. Hence, how the Bureau enforced the laws regarding the Mexican Revolution was fundamentally impacted by changes in US foreign policy. Among other things, the agency had to adjust to the sporadic arms embargoes the US placed on shipments to Mexico, and on two occasions to American military intervention in Mexico. Besides dealing with various Mexican factions struggling for power, the Bureau also dealt with the activities in the United States of reputable businesses and businessmen whose endeavors had a profound impact on the course of the Mexican Revolution. As if all this were not enough, the BI had to deal with agents of foreign powers. In short, the fledgling Bureau of Investigation faced a steep learning curve, and was navigating in stormy and uncharted waters.

Yet, remarkably enough, under the leadership of A. Bruce Bielaski, by 1917 the Bureau of Investigation had become the pre-eminent intelligence agency of the United States government. World War I saw close cooperation between the Military Intelligence Division, the Bureau, and the State Department to maximize counterintelligence capabilities for the war effort. Bielaski resigned once the war ended, in February 1919, and left the Bureau in the hands of less capable leaders. In the early 20s, the agency lacked a clear mission and succumbed to corruption and mismanagement until 1924 when J. Edgar Hoover established his 48-year reign as Director.

The current volume, *The FBI and Mexican Revolutionists*, addresses the newly created Bureau of Investigation's response to the iterations of the Mexican Revolution and their ramifications. Tasked with enforcing the neutrality laws of the United States, the Bureau arguably shaped its intelligence and counterintelligence capabilities with the Mexican Revolution. The Bureau faced considerable challenges. It had to establish its own bureaucratic turf in Washington. The US Secret Service was heretofore the government's premier investigative agency. The historiography touts the competitive and resentful nature of the two agencies, but after the initial inclusion of Secret Service field agents into the Bureau, the two agencies' missions barely intersected. The BI's mission concentrated on enforcing the Mann Act and the Neutrality Laws, while the Secret Service protected the president and pursued counterfeiting investigations. Yet, precisely because the BI was a fledgling agency, both the press and the general public tended to refer to its operatives as "secret service" agents, a description a good number of historians accepted at face value as referring to the US Secret Service.

Information was a valuable commodity which was bought and sold, with the same reports often conveyed to several interested parties. As with other law enforcement agencies, the BI relied heavily on Human Intelligence (HUMINT), often from confidential informants, the difference being that most of these informants were Mexicans, and initially the Bureau had very few agents who could speak Spanish or had any border experience. Special agents assigned from the East sometimes experienced culture shock. The lack of linguistic capability was particularly crippling; most agents had to rely on interpreters, who were of varying accuracy and veracity. Moreover, whereas one hears the term "the fog of war," in this case it was "the fog of rumor;" of trying to sift facts from the cloud of rumors that characterized every facet of the Mexican Revolution—to say nothing of the misinformation, disinformation, and flat-out lies with which Bureau agents had to contend.

Mexican factions were characterized by *personalismo*—allegiance to a leader—e. g. *magonistas* (Ricardo Flores Magón), *maderistas* (Francisco I. Madero), *orozquistas* (Pascual Orozco), *felicistas* (Félix Díaz), *huertistas* (Victoriano Huerta), *carrancistas* (Venustiano Carranza), *villistas* (Francisco Villa), *zapatistas* (Emiliano Zapata), and so on. However, factional loyalty was fragile, and people frequently changed sides depending on who was currently winning. Moreover, with the rank and file "the great trouble was that if the soldiers who get $2/day were offered $3/day by any other faction they would follow the man who had the money."[14] Not only did many Mexicans change their factional loyalty, but changes in United States foreign policy meant that today's allies were the subject of tomorrow's investigations, and vice versa. And in this connection, the Bureau had neither processes nor resources to vet informants.

What hampered a number of important investigations was that the Bureau lacked the capability to translate confiscated documents and letters in a timely manner. Further complicating matters were Mexican revolutionary movements merging into one another, and adherents of a faction being anxious to provide the Bureau with detrimental information about their enemies. In its dealings with Mexican factions, Bureau agents had to guard against being manipulated by one faction against another, and this problem also existed with regard to local political factions along the United States border. Then, there was the matter of public opinion and resentment against federal officials meddling in local affairs. Time after time, Bureau agents would gather evidence for a seemingly ironclad prosecution, only to have a jury acquit the defendants.

A few notes on sources and citations seem in order.[15] The period 1908 to 1914 primarily focuses on the Bureau of Investigation's files on the Mexican Revolution: agents' reports, correspondence, and case files declassified in 1977. Agents' reports have two dates: for the period covered, and for the date the report was submitted. We cite the second date. A problem in BI reports was that Mexican names were frequently misspelled (e.g. "George A. Roscoe" for "Jorge Orozco," or "Magoon" for "Flores Magón"), a situation made worse because Mexican persons of interest sometimes used aliases. A problem with some of the agent reports is that whereas Mexicans have a compound surname, paternal followed by maternal, e.g. Juan García Treviño, BI agents sometimes thought that "García" was the man's middle name and referred to him as "Treviño," while Mexicans referred to him as "García."[16]

The Bureau archive is most decidedly not user friendly. The more than 70,000 documents covering the Mexican Revolution were photographed on microfilm, and the hard copies were destroyed. The twenty-four rolls of microfilm are available at the National Archives as "Old Mexican Files, 232," rolls 851-874. Working directly from the microfilm is problematic. And although the documents are in roughly chronological order, not infrequently the papers relating to a particular day are scattered through several rolls. Therefore, for this study we had the relevant rolls photocopied and then assembled in chronological order, and further complemented the files with agents' personnel files, State, Justice (Court), and military archives. The result amply justified the effort, for there is, for the first time, virtually a day-to-day record of the Bureau's activities. This volume provides an intricate perspective of a fledgling federal government agency that developed and refined its mission, as the southern border of the US became entangled in the upheavals of the century's first social revolution.

Chapter 1: Beginnings

Attorney General Charles J. Bonaparte was frustrated. The Department of Justice (the DOJ) over which he presided had been tasked with an ever-increasing workload, in part because President Theodore Roosevelt was conducting a crusade against "land thieves" in the West and big business "trusts" in the East.[17] The Department of Justice, however, lacked the resources to accomplish its mission effectively. Bonaparte complained that the DOJ's subordinates, records, and library were distributed in a number of leased buildings at considerable distances from each other, which greatly hampered its work and inconvenienced its personnel. More importantly, the DOJ had no executive force and no permanent detective force under its immediate control. The agency had to rely on borrowing Secret Service agents from the Treasury Department to conduct investigations. Bonaparte stated that when emergencies arose requiring prompt and effective executive action, the Department was obliged to rely on the United States marshals. Given this unsatisfactory situation, he recommended in 1907 that Congress create a permanent detective force in the DOJ: "Its number and the form of its organization must be determined by the scope of the duties which the Congress may see fit to intrust [sic] to it."[18]

Congress proved reluctant to do so. The DOJ had used borrowed Secret Service agents to investigate the fraudulent disposition of government-owned land in Oregon, a case involving Senator John H. Mitchell and Representative John N. Williamson. They were indicted for conspiracy in 1905 and convicted.[19] Congress disliked having its members' crimes exposed and retaliated by crippling the DOJ, prohibiting the Treasury Department from loaning its agents to the DOJ and rejecting Bonaparte's request to appoint DOJ detectives.[20] The attorney general then executed a neat end run around Congress while that body was not in session.²¹ Bonaparte, on June 29, 1908, hired ten ex-US Secret Service agents as DOJ employees, paying their salaries through a miscellaneous expense fund. "Then, on July 26, 1908, Bonaparte appointed the Chief Examiner,²² Stanley Wellington Finch, to head this new, permanent investigative division within the Department of Justice."²³ Finch's office was in the Department of Justice offices in the old Baltic Hotel building on 1535 K-Street NW. Such was the inauspicious beginning of what would become a world-famous organization.

Bonaparte explained in his 1908 annual report (which Congress received in January 1909), "Although such action was involuntary on the part of this department [as Congress forbade the use of Secret Service personnel by Justice], the consequences of the innovation have been, on the whole, moderately satisfactory. The special agents, placed as they are under the direct orders of the chief examiner, who receives from them daily reports and summarizes these for submission each day to the Attorney General, are directly controlled by this department, and the Attorney General knows, or ought to know, at all times what they are doing and at what cost. Under these circumstances he may be justly held responsible for the efficiency and economy of the service rendered. The experience of the past six months has shown clearly that such a force is, under modern conditions, absolutely indispensable to the proper discharge of the duties of this department, and it is hoped that its merits will be augmented, and its attendant expense reduced by further experience."²⁴

Figure 2 Charles Joseph Bonaparte. Courtesy Library of Congress Prints and Photographs Division.

For the first time, Bonaparte also explained exactly how many agents he had hired and which funds he used for the new investigative Bureau. "The attorney general's letter states that thirty-four special agents are now employed by the department, and that they are paid out of the appropriation made under the head of 'miscellaneous expenses' for United States courts."[25] Expectedly, Attorney General Bonaparte's action encountered stiff opposition. From the beginning Congress, and especially the House Judiciary Committee, worried about executive overreach of the new "secret service" and its use for political purposes. As Congress had the power to restrict or even to abolish the new agency it threatened the continued existence of the DOJ's special agents.

Chief Finch was of slight build, with a quiet and reserved demeanor. Born in Monticello, New York in 1872, he went to high school in nearby Ellenville, where his father worked as a doctor. Finch attended Baker University in Kansas from 1891 to 1892. He joined the Justice Department in 1893 as a clerk. Over the next sixteen years, Finch worked his way up the rungs of the department, attending college and law school on the side. He completed his law degree at National University Law School (now George Washington University) in 1909, and passed the Washington, DC bar exam in 1911. Meticulous and ambitious, he worked his way up to the position of Chief Examiner, among other things, supervising audits of the federal courts.

Figure 3 Stanley Wellington Finch. Courtesy Library of Congress Prints and Photographs Division.

Finch's deputy was Examiner Alexander Bruce Bielaski, a special assistant to the attorney general, who pursued his law degree as a fellow student at night and on weekends. When Finch traveled, Bielaski became the acting Chief of the BI.

Chief Finch's time as the "grand daddy" of the FBI barely finds mention in the historiography, his legacy wilting in the shadows of the long career of Director J. Edgar Hoover.[26] Yet, it was Finch who persistently lobbied for the creation of the Bureau and imprinted his meticulous, process-oriented professionalism on the organization. Historian Athan Theoharis credits Finch with having "been the Department of Justice's strongest proponent of Justice having its own investigative unit." And that it was Finch who originated, or adopted from other agencies such as the Secret Service "...many of the administrative and organizational policies and procedures later identified with J. Edgar Hoover."[27]

"The day-to-day life of a Bureau agent under Attorney General Charles Bonaparte and the Bureau's head, Stanley W. Finch, differed surprisingly little from that under FBI Director Hoover for most of his tenure."[28] Special Agents worked a six-day week but often went into the office on Sundays to catch up on paperwork, mainly their daily reports. But because they sometimes submitted their daily reports for several days together, the information could not be acted on in a timely manner. They also prepared a monthly report of their expenses. Field offices transmitted these reports via telegraph to the home office. The agents received a commission card in a leather case, a numbered badge, a numbered telegraph code book with instructions, numbered transportation request forms, a portable typewriter for preparing their daily reports—and a .38 caliber Smith and Wesson revolver.[29] Although the DOJ did not officially authorize agents to be armed, in practice agents of the Department generally carried guns for their protection.[30] The Bureau was not averse to trying new technology, but Finch informed the National Dictograph Company, "I regret to state that the dictograph system has not proven satisfactory in this office and I, therefore, have to request that you terminate the arrangement and remove the instruments during the present month."[31]

The first Bureau of Investigation Special Agent was Harry John Jentzer (October 6, 1908), who had made a name for himself conducting investigations for the federal government since 1904. He would retire from the BI in 1926. Edward James Brennan (June 29, 1908) was one of eight Secret Service operatives who were transferred from the Treasury Department to the nascent BI. He would retire in 1924.[32] Marshall Frank Eberstein, one of the Secret Service agents detailed to the Justice Department before the creation of the BI, also officially transferred to the BI in the summer of 1908.[33] As agent in charge of the San Antonio field office he will appear prominently in the following chapters. He retired in 1918 to become chief of police of Omaha.[34] His son, Russell Eberstein, joined the BI in 1918 and had a long fruitful career until his retirement sometime after World War II.[35]

Figure 4 Harry John Jentzer, personnel file, NARA

The Bureau of Investigation grew from thirty-four special agents by the end of 1908 to sixty-four in 1910.[36] On occasion, a special agent was sent abroad on a case—to London, Madrid, Montreal, Havana, and Naples.[37] With the appointment of the lawyer and accomplished political organizer for President Taft's 1908 election campaign, J. Ellen Foster, to the BI in 1909, the Bureau now also had the first female special agent on its staff.[38] Agent Foster assisted in cases involving transport and interrogation of female suspects.[39] Because the BI was new, the press and the public frequently referred to these agents as "secret service" agents, the Secret Service being all they knew. Besides its special agents, the Bureau utilized special employees (usually especially valuable informants.) As was—and still is—standard practice among law-enforcement agencies, the Bureau utilized confidential informants, although its limited budget severely restricted their number and term of employment. For example, Finch authorized the Boston field office to employ an informant for not more than thirty days at a salary of $5 per day and actual expenses, adding that "owing to the limited appropriation I am particularly desirous of keeping expenses of this character at the minimum figure."[40]

The first year of the Bureau's existence produced a massive scandal that threatened to confirm the worst fears Congress had expressed over establishing the agency: overreach of the Executive, in this case involving stacking and tampering with a jury to achieve conviction at all costs. In the history of federal agencies, key events sometimes change the organizational culture forever. The US Navy and Marine Corps will never be the same after the Tailhook scandal that came to light in 1991. The Cartagena scandal of 2012 changed the culture of the US Secret Service forever. The Bureau of Investigation went through a scandal as profound in 1909, and it involved the trial of Charles Wyman Morse. One could argue that the fallout from this scandal precipitated a cultural change within the Bureau that is still palpable even today.

The story of Charles W. Morse's downfall begins when on October 18, 1907, panicking depositors initiated a run on the Knickerbocker Trust Company in New York as a result of careless speculation and brinkmanship by one F. Augustus Heinze. He had tried to demolish John D. Rockefeller's virtual monopoly of the copper market. The effort not only failed, but brought the US banking system, indeed the financial health of the United States, crashing down. John Pierpont Morgan, wealthier than the US government itself, came to the rescue with unprecedented loans. The situation became so tense that Morgan asked New York's clergy to pray for "calm and forbearance." Whether with God or J. P. Morgan's help—or as a combination of both—the great bank panic of 1907 ended as quickly as it had come about. Investor confidence recovered within a month and the recession ended in June 1908, almost exactly a year after it had started.

However, among the many Wall Street schemes that came crashing down were the fortunes of the "King of Ice," Charles W. Morse. The owner of virtually the entire US merchant marine had successfully cornered the ice market a few years earlier, a critical component for shipping perishable goods. He created a monopolistic trust, the American Ice Company. "The price of ice doubled in a week," a newspaper reported in admiration.⁴¹ Badly over-leveraged, Morse's empire of steamship lines and warehouses succumbed to bankruptcy in the panic of 1907. A year later, Morse, who had fled to England but eventually decided to stand trial in the US, came under indictment for creating a monopoly. The disgraced tycoon fought tooth and nail to stay out of prison. Morse lost in the first round. He was sentenced to fifteen years hard time and $5,000 for violating the Donnelly Anti-Monopoly Act.⁴² That did not end his struggle, however. Morse demanded a retrial and alleged that agents of the Justice Department had engaged in jury-tampering. The charge seemed far-fetched.

Figure 5 Charles Wyman Morse, April 13, 1920. Courtesy Library of Congress Prints and Photographs Division.

The problem for the BI was the coverage of its role in this case. An affidavit reported in the *New York Sun* in November 1909, revealed the extent to which agents went to achieve a conviction, leaving everyone in the new Taft administration, from the president-elect on down, aghast. BI agents detailed to guard the jury during trial allegedly provided the jurors with "unlimited quantities of liquor," to the point that outgoing President Roosevelt's personal physician had to attend to a juror who ended up at the "Bellevue alcoholic ward" with the "jumps" as a result of the BI agents' liberal distribution of spirits.⁴³ The affidavit further alleged that one of the jurors had a history of mental illness. One of his agents reported this kernel of interest to Chief Finch who allegedly never informed the court. Morse's attorneys further alleged that agents of the BI influenced individual jurors. One of the special agents took a juror "across the street [from the courthouse] to a saloon and both took a drink of brandy."[44] Topping these allegations, the BI agents also provided the jurors with "all the newspapers every day, some of which contained hostile, incomplete, biased, partial and damaging reports..."[45]

The Circuit Court of Appeals rejected Morse's allegations, as did the Supreme Court. However, the report of the BI's alleged jury tampering was disastrous. Not only did the *Sun* print the charges in Morse's affidavit, but it also outed fourteen of the Bureau's first thirty-four agents by listing their names. Attorney General George W. Wickersham, who just had taken over from Bonaparte, did not waver in fighting Morse's appeal. Interestingly, just a year into serving his sentence, President Taft pardoned Morse who lay on his deathbed, according to his wife. Only days after regaining his liberty, Morse miraculously cheated death, recovered his health, and resumed his Wall Street career. He lived until 1933.

The scandal had a profound impact on the Bureau. The first wave of hires, with a strong Secret Service component, had created a "can-do," sort of "Rough Rider" atmosphere in the new department. This may have been the attitude President Roosevelt and Attorney General Bonaparte instilled in their pioneer investigative force. The new Taft administration did not share this view. Wickersham desperately needed Congressional approval and funding for the Bureau. The special agents already had their hands full establishing their credibility with the courts, law enforcement, and citizens in the many localities where investigations took place. We will see the extent to which local resistance to federal influence ranked supreme in the many prosecutions the Bureau brought. Without holding a moral and legal high ground, the Bureau would not survive Congressional scrutiny for long.

Chief Finch insisted on documenting every move meticulously from 1909 on, accounting for every penny of expenditures. He standardized reporting and accounting, so that it became difficult for agents to engage in extra-legal adventures without the knowledge of Bureau leadership. Although not a perfect system, the BI from 1909 on would not be an agency ostensibly engaged in political hack jobs. While politics surely steered their mission, Finch and Bielaski, as well as their successors, tried to investigate and prosecute by the book, even if, as we will see on many occasions, it meant that convictions could not be secured. Despite hostile judges, blatant jury tampering by locals, and seemingly ironclad cases falling apart, by and large the agents of the BI remained within the bounds of the law.

The immediate effect of Wickersham and Finch's decision to redirect the Bureau was to deflect Congressional retaliation. Wickersham assured Congress that investigations would be confined to uncovering violations of antitrust, banking, and postal laws, or criminal acts directed at the federal government. So, Congress need not bother to define the scope of the DOJ's investigations. Congress not only agreed, but in 1910 lifted the restrictions, allowing appropriated funds to be used for "such other investigations regarding official matters under the control of the Department of Justice as may be directed by the Attorney General."[46] In 1910, the contentious relationship with the legislature ended and the Bureau received Congressional approval, and with it the appropriations that laid the groundwork for a decade of massive growth and development.

Unlike bureaucrats who merrily squander taxpayer funds, Chief Finch was determined to ensure that value was received for every dollar the Bureau spent. He notified one agent that 10 cents had been deducted from his October 12 expense account because he had exceeded the allowance of 15 cents for porterage on a chair car. Porterage of 25 cents was not allowed unless a berth in a sleeping car was taken. He advised the agent to be careful where receipts were not taken, to include the full name and address of the hotels, laundries, etc. used. Another agent was chided for charging 27 days for an informant at $2 per day but only enumerating

26 days. "Please give the exact dates in August when the informant was employed. If only 26 days, a $2 refund is needed."[47] And he notified another examiner that "Regarding the fifty cents disallowed from your last account, this deduction was made because of a charge in your account for 'bath.' I believe the charge read 'For room 2 days, at $2.00 per day ($4.00) and bath 50 cents.' While the charge for room is allowable, even though the room has bath attached, it has been the policy of the Department for a long time not to allow a charge for bath as such."[48]

Finch micromanaged every aspect of the Bureau's activities. When an examiner telegraphed a request for blotters for the clerk's office at Shreveport, Finch promptly notified the Supply Division of the DOJ to provide a blotter for the district court and one for the circuit court, noting that the shipments had been duly entered on the records of the BI office.[49] He notified another agent that "a new roller and ribbon for your folding typewriter will be sent you at an early date."[50]

Writing to Lyn G. Munson, Special Bank Accountant, DOJ, St. Louis, Finch laid out his firearms policy: "I am forwarding by registered mail a revolver for your official use. The Department cannot authorize you to carry it, but it is believed you will have no difficulty as a result of doing so. Agents of the Department generally carry guns for their protection, and we have so far had no trouble from any source as a result."[51] On another occasion he wrote to an agent: "I have sent you a shoulder holster as per your request."[52]

Agents sometimes failed to file reports on a daily basis, causing Finch to reprimand them. He did not hesitate to chastise an agent whom he felt had bungled, but when an agent performed well the Chief was fulsome in his praise.[53] And he instructed an agent to "make your daily reports more complete. Show your work in such detail for me to form an intelligent idea of the case's progress, since I have to report to the Attorney General."[54] And Finch was particular: he required all his agents to use the same paper so that all reports would be on paper of uniform size and weight.⁵⁵ He also required that in their daily reports, agents put each ongoing investigation on a separate page, to keep from mixing them up.

By January 1912, the BI operated from its new headquarters, complete with new furniture, in rooms 602-604 in the Southern Building, 15th and H Street in Washington, DC. There was a filing system for correspondence, daily reports, and other documents, facilitated by a card index. Headquarters had nine support staff, including a filing clerk and stenographers to whom agents dictated their reports.⁵⁶ Special Agent in Charge Daniel Clinton Betjeman would go to the Department of Justice after office hours, collect any telegrams for Chief Finch, telephone them to the Chief at his residence and send the Chief's answers.⁵⁷

Bureau of Investigation agents usually worked under the direction of US attorneys, preparing evidence for prosecutions of cases dealing with: violations of national banking laws; laws relating to fraudulent bankruptcies; the impersonation of government officials with intent to defraud; the bucket-shop (brokerage firms operating unethically by permitting betting on the rise or fall of stocks, etc.) law; thefts and murders committed on government reservations; offenses against government property; offenses committed by federal court officials and employees; the smuggling of Chinese in violation of the Exclusion Act; Customs, Internal Revenue, Post Office, and land frauds; immigration and naturalization cases; violations of the neutrality laws; and as of 1910, the White Slave Traffic Act, better known as the Mann Act, making it a federal crime to transport women across state lines for prostitution or other immoral purposes. In its investigations, the Bureau supplemented its special agents with part-time local officers handling white slave cases, and with special employees, enlisted on an ad hoc basis.⁵⁸

Agents soon found themselves also tasked with enforcing the neutrality laws in connection with unrest in Mexico. Frustrating the agency for years was the fact that purchasing arms and ammunition per se was not illegal; it was only illegal to cross the arms and munitions into Mexico to factions other than the constituted government. Illegal exportation violated the neutrality laws and thus could be prosecuted. Yet frequently, BI agents would prepare a solid case only to have the defendants acquitted by a judge's ruling, or by a jury sympathetic to Mexican rebels, or by a jury resentful of interference in what the locals perceived as being merely business, or by a jury discounting the testimony of Mexican witnesses. A tactic that defense attorneys frequently used was to secure continuances, so that when a case finally came to trial, the witnesses had scattered, gone to Mexico, or, in some cases, had died or been executed in the chaos of civil war.

Chapter 2: Challenge To The Dictator

The Mexican Revolution of 1910-1920 was arguably the first great social revolution of the twentieth century. It erupted to overthrow the dictatorial regime of General Porfirio Díaz, who emerged as a national hero from the French Intervention (1862-1867) when the French tried to conquer Mexico. Díaz seized power in 1876, and behind a facade of constitutional government had himself elected president eight times, during which he seemingly transformed Mexico from a country wracked by foreign invasion, revolution, and economic crisis into a model of a developing nation. He accomplished this by first co-opting or eliminating regional strongmen and suppressing unrest and ordinary crime by employing the *Cuerpos Rurales*, the feared mounted constabulary who dealt out summary justice.

Figure 6 *General Porfirio Díaz, President of Mexico.*
Courtesy Library of Congress Prints and Photographs Division.

Having established substantial internal peace, Díaz made Mexico most attractive to foreign investment, mainly from the United States. Foreign capital financed, for example, the construction of trunk rail lines linking Mexico City with Nogales, Arizona, and El Paso and Laredo, Texas. An outstanding feature of the Díaz years was the impressive development of the northern tier of Mexican states, up to then a relatively neglected area. As the Mexican economy was increasingly tied to that of the United States, Díaz effectively shifted Mexico away from the historic east-west Mexico City-Veracruz axis which had oriented the country toward Europe and replaced it with a north-south axis orienting the county toward the United States. But during the decades of Díaz's rule serious problems accumulated, such as the accelerating concentration of land ownership and growing labor unrest. Moreover, Díaz relied on men of his own generation who had proven their loyalty. By 1910, Díaz was eighty years old, and his regime resembled a geriatric ward. The younger generation of ambitious Mexicans bitterly resented being deprived of access to power and the regime's preferential treatment of foreigners and their money. The phrase "Mexico for the Mexicans" reflected a rising nationalism.

Rising opposition to Díaz emerged by 1900. Journalists such as Filomeno Mata, and especially Ricardo Flores Magón and his brother Jesús published scathing articles attacking the regime. Ricardo Flores Magón was born in 1874 in the state of Oaxaca. He studied law in Mexico City but abandoned his studies to become an activist and crusading journalist. In 1900, he and his brother Jesús founded the opposition newspaper *Regeneración*. The authorities quickly suppressed the newspaper and repeatedly jailed the Flores Magón brothers. After being jailed twice, Jesús Flores Magón decided to leave the movement in 1902 and become an establishment lawyer. He succeeded, eventually becoming a cabinet minister in 1912. The third brother, Enrique, became a rebel like Ricardo.

Ricardo Flores Magón fled to the United States, arriving on January 3, 1904, in Laredo, Texas, as a penniless refugee. Naïvely, "Flores

Magón hoped that the United States government might tolerate revolutionary activity by Mexican exiles if officials could be convinced that they shared the same democratic principles."⁵⁹ He briefly resumed publication of Regeneración in San Antonio and later in St. Louis, where he

Figure 7 Ricardo Flores Magón (left) and his brother Enrique in the Los Angeles County Jail, 1917. Source: Los Angeles Times, Creative Commons.

and his brother Enrique were arrested on a charge of defamation. They jumped bond in March 1906 while awaiting trial, and fled to Canada, first to Toronto and then to Montreal.

While contending with American authorities and Díaz agents, Flores Magón organized a political movement, the Partido Liberal Mexicano, the Mexican Liberal Party (PLM), because the traditional Liberal Party had become indistinguishable from the Conservatives in its support of Porfirio Díaz.⁶⁰ Joining Flores Magón were other leaders of the PLM such as poet, journalist, and printer Juan Sarabia, and schoolteachers Antonio I. Villarreal and Librado Rivera, men described as "intellectuals of low status."⁶¹ An exception was Práxedis G. Guerrero, who came from a landowning family but had rejected his background to work as a common laborer in Arizona and Colorado.

Figure 8 Librado Rivera and Enrique Flores Magón, c. 1910.
Courtesy Library of Congress Prints and Photographs Division.

The PLM on July 1, 1906, issued a sweeping indictment of Díaz and a radical plan of social and economic reform. The radicalism of the PLM—Flores Magón would declare himself to be an anarchist—cost them the support of moderate elements, men who could have contributed substantial sums to further the cause. They left the movement largely dependent on small contributions from Hispanic miners and day laborers in the Southwest and with some assistance from socialists in the United States who supported Flores Magón's attacks on the capitalist system. But the PLM did have an impact in terms of its propaganda, which heightened Mexican workers' awareness of their oppression. The PLM also called in 1906 for a nationwide uprising against Díaz.

Flores Magón left Montreal in August 1906, going to El Paso, a hotbed of *magonista* activity, to direct in person the planned rebellion. What the *magonistas* lacked in military expertise they made up for in enthusiasm: the "Liberal Junta's organizational ability stood in inverse proportion to its ideological fervor."[62] By October 1906, the rebel junta had developed a plan: 200 armed militants would storm across the international bridge from El Paso, seize the barracks, police station, city hall, banks, and customs house in Ciudad Juárez. Then a contingent would take the train and capture the state capital, the city of Chihuahua, and install a rebel governor. The junta in El Paso would continue to provide war materiel, and the triumphant *magonistas* would drive southward on Mexico City, with state after state repudiating Díaz's rule in a domino effect. What could possibly go wrong?

What went wrong was that the Mexican authorities had infiltrated the rebel junta and knew all about the plan. Several officers from the Juárez garrison passed themselves off as *magonista* sympathizers and offered to lead a mutiny. The PLM leaders eagerly accepted the offer and divulged the planned operation in detail. The upshot was that on the night of October 19-20, 1906, one of the agents provocateurs led some twenty true believers into Juárez, where they were promptly arrested, along with all other *magonistas* in town. Not only did the PLM operation collapse, but in El Paso the Mexican consul and several Mexican army officers assisted American authorities in rounding up the prominent *magonistas* Antonio Villarreal and Lauro Aguirre. Ricardo Flores Magón fled from this debacle to avoid arrest. Worse, the PLM's campaign to touch off a nationwide uprising in Mexico quickly sputtered out.[63]

By 1907, the *magonista* leadership had regrouped, this time in Los Angeles, which became Flores Magón's permanent headquarters. He began publishing a new revolutionary newspaper, *Revolución*, but his activities intensified efforts to suppress the PLM. Flores Magón faced opposition from three adversaries: United States authorities, the Mexican government, and American private detectives hired by the Díaz regime.

At issue were the neutrality laws of the United States. Since the Díaz regime was a "friendly government," the neutrality laws were enforced with that in mind. Evidencing the attitude of the United States, in April 1907, Secretary of State Elihu Root asked Attorney General Charles J. Bonaparte to suppress *magonista* activity in order to maintain good relations with Mexico.⁶⁴ And on September 28, 1907, the adjutant general of the army sent a confidential letter to the commanding general of the Department of Texas ordering him to spread the word along the border that the US was prepared to use military force "to enforce the neutrality laws and to protect the territory of a foreign state, with which the United States is at peace, from an invasion by an armed party from the territory of the United States."⁶⁵

The Mexican government not only urged the United States to prevent the shipment of munitions across the border destined for Flores Magón's followers but actively operated against *magonistas* in the United States. Mexico had nothing comparable to the Bureau of Investigation, though, relying instead on Mexican consuls who operated independently with their own secret agents and informers and reported directly to the Secretariat of Foreign Relations. There was created the Office of the Inspector General of Consulates, who directed covert activities against enemies of the regime.⁶⁶

Moreover, the Díaz regime used an 1899 treaty with the United States authorizing extradition in the case of serious crimes in order to harass the *magonistas* by having them arrested. The Mexican government had forty days to present its evidence of such a crime. Even if, as usually happened, Mexico failed to produce such evidence, at least troublesome exiles would have been put out of action for forty days.⁶⁷ But some Díaz officials, such as the consul in Douglas, Arizona, resorted to kidnapping. In 1907, Consul Antonio Maza had mercenaries seize *magonista* Manuel Sarabia, and bundle him across the international boundary to Agua Prieta. Sarabia was consigned to the penitentiary in Sonora. However, the kidnapping caused such an outpouring of public outrage in Douglas that it became an international incident. The Díaz authorities grudgingly returned Sarabia to Douglas.

In addition to deploying its own agents and using diplomatic tools, the Díaz regime hired American private detective agencies to work against *magonistas*. The most noteworthy of these firms was the Furlong

Detective Agency of St. Louis. Its head, Thomas Furlong, was hired by Enrique Creel, governor of Chihuahua, ambassador to the US, Foreign Minister, and unofficial head of Díaz's intelligence service. Furlong not only conducted surveillance on Flores Magón and his associates during their time in St. Louis, but he subsequently tracked down the *magonista* leaders in Los Angeles. Aided by two of his operatives and two Los Angeles policemen, Furlong on August 23, 1907, arrested Flores Magón, Villarreal, and Rivera.[68] Transferred to Arizona, their trial for neutrality violations finally took place in May 1909. They were sentenced to eighteen months in the territorial prison at Yuma. After eight months, they were transferred to the new territorial prison at Florence.[69]

Despite the absence of their leader, Flores Magón's followers continued the struggle. Once again using El Paso as their base, they planned a repetition of the failed 1906 uprising. Práxedis Guerrero went there in January 1908, to take charge and make the preparations. But unknown to the conspirators, they operated at a fatal disadvantage—most of the letters Flores Magón had smuggled out of the Los Angeles County jail were intercepted and delivered to the Mexican authorities. One of these letters contained a detailed account of PLM activities and plans for the renewed offensive in 1908.[70]

Guerrero's painstaking stockpiling of munitions for the projected attack on Ciudad Juárez came to naught. The authorities raided Guerrero's headquarters on June 25, 1908, seizing the war materiel, a mass of documents, and arrested four important *magonistas*. Guerrero managed to escape, and on June 30 he led ten fellow militants in an attack on the border hamlet of Palomas, west of El Paso. The attack was a pointless failure. Although the PLM's efforts in the El Paso area had twice been a debacle, other militants did manage to strike another glancing blow for the cause.

Magonistas under the command of Encarnación Díaz Guerra crossed the Rio Grande from Del Rio, Texas, and, on June 26, 1908, attacked the town of Las Vacas (today Ciudad Acuña), Coahuila. Eleven attackers, ten soldiers, and two customs inspectors were killed, and the surviving raiders soon retreated into Texas. Far from touching off popular uprisings, such a raid served to illustrate the PLM's military impotence.

The raid, however, had important consequences. First, at the October 1908 term of the federal district court in El Paso, indictments for violation of the neutrality laws were handed down against leading PLM figures: Ricardo and Enrique Flores Magón, Antonio I. Villarreal, Antonio de Pío Araujo, Encarnación Díaz Guerra, and Práxedis G. Guerrero. In addition, several *magonistas* who had allegedly participated in the raid at Las Vacas were indicted.[71]

Second, American authorities launched an investigation of the raid. The investigators were: Luther T. Ellsworth, the American Consul at Ciudad Porfirio Díaz (today Piedras Negras), across the Rio Grande from Eagle Pass, Texas; Collector of Customs Robert W. Dowe; US Attorney Charles A. Boynton; US Marshal for the Western District of Texas Eugene Nolte; and Captain C. H. Conrad, commanding the troops at Del Rio. This interagency group conferred in Del Rio on July 1 and the next day went to Las Vacas to meet with Mexican officials. Their conclusion was that between forty and seventy-five men from Del Rio had attacked Las Vacas using firearms concealed on the American bank of the Rio Grande. The neutrality laws had indeed been violated. The investigators recommended the establishment of a special "secret service" to monitor Mexican revolutionary movements and border conditions.[72]

Figure 9 Luther T. Ellsworth.
Courtesy Library of Congress Prints and Photographs Division.

Their recommendation posed a problem for Attorney General Bonaparte. Since he did not yet have agents of his own, Bonaparte had hoped to borrow a Secret Service agent from the Treasury Department to surveille the border, but Congress had prohibited such an arrangement. The person Bonaparte had in mind was veteran Secret Service operative Joe Priest. He not only spoke fluent Spanish, but had experience in the Canal Zone in Panama, in Puerto Rico, in Cuba, and he was also well acquainted with the Mexican border. Bonaparte came up with a clever solution: Congress's prohibition did not apply to the State Department, and Bonaparte persuaded the Secretary of State to pay Priest's salary and expenses from State's neutrality fund and place him under Department of Justice (DOJ) supervision. Congress was thus neatly circumvented, and Joe Priest became a DOJ agent. So did Dan Riley, a Furlong Detective Agency operative employed by the Mexican government for three years. Like Priest, Riley was paid by the State Department but worked for the DOJ. Unlike Priest, Riley may also have remained in Mexican employ as an informer.[73]

Several federal agencies participated in the neutrality enforcement effort. The State Department played the leading role because of the desire to maintain good relations with Mexico, but Justice, War, Treasury (Customs Service), and Commerce and Labor (Immigration Service) were also actively involved. "Since Ellsworth had taken the initiative to investigate the Las Vacas affair, the [State] Department encouraged him to continue his efforts by making him its special representative in matters of neutrality. He conscientiously and enthusiastically pursued his new duties."[74] Ellsworth worked in close cooperation with Joe Priest, whom he considered remarkably well-qualified for the task.

Priest came on board in July 1908, reporting to the US attorney for the Western District of Texas, John A. Boynton. Priest's headquarters were in San Antonio, where on the night of September 27, 1908, he arrested *magonista* Calixto Guerra. But Priest ranged widely. On

November 25, 1908, at Wilburton, Oklahoma, he and a deputy US marshal arrested Encarnación Díaz Guerra, the *magonista* colonel who had led the Las Vacas raid. Priest worked well with Ellsworth and Boynton, but he had difficulties involving jurisdictions with the chief deputy US marshal with whom he had to deal. Priest's activities were severely curtailed on July 31, 1909, when he was struck down by a serious abdominal hemorrhage. Even though confined to bed for months, he translated many of the *magonista* documents the authorities had seized. These included correspondence between the PLM and American socialist sympathizers such as John Murray.

The Treasury Department balked at releasing Priest permanently to direct border security. This, combined with Priest's worsening medical condition, ultimately fatal, prevented him from accepting Attorney General Bonaparte's offer in June 1909, to become "Chief Special Agent of the Department of Justice, Bureau of Investigation, with headquarters in San Antonio, Texas." Leading the San Antonio field office, he was to be devoted entirely to the investigation of neutrality matters on the Mexican border.[75]

Since Priest was unable to accept the position created for him, Consul Ellsworth remained the most knowledgeable official dealing with neutrality matters on the border. In recognition of his abilities, the new attorney general, George W. Wickersham, named him on November 11, 1909, the DOJ's "special representative" to oversee neutrality work, thus making Ellsworth the "special representative" for both State and DOJ in these matters. This was done with the State Department's approval. Ellsworth had to send his reports directly to State in duplicate; if the Secretary so chose, he could forward copies to the Attorney General.

The Bureau of Investigation was now directly involved in enforcing neutrality. The attorney general notified all DOJ personnel that they should cooperate fully with Ellsworth. When the latter complained he was not receiving information that he desired from Bureau agents, Chief Finch instructed special agent Fred Lancaster in the San Antonio field office, to provide Ellsworth with any information the consul might find useful but "in furnishing information contained in daily reports you should, of course, submit to him only such parts as relate to neutrality matters and should indicate on the daily report to this office the fact that such part of the report has been furnished him. While in view of the great variety of the work of the special agents in the Texas district it will of course be impossible for the agents to devote their time exclusively to neutrality matters. It is desired that such agents cooperate as fully as may be with Mr. Ellsworth, to the end that violations of the neutrality laws may be anticipated and prevented if possible. In the event that Mr. Ellsworth desires any special investigations as to neutrality matters, it is desired that, as far as such investigations may be made without seriously interfering with other important work, you have the same made, being careful not to incur any unnecessary expense."[76] The Justice Department furnished Ellsworth a copy of its telegraph code.[77]

Ellsworth's enthusiasm for his neutrality activities caused irritation at the State Department because he spent relatively little time at his consulate in Ciudad Porfirio Díaz and because he was running up expenses. To mollify his superiors at State, Ellsworth agreed to remain at his consular post and use the telephone and telegraph to coordinate with officials in San Antonio rather than go there in person. He also reduced to two the number of his paid informants.[78]

The aggressive enforcement of the neutrality laws produced results. In what had been a major center of activity, the judicial Western District of Texas, *magonistas* were now keeping a low profile. Benjamín Silva, Leocadio B. Treviño, Priciliano G. Silva, and José María Ramírez were arrested in El Paso on June 25, 1908; Silva and Treviño were convicted there on October 24. Antonio de Pío Araujo was arrested in Waco on September 14, 1908, and convicted at San Antonio on January 22, 1909. Calixto Guerra was arrested at San Antonio on September 27, 1908, but the US attorney dismissed his case at Del Rio on March 26, 1909. Encarnación Díaz Guerra pleaded guilty at Del Rio on March 25,

1909, and was sentenced to eighteen months at Leavenworth. Juan Castro, also arrested at Wilburton, Oklahoma, on November 25, 1908, charged with assault and impeding the administration of justice, pleaded guilty on January 27, 1909, and was sentenced on February 6, 1909, at Muscogee, Oklahoma.[79] José M. Rangel and Tomás Sarabia were arrested in San Antonio on August 10, 1909. The Bexar County grand jury had failed to indict Sarabia, who with his attorney went to the Bureau office to reclaim his papers seized at the time of his arrest. They were returned, the Bureau having copied them.[80] Tomás Sarabia was a free man, but his colleague José Rangel was not so fortunate. He was sentenced to eighteen months in Leavenworth on January 14, 1910.[81] This was most gratifying to Special Agent J. Herbert Cole, who had attended the Rangel trial.

The 41-year-old Jay Herbert Cole, a lawyer from Detroit, was not the typical Texas lawman. Born and raised in Michigan, Cole pursued a promising career in politics before joining the Bureau. His engagement in Republican politics earned him several state offices under Governor John Treadway Rich between 1900 and 1906.[82] His wife, Elisabeth, however, contracted tuberculosis in 1903, and doctors recommended that she move to a dry, desert climate.[83] Trying to hold on to Cole's career while caring for his wife, the couple permanently moved to Santa Fe in 1906 after several years of spending the summers there. Elisabeth attended to her illness in the local Sunmount Sanitorium, while Cole took a job as a BI agent. In 1909, Cole became agent in charge of the BI office in San Antonio, where the couple established their new residency.[84]

Figure 10 Jay Herbert Cole, www.fbi.gov/history/field-office-histories/sanantonio.

Cole's skilled investigations added to the fact that, by the end of 1909, the *magonistas* were in disarray and on the defensive. Their leaders were in prison, and the rank and file were demoralized. The Bureau of

Investigation was not just investigating the *magonistas* but especially their links with American socialists and anarchists. The activities of the *magonistas* had taken on a national security dimension in early 1908, when Ricardo Flores Magón, Antonio Villarreal and Juan Sarabia associated with John Kenneth Turner and other prominent socialists in Los Angeles who sympathized with the program of the fledgling PLM.[85] Despite Flores Magón's caution not to acknowledge publicly that he had become an ardent anarchist, prominent American socialists and anarchists, such as Turner, Job Harriman, John Murray, Emma Goldman, and Mary Harris aka "Mother Jones" had taken on "the Mexican cause, personified in Ricardo Flores Magón."[86] By 1909, in the eyes of federal investigators, no matter their public restraint, Flores Magón and his PLM followers had become one with American socialists and anarchists posing a threat to the American economy and political system.

As 1910 opened, *magonista* leaders Ricardo Flores Magón, Librado Rivera, and Antonio I. Villarreal languished in the penitentiary at Florence, Arizona. After serving fifteen months of their original sentence, they were released on August 3, 1910. Presumably, the Mexican government would immediately request their extradition and, if granted, their fate was sealed. To prevent extradition, Flores Magón's prominent radical American supporters launched a campaign to mobilize public opinion.[87] By the time of his release, Flores Magón dropped all pretenses and publicly declared himself an anarchist. "Years of being hounded by government operatives of two countries, and his time in …jails and prisons… had made him cynical about the nature of all governments…"[88] While keeping track of the PLM junta, the BI also kept an eye on Mother Jones: "Agent Scarborough, at Washington, called on Mother Jones, Mexican revolutionary sympathizer and speaker, who, believing agent to be a magazine writer, promised to furnish him with certain data relative to her work for use in a prospective story concerning her."[89]

The US attorney for the Western District of Texas supervised Jay Herbert Cole's investigations in the San Antonio Bureau office. Cole conferred frequently with Consul Ellsworth and with Enrique Ornelas, the Mexican consul in San Antonio, who ran his own network of agents and informers. Cole also employed Hispanic informants, among them Andrés [Santos] Coy, assistant San Antonio police chief, while Cole and his subordinates frequented the *barrios* in hopes of learning about *magonista* machinations.

With the *magonistas* on the defensive, Cole and his men were trying to track down revolutionary figures still at large. One of Cole's men was Agent Fred Hill Lancaster, born in Izard, Arkansas in 1862. Lancaster had become a deputy US marshal in 1905. He had traveled in that capacity from San Antonio to Bloomington, Texas, on the trail of Jesús M. Longoria, wanted in Del Rio for neutrality violations. Through an informant's lead, Lancaster succeeded in locating and arresting Longoria, who was working on a ranch. Longoria freely discussed his role as a captain in the Las Vacas raid in June 1908. Lancaster also seized numerous documents Longoria had on his person. Lancaster joined the BI as a Special Agent in San Antonio on November 16, 1909.[90]

The Bureau especially hoped to get a lead on Práxedis Guerrero, described as "the chief of the Mexican revolutionists," through his fellow militant María Rodarte, with whom Guerrero was said to be infatuated. Agent Samuel L. Geck got the job. Born on April 25, 1866, he was a former Republican County Commissioner in Doña Ana County, New Mexico, just north of El Paso. Geck searched for Rodarte in El Paso and in Las Cruces, New Mexico without result.[91] The Bureau office in San Antonio received a break in January 1910: an anonymous letter enclosing correspondence which Práxedis Guerrero had written from Houston to José Rangel.[92]

Figure 11 Samuel L. Geck, Passport Photo, 1921.

In February, Agent John W. Vann in Houston telephoned Cole that he had located Guerrero at the Hotel Louisiana in that city.[93] John Vann was one of the most experienced agents of the Bureau in Texas. Born in 1860 near San Antonio, Texas, Vann served as tax collector in Kerrville, Texas, in the 1890s, before winning elections to become sheriff in 1900.[94] He served as sheriff and deputy US marshal in Kerrville, until President Roosevelt appointed him Collector of Customs for the port of Brownsville in 1906, in part for his active participation in Texas Republican politics.[95] Vann lost his position after the election of Howard Taft. He joined the BI as a special agent in March 1909 and headed the Houston field office.[96]

Cole immediately dispatched Agent Lancaster and an informant who could identify Guerrero. The Hotel Louisiana turned out to be a seedy rooming house where Guerrero, using the alias of "Manuel Martínez," was living with his wife, son, and a colleague, one Francisco Aguilar. Agents Vann and Lancaster arranged with the Houston police chief to raid the place at dawn on February 12. But when Lancaster called at the police station for an officer to assist in the raid because Vann was ill, the clerk on duty refused to detail a man without the express authorization of the police chief. There was not time to contact the chief, so Lancaster left word for backup to be sent as soon as possible, and proceeded to conduct the raid alone. Perhaps not his best idea that day.

Figure 12 John W. Vann, Passport Photo, 1920.

When Lancaster forced his way into Guerrero's room, a desperate struggle ensued. Guerrero, assisted by the others, managed to escape out a window, sliding forty feet to the ground on a prepositioned rope of twisted bed sheets. Guerrero was reportedly badly injured, but injured or not, he got away. Although his quarry had escaped, at least Lancaster was able to seize Guerrero's suitcase, bulging with revolutionary papers and correspondence. Lancaster then reported that since he was known in Houston and was under counter surveillance by Mexicans, he was returning to San Antonio. The search for Guerrero resumed, the Bureau enlisting the aid of the Houston police and establishing a mail cover on the Louisiana Hotel.[97]

The San Antonio field office took on ever greater importance because the city was a center of *magonista* intrigue. One of the recent additions was Guy Hamilton Scull. Born in 1879 in Boston, Scull joined the New York police department in 1908 as a detective. Two years later, he joined the Bureau of Investigation and was dispatched to San Antonio.[98] With the BI intensifying its *magonista* investigations at the border, Chief Finch decided to replace Cole with a more experienced agent in charge, Marshall Eberstein, to head the San Antonio office.

Figure 13 *Guy Hamilton Scull, Lassoing Wild Animals In Africa*, Inside book cover.

The assignment might not have been to agent Eberstein's liking. He neither spoke Spanish, nor had he had any prior involvement with enforcing the neutrality laws, nor had he ever experienced Hispanic culture. The hot summer weather combined with regular flooding of the downtown area may have added to his discomfort. Eberstein had previously headed the Chicago field office and was one of the original ten Secret Service agents who had joined the Bureau in 1908. Born in Kalamazoo, Michigan, in 1859, the first-generation German-American Eberstein left school after the eighth grade and worked on the family farm and as a butcher before joining the government as a federal investigator in the early 1900s.[99] Eberstein's father, George, had fought in the Civil

War on the side of the Union, as did most German immigrants. Tall, with blond hair and steel blue eyes, Marshall Eberstein cut an impressive figure. He spent his formative years as a Secret Service agent in the rugged Rocky Mountain states, investigating robberies and land fraud. After joining the nascent BI, he quickly rose through the ranks to become chief investigator. One of Eberstein's prized trophies was a .44 Colt "once used by Jesse James for business purposes."[100]

Scull resented Eberstein's authority, which Eberstein asserted by making Scull's life unpleasant. Eberstein led an investigation of weapons shipments consigned to merchants on the border, and he relegated Scull to the prosaic task of examining a seemingly endless torrent of shipping documents. One such case involved the firm of Hibbard, Spencer and Bartlett, that admitted to shipping firearms billed as hardware, but refused to cooperate further with the BI.[101] A technique much favored by the Bureau was that of mail covers; arranging with postmasters to have tracings made of the addresses on envelopes sent and received by persons of interest.[102]

Figure 14. Marshall Eberstein, Omaha Daily Bee, September 4, 1918.

The Bureau's efforts to suppress the PLM included sending Agent Curley D. Hebert from San Antonio to Arizona, where he conferred in Tucson with the Mexican consul and in Douglas with the postmaster, and learned which suspicious Mexicans were receiving mail.[103] Born in Shreveport, Louisiana in 1879, Hebert came to the San Antonio office with a solid law enforcement background. Before joining the BI as special agent, he served as a Deputy Marshal in Louisiana, where he effectively worked on solving counterfeiting and liquor smuggling cases.[104]

Hebert arranged for mail covers at the mining towns of Morenci, Clifton, and Metcalf, while he familiarized himself with revolutionary sympathizers there, for the *magonistas* enjoyed considerable support from

Hispanic miners. Agent Geck was in Tombstone, Arizona, in May, still searching for the Rodarte woman. He also traveled to Ciudad Juárez to interview one Antonio López, who said Guerrero has written to him four months earlier from the mining town of Morenci, Arizona, but he did not know the fugitive's present whereabouts.[105]

Meanwhile, acting on information from Consul Ellsworth that revolutionists were active along the Rio Grande between Brownsville and Laredo, Cole on April 11 sent Lancaster to investigate conditions in heavily Hispanic counties of Nueces, Duval, Starr, Hidalgo, and Cameron. Lancaster arranged with the lawmen there promptly to notify the federal authorities of any suspicious activities.[106]

A serious setback for the Bureau occurred when *magonista* Basilio Ramírez, under indictment in the Western District of Texas for neutrality violation and an important government witness in the case against Jesús Longoria, was shot and killed in Del Rio by fellow *magonista* Juan Morín. Ramírez had turned state's evidence, identifying various *magonista* militants, and despite death threats, had imprudently let it publicly be known that he planned to testify. The matter was important enough for Agent Cole to go to Del Rio to confer with the US attorney, for Ramírez's death meant that the government would probably be unable to secure a conviction in the Longoria case. Cole could not interrogate the killer, Morín, for he committed suicide in the Del Rio jail, a true revolutionary to the end. As for defendant Longoria, he was released on $1,000 bail. The authorities worried that he might jump bond and flee to Mexico, which he did.[107]

Agent Cole in El Paso conferred with the US attorney and the US marshal about revolutionary matters. He also interviewed Benjamín G. Silva, whose father was currently in Leavenworth on a neutrality conviction, regarding information the younger Silva proposed to give about neutrality violations.[108] But Cole was still focused on apprehending Práxedis Guerrero. He communicated with every Mexican consul on the border as well as with police officers and postmasters in nearly every town in southern Texas and southern Arizona.[109] Cole also traveled to Austin to confer with the adjutant general of Texas, who commanded the Texas Rangers, and to receive Ranger reports of neutrality violations. Cole also arranged for the US marshal in San Antonio to receive reports from President Díaz's constabulary, the *Rurales*.[110] What gave impetus to the manhunt was the fact that until Lancaster had tried to arrest Guerrero in Houston, many government officials and some prominent Mexicans in San Antonio had doubted Guerrero's very existence. Agent Geck was in Las Cruces, New Mexico, in June, writing to postmasters in New Mexico and Arizona trying to learn whether Guerrero had been receiving mail under the alias of "Federico Resendes."[111]

The Bureau relied heavily on information that Mexican consuls provided, for the consuls were the core of Mexican government intelligence system in the United States. Each consul ran his own stable of agents and informers, and passed along to the Bureau whatever information he chose. Obviously, there were differences in the effectiveness of consuls and in the veracity of what they learned and what they communicated, but given the BI's limitations of manpower and money, it was grateful for whatever it received. For example, the Mexican consul in Tucson informed Cole in March that Manuel Sarabia, indicted in Arizona for neutrality violations and currently a fugitive, was married to Elizabeth D. Trowbridge, a wealthy Boston socialite and prominent socialist, and that he was living with her either in Boston or somewhere in Canada.[112]

Anticipating the release from prison in Arizona of Flores Magón and Villarreal, Agent Cole traveled to Washington in May and again in June to confer with an assistant attorney general regarding their further prosecution for violations of the neutrality laws.[113] Agent Lancaster had a most productive meeting in San Antonio with informant [Santos] Coy, who not only brought him up to date on renewed revolutionary activity in that city, but supplied photographs of Ricardo Flores Magón, Juan Sarabia, Antonio I. Villarreal, Andrea Villarreal González (Antonio's militant sister), and Librado Rivera. The photos were immediately forwarded to Bureau headquarters. The informant cultivated Teresa Villarreal, another of Antonio's sisters, and convinced her that he was a revolutionary sympathizer. He reported that she intended to publish a revolutionary newspaper, *El Obrero*. She did so, and to the Bureau's annoyance, an early issue contained an article by Práxedis G. Guerrero. Moreover, she confided to the informant that Guerrero was now in Los Angeles with her brother, Antonio Villarreal.[114]

There was a lull in revolutionary activity during July, for the reports emanating from the BI's San Antonio office were replete with phrases such as agents and informers "keeping apprised generally of the revolutionary situation," "keeping in touch generally with the revolutionary situation," and reports from informants "relative to the movements of various revolutionists." But the office was also engaged in translating confiscated *magonista* documents. Agent Cole even returned to S. T. Agis, a friend of Práxedis Guerrero, the suitcase and papers of Guerrero's that agent Lancaster had seized. The Chief reminded Lancaster that "it is probably better to send Ellsworth frequent reports even though you have no evidence of any activities among the so-called revolutionists."[115]

The Bureau was well aware that any lull in revolutionary activity could quickly evaporate upon the release from prison in Arizona of the most important revolutionists: Flores Magón, Villarreal, and Sarabia. The Chief of the Bureau notified Agent Geck, who was still following leads in Las Cruces, New Mexico, that the "Department wants confidentially to ascertain what they contemplate doing immediately after release." Geck was ordered to "proceed immediately to Yuma, Arizona, and take up this matter. Maybe the jailer can give you valuable information. Above all stay in close touch with the situation and keep the Department advised of their actions until further notice. Please keep this matter as quiet as possible."[116]

When Geck arrived in Yuma he learned that the prisoners had been transferred to Florence, to which place he proceeded immediately.[117] When the Mexicans were released from prison on August 3, 1910, after serving fifteen months of their original eighteen-month sentence, Geck rode the same train with them to Los Angeles. They traveled in the company of the American socialist, John Kenneth Turner. They were met at the Los Angeles depot on August 4 by several hundred jubilant *magonistas*. As instructed, Geck endeavored to cover the trio's movements.[118] He trailed Flores Magón and Villarreal to nearby San Pedro, where they solicited money from local Mexicans to resume publication of *Regeneración*. Also, at San Pedro, Agent Geck attended a mass meeting at which socialist John Kenneth Turner spoke, denouncing Attorney General Wickersham for prosecuting *magonistas*. Geck later kept Rivera under surveillance. Another BI agent was also active in Los Angeles—Agent F. D. Simmons attended a revolutionary meeting at which Flores Magón, Villarreal, and Rivera spoke. He reported that the enthusiastic audience contributed a substantial sum to be used in reviving *Regeneración*.[119]

Anticipating an upsurge in revolutionary activity now that Flores Magón was free, American and Mexican authorities decided to cooperate more closely. Agents Vann and Lancaster in San Antonio intensified their efforts to track down fugitive *magonistas*. Not only did the BI agents coordinate their efforts with Consul Ellsworth and informant [Santos] Coy, but Joe Priest's health had improved somewhat in 1910, and he was able to participate in the work of the San Antonio field office.[120] That office received reinforcements—of a sort. Five special agents of the Mexican government reported to Consul Enrique Ornelas, and Ellsworth secured their services as informants. The Mexican agents promptly enlisted five individuals to join the local PLM and report back both to Consul Ornelas and to Consul Ellsworth. Agent Vann also participated in running these men.[121]

A pattern was developing by which the overstretched BI increasingly relied on assistance from Mexican intelligence agents, for the Bureau had little money for informants. On occasion, a PLM turncoat provided useful information. Frank F. Cano, who had run guns into Juárez for the *magonistas* in 1906, found himself in a predicament. He was in jail in Abilene, Texas, on a charge of bigamy. He offered to provide information to the Mexican consul at El Paso, Antonio Lomelí, and to deputy US marshals Stevens and Hildebrand if the charge was dismissed. Agent Vann interviewed Cano in jail, conferred with the state attorney handling the case, and arranged for Cano to become an informant.[122]

Agent Simmons at Los Angeles received a telegram from headquarters that a money order had been mailed by S. T. Agis, fugitive Guerrero's friend, from Bridgeport, Texas, reportedly to Guerrero, addressed to Box 676, Station "C." Simmons arranged to apprehend Guerrero should he call for the money order. Guerrero did not appear; one Pilar A. Robledo cashed the money order and purchased two more, sending one to Paulino Martínez, a militant in El Paso. Simmons arranged for a mail cover on Robledo and "kept in touch" with her. The BI agent also attended a meeting of revolutionists, at which the speakers included Flores Magón, Antonio Villarreal, and John Kenneth Turner. He also checked on a house at 519½ East Fourth Street where *Regeneración* was being printed.[123]

Agent Geck at El Paso mingled with Mexicans and conversed with them—this was important, for the BI had very few agents who could speak Spanish. Geck learned that Rivera had told them to organize a few meetings but that they were afraid to have any open meetings because they believed they were being watched by government officers. Geck reported that no meetings were held.[124] But evidently the *magonistas* were conducting operations of their own against the Bureau; when Geck was investigating in Las Cruces, New Mexico, someone had opened the envelope containing one of his reports. Finch suggested "that you mail your reports in some other place and address them to me at 1435 K Street, N.W., Washington, DC, omitting all reference to the Bureau of Investigation and the Department of Justice."[125] Agent Fred H. Lancaster at San Antonio also had a report intercepted.[126]

The Bureau had performed creditably against the declining *magonistas*, to the point that in October 1910, Finch wrote the special agent in Los Angeles that "After careful consideration of your letter of the 9th instant I do not believe that the Bureau would be warranted in detailing any additional agents for duty at Los Angeles. While it is important that we keep as closely in touch with the actions and proposed actions of the Mexican revolutionists whenever it seems likely that any federal law will be violated, we have no particular interest in their movements or plans at any other time. As long as their agitations do not constitute a violation of our laws, we of course have no interest in them."[127]

But a troubling situation developed along the Mexican border in the fall of 1910. A new revolutionary movement suddenly appeared, seemingly out of nowhere, and the Bureau reluctantly found itself involved.

Chapter 3: A Foreign Policy U-Turn

The Magonistas having abjectly failed to topple him, General Porfirio Díaz seemed firmly in control. But unrest continued. Díaz attempted to quell rising discontent by announcing in 1908 that he would not seek reelection in 1910 for an eighth term as president and would welcome renewed political activity. His announcement was a sensation. As matters developed, the canny Díaz was providing potential opponents the opportunity to reveal themselves, after which he would deal with them. He did so by neutralizing opposition candidates and declaring himself reelected in 1910 for his eighth term, thereby touching off a rebellion that produced a decade of devastating civil war, as well as armed intervention by the United States on several occasions.

Figure 15 Francisco I. Madero. Courtesy Library of Congress Prints and Photographs Division.

The man who initiated the Mexican Revolution was a most unlikely revolutionary. In a culture that valued machismo, Francisco Indalecio Madero was an unimpressive physical specimen—short, slight, a teetotaler, a vegetarian, and a spiritualist. Moreover, he was an aristocrat, a member of one of the wealthiest families in Mexico, a family that had profited enormously by its ties to the Díaz regime. Instead of devoting himself to his extensive landed estates in the border state of Coahuila, Madero got involved in politics. Initially interested in education, he gradually concluded that it was futile to talk of educational reform unless preceded by political reform. So, taking Díaz at his 1908 word, Madero in 1910 became the presidential candidate of the newly formed Anti-reelectionist Party. Díaz initially viewed Madero as a joke. But as Madero drew large and enthusiastic crowds, Díaz became concerned. Accordingly, he neutralized Madero prior to the election by having him arrested on a trumped-up charge of sedition. When the votes were counted, the government announced that Díaz had been handily reelected.

Madero now had to decide whether to accept Díaz's fraudulent reelection and return to a luxurious private life or do what he was most reluctant to do: issue a call for rebellion. As of October, Madero was in the city of San Luis Potosí under police surveillance pending the outcome of the charges against him. He managed to elude the police on October 5, disguised himself as a laborer, and hopped a freight train for the American border. He surfaced in San Antonio, Texas, a major center of revolutionary intrigue.[128] From there, he planned the MexicanRevolution.

Figure 16 Porfirio Díaz Mori. *Courtesy Creative Commons.*

As a revolutionist, Madero differed markedly from Ricardo Flores Magón. He was eminently respectable, not some bomb-throwing anarchist. He believed in liberal democracy and in private property, of which he owned an impressive amount. And he was the underdog. He thus generated a great deal of sympathy among the American public. Madero established his headquarters in the upscale Hutchins Hotel in San Antonio. Not surprisingly, Flores Magón denounced Madero as a fraud, a wealthy amateur playing at revolution, and prohibited his followers from having anything to do with him.[129] Flores Magón was determined to maintain ideological purity.

Madero labored under the handicap that the United States formally recognized Porfirio Díaz as the legitimate president of Mexico.

Not only did the federal government enforce the neutrality laws, but Texas governor Oscar B. Colquitt issued a neutrality proclamation of his own. Madero hoped in vain that the United States would grant belligerency status to his movement, but he was reduced to violating the neutrality laws. The Díaz administration, of course, urged strict enforcement of the laws and was continually frustrated by the United States demanding concrete proof of violations before acting.[130] This policy was more than just a matter of strict legality; Washington's support for Díaz was declining. It was an open secret that Madero was violating the law. Ironically, when Díaz had begun the rebellion in 1876 that elevated him to power, he used American territory—Brownsville, Texas—as his base.

The expanded revolutionary situation required even closer cooperation between Consul Ellsworth and the BI, and such cooperation was forthcoming. Chief Finch instructed Agents Cole and Geck at El Paso and Agent F. D. Simmons at Los Angeles to furnish Ellsworth with copies of such portions of their reports dealing with revolutionary and neutrality

Figure 17 Francisco I. Madero, ca. 1911. *Courtesy Library of Congress Prints and Photographs Division.*

matters, for "Mr. Ellsworth is a representative of this Department in such matters, and it is my desire that he be furnished whatever information may be obtained. You will, of course, be subject to no instructions from him, but will merely furnish him the extracts above mentioned." Agents Lancaster and Vann were already furnishing him reports.¹³¹

Madero's first significant move was to issue the customary revolutionary manifesto denouncing the incumbent and announcing the goals of the rebels, who were commonly referred to as *maderistas* or *insurrectos* (insurgents.) Madero's manifesto, the Plan de San Luis Potosí, called for a nationwide uprising at 6 p.m. on November 20, 1910, the date celebrated in Mexico as the beginning of the revolution.

The manifesto could not very well be entitled the Plan de San Antonio because of the neutrality laws. It was therefore backdated to October 5, the last day Madero had been in Mexico. The neutrality laws would be a major concern of factions in the revolution, which was primarily a northern movement, a logical continuation of the rapid development the border states had experienced under Díaz. With the

Figure 18 Manuel A. Esteva. *Courtesy Library of Congress Prints and Photographs Division.*

notable exception of Emiliano Zapata, who headed an agrarian uprising in the state of Morelos near Mexico City, all the major revolutionary figures came from the border states. Northerners enjoyed the enormous advantage of access to the United States for weaponry, finance, recruits, a ready market for loot, and sanctuary if defeated. Whenever possible, they also sent their families and their money to the US for safekeeping.

Brandishing the slogan of "Effective Suffrage, No Reelection," Madero proclaimed himself provisional president and undertook the herculean task of trying to organize a nationwide uprising against Díaz in a mere six weeks. There was a constant stream of visitors at headquarters to receive orders, begin recruiting and amassing weaponry, and organize revolutionary cells in Mexico.[132] Operatives of the Díaz government were quite active against Madero. The consul general, Manuel Esteva, ran several secret agents, and his government funded William Martin Hanson, a former US marshal in the Southern District of Texas, whose network kept *maderistas* under surveillance. Hanson, who later became the senior captain of the Texas Rangers, had a personal interest in maintaining the status quo in Mexico, for he had acquired an hacienda and, like other landowners, feared revolutionary land reform. The Díaz regime also reportedly bribed R. W. Dowe, collector of customs with headquarters at

Figure 19 José Ives Limantour, Secretary of Finance seated, 1910. Courtesy Library of Congress Prints and Photographs Division.

Eagle Pass, and Sheriff J. J. Allen of Terrell County, whose seat was the border town of Sanderson.

Edward Laroque Tinker, a former assistant district attorney in New York City, now in private practice, was interrogated by the Bureau because he apparently endeavored to secure information from all branches of the government in order to sell same to representatives of the Mexican government. The Bureau obtained information that Tinker had hired operatives of the Burns Detective Agency to shadow important members of the Madero party stopping at the Hotel Astor. Tinker, in fact, was a paid agent of the Mexican government.[133] The meetings that took place in a "special suite of rooms at the Astor Hotel" on Times Square in New York on March 11 and 12, 1911 indeed were important. Secretary of State Philander Knox had sponsored these negotiations between the

Figure 20 The Hotel Astor, Historic Buildings Survey, Photocopy. Courtesy of New York Historical Society, Landauer Collection.

Mexican Secretary of Finance José Yves Limantour, representing the embattled Mexican president Porfirio Díaz, and representatives of the revolutionary leadership under Francisco Madero. Representing Madero were his father Francisco Madero Sr., future Mexican presidents Francisco León de la Barra and Venustiano Carranza, intellectual and future secretary of education José Vasconcelos, physician and future secretary of public instruction Francisco Vázquez Gómez, and the main negotiator on behalf of the Madero faction and American oil interests, lawyer and power broker Sherburne G. Hopkins.[134] The issue at hand was for the negotiators to organize the end of the crumbling Mexican government.

Sherburne Hopkins's eventual stellar career as a premier international lawyer and lobbyist did not follow a straight path from high school to law school to entering his father's law practice. Instead of studying law after high school, the 20-year-old Sherburne tried his luck on the press beat in Washington, DC in 1887. Despite trying his best, he did not find employment with a major paper. So, he decided to mail a fake time-bomb to the Chief Justice of the Supreme Court, Morrison Waite. "Breaking" the story as an "independent" member of the press would certainly land him the desired employment on newspaper row. The plan backfired badly. Instead of landing a job as an investigative reporter, Sherburne landed in jail. The police correctly suspected the young Hopkins as the sender of the "infernal machine," that turned out to be a "canard."[135] Thomas Hopkins used his political connections to bust his son out of jail. In a subsequent trial, Hopkins' conviction resulted in the hefty fine of $100. Instead of jail, he entered the Naval Academy in Annapolis. A seemingly reformed Sherburne joined the Naval Militia of Washington, DC and served as captain of the tugboat *Fern* during the Spanish-American war (in the Chesapeake Bay off Baltimore).[136] Possibly with the support of his father's influential connections, Hopkins retired in 1899 as the head of the Naval Militia of Washington, DC and joined his father's law practice.[137] On the question of loyalty, a military intelligence officer in 1920 mused that it "shifted with his fee."[138]

Hopkins had organized the meetings in New York through his influence with Secretary Knox, who had been a long-time friend of the Hopkins family. The Hopkins (Thomas Snell Hopkins, father) and Hopkins (Sherburne Gillette Hopkins, son) law firm of Washington, DC had been engaged for decades in representing the interests of Henry Clay Pierce, who was one of the largest American investors in the Mexican National Railroad and had significant interests in the oil industry. A second major client of Hopkins was Wall Street giant and "king of trusts" Charles Ranlett Flint who headed the U.S. Rubber Corporation, American Chicle, and Computing Tabulating Recording Company, later better known as IBM. Flint had large investments in rubber plantations and transportation in Mexico and Central America. Serving the interests of his clients, Sherburne Hopkins thus had a hand in literally any rebellion and US military intervention in Central America during the "Banana Wars" of the early 20th century.[139]

Figure 21 *Sherburne Gillette Hopkins, c. 1914. Courtesy Library of Congress Prints and Photographs Division.*

It was only natural that Francisco Madero retained Hopkins as he planned the revolution to overthrow Porfirio Díaz. The basic fee that the Hopkins firm required for legal services was $50,000 (approximately $1 million in today's value). Sherburne Hopkins could trace his family to England. His ancestor, Stephen Hopkins, landed in Plymouth onboard the *Mayflower*, a fact that made the Hopkins family "American nobility." And Hopkins certainly looked the part: a handsome, well-coiffed, tall, and slender man with a high forehead and pronounced chin. Always impeccably dressed, Hopkins exuded professionalism and class, especially when seated at the desk in his father's office in Washington, DC in the prestigious Hibbs building on 15th Street, a three-minute walk from the White House. With Hopkins arranging the sale to Flint of rubber plantations the Maderos owned, he helped raise the initial cash needed for the revolution. Hopkins' first task was to arrange the purchase of arms and ammunition, as well as create "confidential agencies" in New York, Washington, DC, San Antonio, and El Paso.[140] These became the hubs of *maderista* activity the Bureau watched so closely.

For reasons not fully documented, the Bureau did not have any of its agents on the ground in the Hotel Astor. However, evidencing the fact that the Bureau understood the importance of these meetings and the need to gather details, Division Superintendent Mitchell personally interviewed Tinker.[141] And Mitchell assigned Agent Scully to continue investigating Tinker, while agents in San Antonio and El Paso observed *maderista* movements.

The Bureau's response to the Madero rebellion was twofold. First, monitoring, and, if possible, infiltrating, *maderista* cells. Second, combatting recruiting and arms smuggling. BI agents in San Antonio began trying to get a handle on this new crop of revolutionists, mainly by working their informants and attending meetings of revolutionary sympathizers.[142] The field office also employed a stenographer, Miss Alice Whiting, "who is familiar with both the English and Spanish languages."[143]

At El Paso, where some ninety percent of the population supported Madero, BI agents Cole, Lancaster, and Vann coordinated with the Mexican consul and with Consul Luther Ellsworth, deputy US marshals, customs inspectors, and Texas Rangers. They also arranged with railroad officials to receive notification when munitions were shipped to border businesses such as hardware stores. Of particular interest were the two leading hardware firms: Krakauer, Zork & Moye, and Shelton-Payne. Krakauer was the largest munitions dealer in the Southwest. The head of the firm, Adolph Krakauer, was not just a hardware dealer—he was one of the most prominent businessmen in El Paso. His competitor Shelton-Payne would supply much of the *maderistas*' armament. These firms epitomized the views of many border businessmen whose attitude was that "if the Mexicans were determined to kill each other they should be provided with ample weaponry at a price they could afford."[144] Adolph Krakauer, for instance, made his position quite clear when testifying to a Senate subcommittee: "Our business is supplying arms and ammunition, it has been for the last 25 years, and I do not propose on account of this revolution to stop it."[145] As with Prohibition and more recently with drugs, if there was no demand there would be no supply.

The head of Madero's junta in El Paso was Abraham González, whom Madero had named the revolutionary provisional governor of Chihuahua.[146] González, scion of a wealthy Chihuahuan family, had graduated from Notre Dame University, was a gentle giant of a politico, and a master organizer. It was he who had recruited Francisco "Pancho" Villa as an *insurrecto* chieftain. Under the leadership of González, the junta was supplying the *insurrectos* in Chihuahua with an ever-increasing flow of munitions and supplies. And despite González's public assurances, the junta was daily violating the neutrality laws. Further, in order to combat the Mexican consul's operatives, González hired the Thiel Detective Service, an international firm.[147]

Yet another player on the intelligence scene in El Paso was the foreign-owned Mexico Northwestern Railway (MNW), whose tracks ran from El Paso in a loop through the Sierra Madre to the city of Chihuahua. Since the railroad's track, rolling stock, and facilities were vulnerable to attack by *maderista* guerillas, the MNW hired private detectives to report on revolutionary conditions: brothers Thomas Branham Cunningham and Ed B. Cunningham. Thomas B. Cunningham, incidentally, was a former Bureau of Investigation agent.[148] The Cunninghams ingratiated themselves with the *maderista* junta, sending the MNW reports of real value, including Standard Oil Company's offer to finance the Madero rebellion in return for concessions should Madero prevail. But at the same time, the brothers were working for Consul Torres. In fact, they were his most important agents, signing their reports as "Your Informants." And they also supplied information to the Bureau of Investigation.[149] Many secret agents reported to more than one master.

The New York office of the Bureau, the largest of the field offices with around a dozen agents, monitored the munitions pipeline as best it could. Division Superintendent Mitchell dispatched Agent Charles J. Scully fifty-five miles up the Hudson River to Bannerman's Island. Francis Bannerman was the leading arms dealer in the country. He had purchased most of the Spanish army's weapons and ammunition in Cuba after the Spanish-American War and had transported them to his island, where he built a literal castle and from where he conducted business in complete security. As Scully reported, "the island on which the stores are kept by Bannerman is practically inaccessible as even an inspector of the Bureau of Combustibles is compelled to make an arrangement for a visit to the island several days prior thereto."[150] However, Scully arranged with the New York Central railroad's agent at Newburgh, New York, to notify the Bureau's New York office in the event Bannerman attempted to ship ordnance to the border.[151]

The person handling arms shipments to Madero from New York City was Ed Maurer, a wealthy import-export broker who had had extensive business dealings with the Madero family before the revolution and now received funds from Hopkins and Flint. Maurer supplied virtually all the munitions the firm of Shelton-Payne received in El Paso.[152] Maurer was shipping arms through the Bush Terminal Company in Brooklyn, and Superintendent Mitchell assigned Agents Scully, Dotzert, Craft, and Dyer to monitor this traffic. They followed the trucks transporting munitions from Bush to steamship companies' wharves, from where the armament would usually go to Galveston for transshipment by rail to dealers in places such as El Paso. Scully, for example, tracked seven bales marked "furniture fixtures" but which contained cartridges sent to El Paso and destined for the *maderistas*.[153] The shipment was consigned to one "Frank Cody," an alias for Harvey J. Phillips, an employee of Sherburne G. Hopkins. Bureau agents failed to apprehend Phillips, and the munitions reached the *insurrectos* through the Shelton-Payne hardware firm. The Bureau eventually tracked down Phillips, who pleaded guilty to violating the neutrality laws and was fined a mere $100 and costs. (His neutrality violation was not held against him when he became a Bureau special employee in 1912.)

What the increasing flow of weaponry illustrated was that as a revolutionist Madero had something Flores Magón always lacked: money. Madero had something else Flores Magón lacked: courage. Whereas Flores Magón remained safely in his Los Angeles headquarters while urging his followers to risk their lives in Mexico, Madero decided to lead the rebellion in person. He slipped out of San Antonio and made his way to the border at Eagle Pass, where on the night of November 19, the eve of the rebellion per the Plan de San Luis Potosí, Madero crossed the Rio Grande to take command of the rebel force awaiting him. He was shocked to discover that despite the assurances he had received, there was no rebel force. A chagrined Madero returned to San Antonio to await developments.

It seemed the rebellion was stillborn. But in the state of Chihuahua, rebels such as Pancho Villa and Pascual Orozco were raising guerrilla bands and taking on units of Díaz's army. The revolution began to show signs of life. Madero's followers in El Paso were busily recruiting volunteers, raising money, and acquiring munitions which they easily smuggled across the shallow Rio Grande. Smuggling was such an ingrained aspect of life on the Mexican border that it merits a scholarly history.[154] The Díaz administration took the position that it was the responsibility of the United States to interdict the flow of munitions across the extremely porous border.

The Bureau became more concerned as the Mexican Revolution gained momentum. Chief Finch was not just a desk-bound bureaucrat. He traveled to Austin, Texas, to confer on February 4, 1911 with Agent in Charge Cole, US Attorney Charles Boynton, and US Marshal Eugene Nolte about conditions on the Texas border. Two days later, Finch was in San Antonio conferring with Marshal Nolte, Consul Ellsworth, and the commanding general of the Department of Texas. The Posse Comitatus Act prohibited the military from enforcing civil laws, but on occasion the army detailed soldiers in plain clothes to assist the Bureau by conducting surveillance, and on one occasion the commanding general in San Antonio arranged to send a few soldiers to the Buckhorn Saloon as agents provocateurs with instructions to create the impression that their terms of service would expire in a few days, and that they were amenable to being recruited by the *maderistas*.[155] Chief Finch, accompanied by Ellsworth and Cole, visited Eagle Pass, Del Rio, and El Paso to confer with various officials.

The Bureau was developing some expertise in running covert operations. Although the agency had few undercover assets, one of the best was John C. Wilbur, assigned by Chief Finch himself. Wilbur, who reported to the San Antonio field office, was an ex-soldier (Troop A, 5th Cavalry, 1897-1900) who had spent time in South America and in Mexico. He could speak Spanish fluently, at a time when few Bureau operatives could. Wilbur was living in San Antonio and became acquainted with Francisco Madero and his brothers, Alfonso and Julio, "after the Chief ordered me on the case in January 1911." He gained the confidence of the local *maderista* junta, which was contemplating launching an expedition to Yucatán and recruited Wilbur to help organize the venture. The plan was ludicrous: a force of fifty *insurrectos* under a captain would sail from New Orleans in a chartered vessel for Yucatán at the southern end of Mexico with 500 rifles and ammunition and would liberate and arm the political prisoners in a penal colony, thereby opening a second revolutionary front.[156] The proposed operation was repeatedly changed and postponed, and finally abandoned.

Wilbur continued to pose as an ardent *maderista*, but his cover was jeopardized by one James Henry McCloskey, with whom Madero's brother, Alfonso, had been negotiating purchases of munitions. Alfonso Madero instructed Wilbur to work with McCloskey. Knowing that McCloskey, who had been reporting to Mexican Consul Ornelas, was absolutely unworthy of confidence, and fearing that Wilbur's connection with the Bureau would be revealed if he dealt with McCloskey, Agent in Charge at San Antonio Marshall Eberstein directed Wilbur to tell Alfonso Madero that he had received information that McCloskey was really working for the Mexican Government. Wilbur later reported that Madero thanked him very kindly for the information and directed him to have nothing to do with McCloskey.[157]

With Wilbur's revolutionary credentials thus enhanced, Alfonso Madero offered Wilbur a captain's commission in the *insurrecto* army and sent him in February to the small Texas border town of Sanderson. The San Antonio junta hoped to launch a military expedition from Sanderson into Madero's home state of Coahuila. To that end, they planned to smuggle a sizeable shipment of munitions to Sanderson, and Wilbur was their key operative. The junta also tasked BI informant Wilbur with surveilling BI agent Guy Hamilton Scull, who had shadowed on the train from San Antonio a *maderista* conveying a shipment of saddles to Sanderson. Presumably, Scull was delighted to be working in the field instead of reviewing waybills.

Complicating matters, J. D. Womack, a private detective who was a Mexican government agent recruited by William Hanson in San Antonio, appeared at Sanderson eager to combat *maderistas*. His presence threatened to wreck Scull and Wilbur's operation. Agent Scull remonstrated strongly with Womack, persuading him to leave Sanderson.[158] Womack, still working for Consul Ornelas, reappeared at San Antonio, where he seized from Mexicans at the Southern Pacific depot guns and ammunition being loaded on the train for Sanderson. Wilbur reported that Alfonso and Julio Madero were quite upset over the incident. Agent in Charge Eberstein issued a public statement that the government had nothing whatever to do with Womack's action and advised Consul Ornelas that his man Womack's interference with BI investigations was harming the interests of both the United States and Mexico. Ornelas apologized for Womack and agreed to furnish the Bureau with copies of the reports that Womack and his other operatives furnished him.[159] Alfonso Madero, still believing Wilbur to be a committed *maderista*, instructed him to return to Sanderson, taking with him two *maderistas* and two trunks of guns and ammunition. Agent Eberstein had the serial numbers of the bills Madero gave Wilbur for expenses and the serial numbers of the rifles carefully copied for future reference.[160]

The Bureau's Sanderson operation was still on track, but further interference came from the army. Agent in Charge Eberstein reported he "was in telegraphic communication with Agent Scull at Sanderson, Texas, regarding the presence of Captain Conrad, of the United States Army, who had arrived in Sanderson for the express purpose of investigating and reporting on the situation there, particularly as to Informant Wilbur. Mr. Scull declined to give the captain information as to the informant, referring him to Mr. Eberstein. The matter was taken up by telegraph with this Bureau and arrangements were later made with the War Department which it is believed will prevent further interference of this character."[161]

Matters moved to a climax in March as preparations for the expedition neared completion. Agent Scull advised that it was imperative to act. Wilbur helped transport the arms and ammunition to the Rio Grande, having notified Bureau agents Clyatt and Scull of the route. They swooped down and arrested everybody, thereby preserving Wilbur's cover. The leader of the proposed expedition frantically began tearing up the incriminating documents he imprudently carried on his person. Wilbur obligingly lent a hand, tearing up the envelopes but secreting the papers.[162] Twelve men were arrested and eleven pack animals, fifty-six rifles, and 10,000 cartridges were seized.[163]

Wilbur was later approached by the individual who had sold him the munitions "who intimated to me that it would be very much to my interest in a financial or any other way, if I were not a Govt. witness in the coming trial against the bunch that was arrested in Sanderson." Wilbur, Agents Clyatt and Scull received death threats from the gang of smugglers, but talk was cheap.[164]

Unfortunately, the press revealed Wilbur's connection with the government, and his usefulness as an informant against the *maderistas* was destroyed. He was reassigned to Dallas to work under the US attorney, and in May returned to San Antonio to testify before the grand jury. His cover blown, Wilbur was then assigned to assist Agent Scull openly in Laredo trying to locate revolutionists. Wilbur was a competent secret agent and perhaps became intoxicated with the excitement and danger involved.[165] He was indicted in San Antonio in January 1913, for impersonating a Bureau of Investigation agent.[166] However, he was evidently exonerated, for he later became a "Local Officer" BI agent assigned primarily to enforcing the Mann Act.

Agent in Charge Eberstein directed Agent Clyatt to join him in San Antonio, while Agent Scull was again relegated to inspecting waybills, this time in Laredo. To Eberstein's surprise, Scull resigned. What the agent in charge had not known was that the special agent he had banished for months into the most remote Texas towns to scan freight bills, was surprisingly accomplished. Eberstein seemed not to have been aware of Scull's resume: a Harvard graduate, class of '98, who counted Theodore Roosevelt among his close friends. As the famous Rough Riders, they had stormed San Juan Hill in Cuba during the Spanish-American War. From his service in Cuba, the rough riding captain also became friends with General Leonard Wood. In the early 1900s, Scull became a war correspondent in the Russo-Japanese war in 1905 and in the Dominican Republic.[167] He traveled extensively, almost died in a boat wreck during a hurricane in the Caribbean, hunted big game in Africa, and shared the harrowing tales of his adventures with his Harvard Club friends in New York and in American magazines and newspapers.[168]

Scull was in the headlines with a bestseller in 1911, just as he joined the BI. The book described Scull's experience as a field manager of the Buffalo Jones African Expedition with the title, *Lassoing Wild Animals in Africa*, with an introduction from his Rough Rider presidential friend.[169] He may have had fantasies of exploring the Mexican border on horseback and lassoing neutrality law violators, as his friend Jimmy Hare, the legendary war correspondent for *Colliers Magazine* who spotted him in San Antonio, teased him in the Harvard Club in 1911. Months of checking waybills—the only excitement being the infrequent passing through of a train—obviously wore out his patience. Scull moved to Washington, DC, where the State Department obviously appreciated Scull's abilities and command of Spanish more than the BI, and sent him to Nicaragua in 1912 as an advisor to the government with the task of creating a national police force.[170]

Agent in Charge Eberstein, according to Scull's biographer, only learned of his agent's celebrity shortly before the latter resigned. "It left me flabbergasted," he is quoted as saying.[171] Supposedly, the two made up some time later and became fast friends. Whether Eberstein indeed had been unaware of Scull's background, or whether that knowledge precipitated the treatment he gave to his charge, remains unknown. Had he really been unaware, this certainly would shine a negative light on the communication between headquarters and the field offices. It would also allude to an attitude of surprising modesty on the part of Scull as he spent the better part of a year tending menial assignments.

The Sanderson operation had been a resounding success, but it paled beside the Bureau's activities in El Paso, which remained the center of revolutionary action. There, Agent in Change Cole supervised Agents Lancaster and Vann as well as Agent Geck, currently investigating in nearby Las Cruces, New Mexico.

The Mexican consul in El Paso, Antonio Lomelí, ran his own secret agents against the *magonistas* and the *insurrectos*. He sometimes shared information with the Bureau. The Bureau distrusted the Mexican consul and conducted its own surveillance of the *magonistas* and *insurrectos*. These revolutionary factions conducted counter-surveillance on the consul and the Bureau. The Bureau's skepticism about Consul Lomelí proved justified, for a representative of the *maderista* junta suborned the consul, who provided information about Díaz troop dispositions and a cipher in exchange for $3,000, paid in weekly installments. The Díaz government also became suspicious of Lomelí, replacing him in March 1911, with Tomás Torres, whose operatives included Jesús María Arriola, who would become head of the Mexican government's intelligence service in the United States in 1916. The man who suborned Lomelí, Charles Francis Louis Zeilinger Caracristi, was one of the most exotic players in revolutionary intrigue. A PhD in geology from Virginia, Caracristi was familiar with Latin America and had an ego the size of Texas. He continually invoked the names of the rich and powerful whose wrath he could call down on anyone who crossed him.[172]

Figure 22 C. F. Z. *Caracristi*, Tacoma Times, March 13, 1911.

Francisco Madero slipped out of San Antonio for El Paso because the fiction that he was not violating the neutrality laws had worn dangerously thin. On February 11, 1911, the US Commissioner in El Paso, George B. Oliver, issued secret federal warrants for the arrest of Madero and Abraham González.[173] But even as Agents Lancaster and Vann tried to serve the warrants, the press broke the story. Both Madero and González managed to slip across the Rio Grande and join their jubilant supporters.[174]

Madero courageously led his followers into battle in the state of Chihuahua. Unfortunately, he knew nothing about warfare. At the town of Casas Grandes on March 5-6, Díaz forces routed the rebels, and Madero himself was slightly wounded in the arm as he rode at the head of his troops. Máximo Castillo, at that time Madero's bodyguard, was rather impressed with his chief's bravado. After the battle, he commented, "...he either does not know that bullets kill, or he is extremely courageous."[175] Having proven his valor, Madero left command of the *insurrectos* to those who knew what they were doing, such as Pascual Orozco and Pancho Villa.

While recovering at Hacienda Bustillos, Madero received his commanders Orozco, whom he promoted to brigadier general, and Villa, now colonel. American correspondents also received audiences to conduct interviews. Among Madero's visitors at Bustillos was the German mining engineer Felix A. Sommerfeld, at the time resident of Chihuahua City. While he proclaimed to correspondents and American investigators in later years that he worked as a stringer for AP News, he was in actuality a German naval intelligence agent. Sommerfeld, who appears in most accounts of the Mexican Revolution as a shady, unsavory character, had apparently crafted his cover story well enough to withstand most historians' prying.[176] The German government took no chances as to having a source close to whoever would succeed the aging Mexican dictator. After all, Mexico was a major trading partner and international debtor to the German Empire. Sommerfeld was the man to cover Madero for Germany. His handler in Mexico City, German Commercial Attaché Peter Bruchhausen, hit the jackpot with dispatching the 31-year-old army veteran and fluent Spanish speaker to Hacienda Bustillos. Sommerfeld would become the highest-level secret agent in North America for the German Empire during the Mexican Revolution and World War I. Madero and Sommerfeld took an immediate liking to one another, and the German agent would not leave Madero's side thereafter.

Sommerfeld's official mission at Bustillos was to interview Madero about two German mercenaries who had fought on the side of the *insurrectos* at the Battle of Casas Grandes and were captured. The federal commander sent them to Chihuahua to await trial and probable execution.[177] The two adventurers languished in prison until the revolutionary governor, Abraham González, freed them a year later.

Important to the present study is the fact that without question, Francisco Madero and his entourage knew literally from the first meeting that Felix Sommerfeld was a German agent. Despite this knowledge or maybe because of it, Madero kept Sommerfeld close, connected him with Sherburne Hopkins, and made him head of the Mexican Secret Service. It will be evident throughout this book that Sommerfeld continued to serve several factional leaders who undoubtedly knew his true background. In March 1911, however, and for the better part of the year, the Bureau had no idea of who this newcomer on the revolutionary scene was. Thereafter, BI agents periodically shadowed Sommerfeld but were never able to build a solid case, and in fact, often relied on Sommerfeld's extensive network and willingness to trade intelligence.

The Bureau learned in April that Francisco Madero's father, his brother Alfonso, and several of their aides had left San Antonio for El Paso, registering at the Sheldon Hotel, a major venue of revolutionary intrigue. Agent Lancaster covered the movements of the Madero party, while Agent Vann went to the downriver town of Fabens to investigate a *maderista* smuggler, William P. "Red" Stratton, a former customs inspector at El Paso, who had been fired for accepting bribes to smuggle in Chinese laborers. Now, Stratton was bribing soldiers guarding the river to let him pass supplies through their lines.[178] Vann also conferred with Consul Torres and with José María Arriola, the Mexican government agent, about that government's efforts to secure evidence of neutrality violations. Agent Cole received reports from informant Bryan Cunningham about *maderista* recruiting efforts. On occasion, Cole and Lancaster visited Ciudad Juárez to learn of conditions there. The Federal garrison in Juárez was becoming increasingly apprehensive, for the *insurrectos* were gaining control of the state.

Agent Cole had his hands full trying to keep up with the swarm of colorful mercenaries involved in the revolution, people such as Giuseppe Garibaldi, General Benjamin Johannis Viljoen, John M. "Dynamite Slim" Madison, and Jack R. "Big Dude" Crum. Bureau agents compiled lists of some twenty Americans serving as a kind of foreign legion with Madero.[179] El Paso also boasted a senior revolutionist in residence, Victor Leaton Ochoa, who in 1894 had led a disastrous expedition in the state of Chihuahua against the Díaz regime. Thereafter, Ochoa had continued plotting, and he would do so during the rest of the revolutionary decade.

Bolstered by the increasing volume of recruits and supplies being smuggled to them from the El Paso area, the *insurrectos* had advanced to within a few miles of Ciudad Juárez by May 1911. Besides smuggling munitions directly across the Rio Grande near El Paso, *maderistas* easily smuggled shipments across the adjoining New Mexico section of the border, which consisted of an imaginary boundary, since the Mexican government maintained no customs organization or force of *Rurales* there. Among the *insurrectos* operating in New Mexico was Paul Mason, a noted soldier of fortune. American soldiers arrested him on the border at Columbus, New Mexico. When he was taken before the US commissioner at Las Cruces, the case against him was dismissed for insufficient evidence.[180] Mason would continue to plot.

Agent Cole visited Madero's headquarters at the rebel encampment upriver from Juárez across from the El Paso smelter and interviewed members of his staff. Agent Vann also went to Madero's camp to help one William Hill retrieve his eleven-year-old son, who had run away to join the *insurrectos*. They found the boy proudly equipped with a rifle and cartridge belt. Hill took him home.[181] Among the *maderistas* flocking to Madero's camp was Venustiano Carranza, who would figure prominently in the Mexican Revolution, eventually becoming president of the republic. Madero was engaged in peace talks with representatives of the tottering Díaz government, and although Díaz's emissaries agreed to some of the rebels' demands, the talks failed because Díaz refused to accept Madero's principal demand: that Díaz step down as president.[182] The issue would be decided on the battlefield.

The struggle took a dramatic turn on May 10, 1911, when after two days of intensive combat, Madero's forces captured Ciudad Juárez, the largest Mexican border town. Agents Eberstein, Lancaster, and Thompson promptly visited Juárez ostensibly to assess the situation but mainly out of curiosity. Because the defeated Federal commander, General Juan Navarro, had executed captured *insurrectos*, the victorious rebel commanders Orozco and Villa were determined to execute him. But on Madero's orders, Garibaldi spirited the general across the Rio Grande to El Paso. Villa went there reportedly to kill Navarro, but was expelled from the city as General Navarro hid in the basement of a department store.[183]

The Mexican consul alerted Agent Eberstein, who on his own initiative, proceeded to protect the fugitive general. Eberstein reported: "This was a new stunt for me and looked like a rather large stunt for a Special Agent, However, since consul had made this request, I told him I'd furnish a guard until I could advise Department and request instructions." While Eberstein wired the Department for instructions, Agent Lancaster secured the services of a friend of his who had an automobile (an instance of the Bureau's lack of transportation), who drove Lancaster to General Navarro hiding in the basement. Lancaster and Thompson remained with Navarro until Eberstein received a telegram from the Chief informing him in no uncertain terms that the Bureau had no authority for such action. Eberstein turned the protection of Navarro over to the El Paso police, who lodged him in a safehouse because there were a lot of *maderistas* in El Paso who wanted Navarro dead. A chastened Eberstein informed the Chief that "I am not certain that I did perfectly right in this matter, but I feel that it was an emergency case and the least we could do was to protect him until I could get further orders."[184]

The stunning *insurrecto* capture of Juárez demonstrated that Porfirio Díaz was a paper tiger. His regime collapsed within two weeks. Leaving Francisco León de la Barra, formerly his ambassador in Washington, in charge of an interim regime, Díaz went into European exile. He settled in Paris, where he died in 1915. In his hour of triumph, Madero stepped down as provisional president and began preparing to be a candidate in a forthcoming free presidential election. Unfortunately for Madero, most of the Díaz structure was still in place although Díaz was gone, and De la Barra did what he could to frustrate revolutionary reform. Since he was now merely a private citizen, all Madero could do was to suggest and complain. His popularity began to erode.

In view of Madero's victory, Chief Finch was anxious to reduce the Bureau's costs as quickly as possible. Although Attorney General Wickersham himself authorized the continued employment of an informant for five days at three dollars a day, Finch wired Agent in Charge Eberstein at San Antonio: "Appointments Thompson, Clyatt, Ross, Whiting, Clark, and Wilbur expire May 31; in view present conditions wire whether services of any of above employees can be dispensed with after 31st."[185] Eberstein replied that it was difficult for him to give an intelligent answer because revolutionary plotting and arms shipments to Mexico were continuing, and he would need all the personnel he currently had. He suggested that Finch maintain the present force at least until mid-June, but if nothing noteworthy occurred within the next few days he would instruct all agents and informers to proceed to their assigned stations. (He also requested from Finch a supply of blank transportation requests, assorted envelopes, report paper, and letterheads.)[186] Finch instructed him to "discontinue services informants at close present month, or earlier if practicable."[187]

One of the agents Eberstein requested to remain on staff and who would eventually succeed him as agent in charge of the San Antonio field office was Hy (Henry or Hayman) A. Thompson. He remains somewhat of an enigma. Military records indicate that he was born around 1865, most likely in California. He joined the California National Guard in 1886.[188] A year later, a local newspaper mentioned the young soldier, now stationed at Fort Keogh near Miles City, Montana, as having "powerful influence over [the] Cheyennes," as he motivated four members of the tribe to surrender to law enforcement.[189] Thompson worked in 1889 for the Thiel Detective Agency, known for their knack as strike-breakers on a national scale, and set up regional field offices.[190] It is unknown how long he worked for the Thiel agency. Between 1906 and 1908, Thompson worked as an investigator for the Frisco Railroad System in Sapulpa, Oklahoma.[191] It may have been just a coincidence that Secret Service agent Marshall Eberstein, under whom Thompson worked in 1911, investigated a land fraud case in Omaha at the same time.[192] Between 1909 and 1910, Thompson joined the Bureau in the Kansas City, Missouri, field office. He transferred to the BI office in El Paso, Texas in March 1911.[193] Thompson's pedigree, both as a Thiel detective (several of his colleagues, for example Agent L. E. Ross came from that organization), and railroad special agent seemed sufficient for the BI to promote him agent in charge for the important San Antonio office when Eberstein transferred to Omaha, Nebraska in the fall of 1911.[194]

The Treasury Department, believing the Mexican Revolution to be over, directed in May 1911, that ports of entry be open for all traffic into Mexico. This meant that arms and ammunition would legally be shipped if properly manifested. A flood of properly manifested munitions, a good part addressed to fictitious consignees, ensued. Almost overnight the Bureau, which had been cooperating with the Díaz government in combatting *maderista* violations of the neutrality laws, now faced a situation in a state of flux. An interim regime under Francisco de la Barra tried to hold the country together until a presidential election could be arranged. Agent Lancaster went to Ciudad Juárez and spoke with Madero, assuring the revolutionary leader that although there was a warrant against him for neutrality violations, the grand jury had passed one term and Madero had not been indicted. The assistant US attorney stated that, under the circumstances, Madero would not be molested if he traveled through US territory while returning in triumph to Mexico City to prepare his candidacy for the presidency.[195] Riding the wave of popularity, Madero was a shoo-in to win the forthcoming election.

Even while focusing on Madero, the Bureau had to concern itself with other revolutionary matters. For one thing, the *magonistas* were showing renewed signs of life. Flores Magón, who publicly proclaimed himself an anarchist, had come up with a new strategy in 1911 to sideline Madero and emerge as the true revolutionary leader: seize control of the Territory of Baja California, a sparsely-inhabited backwater of the Republic of Mexico, and use it as a base for overthrowing the government. The strategy was grandiose, and the result was predictable—another PLM fiasco. Flores Magón began trying to organize a filibustering expedition from his Los Angeles headquarters to invade Baja California. He counted on being close enough to the border to facilitate logistics and, if things went wrong, to provide his followers asylum in the US. He appealed to radicals everywhere while walking a fine line to avoid violating the neutrality laws. Most of his support from American radicals came from the militant labor organization Industrial Workers of the World, the IWW, or "Wobblies," as they were commonly called, who smuggled munitions into Baja California.[196] Agent Simmons was promptly dispatched to Calexico to monitor the *magonistas*' activities, with the local Mexican consul's assistance.

Initially, the PLM's campaign looked promising. In January 1911, twenty of its filibusters under Simon Berthold seized Mexicali. Berthold told a reporter that he had enlisted about fifty men, but an essential shipment of rifles had been delayed to long that by the time the shipment finally arrived, most of his men had left him; only twenty accompanied him to Mexicali.[197] In the high point of the campaign, IWW militants under a Welsh mercenary, "General" Caryl Rhys Pryce, seized Tijuana. Pryce, who was a British subject and a resident of British Columbia, had fought for Britain with distinction in several campaigns in South Africa.

But after these initial victories, the filibusters' campaign began to unravel. Agent in Charge Clayton E. Herrington filed a criminal complaint at San Francisco for violation of the neutrality laws against "General" Pryce, who had just been indicted in Los Angeles. The US commissioner then issued an arrest warrant and delivered it to the US marshal, who arrested Pryce and held him for trial in Los Angeles. He admitted his connection with the insurgent forces but insisted that he never enlisted any men or secured any munitions in the United States.[198]

Clayton Herrington was not a typical BI agent. Born in 1856 in Milwaukee, Wisconsin, Herrington grew up in Pennsylvania. In 1877, he joined the law school at Iowa College in Iowa City (today University of Iowa).[199] Married with two children, he practiced law in Des Moines through 1897, when the young family moved to San Antonio, Texas. Herrington took a job as railroad claim agent. He moved to San Francisco in 1911 and joined the Department of Justice as a lawyer and BI special agent.[200]

A slick empresario and publicist, Dick Ferris, who had been a promoter of various enterprises, including theatrical companies, aviation meets, and night baseball, now styled himself a general, and proclaimed the "Republic of Baja California," which further confused the issue. Agent Herrington conferred with the US attorney and the Mexican Consul General to build a case against Ferris by having informants report to Ferris for enlistment in his proposed venture. Having informants enlist in revolutionary factions was a standard BI technique for obtaining evidence of neutrality violations. To Agent Herrington's frustration, Ferris's secretary always told the prospective recruits that Ferris was out of the office. However, an informant told Herrington that he had called on Ferris, who told him that the movement of US troops to the border had interfered with his plans, but that he had intended to take possession of Baja California in the event the present government of Mexico should be overthrown by the *insurrectos*. Furthermore, Ferris told the informant that he had not enlisted any men but had the addresses of a number upon whom he could call at any time to join his expedition. Herrington had the informant prepare an affidavit concerning his interview with Ferris.[201]

Agent J. A. Baker inquired in New York City at the offices of the *New York Herald* regarding an advertisement in that newspaper on February 14: "General" Dick Ferris called for 1,000 men to go to Mexico. The agent was informed that the original advertisement had been destroyed and that they did not keep a copy. Furthermore, he learned that the *New York Times* had run the ad once but had dropped it as objectionable. Baker had better luck at the *New York American*, where upon the advice of their attorney, the newspaper delivered their copy of the advertisement. It turned out, however, that the advertisement came from an advertising agency and the clerk who had written the original was no longer employed there. The BI tracked the clerk down at his residence in Kansas City, but he could not remember who had paid for the advertisement.[202] Ferris's farcical Republic of Baja California proved ephemeral. "General" Pryce absconded with all the cash he could lay hands on, and American newspapers portrayed Flores Magón as incompetent at best and essentially ridiculous.[203]

Agent James Ganor in Los Angeles was a former customs officer. He located and spoke with Dick Ferris and submitted statements of two Mexicans who applied at PLM headquarters there for enlistment and transportation to Baja California to join the insurgents. They stated they were told that if they would secure guns and ammunition and agree to pay their own expenses, arrangements would be made for them to join the revolutionists in Mexico.[204] Agent Ganor and the US marshal raided the *magonista* headquarters at $519\frac{1}{2}$ East Fourth on June 14, arresting the members of the junta: Ricardo Flores Magón, president; Enrique Flores Magón, secretary; and Anselmo L. Figueroa and Librado Rivera. Enrique Flores Magón attempted to destroy documents, but the agent overpowered and handcuffed him. The officers seized all the documents they could find, but as they left "it became necessary for US Marshal and Agent to draw revolvers to protect themselves from the crowd who were in and near office at the time of Enrique Magon's [sic] arrest." The agent spent the following days in the office with the assistant US attorney going over the books, newspapers, and documents seized.[205] Furthermore, the US marshal's deputies located and confiscated three two-inch-bore fieldpieces under construction for the insurgents.[206]

Antonio de Pío Araujo, also indicted in connection with the Flores Magón case, remained at large. The Bureau contacted Leavenworth Penitentiary and the Special Agent in Charge in El Paso for a photograph and description of the fugitive, since he had been convicted there on January 22, 1909, of neutrality violation and sentenced to a fine of $1.00 and thirty months at hard labor in Leavenworth. Araujo no sooner had completed his sentence than he reverted to his old *magonista* ways. Agent in Charge H. A. Thompson in El Paso sent a photograph and description of Araujo to Los Angeles as requested.[207]

Ricardo Flores Magón, Enrique Flores Magón, Librado Rivera, Antonio de Pío Araujo, and Anselmo Figueroa were indicted on July 8, 1911, for neutrality violations. Their trial began on June 4, 1912, and they were found guilty as charged. On June 25, 1912, they each received a sentence of one year and eleven months in the federal penitentiary at McNeil Island, Washington. They applied for executive clemency but were denied. The pardon attorney recommended that they serve their full sentence.[208] Besides visiting the Mexican *barrio* in Los Angeles, "where speeches were being made by Magon faction," Agents Simmons and Ganor continued to evaluate the trove of papers seized from the junta. The agents asked Mexican Consul General Arturo M. Elías for help coping with this formidable task, and he quickly provided a Spanish translator in the person of his assistant.[209]

Also at Los Angeles, Consul Antonio Lozano had managed to intercept *magonista* communications. Flores Magón and his associates had been laboriously writing messages and personal letters on strips of cloth and smuggling them out of the Los Angeles County jail in their dirty laundry. Lozano not only obtained and photographed these communications, but he also photographed incoming messages, providing copies of everything to the Mexican Ministry of Foreign Relations and the US attorney.[210]

Yet relations between the BI and Consul Lozano were fraught, for the information his agents shared with the Bureau was vague and usually inaccurate. As Agent Ganor commented: "Agent informed officers that within the last year they have employed a large number of men for secret work, and they are unable to give this department any assistance. As to the evidence all that has ever been secured were [sic] by Agent Simmons and myself."[211] Even the Mexican government's attorney was unable to persuade the consul to provide the Bureau with useful information.[212]

A further irritant was that Mexican consuls Arturo Elías and Antonio Lozano in Los Angeles, as well as Consul J. Díaz Prieto in San Diego, were busily—and blatantly—recruiting men to combat the insurgents in Baja California.[213] And Mexican government sympathizers led by Dr. Horacio E. López and Carlos V. Mendoza were raising money and conducting propaganda. Mendoza was prominent in an organization at San Diego called the "Defenders of the National Integrity," dedicated to inducing Mexicans in the US to proceed to Ensenada in Baja California to protect that place from insurgents.[214]

Flores Magón's sympathizers repeatedly brought all this to the attention of United States authorities, urging them to enforce the neutrality laws equally. In response, Attorney General Wickersham had the US attorney investigate. The result was that on May 25, López and Mendoza were arrested at the docks in San Diego as a band played the Mexican national anthem, and a vessel with volunteers prepared to depart for Baja California. The interim Mexican government strongly protested the leaders' arrests, and in order to maintain good relations, the American authorities ordered López and Mendoza released, on May 31. As for the volunteers, most made it to Ensenada—some 150 were there by the end of May.[215]

The invasion of Baja California collapsed in June 1911, because of disputes among the rebels, a counteroffensive by forces of the interim government, logistical problems, and the antipathy of the United States. This ill-fated campaign by a couple of hundred fighters, many of them foreigners, had been the high point of *magonista* military participation in the Mexican Revolution. Thereafter, this faction was increasingly marginalized, their strong suit continuing to be propaganda.

During the debacle, those insurgents who could, sprinted across the border seeking asylum in the United States. The army arrested them. At Fort Rosecrans outside of San Diego, 105 dispirited rebels were being held pending the action of the US marshal and US attorney.[216] Agents Simmons and Ganor questioned them while their attorney "remained with them during day making speeches and instructing them to remain silent."[217] The agents also interrogated those insurgents in the county jail who had been arrested as they crossed the border. Some were rank-and-file insurgents and gave little information of value. Three insurgent smugglers were taken to Los Angles to testify before the grand jury.[218] One insurgent in custody since his arrest in April near San Diego decided to plead guilty to violating the neutrality laws. He was sentenced to six months in the county jail. Agent Ganor also questioned his informant regarding Richard Ferris, who had also been indicted in the Flores Magón case.[219]

As of March 1912, Agent Ganor was still working through the mass of *magonista* documents seized from the junta, as well as meeting with the Mexican government's attorney regarding Flores Magón's forthcoming trial beginning April 18. Ganor spent considerable time trying to locate important witnesses that the US marshal's office had failed to find. And he also made a point of wandering through crowds in the Hispanic *barrios* to get some idea of popular sentiment regarding events in Mexico.[220]

New Orleans was yet another center of revolutionary activity. Agent Billups Harris reported that the steamship *Sonora* left for Veracruz with a quantity of ammunition loaded at a place not inspected by customs officers. The agent checked, found a locked warehouse, and began watching it sporadically for possible violation of neutrality laws. And when the Mexican ship *Puebla* docked in New Orleans, Agent Harris had Customs place it under constant surveillance in case it loaded munitions for Mexican ports.[221] The arms traffic through New Orleans was picking up; the SS *Dunkeld* departed for the port of Progreso in Yucatán with 48,000 cartridges and three cases of rifles not on the manifest. The Mexican ambassador claimed the governor of Yucatán was preparing a rebellion. The US attorney's opinion was that such shipments were in the regular course of commerce and refused to stop the shipment. But the Mexican Steamship Lines in New Orleans received instructions to transport no more war materiel to Mexico. Nevertheless, Agent Harris tried to have the wharves and docks watched. An unsettling bit of information was that the agent learned from a clerk at the hardware firm of Stauffer, Eshleman & Co. that a large shipment of arms and ammunition would soon go to Mexico. Among other things, Harris arranged for a mail cover.[222] Given the disreputable crowd with whom he had to deal, Agent Harris became apprehensive, for he telegraphed Bureau headquarters to "Please send revolver, automatic preferred."[223]

Besides trying to monitor Mexican revolutionary activity, the overworked Bureau agents at New Orleans also had to keep an eye on persons suspected of plotting revolutions in Central America, especially Honduras. They focused on the mercenary, Lee Christmas, who was indeed instrumental in overthrowing the Honduran government in 1911. Furthermore, Agent Brett H. Dorey informed the Chief that "at present I am greatly handicapped by not having the convenience of an office—in addition to losing much time in going to and fro between my apartments, where my official papers and documents must be kept in a trunk, and the Federal Building. The status of the office question is indicated by the enclosed letter from the Custodian of the Federal Building. If cases are important, request authority to employ two informants, one at $4 per day and one at $2.50, leaving it [to] my discretion as to how the total sum of six dollars and fifty be divided between them, and that these men be paid on regular vouchers as are the Special Agents, if this be not incompatible with the practice of the Disbursing Officer, and that they be required to render the regular written daily reports required of Special Agents. My reasons for this recommendation are that I fear that my individual work along several lines simultaneously may result unsatisfactory to the Department, and that the hiring of informants by myself who would look to me for their payments might become financially embarrassing to me personally."[224]

Figure 23 Portrait of General Bernardo Reyes, c. 1901. Source: The World's Work, 1901.

Agent Harris's worries increased when on October 5, 1911, General Bernardo Reyes arrived on the steamship *Excelsior* from Havana. Alerted by a telegraph operator as to the date of Reyes's arrival, Harris wired the Chief and was at the dock when the Reyes party landed. Reyes was the most distinguished soldier in Mexico. He had served as Porfirio Díaz's minister of war and had been viewed by many as the dictator's probable successor. Because of Reyes's prominence, Díaz had viewed him as a potential rival and had neatly neutralized him by sending him on an extended inspection trip to Europe. Reyes did not return to Mexico until after Madero had overthrown Díaz. Recognizing General Reyes's prestige and his ability to cause trouble, Francisco Madero offered Reyes the position of Minister of War if Madero was elected president, but many of Madero's followers viewed this as a betrayal of the revolution, given Reyes's prominence in Porfirio Díaz's regime, and the overture failed. Reyes decided to run for president against Madero in the forthcoming presidential election but dropped out the of the campaign, charging intimidation and that Madero had the election rigged. He left Mexico in disguise, alleging that his life was in danger.

Reyes, accompanied by his attorney David Reyes Retana and his secretary Manuel Quiroga, was met at the dock by an enthusiastic crowd which included soldier of fortune Paul Mason and F. A. Chapa, the most prominent Hispanic politician in Texas. Reyes, his entourage, and his leading supporters checked in at the St. Charles hotel, where Chapa had already registered under the alias "F. A. Carson." General Reyes told reporters that he would not rebel against Madero, and that he would soon leave for San Antonio where he might protest Madero's election, but had no intention of organizing a revolutionary junta.[225]

Figure 24 Francisco A. Chapa, 1894. Courtesy University of Texas at San Antonio.

Reyes, of course, was plotting a rebellion against Madero.

Chapter 4: Thwarted Ambition

M'ADERO INDEED BECAME PRESIDENT, in the cleanest election yet in Mexico. He was sworn into office on November 6, 1911, and the United States formally recognized him as the legitimate president.

This meant a dramatic reversal of policy for the Bureau. As long as the United States had recognized Porfirio Díaz as Mexico's legitimate president, the Bureau had been tasked with investigating Díaz's enemies, primarily Madero. Now, Madero was recognized as president, and the Bureau was tasked with investigating Madero's enemies. And they were many, beginning with General Bernardo Reyes.

Figure 25 Bernardo Reyes in 1911.
Courtesy Collection of Dr. Carlos Martínez Assad.

Reyes arrived in San Antonio on October 7, 1911, to the cheers of some 400 to 500 jubilant followers who received him at the railroad depot.[226] He took a page straight out of Madero's playbook, using San

Antonio as his base from which to organize a rebellion against Madero, who was duly elected president in October.

Like Madero before him, Reyes had to circumvent the neutrality laws while plotting rebellion. When he reached San Antonio, Agent in Charge H. A. Thompson assigned informant John Wilbur to cover his movements. Wilbur reported that Reyes was staying at 817 San Pedro Avenue, the home of his friend Miguel Quiroga, meeting with a continual stream of people. "Everyone was talking politics and denouncing Madero." There was a rumor that Enrique Creel, Porfirio Díaz's unofficial spymaster and former member of the dictator's cabinet, was due to arrive shortly. "Mr. Creel is head of the Científico party [Porfirio Díaz's adherents] and is the same man who subscribed himself for $250,000 on his former visit to San Antonio. This subscription was to be used to further a counter-revolution against Madero."[227]

The stream of visitors included Francisco A. Chapa, a prominent San Antonio druggist, who was on the military staff of Governor Oscar Colquitt of Texas. Governors appointed twelve of their closest political supporters as lieutenant colonels in the Texas National Guard.[228] Chapa, the only Hispanic on Colquitt's military staff, had received this signal honor because he was the leading Hispanic politician in Texas and could deliver the Hispanic vote in San Antonio. He was among Reyes's most frequent visitors. Others included Dr. Samuel Espinosa de los Monteros and Ildefonso Vázquez, who had directed Reyes' political campaign in Mexico. According to Wilbur, the town was full of strange Mexicans, and they seemed to be well supplied with money.

There was the usual dense cloud of rumors—one was that there were 30,000 rifles hidden in San Antonio. Wilbur believed firearms were cached at 913 and 915 San Luis Street but was unable to verify this. Also, a prominent *reyista* from Monterrey, Carlos del Rio, who supposedly handled the financial affairs of the Reyes junta, arrived in town and reportedly deposited $180,000 in gold and travelers checks in the Alamo National Bank. Wilbur tried to verify this, making the rounds of the banks only to be told that none of them had such a depositor. Wilbur's surveillance was badly hampered for lack of an automobile, an important Bureau deficiency. When Reyes left the house, Wilbur was unable to follow. He did learn that on at least one occasion Reyes visited 1022 Houston Street, the residence of Julio Falomir, a professed *reyista*, while Andrés Garza Galán, who had been a prominent politician in the state of Coahuila under Porfirio Díaz, visited Reyes at his home.[229] Agent in Charge Thompson received intelligence from informant Captain Andrés [Santos] Coy, the assistant San Antonio police chief, and from Samuel Belden, Madero's attorney in that city.[230]

The Bureau in San Antonio got a crucial break. Agent Lancaster related that "William Chamberlain came to the office. Chamberlain is very close to General Reyes and showed me letters received from General Reyes when Reyes was in Europe. I have already furnished the Department with copies of one or two of these letters, and I know that Chamberlain is very close to General Reyes." Reyes had strong backing from supporters of ex-President Díaz, both civilians and army officers. His strategy involved launching attacks from Laredo, El Paso, Eagle Pass, and Brownsville. "Mr. Chamberlain asked that this information be kept strictly from the Mexican Government, as this would cut off the resources [sic] of his information to this Department."[231]

The walk-in informant, William Chapman Chamberlain, indeed moved in elevated circles. He was born in Brownsville, Texas, on October 2, 1850, the son of a Presbyterian minister who was a chaplain in the United States army during the Mexican War and who settled in Brownsville, becoming once again a chaplain, in the Confederate army during the Civil War. William C. Chamberlain grew up in Cameron and Nueces counties, the protégé of his brother-in-law Richard King, the cattleman who founded the legendary King Ranch. Chamberlain received a first-class education, served in the Confederate army, and in 1872 married Cármen Pizaña, with whom he had seven sons and one daughter. Chamberlain moved to Laredo in 1894. He spent considerable time in

Mexico, where he had extensive investments in valuable mining properties, mainly in the state of Durango.²³² On his trips to Mexico, Chamberlain met with a variety of personages up to and including President Porfirio Díaz. As of 1910, Chamberlain lived in San Antonio at 622 Avenue E. His stated motive for contacting the BI was that "he places his citizenship in the United States above any relationship existing between him and the Mexican Government."²³³ Through Chamberlain the Bureau gained invaluable access to the inner councils of the Reyes movement.

Informant Wilbur, meanwhile, continued his surveillance. General Reyes, Andrés Garza Galán, Miguel Quiroga, and Dr. Espinosa de los Monteros conferred for several hours and met later at the International Club (of which informant William Chamberlain was a member, also keeping an eye on Reyes.) Besides information, Wilbur had good news to deliver: "Have made arrangements to join the *Reyista* party. The party who is going to introduce me into the party, a man named Ortiz, says it will take about a week."²³⁴ Although not as valuable an informant as Chamberlain, Wilbur provided useful intelligence, such as that Quiroga and Garza Galán would soon start a newspaper, *El Porvenir*, to build public support for Reyes. And that Garza Galán was holding *reyista* meetings in an empty house belonging to F. A. Chapa. There were rumors that arms were stored in that same building.²³⁵ Another item was that Reyes feared assassination and was always surrounded by half a dozen friends when he left home.

The most intriguing item that informant Chamberlain reported was that Reyes, Miguel Quiroga, and F. A. Chapa went to Austin to meet Governor Oscar Colquitt. Reyes told Chamberlain that the object of the trip was to persuade Colquitt not to use the Texas Rangers against Reyes's conspiracy.²³⁶ Chamberlain subsequently reported that "General Reyes states that he was heartily received by Governor Colquitt, and that the Governor offered him all protection while on Texas soil...Reyes stated he informed Governor Colquitt he was not here to start a revolution, but Chamberlain says this is only a bluff."²³⁷

Governor Colquitt's attitude toward Reyes and the rebellion he was organizing was interesting. Colquitt had been quite energetic in attempting to suppress *maderista* activities in Texas, even issuing a neutrality proclamation of his own, but now he turned a blind eye to the Reyes conspiracy. The reason had to do with Texas politics. In his 1910 reelection campaign, Colquitt had received significant support from Amador Sánchez, the former mayor of Laredo and currently sheriff of Webb County, who as political boss turned out the Hispanic vote and campaigned for Colquitt. More importantly, F. A. Chapa delivered the Hispanic vote in San Antonio for Colquitt.

Figure 26 Oscar B. Colquitt. Courtesy Library of Congress Prints and Photographs Division.

Sánchez and Chapa were not only strong supporters of Colquitt but also of Bernardo Reyes, and they were deeply involved in his revolutionary intrigues. Sheriff Sánchez, for instance, was stockpiling *reyista* weapons in the Webb County jail. Their involvement created a problem for the governor. Agent Lancaster speculated that Chapa might use his influence with the governor to get men appointed whom he thought could be bought or controlled by political influence in the event of a revolution along the border. Although the meeting with Reyes was described publicly as being brief and formal, it was later revealed that Colquitt and the Mexican general had met privately at some length. The evidence suggests that Colquitt saw to it that the Texas Rangers, who were under the direct control of the governor, did nothing to hinder Reyes's conspiracy, especially in Laredo. Colquitt continued to pay lip service to enforcing neutrality and announced that the Texas Rangers would enforce the laws to the letter.[238]

Agent Lancaster was called to the home of Chamberlain, who had just returned from a visit to Reyes's headquarters. Chamberlain stated that Reyes wanted the good will of the American public for his rebellion, and the general was confident of obtaining ample weaponry, mainly surplus from the Spanish-American War, at New York, (from Francis Bannerman) and transporting the munitions to Tampico and Veracruz. Reyes further stated that he now had plenty of money and backing to carry on a revolution successfully.[239]

Lancaster pursued other lines of inquiry. At the post office he learned the addresses where *reyistas* received mail, and also which suspicious Mexicans had applied to rent post office boxes. Furthermore, he met at city hall with a certain M. M. Flores, "one of the men that guarded the 100 guns and 75,000 rounds of ammunition when the Revolution first broke out last November. Flores informed me he is well acquainted with Antonio Magnón and would go to the Gunter Hotel and would have a conversation with him in regard to the revolution and as soon as he secured what information he could from Magnón he would come to the office and inform me. Magnón is one of General Reyes' private detectives that he used for many years when he was Governor of the State of Nuevo León. I am well acquainted with Magnón myself as he was at one time a river guard [customs inspector] at Laredo, Texas, and is a very bright Mexican."[240]

Agent Lancaster called on the Mexican consul general, Manuel A. Esteva, for that government's views on the Reyes conspiracy. Rather discouragingly, Esteva said that he had several secret agents working but they had been unable to uncover anything. "He stated that they knew the Reyistas were getting quantities of arms and ammunition, but where they are stored he does not know, but thinks they are to be moved at any time; stated that if he could learn where they are and when they are to be moved he would advise me further." But evidently an audacious unnamed government secret agent sent from Mexico City was considerably more effective. The next day the Bureau was told that Reyes's headquarters were in an uproar because they had learned that "a Mexican Government Spy had worked into their quarters and had attended some of their meetings, an[d] in fact had held a private conversation with the General under the pretext of being one of the Treviños [General Gerónimo Treviño commanded the garrison in Monterrey and reportedly was a supporter of Reyes], who was expected here and why was unknown to the General. This fellow secured from General Reyes a vast amount of information including some of his important plans, and during his stay here made a trip to Austin and interviewed the Governor with reference to the meeting he had with General Reyes; he then returned to Mexico, and the Reyistas believe he has caused the arrest of a large number of their friends and followers now in Mexico."[241]

Informant Wilbur's cover was again blown. As he reported, on October 18, "I was approached by an Agent of Fernando Ancira, a millionaire of Monterrey, Mexico, who is now stopping at the St. Anthony Hotel in this City and was offered $2,500 if I would come over to their side, at the same time keeping my position with this Department. All I was to do was to keep them supplied with information regarding actions of our Department, orders issued and what the Mexican Government is doing through their Consul General here. Reported the facts to Agent in Charge Thompson and received instructions to go ahead and develop things. Am to give Ancira my answer in a day or two." However, Wilbur "had an appointment with Ancira, the man who wanted to bribe me but did not get to see him." Still, Wilbur informed the Bureau that the San Antonio *reyistas* were sending many coded telegrams to Mexico; he would try to get the key to the code and, hopefully, copies of the telegrams.[242]

A week later, Wilbur, in his persona of a corrupt government operative, had an interview with General Reyes himself regarding a proposition Wilbur had made to one of Reyes's agents. Wilbur reported that he had offered to smuggle arms and ammunition to a point that Reyes designated. When asked how much he would charge, Wilbur said he left that up to Reyes, but if it were not enough, he would so tell the general. "We talked a good deal about the methods and ways of getting the stuff over. At last, he told me he would think over the proposition and would let me know in a few days whether he would accept it or not."[243] Were the question of entrapment ever to come up, the Bureau could maintain plausible deniability by stating that Wilbur was not a Bureau agent.

Per instructions from Chief Finch to cover General Reyes and any other revolutionists, Agent in Charge Thompson sent him a detailed account of the San Antonio field office's activities, mentioning especially the valuable intelligence that William Chamberlain was providing. Thompson wrote three days later that Reyes's uprising was imminent; Chamberlain reported Reyes as saying on October 21, "We will be in Mexico in less than ten days."[244]

General Reyes was quite visible, not only frequenting the International Club but, at the invitation of the commanding general, reviewing the cavalry at Fort Sam Houston. He was also the guest of the local Masonic lodge. But mainly he plotted. Chamberlain notified Lancaster on October 28 that Sheriff Amador Sánchez, accompanied by Reyes's partisan Antonio Magnón, had been in Reyes's headquarters when Chamberlain arrived there. The headquarters were a beehive of activity, with well-dressed Mexicans coming and going, a steady stream of telegrams arriving, and several secretaries busily typing. Chamberlain also supplied the Bureau with a lengthy pamphlet entitled, *Truth and Justice: Gen. Bernardo Reyes and His Detractors*, translated from the newspaper *La Voz de Nuevo León* in Monterrey, extolling Reyes's career and virtues.[245]

In view of his invaluable assistance, Agent in Charge Thompson thought it only fair to obtain some monetary compensation for Chamberlain. He mentioned specifically reimbursing him for his daily trolley fares. Chief Finch approved, authorizing a "reasonable sum" entered on Thompson's expense account. But if Chamberlain's work continued for some time, further authorization would be necessary.[246]

The San Antonio BI office received a reinforcement in the person of Agent Isaac F. Lamoreaux. Born April 8, 1851, the sixty-year-old agent was born in Canada but had settled in Grand Rapids, Michigan in the 1870s. There, he started his career with the Pinkerton Detective Agency, then served as a deputy sheriff for four decades, with short interludes when he held elected offices, collector of taxes, and city clerk.[247] He, his German-American wife, and three children moved to Salt Lake City in 1910 to work in the field office of the BI. When the BI reassigned him to San Antonio, Lamoreaux brought lots of law enforcement experience to the department, but he neither spoke Spanish nor did he have much taste for the southwestern United States. Only a year after his assignment, the BI sent him back to Utah to work on white slavery cases.[248] After he lost his son in Germany in 1919, and having retired from the BI, he moved back to Grand Rapids where he died in 1924.[249]

After receiving a briefing from Agent in Charge Thompson, he accompanied him to Fort Sam Houston, where they had a long interview with General J. W. Duncan regarding conditions on the border. Lamoreaux considered renting a room in order to keep Reyes's headquarters under surveillance, but Agent Thompson informed him that he had "Reyes Headquarters so completely and satisfactorily covered that it does not appear possible for any important move to be made there without his being informed." Lamoreaux called on Bureau informant Chief Deputy Sheriff Charles Stevens (a future Texas Ranger captain), who recommended a reliable Mexican informer, and on the Mexican consul, who provided considerable information on current conditions. However, just as Lamoreaux was beginning to find his way around San Antonio, Agent Thompson assigned him to Del Rio.[250]

Although many of his supporters encouraged him to strike immediately, General Reyes decided to wait until Francisco Madero had formally been sworn in as president on November 6, 1911, so as not to embarrass Reyes's friend, interim president Francisco León de la Barra.²⁵¹ On November 10, the Mexican ambassador notified the State Department of Reyes's activities, asserted that they violated the neutrality laws, and formally requested that American authorities suppress the revolutionary movement in San Antonio. A few days later, the ambassador made the same request in person to Assistant Secretary of State Huntington Wilson, who replied that the neutrality laws did not allow conspirators to be arrested merely on suspicion, and action could be taken only on evidence that an actual violation had occurred. The Madero government was busy trying to amass such evidence. Not only were the international bridges on the Rio Grande closely watched for *reyista* agents, but Madero consuls were employing their own secret agents, such as J. J. Mahan in San Antonio.²⁵²

Thompson notified Chief Finch that the attorney in San Antonio representing Madero, Samuel Belden, had called on him, stating that he and Consul Esteva "were fixing to pull off some kind of a deal that would give them inside information and indicated to us that it might be some kind of a raid on the Reyista quarters. I was unable to get just what he intended to do but I see no way by which they could do this, and this Department will take no part in anything of that kind without first receiving your authority."²⁵³ Thompson further informed Finch that Esteva and Belden were trying to keep up with Reyes's movements but with little success. "They have a good many secret service agents here and with the exception of one, none of them have been able to gain an entrance to the Reyista councils. They state to our informants that the Reyistas have all the arrangements made for their arms and supplies and that they are now only perfecting their plans and organization preparatory to one final movement when the opportune time arrives."²⁵⁴ Consul Esteva finally did achieve something, using operatives Juan Leets and Francisco Villavicencio to penetrate Reyes's headquarters. Villavicencio was so adroit that he was given money to purchase arms for the rebellion.²⁵⁵

General Reyes's confidence increased. He boasted to William Chamberlain that the entire Federal army and all the large landowners in

Mexico were with him. When he crossed the Rio Grande, it would all be his. He even urged Chamberlain to accompany him. Reyes was particularly pleased to read in the newspapers that Madero was to appoint General Lauro Villar as Minister of War—Villar was an old friend of his.[256] Not only was Reyes's support in Mexico solidifying, but at Laredo Sheriff Amador Sánchez "has promised to give General Reyes all the protection that can be afforded him while he is in that County."[257]

Reyes was unaware of the extent to which his movement had been penetrated by the Bureau. William Chamberlain was now not just providing intelligence but was submitting his own reports, including a mention that Reyes and Chapa spent the morning at the Frost National Bank, and that "General Pascual Orozco of Chihuahua is with the Reyes party, notwithstanding reports to the contrary." Chamberlain was reporting from Reyes's headquarters, where F. A. Chapa was a frequent visitor.[258]

As matters moved toward a climax, some *reyistas* were singularly lacking in subtlety. Walking along a downtown street on the night of November 15, Agent in Charge Thompson noticed "two Mexicans dressed in khaki uniforms with canteens and other equipment necessary for field duty and in their possession six rifles, each carrying three, apparently .30 .30 rifles wrapped in newspaper and each one wrapped separately." He followed them to a French restaurant, where about twenty "well-to-do Mexicans of the better class" were dining. Thompson detailed Agent Hebert to watch this bunch. Hebert followed six of them to the railroad depot carrying rifles in cases as well as suitcases. Hebert later spotted another ten having dinner in a Mexican café, with ten rifles and suitcases leaning against the wall. He reported that "This is the first indication I have noticed that looked like a real revolutionary movement."[259] It was indeed. Agent Thompson reported that "There was a large move during the evening for the border; there seemed to be a great deal of stir, and every person who has been interested in the Reyes movement was out watching everything. Naturally we were very much interested, as we have expected for several days that the General would attempt to move, and this is the first concerted movement that has taken place."²⁶⁰ Reports came in that strange, well-dressed Mexicans were arriving in Marfa, Del Rio, Rio Grande City, and Brownsville.²⁶¹

But Laredo was the real center of action. A federal grand jury began returning bills of indictment for neutrality violations on November 16.²⁶² Once the federal authorities had forced his hand, Governor Colquitt went through the charade of suddenly discovering that Reyes had been plotting. With Reyes's conspiracy now collapsing, Colquitt wanted to get as much credit as he could for smashing it. Texas Adjutant General Henry Hutchings arrived on November 19, accompanied by Texas Ranger Captain John Sanders; Colquitt had ordered them to clear Laredo of Mexican plotters. In yet another instance of the army assisting the Bureau, Major Charles B. Hagadorn, commander at Fort McIntosh in Laredo, detailed troops to help Agent Lancaster and deputy US marshals conduct a series of raids that uncovered caches of *reyista* arms, ammunition, and equipment.²⁶³

Agent in Charge Thompson filed a criminal complaint with the US Commissioner, and General Reyes was arrested in San Antonio on November 18.²⁶⁴ F. A. Chapa promptly posted his $5,000 bond and the general was released for appearance at Laredo. (Chapa would post a $5,000 bond for himself when he was arrested on December 11.) Reyes put on a brave face as his movement disintegrated, maintaining his daily routine and informing his associates that he was reorganizing his forces for a new offensive.²⁶⁵

On the day of Reyes's arrest and release, Felix A. Sommerfeld suddenly appeared for the first time on the radar of Bureau agents. He personally called Agent in Charge H. A. Thompson in the middle of the night on November 18 and identified himself as "a special service agent for the Mexican Government."²⁶⁶ In the following days, Sommerfeld produced a letter from President Madero giving him a roving commission and unconditional support from all Mexican officials.²⁶⁷ He also gave Thompson his personal code (for decoding telegrams) and a present from the President of Mexico, "a very fine watch."[268] Even acknowledging that identifying a foreign spy is complicated, Thompson certainly did not seem to question Sommerfeld's background. The German citizen and army reservist, mining engineer, and sometimes journalist who, from obscurity, suddenly showed up at his doorstep as the friend and personal representative of the Mexican president should have raised some flags.[269] Sommerfeld proudly testified to his military service in China and occupations before and during the Revolution. However, the BI not only lacked an even rudimentary vetting process, but local offices also lacked financial resources, linguistic capabilities, and personnel. It is no wonder that this German naval intelligence agent had no problem infiltrating the enforcement arm of the US federal government and appeared in San Antonio's BI office as a godsend, bringing not only literal gifts but also valuable intelligence and badly needed investigative resources.

Madero's special representative now set out to help the Justice Department build a solid case for prosecuting the rebels and ending the conspiracy against the Mexican government. He immediately briefed agents Thompson and Lamoreaux on all the information Mexican intelligence agents in San Antonio and El Paso had gathered. Sommerfeld also quickly proved to anyone doubting his authority that he was now in charge. "I have expressed the opinion [to the Mexican president] that some consuls should be removed." Within weeks, Sommerfeld personally fired most consuls along the border, calling them "drunkards," and "no good in office."[270] The replacements included people like Enrique Llorente in El Paso, a protégé of Francisco León de la Barra, the interim president of Mexico, whom Madero had just replaced. Llorente clearly understood the distribution of power and worked closely with the German agent on all intelligence matters. Manuel Esteva obviously was not a drunkard or inept in Sommerfeld's estimation and remained at his consular post in San Antonio. The two developed a close personal friendship that lasted for years to come.

Sommerfeld turned out to be an adept organizer. The task of ending the Reyes conspiracy in his estimation required close cooperation with US authorities in general and the BI in particular. Hence the call on Thompson as his first act upon arrival. He told American investigators in 1918 that when he arrived, federal agents were already watching Reyes and his conspirators. "It was simply a question of getting in touch because I believed it was necessary to work hand-in-hand and with the authorities of the United States."[271] And hand-in-hand they worked. According to the disgruntled BI agent Curley D. Hebert, "I have seen Mr. Thompson take the daily reports of special agents and go to the hotel at San Antonio and meet the Mexican consul, Mr. Esteva, and go through those reports with him, and the consul would take notes from them."[272] Using H. A. Thompson in San Antonio and Louis E. Ross in El Paso as his main contacts, Sommerfeld indeed created unique and effective cooperation between Mexican and US intelligence organizations, freely sharing information, personnel, and even an automobile when necessary.

Agent in Charge Thompson was now busy assisting the US attorney preparing cases for violation of the neutrality laws against Reyes, F. A. Chapa, Miguel Quiroga, David Reyes Retana, and lesser *reyistas*, such as Sheriff Amador Sánchez, Antonio Magnón, José Sánchez, and Severo Villarreal. José Sánchez and Severo Villarreal were released on $5,000 bond each.[273] From Agent Lancaster, Thompson received a copy of General Reyes's verbose revolutionary manifesto in which he proclaimed himself provisional president of Mexico. To skirt the neutrality laws, the manifesto was dated on November 16, 1911, at Soledad in the border state of Tamaulipas, Mexico. The US attorney asked Thompson to have it translated. Thompson had stenographer A. G. Brown assist Alice Whiting "get out this very difficult translation, as no one in the building is able to translate our matters but Miss Whiting, and as she is the only translator in this Department here, it was necessary to secure an extra stenographer to take the dictation and typewrite the proclamation while she did the work of translating."[274] The manifesto, it turned out, was printed on the presses of *El Imparcial de Texas*, the newspaper owned by the fervent *reyista* F. A. Chapa.[275]

Agent in Charge Thompson accompanied the US marshal to inspect a boxcar shipped from New York consigned to fictitious persons in Laredo. They uncovered a bonanza: 510 Winchester rifles and 1,110,000 cartridges. Felix Sommerfeld called at the Bureau office and dictated several telegrams addressed to Madero and General Treviño, advising them that the United States authorities were holding the boxcar and requesting information about the consignees. It was decided to release the car and have the Mexican authorities seize it in Nuevo Laredo.

Thompson also mentioned that Major Hagadorn in Laredo (another recipient of a watch from the Mexican President via Sommerfeld) was refusing to furnish Agent Lancaster with the statements by *reyistas* whom the army had detained. Thompson hoped to end this frustrating interagency rivalry by appealing to General Duncan, commanding the Department of Texas. Agent Lancaster did get to accompany the Mexican consul and a deputy US marshal to Fort McIntosh to take a witness's statement.[276] Lancaster assisted the US attorney in interviewing witnesses, one of whom implicated Sheriff Amador Sánchez.[277]

Among the missing was the prominent *reyista* Dr. Samuel Espinosa de los Monteros, for whom a fugitive warrant was issued. Agent Lancaster participated in a search on November 27 of the doctor's room at the Kelly House, a rooming house in Laredo, which uncovered firearms and telegraphic equipment. More importantly, the next day Major Hagadorn and a deputy US marshal searched the room again, and in a just-delivered trunk found a list of Reyes's clubs in Mexico and the United States, "also the names of all his leaders and some other papers." The loose-leaf book was divided by Mexican states, listing both *reyista* clubs and their locations, and individuals and their residences. One name that stood out was that of General Pascual Orozco. Lancaster sent a copy of the notebook to Agent Thompson, and in a gesture of interagency cooperation, he gave two copies to Major Hagadorn, who thought it might be useful in case of

United States intervention in Mexico. In a further warming of relations, Lancaster met in his room with Major Hagadorn and Raúl Madero, one of President Madero's brothers.[278] Interestingly, Agent Lamoreaux, recently assigned to Laredo, mentioned that Major Hagadorn "has sent some of his men in plain clothes working about the city."[279] Once again, the military was assisting civilian authorities.

In San Antonio, Agent in Charge Thompson was taking action to subpoena the records of the L. Frank Saddlery Company, suspected of having sold saddles to the *reyistas*.[280] And the BI sent an examiner to San Antonio to review Reyes's account at the Frost National Bank and, if possible, to secure cancelled checks. The examiner went through the accounts of Bernardo Reyes, B. Reyes Retana, Adolfo Reyes, and Manuel Quiroga not only in the Frost Bank but in the other national banks in town and in state banks as well. One of the Bureau's most effective tools was the subpoena duces tecum, requiring a firm or individual to produce certain items. The Bureau thus secured from Western Union copies of coded telegrams that Miguel Quiroga and David Reyes Retana had sent to parties in Laredo and in Mexico. Thompson was confident of being able to produce a clear text, using the key to the *reyista* code that the Bureau had obtained in El Paso.[281] The government was building an airtight case for violation of the neutrality laws.

Still reporting to the Bureau from Reyes's headquarters at 701 San Pedro Avenue, Chamberlain wrote that Antonio Magnón and Amador Sánchez had arrived from Laredo together with Marshall Hicks, the general's attorney. Hicks was a prominent San Antonio lawyer, former mayor, and a delegate to the 1912 Democratic national convention that nominated Woodrow Wilson for president. Together with Magnón, Sánchez and Hicks, Chapa joined the discussion about resurrecting the *reyista* movement. Chamberlain reported that Reyes had told him he planned to focus on his supporters at Douglas, Arizona, and El Paso, for he did not believe he could cross any large number of men across the lower Texas border because of the close surveillance by United States officials.[282]

The Madero regime was worried about the situation on the Arizona border, particularly the smuggling of arms for an attack on the town of Agua Prieta, Sonora across from Douglas, Arizona. There was reason to worry. When the Agua Prieta garrison had been ordered in October to take the field against a rebel chieftain named Escobosa who had some 300 followers, the troops mutinied, and in the fighting one soldier was killed and six were wounded.[283] Not only were the troops reluctant to fight, but their officers were said to be strongly against President Madero and supporters of General Reyes. So, should Agua Prieta be attacked they would surrender the town without resistance. Agent Hebert accompanied Consul Torres in making the rounds in Douglas looking for revolutionary activity.[284] As matters developed, Reyes's partisans in Arizona were unable to launch any significant operations. It must have been distressing when Reyes received a telegram stating that six influential *reyistas* in Sonora had been executed by the government.[285]

Another indication that Reyes's new strategy would not work occurred in El Paso, where the *reyistas* were well organized and financed; their club initially claimed a membership of sixty. Dr. Rafael Limón Molina headed their junta, and he had forged a cynical alliance with the *magonistas*: the *reyistas* would provide the money and the *magonistas* the cannon fodder. But the junta had been thoroughly penetrated: Madero's spymaster in El Paso who now reported to Sommerfeld, Abraham Molina, suborned the treasurer and general purchasing agent. A task force of eight Texas Rangers, a deputy US marshal, Molina, and Agent L. E. Ross swooped down on the junta on November 30, making fourteen arrests. Two of those arrested revealed themselves to be Molina's operatives.[286] The participation of Texas Rangers indicated the major reversal of sympathies by Governor Colquitt. Sommerfeld had lobbied the governor intensely on behalf of the Madero government, but the shrewd politician had also realized that continued support for Reyes and his conspiracy had become a political liability.

Agent in Charge Thompson was confident Reyes could make no move without the BI knowing about it, but, crucially, Thompson lacked an automobile to shadow Reyes when the general was being driven around town. On one of these trips, Reyes simply jumped bond and disappeared. An anxious Chief Finch telegraphed Thompson that the State Department had received a report that Reyes had left San Antonio and his whereabouts were unknown; it was believed he intended to cross the Rio Grande at Del Rio. A chagrined Thompson had to telegraph Finch that indeed Reyes had left on the night of December 3 accompanied by his secretaries. "He left by automobile and from information in our possession intends to cross near Rio Grande City. Telephone message just received says he has been seen enroute and that every effort is being made to apprehend him."[287] Chamberlain reported on December 4 that Reyes had not been seen in San Antonio, nor had Rodolfo Reyes, Miguel Quiroga, and attorney David Reyes Retana. "I am pretty certain they have left the city in the automobile for the border."[288]

Informant Chamberlain went to the BI office on December 6, and told Thompson he had just come from Reyes's residence where he had seen a telegram from Reyes to his wife informing her that he had crossed the Rio Grande at the hamlet of Samfordyce [sic], Texas, during the early morning hours of December 5. The general mentioned that he had experienced considerable difficulty in crossing because United States cavalry were patrolling the river, but once across he had been enthusiastically received by his partisans. The telegram, sent from Camargo, Tamaulipas, was in code but Chamberlain had been given the key with which to decipher it. *Reyistas* were now leaving San Antonio for the border in droves, making little effort to conceal their movements and, in many cases, carrying their weapons.

Chamberlain visited the rooming houses in San Antonio utilized by *reyistas*, learning that Reyes was reportedly in the mountains in the state of Nuevo León. Chamberlain also attended meetings of *reyistas* held to assist financially their refugees in Texas. He urged the Bureau to "Please keep this strictly confidential, as if there is a leak it would bar me from attending these meetings, which I consider important...The Reyistas have plenty of money now; they were running short."[289]

General Reyes remained a fugitive in Northeastern Mexico. Whatever popular support for his rebellion he expected simply did not materialize. Having no stomach for the hardships of being an outlaw, he surrendered to the Madero government at Linares, Nuevo León, on December 25, 1911, and was taken off to prison in Mexico City. This was probably the best Christmas present President Madero received. Sommerfeld commented on the incarceration of Reyes in later years as one of Madero's crucial mistakes. "They should have shot him," he testified matter-of-factly. As subsequent events will show, he may have been correct.[290]

Chapter 5: Aftermath

The aftermath of the Reyes movement included a series of sensational trials. A federal grand jury in Brownsville on December 9, 1911, indicted General Reyes and thirty-seven other individuals for violation of the neutrality laws.[291] Chamberlain reported that "The Reyistas are delighted that their compatriots who are in jail at Laredo, Texas, were not turned over to the Maderistas who would have shot them."[292] Chamberlain and Agent Lancaster were subpoenaed as government witnesses in the forthcoming neutrality trials. And Madero's special intelligence representative, Felix Sommerfeld, was in Laredo observing the proceedings and conferring with American officials.[293] Agent in Charge Thompson instructed Agent Isaac F. Lamoreaux to join the party of defendants and witnesses going from Laredo to Brownsville and assist Lancaster and Hebert in the neutrality trials. He also dispatched to Brownsville his stenographer, Alice Whiting, to testify about translating *reyista* documents.[294]

The trials began in Brownsville on January 1, 1912. A former Texas Ranger captain, Tom Ross, was the court interpreter.[295] Even by the peculiar standards of South Texas justice, the trial of the *reyistas* was unusual. Twenty-three of the thirty-seven men indicted were present. They were represented by an impressive display of legal talent. The lead attorney for all defendants except Chapa was Marshall Hicks. Leading Chapa's defense team was Jacob F. "Jake" Wolters, a formidable Houston attorney who had been Governor Colquitt's campaign manager and, like Chapa, was a lieutenant colonel on the governor's personal staff.

The *reyista* trial attracted national publicity because of some of the participants' prominence, but mainly because it was a major test of the government's ability to enforce the neutrality laws. Defendants were charged with multiple counts of conspiracy to organize a military expedition against a friendly government. The prosecution presented an overwhelming case. There was a boxcar-load of confiscated guns, saddles, and munitions.²⁹⁶ The government's sixty-nine witnesses included William Chamberlain and a number of defendants who had agreed to turn state's evidence. Besides testifying, Chamberlain assisted in translating *reyista* telegrams, ninety-three of which the prosecution introduced as exhibits.²⁹⁷ As if this were not enough, the government produced three Reyes manifestos and proved they had been printed by Chapa's newspaper *El Imparcial*. But what was really embarrassing was when Governor Colquitt's private secretary, John T. Bowman, admitted that, in fact, the governor had met privately with Reyes and his associates.

Perhaps to avoid any more embarrassing revelations, the trial took a surprising turn on January 8. Following a closed-door plea deal between the prosecution and defense, Marshall Hicks changed from "innocent" to "guilty" the pleas of Amador Sánchez and twelve other defendants. The prosecution then announced that it was dropping all charges against nine more defendants.²⁹⁸ Agent in Charge Thompson reported: "I was also advised by persons coming from Brownsville, Texas, where they had been as witnesses in the trial of our neutrality cases, that the defendants who were discharged by Judge [Waller Thomas] Burns, at the time some of the parties plead guilty, were each given a slip of paper by Col. F. A. Chapa and Amador Sánchez, telling them where to go and who to see, and what arrangements had been made to continue the revolutionary movement."²⁹⁹

Figure 27 Waller T. Burns.
Source: Texas Jurists Collection.

As a result of these dramatic developments, the only remaining defendant was F. A. Chapa, who readily admitted his friendship with

Reyes but denied knowledge of any conspiracy. His attorney, Jake Wolters, argued that Chapa was the victim of a political frame-up. But despite Wolters' eloquence, and after taking repeated ballots, the jury found Chapa guilty. They had been deadlocked at eleven-to-one for conviction, but the deadlock was broken when Judge Burns assured the jury that he had no intention of sentencing Chapa to prison, and that they could reach a verdict by majority vote.

The actions of Judge Burns are the most intriguing aspect of the *reyista* trials.

Back in December 1911, when the grand jury was preparing indictments, he had charged them to be especially vigilant regarding neutrality violators, and he promised to impose sentences commensurate with such offenses. During the trial, however, he was a defense attorney's dream. His whole attitude was that of solicitude for the defendants. On the first day of the trial, he asked the accused whether their accommodations in the Cameron County jail were comfortable and, when told that they could use additional blankets, he ordered the sheriff to provide them forthwith. Judge Burns then released the defendants on their own recognizance, and throughout the trial they mingled freely with the witnesses, causing the Bureau agents real headaches as they tried to prevent witness tampering. During the sentencing phase it was discovered that defendant Anastacio Herrera had fled. Burns sent another of the defendants, José Bonales Sandoval, out to look for him. Bonales Sandoval did return and informed the judge that Herrera was indeed missing. Agent Hebert later went to Matamoros, across the river from Brownsville, to try to locate Herrera, but without result.[300]

The sentencing phase itself merited puzzled comment by the press. In sentencing Chapa, Judge Burns told him, "I am well disposed toward you...and will not send you to the penitentiary, as that is not a place for men of your kind." He imposed a fine of $1,500 which Chapa paid on the spot, still proclaiming his innocence. Miguel Quiroga pleaded "guilty," and Judge Burns fined him $1,500 and costs.[301]

Regarding those who had pleaded "guilty," they requested the minimum sentence. The press reported Burns as stating: "It was not the purpose of the court to sentence any of the defendants who had admitted their guilt to the penitentiary. To do so would be to give them a status which they neither had earned nor deserved. Personally, Judge Burns said, he regarded the prisoners with pronounced favor, but the law exacts a strict demand that the neutrality regulations not be violated and hence regards the offense as serious. It distresses the court, Judge Burns continued, to impose a penalty..." As for Amador Sánchez and Antonio Magnón, the judge described them as "two strong, clean, men, citizens of Webb County, for whom as individuals the court has a great warmth of kindly feeling." In glowing terms, he recounted Sánchez's accomplishments and his ancestors' contributions to Texas. Judge Burns then imposed a fine of $1,200. José R. Sánchez, the sheriff's brother, was "a youth of tender years and perhaps unconscious of the fact that his actions were in violation of the law." He was fined $600, as was each of the remaining defendants.

Sheriff Sánchez and several others were able to pay their fines; eight of the defendants could not and faced six months in jail. Burns ordered them to the Nueces County jail in Corpus Christi, but their spokesman asked whether they could serve their time in the Webb County jail in Laredo instead. The judge readily agreed, adding that: "When their time of detention had expired, they would be welcome to Houston and his home and, further, that at the proper time and without delay he would endeavor through the proper government channels to assure to each one of them the opportunity of returning to their homes in Mexico with full guarantees of personal protection. He also said that he would request the sheriff of Laredo to permit each of them two hours in the yard each day and expressed the hope that their period of detention might be brief."

The sheriff at Laredo, Amador Sánchez, had been uttering threats and making things as difficult as possible for government witnesses and those who had been helping to enforce neutrality.[302] And he did more than permit his fellow conspirators a daily exercise period in the yard. Besides allowing them all kinds of privileges, he let those who were Laredo residents to go home at night. Even more blatantly, he put his brother José on salary as jailer to guard his fellow conspirators. The *reyista* prisoners were on vacation in the Webb County jail. One of them, José Bonales Sandoval, however, presented to Judge Burns in February that his wife had died, and he urgently needed to return to Mexico City to care for his young children. He asked for a $600 loan in order to pay his fine and secure release. Judge Burns not only loaned him the money but invited him to Houston as his guest. Bonales Sandoval stopped briefly in Houston to thank Burns personally, then returned to Laredo to pay the fines of all his colleagues with money he had just received from the eldest son of General Reyes. A bemused reporter described the whole affair as "the most unusual occurrence ever chronicled in a court of justice in this section of the country."

The Bureau of Investigation agents who had worked tirelessly on the Reyes case were presumably in a state of shock and despair. They had put together an airtight case and the defendants had received only a figurative slap on the wrist.[303] Obviously furious with Judge Burns, Thompson also railed against a deputy US marshal who procrastinated in transporting to jail the defendants who had not yet paid their fines. Thompson believed this "proves conclusively that these officers are doing everything within their power to protect these criminals and to hinder the process of the law. These things are known publicly here and have a serious effect in the minds of the people towards an enforcement of neutrality law, making it almost impossible to accomplish anything in this section of the country."[304]

Sommerfeld, who had not only observed the proceedings in Waller T. Burns's court but actively supported the BI with pertinent information, was just as frustrated as H. A. Thompson and the other agents as one after another of their cases fell apart. Apparently, Sommerfeld rendered a bit more than just investigative support. The prosecutor in the Reyes case, Lock McDaniel, reported to the Attorney General in July 1912, that his assistant, US Attorney Noah Allen, "...had been in communication with President Madero and...was the recipient of a valuable scarf pin which had been presented to him by the President through one F. A. Sommerfeldt [sic]."[305] The token of the Mexican president's appreciation for the hard work of the assistant prosecutor did not change the direction of the proceedings. Instead, Sommerfeld knew, as the frustrated BI agents certainly did, that the enforcement of the neutrality laws lacked teeth.

The German agent traveled to Mexico City on December 3, to brief President Madero on the trials in Laredo.[306] The result of Sommerfeld's meeting in Mexico was that Sherburne Hopkins lobbied the Taft administration for an amendment to the neutrality laws through executive action. Once again, Hopkins enlisted his old friend Secretary of State Philander C. Knox to approach the president. The lawyer suggested an increase in fines and penalties for violators of the neutrality laws. Most importantly, Hopkins wanted federal authorities to have the ability to seize contraband on the suspicion of a neutrality violation, rather than meeting the high burden of catching violators *in flagranti*. Finally, Madero's lawyer suggested the imposition of an arms embargo for any party other than the constitutional government of Mexico. Justifying the worth of his astronomical fees, Hopkins's lobbying succeeded. On March 12, 1912, President Taft issued an executive order amending the neutrality laws as Hopkins had outlined, and on March 16 imposed an arms embargo against all factions other than "the constituted government of Mexico."[307]

Despite the frustration with juries and especially with the courtroom antics of Judge Waller T. Burns, the prosecution of the Reyes conspiracy produced some lessons and intangible changes for the BI's work along the border. The federal agents now had more leverage with respect to arms and ammunition smuggling, although local juries still hampered their prosecutorial success. The Mexican consuls and the Mexican secret service organization under Sommerfeld countered the apparent lack of control over local court proceedings and began closely cooperating with the BI on investigative and operational levels. Sommerfeld and the consuls provided manpower, intelligence, and the ability of US authorities to incarcerate suspects under the 1899 treaty with Mexico for forty days until the Mexican government submitted evidence to initiate extradition proceedings. The evidence from the Mexican government was rarely forthcoming, but the delay provided the BI with more time to develop cases against the suspects. This arrangement between the Mexican consulates and the BI circumvented local courts for at least forty days, and at the same time effectively interrupted the plans of neutrality violators.

But regarding the Reyes matter itself, adding insult to injury was that both F. A. Chapa and Amador Sánchez received presidential pardons. The necessity for such pardons arose from Judge Burns's perverse interpretation of the neutrality laws. He had construed the neutrality offenses to be misdemeanors when, in fact, they were felonies. Chapa and Sánchez were thus convicted federal felons. As such, Chapa had the grace to resign from the governor's personal staff the day after his conviction, but Sánchez had no intention of giving up his office. Only executive clemency would save the careers of the beleaguered pair. Chapa promptly mobilized all the political influence he could muster. Texas Senator Joseph Weldon Bailey discussed Chapa's plight with Attorney General Wickersham, who told him that if Governor Colquitt would recommend to President Taft that Chapa be pardoned, Wickersham would recommend that Taft grant the pardon. But when the pardon attorney whom Wickersham assigned to prepare the brief reviewed Chapa's record, especially Agent Thompson's reports, he balked.

The problem was solved in an unusual way. The US attorney for the Western District of Texas informed the Attorney General that a man impersonating a Bureau of Investigation agent had induced Chapa to endorse a check for $150; the check proving to be worthless.[308] The man had been indicted in San Antonio, and Chapa's testimony was essential for the government to secure a conviction. Chapa as a felon, however, had lost his civil rights, and could not testify. The US attorney urgently recommended an immediate pardon for Chapa. The Assistant (and future) Chief of the Bureau of Investigation, A. Bruce Bielaski, also informed Wickersham that Chapa's testimony was crucial. Significantly, Bielaski sent him a drastically amended report from Thompson stating that his previous reports had been based on rumors, and that Chapa was not involved in a revolutionary conspiracy. A relieved Attorney General Wickersham seized on this solution, which had the added advantage of waiving the two-year probationary period required in pardon cases. On May 29, 1912, President Taft granted Chapa an unconditional pardon.

Obtaining a pardon for Amador Sánchez proved more difficult. His conviction had no effect on his activities. Not only did he remain as sheriff, but he served as president of the Webb County school board. He continued to campaign vigorously for Governor Colquitt and in 1912 attended the Democratic national convention in Baltimore accompanied by his attorney Marshall Hicks, the national committeeman from Texas. Both Sánchez and Hicks were strong supporters of Woodrow Wilson at the convention. And after his return to Laredo, Sánchez won the Democratic primary for sheriff even though his name did not appear on the ballot. But despite his political connections, Sánchez encountered a serious obstacle: the Mexican ambassador vigorously protested to the State Department because Sánchez was a proven enemy of the Madero government. Nevertheless, the sheriff submitted his pardon petition, alleging that he had not been aware that he was violating the law by assisting his lifelong friend General Reyes. "This custom of purchasing arms, horses, and munitions of war along the Rio Grande for revolutions in Mexico has prevailed ever since I was a boy, and no one has ever been prosecuted for it until the beginning of what was known as the Reyes Revolution."[309] Moreover, he had pleaded guilty because Judge Burns had assured him the offense was only a misdemeanor and, in fact, had so stated in the judgment. Lastly, Sánchez claimed he was an honorable family man and a public official who was descended from an honorable family.

Sánchez submitted fulsome letters of recommendation from the US attorney who had prosecuted him, from Judge Burns, from Governor Colquitt, from Congressman John Nance Garner, and from Texas Senator Charles A. Culberson. Attorney General Wickersham again found himself in a dilemma: the Mexican ambassador visited him in person to protest against any pardon for Sánchez. Regarding the pardon, Wickersham reluctantly wrote to Taft, "I doubt the wisdom of this." Furthermore, Sánchez's troubles at home were increasing. The US attorney in Texas withdrew his recommendation because Sánchez had abandoned his family and was "openly and shamelessly" living with a known prostitute. Sánchez's bitter enemy, John Valls, the longtime Republican district attorney in Laredo, petitioned Taft not to grant the pardon. When Sánchez handily won reelection as sheriff, Valls filed suit to prevent him, as a convicted felon, from continuing in office.

Still, Sánchez had powerful friends, and they continued to lobby on his behalf. In February 1913, Judge Burns reopened the pardon matter, writing a veritable catalogue of Sheriff Sánchez's virtues, even mentioning that one of his ancestors had fought for Texas independence with Sam Houston at the Battle of San Jacinto. Burns suggested that "the time has come when the president can act in this matter." An unenthusiastic Wickersham resubmitted the pardon application on February 13. On February 21, Taft wrote on the pardon application, "Let the pardon be granted." Taft was about to leave office, and Sánchez would be Woodrow Wilson's problem.

An important lesson from the Reyes conspiracy was that it was one thing to build an airtight case and secure an indictment, but something else to secure a meaningful conviction.[310] The locals had a much more tolerant attitude toward Mexican revolutionary conspiracies than did the federal government. But the ramifications went beyond Judge Burns's bizarre behavior. In this major test of the government's ability to enforce the neutrality laws, the message seemed to be that those laws need not be taken too seriously if one had the right connections. Bureau agents would be working under this considerable handicap for years to come. It should be noted, however, that the Bureau itself contributed to this attitude. By bowing to political pressure, Agent Thompson's drastically amended report absolving F. A. Chapa from involvement in the Reyes conspiracy, and the Bureau's use of this report, seriously undercut the government's credibility in enforcing neutrality.

Agent in Charge Thompson at San Antonio supervised the collection of further evidence against the imprisoned General Reyes in case he ever returned to the United States. As the BI, the army, and local law enforcement had managed to disassemble Reyes's conspiracy, albeit exposing the challenges hampering a unified and effective law enforcement process—personnel, local resistance, lack of funding, local and federal political influence—revolutionary realignments from the wreckage of this movement soon appeared.

The Bureau required new leadership in meeting these challenges. Chief Stanley W. Finch resigned to become "Special Commissioner for the Suppression of White Slave Traffic" in the Department of Justice.[311] Not only have Finch's organizational achievements been largely overlooked, but not the least of his accomplishments was grooming his successor A. Bruce Bielaski.[312]

Chapter 6: Youthful Leadership

ALEXANDER BRUCE BIELASKI TOOK OFFICE as the new Chief on April 30, 1912, after he had been serving as Finch's assistant and had considerable experience handling day-to-day matters regarding agents.[313] Bielaski differed quite markedly from his predecessor. Born in southern Maryland of a Lithuanian immigrant turned Methodist minister and a Jewish mother, Bielaski, whom his parents called Bruce, so not to confuse his first name with that of his father Alexander, was an achiever both in academics and in sports. While in high school, he played baseball and football, in addition to winning "the inter-high school one-half and one-mile races" as a track runner.[314] When he joined Columbian College, renamed George Washington University in 1904, he not only finished his law degree at age 22 (class of 1905), but he also became a celebrated college football star. When George Washington University inducted Bielaski into the Athletics Hall of Fame in 1959, the list of accomplishments included team captain 1903 and 1904, and two touchdowns against Randolph-Macon in 1904 through "splendid" interference.[315]

The new lawyer joined the Justice Department as a clerk. He passed the Washington, DC bar in 1907.[316] At five foot, eleven inches, and 162 pounds, he was handsome, athletic, and a team player, who knew how to inspire others.[317] When Attorney General Bonaparte appointed Stanley Finch to head the new investigative unit, Finch chose his fellow Washington University graduate Bielaski to be one of the first thirty-four agents. His title was "Special Examiner," one level above the "Special Agent" designation of the other staff. With the bar exam under his belt and securely employed, he married the love of his life, Amelia Benson, in 1909. They would remain married for 55 years, until his death in 1964. While the government job was somewhat prestigious, Mrs. Bielaski had to supplement her husband's annual $3,500 salary as a physics teacher in a local high school.[318]

Bielaski's first assignment as a federal agent was Fort Leavenworth, Kansas, where he investigated the prison staff after a disgruntled guard had submitted to Washington allegations of corruption. Later in 1909, an article in the *Washington Evening Star* had no important news to report about this assignment, other than "there is no scandal whatever at Leavenworth," but more importantly that the man personally sent by Attorney General Wickersham "was once one of the crack base ball [sic] players of the Departmental League."[319] Bielaski returned to Washington by year's end and became Finch's trusted deputy. A little over a year later, in April 1912, he became the Attorney General's natural choice to succeed Finch. Bielaski was 29 years old.

Figure 28 A. Bruce Bielaski. Courtesy Library of Congress Prints and Photographs Division.

Bielaski's tenure as Chief of the Bureau of Investigation finds only cursory mention in the historiography. Most likely, this is an effect of J. Edgar Hoover's obsession with a legacy of having created the modern FBI. Even the current leading historian of the FBI, Athan Theoharis, has a surprisingly brief entry (four lines) for Bielaski.[320] Hoover's tenure covered Prohibition, World War II, the Red Scare, and the Cold War, and, according to his personally chosen FBI historian, Don Whitehead, with success. Whitehead reserved four mentions for Bielaski in the entire *The FBI Story*, with a foreword by J. Edgar Hoover.[321] While Director Hoover certainly deserves credit for his decades of leading the FBI, Bielaski's tenure was remarkable in many ways.[322] He took over an organization with a limited focus, mainly on white slavery and land fraud, and within six years turned it into the country's premier law enforcement, intelligence and counterintelligence agency.

As the new Chief settled in his job in the spring of 1912, the Mexican border teemed with smugglers, revolutionaries, and foreign agents. Enforcing the US neutrality laws was an immediate priority when he took the helm, and the first step towards a focus on counterintelligence in addition to law enforcement. The new Chief took trips into the field, communicated directly not only with the agents in charge in the various field offices, but also sent and received information directly from certain field agents. Famous for the communications, "Tickler from the chief," the field received one-page messages with specific questions, tasks, and information from Bielaski on a daily basis.[323] For instance, when Agent Eli Murray Blanford in Los Angeles advised that the *magonista* newspaper *Regeneración* had resumed publication in October 1915 with Enrique Flores Magón as editor, his predecessor, Anselmo L. Figueroa, having died. Bielaski instructed Blanford to establish definitively that Figueroa was dead, and not to rely just on Figueroa's obituary in *Regeneración*.[324] He personally hired and fired agents, actively shaped his organization, and took the existing filing and management processes he had inherited to a level that could handle the flood of reports and intelligence reaching the Bureau on a daily basis.

For a historian, digging through the tens of thousands of documents, often seemingly disorganized and spread across different microfilm reels, it is hard to fathom today how Bielaski stayed on top of the information and focused his investigative force with such effectiveness. Amazingly, without a huge staff or computers, he kept the Bureau's fingers on the pulse of what was happening in the Mexican Revolution and during World War I. In today's world, the Chief would have an army of analysts working to sift through the raw intelligence, digest, and condense it to allow assessment and decision-making. By all accounts, Bielaski only had a handful of stenographers and two or three administrative assistants at his disposal. What seems to be the case was that agent reports from the field offices went through a process whereby administrators circled or highlighted names in the reports. Based on the importance of these names, the staff created a card filing system, allowing search either by name or date or case. In addition, for more important cases, the staff used the information in the investigative case files to create numeric files, again the file names being searchable in the card filing system. The numeric files contained important targets of investigation, such as prominent Mexican revolutionaries, foreign agents, foreign diplomats (especially Mexican), German saboteurs, and IWW, as well as union organizers. Periodically, likely on the order of the Chief, staff assembled names of suspects and persons of interest on lists. Each of the names on the list had a case file that could be called upon request from field offices or the Chief. Bielaski now could quickly scan the newest field reports with highlighted names, and then decide whether he needed further information from the numeric files. This system proved to be as simple as it was brilliant. Clearly, Bielaski also had an incredible ability to relate names and cases, as well as remember relationships between different investigations. Basically, sitting in his DC office with less than ten staff members assisting, he steered the Bureau through unprecedented growth, focused with ever increasing precision on creating an effective law enforcement and counterintelligence organization.

Bielaski was about to assume his new position as Chief when a counterrevolution against the Madero government began to develop in Texas. This newest conspiracy was different, as its leaders came from the revolutionary movement in Mexico and not the reactionary group around the deposed dictator Porfirio Díaz. San Antonio Agent in Charge H. A. Thompson wrote on March 4, 1912, that the enforcement of neutrality was "requiring the attention of all of the agents of this division at this time."[325] Emilio Vázquez Gómez had been Madero's *Ministro de Gobernación* (Department of Interior, the most powerful post in the cabinet) but had been dismissed. He took it personally. Vázquez Gómez established his residence in San Antonio and, like Madero and Reyes before him, began plotting.[326]

Illustrating the propensity of the political "outs" to combine against whoever was "in," (and then double-cross their erstwhile allies if possible) Madero's agents in San Antonio reported that Emiliano Zapata, who was leading an agrarian uprising in the state of Morelos against Madero as he had against Porfirio Díaz, had allied himself with Emilio Vázquez Gómez. Agent Lancaster sent headquarters the translation of a seized letter signed by Zapata on March 14, 1912, to Vázquez Gómez at San Antonio, hoping to combine their revolutionary movements.[327] The only thing an upper-class professional politician such as Vázquez Gómez would have in common with a bunch of peasant agrarian rebels was their mutual opposition to Madero. While a rebel, Madero had raised the public's expectation of reforms to an unrealistic level. He had deposed General Porfirio Díaz, but most of the Díaz structure remained intact. Now as president, Madero proved unable to solve the nation's problems, and his popularity plummeted.

Figure 29 Emilio Vázquez Gómez. Courtesy Library of Congress Prints and Photographs Division.

Vázquez Gómez began issuing commissions, among them one to José Morín, who was a recruiter, and to Colonel Viviano Zaldívar Cervantes at Brownsville, who was to operate in the state of Tamaulipas. Madero Consul General Manuel Esteva turned over to the Bureau five letters written by Vázquez Gómez, several of them to Zaldívar Cervantes.[328] Although Vázquez Gómez claimed that his revolutionary movement against Madero was distinct from that of Reyes, there was considerable convergence. Now with Reyes languishing in prison, Mexican conservatives were reduced to rallying around Vázquez Gómez, whose followers were called *vazquistas*.

Andrés Garza Galán was a case in point. He had been the *Jefe Político*, or district political boss, at Piedras Negras under Porfirio Díaz, and he was an intransigent enemy of Madero. He had been trying to form his own counterrevolutionary movement in San Antonio but with unimpressive results. The Madero administration tried to neutralize Garza Galán by requesting his extradition. He was jailed for forty days under the 1899 treaty[329] but was released in February 1912, when the State Department held that the offense with which he was charged was a political one and was not extraditable. He now joined Vázquez Gómez, as he had earlier attached himself to Reyes.[330]

An important Bureau development in coping with this new iteration of the Mexican Revolution was the assignment of Special Agent Robert E. Lee Barnes to the San Antonio field office on February 12, 1912, from the Houston office. Born in Prentiss, Kentucky, on October 7, 1879, Barnes was a stern, no-nonsense, mustachioed lawman with administrative as well as investigative skills. He succeeded H. A. Thompson, who resigned in December 1913, as Agent in Charge in San Antonio.[331] Barnes was an exceptionally capable agent, although on one occasion he was duped by an informer, as we shall see.

Special Agent Barnes called at Vázquez Gómez's residence at 501 South Presa Street hoping for an interview, but was told he was ill. As the Vázquez Gómez movement took shape, Barnes kept watch over two trunks of ammunition that arrived in San Antonio, but no one claimed them. He subsequently traveled to Eagle Pass, where a *vazquista* junta had formed. There, Barnes received a visit from Juan Leets, the Mexican government agent, who was ostensibly investigating the loyalty of officials in Piedras Negras across the river.[332]

Barnes assigned Agent Curley D. Hebert to the investigation. Hebert was a thirty-three-year-old Louisiana native. He was appointed on March 18, 1909, making him one of the original thirty-four BI agents.[333] Now stationed in Laredo, Hebert learned just how precarious Madero's hold on northern Mexico was. Customs Inspector Pete Edwards told Hebert that the customs collector in Nuevo Laredo favored the *vazquistas*, and that the first boxcar of rifles and ammunition for Madero coming through that port would immediately be turned over to the rebels.[334] But Agent Hebert did not rely entirely on receiving intelligence. On the night of March 30, he and a customs inspector were staked out on the Rio Grande watching for munitions being smuggled into Mexico. They spotted a man carrying something on his shoulder, and when he saw them, he dropped his load ran. His load proved to be five new Mauser rifles and twenty-five cartridges tied up in a cloth. The officers were somewhat unusual in that the "man got away as we could not stop him without shooting him which we had no right to do." Agent Hebert came down with pneumonia as a result of the stakeout, and Thompson instructed him to go to San Antonio as soon as he was able to travel.[335]

Agent in Charge Thompson had interesting dealings with Antonio Magnón, the former *reyista*. Magnón had been approached to sell some of the rifles left over from the *reyista* movement but stated that he would not sell them without the Bureau's permission, as "he knew what they were wanted for and did not want any further trouble." Magnón eventually claimed he had arranged to sell to the Mexican government all the Reyes arms and ammunition that US authorities had seized, and which the court had released. Conducting the negotiations was Magnón's attorney, Marshall Hicks. However, the Mexican government denied it had entered into any contract to purchase anything.[336]

Another former *reyista* interested in firearms was F. A. Chapa, who called at the Bureau office and said certain parties had offered to buy 8,000 Mauser rifles. "He stated he was the owner of a hardware store on South Presa and would like to do this piece of business if it could be done legally, stating that he had been a Reyista, but was not a Vazquista, and he was ready to assist the Government."³³⁷ Chapa was disingenuous; he was later spotted deep in conversation with General Reyes's son Alejandro, Miguel Quiroga, Ismael Reyes Retana, and Andrés Garza Galán, flashing a large roll of bills, which they were using to pay their recruits at a rate of $2.50 per day.³³⁸

Chapa's drugstore, at the corner of West Commerce Street and Santa Rosa Avenue, was where he conducted ordinary business. He also had a little office a few blocks away where he conducted most of his revolutionary business. Admission was by giving one hard rap on the door, waiting, then rapping again three times in rapid succession. It was there that Chapa contracted with a certain H. C. Buckholtz, recently dishonorably discharged from the army, to work as a machine gunner for the *vazquistas* for four months and receive $1,800. Barnes obtained a copy of the contract, put pressure on Buckholtz, and made him an informer at $3 per day to investigate recruitment by the Madero government as well as the *vazquistas*. But Barnes soon discontinued Buckholtz's services for lack of results.³³⁹

Vázquez Gómez's headquarters, at 113 City Street, were the scene of continual activity, with the leader dictating to his secretary and meeting with a stream of visitors. Agent Lancaster wrote that "Vice Consul Francisco Espinoza y Rondero came to the office and said that Francisco I. Guzmán and Manuel Garza Aldape were sending a considerable number of telegrams but that they were in code. He stated that he would like to find someone who could get in with these parties and secure a copy of the code if possible. He stated he would be willing to pay an informant in case we could find one. I, knowing that Mrs. Beatrice Warmbold was in with these people, suggested that he might get her to undertake this work. Mrs. Warmbold is the woman that gave me the first information as to the Vazquistas, when they left the Ohio Flats last fall and moved to 113 City Street. I phoned for Warmbold and she came to the office and Mr. Espinoza employed her to undertake this work—find out what she could about the Vazquista movement. Warmbold is to furnish me at the office such information as she may get from these parties, as the Consul and I thought it unsafe for her to go to his office for fear she might be detected by Mexican Revolutionists."[340]

Vice Consul Espinoza informed Agent Lancaster that he had received a telegram from the Mexican consul in El Paso stating that a *vazquista* courier, supposedly carrying a document for Vázquez Gómez, had left El Paso and would arrive at San Antonio at 9:30 p.m. on April 7 and gave the man's description. Lancaster contacted detective John J. Mahan, who was working for the Mexican consul. Mahan said he would cover the train's arrival with two other Mexican agents and learn whether the party had arrived, and if so, shadow him. Mahan advised that he had met the train, had seen the courier with Garza Aldape, and had followed them to the latter's house.[341]

In his effort to penetrate the *vazquista* junta, Agent Thompson used a certain Indalecio Ballesteros, Jr., a relative of the Garza Galán clan who was currently part of the *vazquista* movement. Ballesteros said his motive for informing was that "if he got in a bad light with the Mexican Government, his wife who has large holdings in Mexico, would be apt to lose out if he turned against his Government." Ballesteros was willing to be an informant, for a nominal sum. Thompson "told him to go ahead and get all he could concerning their movements and give me the information and if this information was really valuable, I would be glad to take care of him. I believe this young man is the party I have been looking for to put into the [Vázquez] Gómez headquarters, and if he deals fairly, I feel sure we will be able to get some information in the near future that will justify us in getting warrants for these people, which we have been unable to do so far. We have ample testimony to prove a conspiracy, but they have been very careful about organizing any expedition or doing anything that could be identified with their movement."[342]

Ballesteros did, in fact, become an informer. Thompson reported that he had a man in the *vazquista* organization in San Antonio named

Anastacio [sic, Indalecio] Ballesteros, who was keeping him advised of their movement, a combined Emilio Vázquez Gómez and Andrés Garza Galán enterprise. Whenever they attempted to launch an expedition, Thompson would arrange for Ballesteros to accompany the plotters to the border where Agent Barnes and other officers would intercept them at the river.[343] The presence of Mexican agents operating in the United States was becoming an issue. Consul Luther Ellsworth, for one, had become increasingly strident in denouncing them. He specifically mentioned Ballesteros, Abraham Molina, Teódulo R. Beltrán, John J. Mahan, and Manuel Mata as agents of the Madero government.[344]

Regarding the actions of informant Ballesteros, a noticeable lack of tradecraft is evident—he sometime made his reports at the Bureau field office. There he informed Agent in Charge Thompson that Garza Galán and Vázquez Gómez had assigned José Cruz Aguilar to take charge of the weapons they planned to smuggle across near Eagle Pass; also, that Nicanor Valdez, Manuel Garza Aldape, and Juan Pedro Didapp were prominent *vazquistas*. Didapp, claiming to be a reporter for the *Washington Post*, had been a consul general under Porfirio Díaz.

Ballesteros either had a change of heart or was a double agent all along, for he later alleged that his reports concerning the *vazquistas* had been submitted because the Bureau had threatened him. This shocking development effectively destroyed any value he might have had as a government witness in neutrality cases. Even worse, he became an active *vazquista*, attending clandestine meetings and furnishing the money for Andrés Garza Galán and his relatives to purchase rifles in San Antonio.[345]

Revolutions require financing, and Agent in Charge Thompson reported that attorney "Manuel Garza Aldape who lives at 917 Salinas Street, has negotiated a loan in the sum of $475,000 gold at Detroit, Michigan, securing the loan from Walter C. Parker, who owns the Coahuila Mining and Smelting Company and the Mexican Crude Rubber Company." The loan was secured "ostensibly for lands and Treadwell, their local manager, and a friend of Manuel Garza Aldape, put the deal through. [Garza] Aldape is an attorney for this Company in Mexico. Mr. Mayo an American who owns large interests in Mexico and Harvey Stiles, who are now at the Menger Hotel, know about this deal, and state positively that this money is for the Vázquez [Gómez] movement."[346]

Some of the money was used to purchase arms in San Antonio. Manuel Garza Aldape had hidden at his residence 600 rifles for use against the Madero regime and had contracted with the L. Frank Saddlery Company for 300 saddles, for a proposed expedition into Coahuila led by Garza Galán. This from Madero agent Teódulo R. Beltrán, who operated the Alamo Safe and Lock Company in San Antonio.[347] Thompson notified Agent Barnes at Eagle Pass that the *vazquistas* had weapons boxed and ready for immediate shipment. Barnes intensified his surveillance of the local junta, but the arrival of a troop of the 3rd US Cavalry coupled with the difficulties the *vazquistas* were experiencing in recruiting, drastically reduced the chances of an armed expedition from Eagle Pass.[348] Undaunted, Vázquez Gómez and his closest advisors met and began planning an attack on Las Vacas, across the river from Del Rio.[349] Vázquez Gómez was doubtlessly heartened by scattered, small uprisings on his behalf in Chihuahua.[350]

Special Agent Barnes at San Antonio in the guise of a prospective employer who had taken over the publishing business of Bureau informant L. F. Daniels called on a certain Mrs. Josefina B. de McTeague, who was working for Vázquez Gómez. Daniels had written a letter of recommendation for Barnes. Mrs. McTeague was remarkably forthcoming, saying she had carried to Laredo 200 rounds hidden in a special skirt as well as a personal message from Vázquez Gómez to General Pascual Orozco which Vázquez Gómez would not commit to writing. Barnes arranged for her to make another trip, the government having agreed to pay her expenses and promised not to prosecute her. Barnes interviewed her again, and she disclosed that Jesús Hernández was the head of the *vazquista* junta in San Antonio, and that on her trip to Laredo the password was "latch." She was given a safe conduct at Laredo signed by Vázquez Gómez. She carried it and other important papers in a secret pocket in her underskirt. She made other trips as a courier for Vázquez Gómez, and the Bureau felt she would make a good witness against him.[351]

One of the Madero administration's countermeasures to the *vazquista* threat was to have an agent in Laredo, newspaper publisher Emeterio Flores, purchase horses, recruit men (at $1.50 per day), issue each one a horse, a rifle, and 100 rounds of ammunition, and send them across the river to join the Mexican army. Flores was thinking big—he was trying to buy 1,000 horses. So far, he had acquired ninety, but when he went to the customs house and asked whether he could take them across the Rio Grande for use by the Mexican army, he was told that he could not take horses across for any reason whatsoever.[352]

The matter of recruitment was complicated. For instance, Agent in Charge Thompson was informed that José Morín was recruiting men in San Antonio near F. A. Chapa's drugstore, claiming to be working for the Mexican government. Mexican Consul General Manuel Esteva assured Thompson that his government was making no effort to enlist Mexicans in Texas, although this was not the case. Thompson was convinced that Morín was running a "false flag" operation, actually recruiting for the rebels: "An Agent will be assigned to cover this movement and ascertain if possible what the recruiting is being done for, and if necessary, to accompany this [sic] persons to the border and if they attempt to cross as an expedition arrangements will be made for their arrest and detention for the violation of Section 10, Chapter 8 of the Criminal Code."[353]

As usual, local sentiment was a factor in neutrality cases. Agent Hebert attended the trial of *maderistas* Emeterio Flores and C. J. Fierros at Laredo, reporting that Immigration Inspector Hardy Jeffries and mounted Customs Inspector Robert Rumsey talked with jurors, telling them what a fine man Flores was, saying Flores had been framed and was innocent. Hebert repeatedly reported this outrageous jury-tampering to US Attorney Lock McDaniel, naming the jurors whom Jeffries and Rumsey had approached. But Flores and Fierros plead guilty to violating the neutrality laws and were fined: Flores $1,200, and Fierros $600. Flores paid immediately; Fierros lacked the money, and the US marshal took him in charge.[354]

Also in Laredo, Agent Hebert reported that he had had a long talk with one R. S. Aldana [sic] from San Antonio "who said he was working for Vázquez Gómez and was in Laredo to stir up public sentiment against the Madero government. He said [a] regular rebel meeting place in San Antonio was in a room on the second floor of the Laclede Hotel. They met late at night so that the room could not be searched. "Aldana claims it's against the law to search a house at night! When they leave the room, they take all their correspondence with them. Aldana claims a stenographer takes everything down in shorthand and types it up the next day."[355]

Curtailing the flow of munitions was a priority. Agent Thompson reported: "We need additional help to cover constant traffic between here and Eagle Pass, for an attack on C[iudad] P[orfiro] Diaz [today Piedras Negras] is expected soon. Would like one or two competent informants to cover SP, I&GN, and SA&AP stations so agents can cover movements of munitions. Our principal work from now on it seems will be of this class as the rebels without supplies are unable to fight, and to make it extremely difficult for them to get these supplies and reduce the exportation to the minimum, is our desire." Thompson stated that munitions were hidden in many places in San Antonio and those places "are being covered by Mexican informants employed by the Mexican Government, but their information is very unsatisfactory, and especially so now when there is so much disorganization among their officers," referring to the replacement of Porfirio Díaz regime operatives by those of the Madero government.[356] One of the *maderista* operatives working against Vázquez Gómez was John J. Mahan, employed from June to September, who said that on one occasion he spied "through a window, the blind of which was drawn" on Miguel Garza Aldape, David de la Fuente, and Vázquez Gómez poring over maps.[357]

The Bureau needed its own informants. The Chief authorized the employment of one or two informants "keeping expense as low as possible." Thompson was frustrated because while he could prove that munitions were purchased, he was unable to prove that they were actually transported to the border or taken across the border. The last he knew was that they were still in San Antonio, and it was clearly shown that they were purchased for the proposed Garza Galán expedition.[358]

The Bureau was amassing considerable evidence against revolutionists through use of the subpoena duces tecum, which required a firm or individual to produce specified items, which could then be presented to a grand jury. These subpoenas were principally sent through the Bureau offices in San Antonio, El Paso, Eagle Pass, and Laredo. They were particularly effective when served against companies such as Western Union, for revolutionists conducted much of their communications by wire, both in the clear and in code. Making translations, though, was another matter. A lack of translators meant that often batches of documents could not be analyzed on a timely basis. And sometimes subterfuges were employed, as when Andrés Garza Galán sent telegrams in the name of the illiterate porter at the International Club in San Antonio.[359]

The Bureau in January 1912 had assigned as its new resident agent Louis E. Ross, one of the most capable operatives on the border, to monitor the munitions traffic in El Paso. Ross spoke, read, and wrote Spanish, a rarity in the BI. And he had considerable border experience, having worked in the office of the Sonora Packing Company at Cananea, Sonora, before the Revolution and having been a Thiel Detective Service operative in 1911.[360] Now he worked closely with his counterpart, Abraham Molina, a former freelance purveyor of intelligence whom in September 1911, the *maderista* governor of Chihuahua, Abraham González, had appointed as intelligence chief in El Paso. Ross and Molina had to spend much of their time running down what proved to be false reports of revolutionary activity. For instance, Ross reported that "Molina received information that two Americans were making bombs in a room at 8th and El Paso Sts. We inspected this place tonight and found that the men are making ink instead of nitroglycerine."³⁶¹

Ross and Molina made an effective team against the *vazquistas*. They were particularly interested in the hardware firm of Krakauer, Zork, & Moye, who reportedly were under contract to deliver 750,000 rounds and 1,000 rifles. Although some shipments got across the Rio Grande, Ross and Molina, with the assistance of the army, customs inspectors, and the Texas Rangers, managed to curtail the flow of munitions significantly.³⁶² They received valuable information from Henry C. Kramp, manager of the Thiel Detective Agency's local office.³⁶³ The Thiel agency, which had been hired in 1911 by the regime of Porfirio Díaz against the *maderistas*, was now working for the Madero regime.

While thus making some progress on several fronts, Thompson was also dealing with a most disturbing development. "During the day Mrs. Luther T. Ellsworth came in from Eagle Pass. She registered at the Gunter Hotel and at once sent for Andrés Garza Galán and had a long conversation with him. She stated to the telephone operator who put in the call for her that she had important messages for Mr. Galán from C[iudad]. P[orfirio]. Díaz."³⁶⁴ A week later, while still an informant, Indalecio Ballesteros wrote that Garza Galán boasted that the *vazquistas* had nothing to fear because "he had friends at present in the Secret Service [sic, the BI] who would give him opportune warning, and besides he understood the laws of this country and would be ready for them." Agent in Charge Thompson immediately informed the Chief: "I wish to call your attention further to the statement made by them, where [Garza] Galán said that he had friends in the Secret Service Department who would keep him advised of any papers made out for his arrest and any other facts regarding his violating Neutrality Laws. Now, this information Ballesteros told me came to [Garza] Galán in a letter written to him and Valdez³⁶⁵ by Mrs. Luther T. Ellsworth, in which she stated that Mr. Ellsworth her husband was doing everything in his power to assist Messers [Garza] Galán and [Nicanor] Valdez; and further along this line, Agent

Barnes writes me and desires to know if there is any means by which the interference with his affairs at Eagle Pass, by Consul Ellsworth, can be avoided. It makes it very hard for us to obtain information when we are opposed by persons connected with this Government who should be assisting us."[366]

The State Department had also been receiving complaints that Ellsworth was partial to President Madero's opponents. Ellsworth defended Garza Galán and Valdez against accusations that the pair were smuggling arms to anti-Madero rebels. The consul declared that Mexican secret agents had hounded the unpopular pair and tried to frame them for a crime of which they were innocent. Ellsworth stoutly proclaimed his own impartiality, enclosing letters from some border officials stating that he unfailingly cooperated in neutrality enforcement. Consul Ellsworth's defense of Garza Galán and Valdez stemmed in part from his antipathy toward Madero's secret agents operating in the United States. When Bureau agents cooperated with them, Ellsworth considered this a betrayal of United States policy. But his defense of the conservative Mexican plotters also reflected the fact that Ellsworth was no longer neutral. Whereas he had initially viewed Madero favorably, his opinion had changed dramatically, and in his dispatches to the Department of State he did what he could to discredit the *maderistas*.[367] Despite Ellsworth's protestations, the fact was that Garza Galán and Valdez were plotting revolution.[368] And they continued to do so. As of October, they were openly recruiting men at Marathon, Texas, and sending them into Mexico. Garza Galán decided, however, to cease, at least temporarily, smuggling munitions across the river.[369]

Even more troubling, Thompson wrote that although Consul Ellsworth was "located where there's much revolutionary activity but he's never given this Department one scrap of information concerning the movements there. On the other hand, we can show beyond a reasonable doubt that he has placed everything possible in our way and do [sic] everything possible he could to interfere with our work in accomplishing what we have set out to do—namely the enforcement of the law." Thompson attached a letter from Agent Barnes, investigating at Eagle Pass and Del Rio, stating that Ellsworth was continually interfering with his work, that Ellsworth was consulting and conferring with the rebels, that Ellsworth regularly attended their junta, and that Ellsworth had even gone to the extreme of pointing out Barnes to the revolutionists and telling them what he was there for. Barnes asked Thompson if something could not be done to prevent Ellsworth's activities. Ellsworth "openly admits that he is opposed to the Madero government and in sympathy with the other people and this accounts for the fact that they go to him to make these complaints." Thompson added that Madero's Consul General Esteva had been complaining repeatedly to him about Ellsworth.[370] As of May 15, though, at Ellsworth's request, Agent Lancaster met him at Eagle Pass and accompanied him across the river to Piedras Negras.[371] The Bureau became disenchanted with Ellsworth and ceased sharing information with him, but maintained contact. As of November 19, Agent Palmer, stationed at Eagle Pass, called at Del Rio on Ellsworth, who discussed border conditions, especially neutrality, and offered his assistance at any time Palmer asked for it, and suggested that the representatives of the two Departments cooperate.[372] The Bureau was unwilling to do so.

A dramatic event in Washington, DC had decisively changed the course of the Mexican Revolution. A joint resolution of Congress on March 14, 1912, empowered President Taft to impose an arms embargo on shipments to Mexico, an embargo that was lifted on March 25 for the Madero government.[373] As Madero had done, his enemies now had to evade the Bureau in smuggling munitions and recruiting fighters. The joint resolution of Congress and President Taft's subsequent exception for the Madero government was the result of an important player in Madero's orbit: Sherburne G. Hopkins. Hopkins, Madero's lawyer and lobbyist in Washington, DC, was close friends with Secretary of State Philander C. Knox. Together they lobbied for the embargo and the Madero exclusion.

While Madero's people under the leadership of Felix A. Sommerfeld and the Mexican consuls along the border supported the BI with men and resources to prevent smuggling attempts, Hopkins effectively lobbied for and achieved a change of US foreign policy to advance the same goal: Undermine Madero's opposition.[374]

Agent Barnes at Eagle Pass requested instructions as to whether food and clothing destined to Mexican points in quantities such as to raise a conclusive presumption that they were not for the individual use of the consignee, were to be construed as 'Munitions of War' within the meaning of the President's proclamation. The administration decreed that food, hardware, dry goods, and clothing could be exported in the ordinary course of legitimate commerce when properly manifested. The general rule was that "everything used by an army, except ordinary clothing and food, are considered munitions of war."[375]

Faced with the refusal of the United States to grant his movement belligerent status and with the President's proclamation, Emilio Vázquez Gómez decided that he must do something decisive to solidify his credentials as a revolutionary leader. Accordingly, in May he and two companions traveled by train to El Paso. Alerted by Agent in Charge Thompson about Vázquez Gómez's plans, Agent Ross was too busy investigating illegal recruiting by the Mexican government (the Bureau was proceeding very cautiously in this regard) to attend to Vázquez Gómez. Ross asked Abraham Molina to meet Vázquez Gómez's train. Molina did so, causing the Mexican politician's immediate arrest. Ross quickly secured his release because there were no charges pending against him, but he arranged for informants to keep Vázquez Gómez under surveillance.[376]

Vázquez Gómez quickly crossed over to Ciudad Juárez, where the garrison in February had mutinied in his favor. There he proclaimed himself provisional president of Mexico and installed himself in the customs house, now presidential palace, naming David de la Fuente commander in chief of his revolutionary forces.

An indication of Madero's eroding authority was Agent Hebert's report from Douglas that he had consulted "with Manuel Cuesta, Mexican consul here and Consul Lozano from Laredo. Both were pleased Vázquez Gómez had at last gone to Mexico, and both expressed the hope that the rebels would now be recognized as belligerents by the US. In conversation they both committed themselves as being in accord with Vázquez Gómez and his followers."[377]

Vázquez Gómez's stay in Mexico was brief. The putative provisional president found conditions in Chihuahua to be very different from what he expected. Not only was there dissention among the rebels, but many were now antagonistic toward him. Agent in Charge Thompson reported: "He and General Orozco and his aide Gonzalo C. Enrile couldn't agree as to the terms upon which he was to enter that country as its provisional president and there seemed to be some difficulty as to the former understanding between them. At any rate he returned very much dejected, and I'm inclined to believe his revolutionary activities are about at an end." [378] Not so. Vázquez Gómez's former ally, General Pascual Orozco, had taken over leadership of the rebellion, as we shall discuss in the next chapter.

Vázquez Gómez returned to San Antonio to sulk. He tried to revive his movement, still clinging to the illusion that he was a major player in the revolution. He dispatched one of his principal assistants, Dr. Policarpo Rueda, as his Diplomatic Agent to Washington in a futile effort to secure United States support. And he continued to issue proclamations.[379] His new junta in San Antonio was quickly penetrated by Consul General Esteva, one of whose agents became a member. Through this agent, Esteva obtained letters and telegrams, which he loaned to the Bureau to be photographed. This was welcome, but Lancaster had no one to translate the documents; he had to send the photographs to El Paso for translation by Agent Ross, who spent days doing so.[380]

The Bureau continued to build a neutrality case against Vázquez Gómez, securing copies and translating numerous telegrams covering from October 1, 1911, through April 30, 1912, that the local Western Union manager provided under a subpoena duces tecum. These documents were then supplied to the federal grand jury.[381] In addition, Dr. José S. Saenz, who had been the *vazquista* financial agent in Douglas, was a Bureau informant, revealing that Vázquez Gómez received his San Antonio mail at P. O. Box 1068 and at 113 City Street under the name of W. Castor.[382] Francisco Pérez, a member of the *vazquista* junta in Douglas who carried messages to Vázquez Gómez at San Antonio, delivered these letters to Agent Thompson, who had them photographed. Pérez then took the letters to Vázquez Gómez and did the same with the latter's replies.[383] A reporter for the *San Antonio Daily Light*, Louis DeNette, attended a junta at *vazquista* headquarters and was given certain documents, which he promptly turned over to the Bureau for copying and translation by Ross.[384] Agent Ross's linguistic capabilities were invaluable. He also received for translation documents the Bureau had obtained in Arizona.

The US marshal and one of his deputies on the night of July 20 in San Antonio arrested Emilio Vázquez Gómez, Francisco I. Guzmán, Dr. Policarpo Rueda, Manuel L. Márquez, Francisco Pérez, and Felipe Fortuño Miramón, seizing commissions and other documentary evidence. They were charged with conspiracy to set on foot a military expedition. Vázquez Gómez's bond was set at $10,000, Francisco Pérez's at $2,500, and the rest at $3,000. Initially, only Vázquez Gómez was able to post bond. Lancaster wired Chief Bielaski requesting permission to employ a stenographer and translator to prepare the evidence seized. Bielaski authorized the employment—just for a few days, keeping expenses as low as possible. Mary A. Desmarets was hired, at $3 per day.[385]

The prominent *vazquista* Felipe Fortuño Miramón did not remain in the county jail long. He escaped on the night of September 14. When the Bureau investigated, it turned out that the *vazquista* prisoners were housed on the first floor of the jail, not the second as was proper procedure, and that they received many privileges. The cell occupied by Miramón and Francisco I. Guzmán, the only two who had not been able to post bail, was unlocked day and night. Miramón secured a key to the front door from an assistant jailer who was a *vazquista* sympathizer, used the old trick of leaving a dummy in his bed that night, unlocked the front door, and strolled out. Guzmán declined to escape. Officers raided the home of "G. Adams" (G. Z. Adame [sic]), arresting him for helping Miramón escape. Adame gave a statement that after escaping, Miramón went to Adame's house where he was concealed until September 18 when he was driven to the railroad station in a small town south of San Antonio, where he caught the train to Laredo.[386]

In the county jail, Agent Barnes interviewed Aldame who claimed to have been a law student in Mexico City who had left for political reasons, arriving in San Antonio in November 1911, and was currently unemployed. Barnes also spoke with police captain Charles Stevens (the former deputy sheriff who had been a Bureau informant for years.)[387] and determined that the prisoner's real name was Gonzalo Zúñiga Aldame [sic]. He admitted having hired a chauffeur for $10 to drive him and Miramón to the town where he caught the train. Miramón got out about a mile from there and walked the rest of the way, Zúñiga Aldame having been driven to the railroad station to check for peace officers. When Barnes went to Zúñiga Aldame's residence he found it vacant, and all he picked up were a few papers in Spanish. "From all indications, it would appear that the inmates of this place were revolutionary sympathizers," and Barnes hoped to locate them through the post office. Barnes interviewed a pawnbroker who said one A. González had pawned a diamond scarf pin on September 17 for $11. "A. González" was one of Zúñiga Aldame's aliases, and the money was probably used in Miramón's escape. Barnes took the pawnbroker to the jail where he identified "A. González" as Zúñiga Aldame, who was charged with aiding a federal prisoner to escape. The US commissioner placed him under a $1,000 bond which he could not post, and he was remanded to jail. Miramón finally made it all the way to Mexico City, where he was arrested by the Madero authorities.[388] His stay in a Mexican prison was considerably less pleasant than in the San Antonio jail.

The Bureau struck at Vázquez Gómez's followers in El Paso on July 21, arresting Victor Ochoa, Flavio Sandoval, José Trujillo, Dr. José Saenz, and Paulino Martínez, the head of the local *vazquista* junta, seizing a code and an impressive quantity of letters, documents, and telegrams, "which implicate numerous others and will disclose other overt acts." Dr. Saenz, who was the secretary of the junta—and a Bureau informant—was arrested at his own request to preserve his cover. The defendants were placed under a $3,000 bond each.[389] As soon as he posted bail, Dr. Saenz resumed his *vazquista* activities—and resumed informing the Bureau.[390]

A subsequent arrest in San Antonio was that of the delightfully named Dr. Luis (Ludwig) J. Snowball on July 26. He had rented a room over a drug store, had hired a stenographer, and had been churning out documents for distribution. Snowball had been in hiding since the wave of arrests began. At Snowball's hearing, Agent Hawkins represented Lancaster, who had injured his shin and was confined to his room. Snowball waived his hearing, and his bail was set at $1,500, which he posted. He was to appear in federal court on January 2, 1913, and to report to the US marshal on first of each intervening month, as the case might be called before the January term of the court.[391]

Discouragingly, Thompson informed the Chief in August that "those vazquistas who've made bond in San Antonio are again active and are organizing at Del Rio, Eagle Pass, and Brownsville, all of which should be covered by an active agent who could keep in line with their movements."[392]

Vázquez Gómez's associates David de la Fuente, commander in chief of his forces, and politician Ricardo Gómez Robelo fled from San Antonio to El Paso before arrest warrants for conspiracy could be served on them. It was learned they were hiding in the home of *vazquista* Paulino Martínez. De la Fuente was arrested with a code on his person. He posted a $2,500 bond and was released from jail. Mexican government authorities immediately had him rearrested on an extradition warrant, charging him with having robbed a bank in Chihuahua—the forty-day ploy.[393] Gómez Robelo managed to slip across the river to Juárez, but the Bureau kept his luggage left at the Linden Hotel under surveillance in case he was stupid enough to return for it. He was. Thompson had Gómez Robelo arrested at the international bridge and consigned to the county jail.[394] Agent Ross had him temporarily released from jail, however, in order to meet quietly with Senator Albert B. Fall of New Mexico, who was trying to broker peace in Mexico in return for lucrative concessions. Assistant US Attorney S. Engelking also attended the meeting and reported the substance to Ross. On September 3, there was a hearing for Gómez Robelo before the US Commissioner, and he was released. Gómez Robelo departed hurriedly for New Orleans.[395] By September, though, he was back in El Paso, living at 609 Third Street and plotting away.[396] He slipped off to San Antonio, but informers quickly alerted the Bureau. Agent Thompson phoned the US attorney for instructions whether or not to arrest Gómez Robelo, and was told to file a criminal complaint before the US commissioner charging violation of Section 37, Chapter 4 of the Criminal Code. The US marshal received an arrest warrant but had not located Gómez Robelo.[397]

The net of arrests widened. A notable case was that of Juan Pedro Didapp. In its efforts to enforce neutrality, the Bureau received assistance from none other than Harvey J. Phillips, whom we last saw convicted in 1911 of supervising arms shipments to the *maderistas* for Sherburne Hopkins, insurgent Madero's attorney. In 1912, Phillips was still working for Hopkins, who was now President Madero's attorney. And Phillips was now a Bureau special employee. He ingratiated himself with the *vazquistas* in New York to the point that one of their leading partisans, Juan Pedro Didapp, enthusiastically recommended him to the *vazquista* junta in San Antonio, providing him with a letter of introduction to Dr. Policarpo Rueda.[398] Phillips provided Agent Thompson with a letter on the letterhead of the "Embajada Especial de la Revolución de Mexico" (the

Special Embassy of the Mexican Revolution), 103 Vermont Avenue, Washington, signed by Didapp, stating he had received a telegram from Emiliano Zapata's headquarters that if US troops intervened in Mexico, American lives and property there would be in jeopardy. Although Phillips was useful, Bielaski became wary of him, suggesting Thompson have as little to do with him as possible.[399]

As for Didapp, the Bureau in San Antonio filed a criminal complaint against him for neutrality violations. Ross located Didapp in El Paso and arrested him in a drugstore while sipping lemonade, and turned him over to a deputy US marshal. Ross went to Didapp's room in the Angelus Hotel and went through his luggage, finding a mass of documents which he took to the BI office to translate. The US Commissioner fixed Didapp's bail at $3,000, which he could not post, and was remanded to jail.[400]

Warrants were issued for the arrest at Douglas, Arizona of Teodoro Rodríguez, Ramón E. Vázquez, Candelario Izuñza, and Antonio M. Franco. Agents Barnes and Hebert conducted a series of arrests on July 28 of *vazquistas* charged with conspiracy to set on foot a military expedition, starting with Ramón Vázquez, head of the junta, and Teodoro Rodríguez.[401] Rodríguez promptly sent for the Mexican consul and said if the consul could secure his release; he would furnish complete information about the local junta, including names, and would tell where all papers, correspondence, etc. relating to the junta could be found. Agent Barnes also obtained through a subpoena duces tecum copies of the numerous telegrams Vázquez had sent and received during the past two months.[402] Agent in Charge Thompson traveled from San Antonio to be present at the preliminary examination of Rodríguez and Vázquez.[403]

Acting on Agent Lancaster's information and under US Attorney Charles Boynton's direction, on January 9, 1913, the grand jury in San Antonio indicted Emilio Vázquez Gómez and thirty-eight others, several of whom used aliases, "for conspiracy to set on foot and provide and prepare the means for a military expedition and for the enlistment of men and for the purchase of supplies in pursuance of the conspiracy to violate Sections 10 and 13 of the Penal Code."[404]

The Bureau had gathered a mass of letters and documents which were introduced as evidence, and the assistant US attorney was confident of convicting the majority of the defendants.[405] Some defendants were out on bond, and Thompson reported that people held in San Antonio for neutrality violations were forfeiting their bond and fleeing to Mexico, nullifying chances for their prosecution. Most of the rest were scattered from Los Angeles to New Orleans. Several were arrested in San Antonio and El Paso.[406] The case would not be tried until the October term of court. Keeping track of the defendants and witnesses until October would be a major challenge for the Bureau.[407]

Vázquez Gómez's rebellion was foundering in Texas, but he hoped to revive it by opening a new campaign in Sonora. Such a campaign would necessarily involve acquiring the necessary munitions and supplies from Arizona, principally through Douglas. As Agent Hawkins pointed out, it was most difficult to prevent smuggling—sixty miles of the invisible international boundary were patrolled by two mounted customs inspectors.

As for Douglas itself, Agent Barnes, temporarily in Douglas reported: "Concerning the enforcement of the neutrality [laws] at this point, there is practically nothing to hinder wholesale smuggling of arms and ammunition. The Custom House closes at 4:30 p.m. The military force has recently been augmented but so far, the officers have not seen fit to take any steps toward the prevention of smuggling contraband articles. Such steps, however, are not so necessary now so long as this vicinity is in the hands of the Federal forces."[408]

Initially, Agent Earnest Hawkins covered Douglas, but as Agent in Charge Thompson wrote, "Hawkins is the only agent available at present, but owing to the fact that he is not familiar with conditions along the border and not fully advised as to Neutrality Law and its provisions, I am endeavoring to make a change and send some other Agents there or take up this work myself at El Paso where I feel that it is much more important for me to be at this time than in San Antonio."[409]

Hawkins received intelligence from the Thiel Detective Agency's Douglas office. Its manager was none other than Thomas B. Cunningham who, during the *maderista* phase of the revolution, had simultaneously reported to Thiel, to the *porfirista* consul, and to the BI. Cunningham ran his own stable of operatives and informants covering, among other things, the Phelps-Dodge Company, which also owned the Moctezuma Copper Company and the Nacozari Railroad in Sonora. One of these operatives worked directly for James Douglas, in charge of the company's store in Douglas. This operative had an informant who was a rebel courier and who described how ammunition was being smuggled to Douglas from El Paso. Two to five men carried ammunition in sacks from El Paso to one of the small stations on the El Paso & Southwestern Railroad; a confederate purchased a ticket on a daily EP&SW train carrying both passengers and freight, usually cars with coal or coke and stopping whenever flagged at a station. When the confederate had the train flagged to a stop in order to get off, the waiting smugglers scrambled aboard the coal cars and concealed the ammunition beneath the coal. They all returned to El Paso and repeated the procedure.[410]

Hawkins also exchanged information with Mexican consul Cuesta, Deputy US Marshal Arthur A. Hopkins, an Immigration inspector, and Madero agent Henry N. Gray, among others knowledgeable about revolutionary matters. He commented that "the air is full of all sorts of rumors of unusual activity on the part of revolutionists on the Mexican side of the border, but as is usually the case in times of excitement and speculation, the bulk of them are probably without substantial foundation." Some rumors did have foundation, though. Hawkins filed criminal complaints against several Mexicans for smuggling ammunition and for recruiting.[411] Particularly concerning was the possibility of *vazquistas* storming Agua Prieta, which had a small garrison whose officers' loyalty to Madero was questionable.

Agent Hawkins soon focused on Manuel Mascarenas, Jr., whom Vázquez Gómez had commissioned as provisional governor of Sonora. Mascarenas belonged to a wealthy Sonoran ranching family which had been prominent in the Díaz administration. For months, Mascarenas had rented a room at the rear of the National Hotel in Nogales, literally a few feet from the international boundary. He had recently crossed a shipment of rifles for the rebels after having had them sent to the American Drug Store in Nogales and then delivered to the National Hotel, from where they were smuggled into Mexico at night.

Mascarenas arrived in Douglas in early April, accompanied by J. B. Larrazolo, an undistinguished lawyer from El Paso who was the *vazquista* provisional vice governor. They stayed in the upscale Gadsden Hotel, where they opened an office for one month, ostensibly as brokers handling land, mines, and cattle. Hawkins had been unable to connect them directly with any shady transactions or violations of the neutrality laws, but Madero agents, including H. N. Gray, were watching them closely and had promised to communicate anything incriminatory they discovered. The pair hurriedly left town on April 18 because of articles in the local newspaper identifying them, and corroborating what was common knowledge. Pathetically, Larrazolo had offered the reporter who wrote the story five pages of advertising for their brokerage business if he killed the story. The reporter refused.[412]

The situation at Douglas was rather loose, according to Agent Curley D. Hebert, recently assigned there from Laredo to replace Hawkins, and cover both Douglas and Nogales.[413] General Giuseppe Garibaldi, who had been on Madero's staff in the initial struggle against Porfirio Díaz, was busy recruiting men for the Mexican army, but the Agua Prieta garrison was less than combat-ready. Hebert said all the Mexican officers spent most of their time in the lobby of the Gadsden Hotel, and that Federal soldiers from Agua Prieta were in town most of the day and until late at night drinking and carousing.[414] Not surprisingly, smuggling into Agua Prieta continued.

The Phelps-Dodge Company's Copper Queen store (subsequently named the "Phelps-Dodge Mercantile Co.") in Douglas, was of particular interest to Agent Hebert.[415] The store's manager threatened the clerks with instant dismissal if they said anything about anything sold there. Hebert kept the store under surveillance and persuaded the clerk who handled arms sales to describe how this smuggling scheme worked. All the sales were to Roberto Pesqueira, who would come in and purchase some small item of hardware and ask for it to be delivered to him. If he bought two articles, this meant 2,000 rounds were to be taken out the back of the store to the alley behind the Gadsden Hotel and delivered to a driver, who put them in his car with a lap robe to cover them, then drove around to the front of the hotel, picked up Pesqueira, and from there drove across to Agua Prieta. The clerk claimed that Pesqueira had crossed as many as 4,000 cartridges in a day. Agent Hebert had seen Pesqueira go into the store, buy small articles, and walk out, and would later see him being driven to Agua Prieta, but he had failed to connect the dots.[416]

Hebert had to rely on an interpreter. The American consul in Agua Prieta wrote: "I cannot too strongly recommend that, if possible, an Agent of the Department of Justice be sent to this place [Douglas], who has some knowledge of the Spanish language and some experience in dealing with Latin races..."[417] Hebert was frustrated. He complained that Mexican secret agents informed him several times a day about nefarious activities but when investigated, these reports invariably turned out to be false. "Agent has never had one of the Mexican Secret Service men to give him correct information about a case."[418] Hebert's opinion did not improve. When a new Mexican secret service man named Joseph Rothman, who claimed to be a former Bureau agent, arrived on the scene, Hebert claimed Rothman "can find more false information than most of the Mexican Secret Service agents who have been in Douglas."[419] Agent Barnes, however, stated that Rothman was also an informant for the Bureau.[420]

Hebert also complained that local officers, the US commissioner, US attorney, and Deputy Marshal A. A. Hopkins, along with other federal officers, were not doing their duty. Men arrested were released without bond or had their cases dismissed entirely, and the commissioner had absolutely refused to issue warrants for persons attempting to export munitions. Hebert emphasized that it was impossible to enforce the law without the help of local officers, especially in a place like Douglas, where most residents sympathized with the rebels. No one was searched going into Agua Prieta, there was no inspector on duty at the customs house after 9 p.m., and, even when someone was on duty, Mexicans just crossed 100 yards from the customs house. At least one more agent was needed to cover the Douglas-Nogales section.[421]

However, some of Agent Hebert's complaints should be placed in perspective. For example, the federal judge at Douglas refused to issue a warrant for vagrancy for two Mexicans as requested by Powell Roberts of the Madero intelligence service, stating that since Roberts worked for the Mexican government he would be treated as a Mexican, and the judge did not believe in a Mexican officer trying to enforce the laws of the United States. "The Judge also claims that there's been too much searching of people and houses by Mexican officers in and around Douglas for the past few months and that he'd see that a stop was put to it."[422]

Neutrality enforcement received a stunning blow from federal judge Thomas Sheldon Maxey on October 7, 1912, in the case of US v. Arnulfo Chávez charged with transporting rifle ammunition between two points in El Paso with intent to export.[423] Maxey quashed the indictment, ruling that in order to constitute an offense an individual must actually transport munitions to Mexico.[424] Since the Bureau had requested clarification of the law, the attorney general telegraphed the US attorney in Arizona: "Difference between you and Department is apparently on question of fact not law. Where a person is discovered actually carrying arms or munitions of war from the United States into Mexico it is not necessary in my opinion that he get across the border before the offence is complete. He is engaged in the act of exporting, not in an attempt to export when he is proceeding with the prohibited arms and munitions from a point in the

United States towards the Mexican boundary with intent to cross into Mexico. To hold otherwise would be to make the enforcement of the law impossible. Please be governed accordingly."[425] The US attorney in Arizona was still reluctant to comply. Hebert hurried to El Paso to confer with Agent in Charge Thompson about the situation in Douglas and ask his assistance regarding the large backlog of neutrality cases. Judge Maxey's ruling requiring in flagranti violations of the neutrality laws in order to make an arrest, and the legal challenge of the ruling by the Texas attorney general created the backlog of cases. The Supreme Court eventually overturned Maxey's ruling.

Hebert returned to Douglas to monitor closely conditions in Agua Prieta; a munity was suppressed in the Federal garrison involving former rebels who had recently been recruited by General Garibaldi for the Madero army. Loyal officers disarmed more than 100 of these men, rapidly sending munitions back to Douglas to prevent rebels from seizing them. Everything seemed to be in an upheaval—disagreement among the officers, and soldiers deserting every day and crossing to the US seeking work.[426] Yet amid all these developments, Hebert wrote: "All quiet except for lots of wild reports by Mexican Secret Service men."[427]

In a welcome development, the freight agent of the EP&SW railroad promised Agent Barnes to send daily transcripts of all incoming arms and ammunition, while the manager of the Phelps-Dodge Mercantile Co. agreed to furnish a daily copy of their sales of munitions, in addition to a list of rifles sold since January. The manager of the Douglas Hardware Co. agreed to provide information on future sales to rebels, provided this information was treated confidentially.[428]

Barnes also traveled to the little town of Naco, Arizona, to investigate neutrality violations. Naco was an ideal venue for smuggling: two railroads intersected there, and the invisible international boundary separated Naco, Arizona from Naco, Sonora. The Mexican consul in Naco, Arizona, was most forthcoming, providing names of rebels in the local junta and those of others at Bisbee, Benson, and other Arizona locations.

Barnes crossed to Naco, Sonora, and interviewed the police chief, who provided much the same information.[429]

Apprehension grew regarding the Mexican government's ability to retain Agua Prieta. The rebels could easily take the town because it had a small garrison whose loyalty was questionable at best. A night attack would be particularly successful, for most of the federal officers slept in Douglas, preferably at the Gadsden Hotel. One officer was quoted as saying they did not intend to make any resistance if attacked.[430]

Barnes had to return to San Antonio, leaving Hebert once again to cover Douglas. But Hebert was deemed unsatisfactory. Agent in Charge Thompson informed headquarters on September 7 that there was much activity in the Douglas-Agua Prieta section, mostly on the Mexican side of the boundary, but "Agent Hebert, stationed there, has been unable to get any information for us concerning movements of parties on this side of the border, in which we are especially interested." Thompson then quoted a telegram from the US attorney in Arizona suggesting prompt action in the Hebert matter. Hebert, as we have seen, complained about both US and Mexican officials in Douglas and was unable to work with them. "For this reason, he has been instructed to return to El Paso and another Agent will be assigned to cover this section of the country as soon as one is available."[431]

The Hebert affair became nasty. Hebert told a reporter for the *Douglas Daily Dispatch* that he had been "harassed by the Mexican consuls at Douglas, El Paso, San Antonio, and Laredo, and Felix Sommerfeld until things got unbearable and I could not stand for it any longer. All my confidential reports to the Department of Justice became the public property of the Mexican consul at El Paso and from there were given out to the various Mexican consuls located along the border. [Manuel] Cuesta [Mexican consul at Douglas] was no exception, he himself having informed me that he secured all the information I turned in to my Department. Not only did the Mexican consuls attempt to have me removed but they were also assisted by Agent in Charge Thompson of San

Antonio as well as United States officials in Arizona. Thompson himself informed me that the United States Attorney Morrison had requested him by letter to remove me from Douglas and substitute Special Agent R. L. Barnes or some other agent who would cooperate with Mexican Consul Cuesta in this city." Hebert cited Sheriff Harry C. Wheeler who not only refuted the allegation that Hebert sympathized with the rebels but "asserted that Agent in Charge Thompson and L. E. Ross of El Paso, at that time special agent for the Department of Justice, were both receiving compensation from the Mexican government for services rendered the Madero government." Hebert stated that he had learned of Consul Cuesta's duplicity early in 1912 and had reported it to the Department, only to be informed later by Cuesta and Consul Antonio Lozano at Laredo that they had received copies of the report. "For these reasons I resigned from the Department rather than be harassed by my own brother officers in Arizona and Texas."[432]

Special Agent in Charge Thompson wrote a "PERSONAL AND CONFIDENTIAL" letter to Chief Bielaski refuting Hebert's charge that he and Agent Ross had accepted bribes from the Mexican government, particularly from Consul Llorente in El Paso. "There has been no relationship whatsoever between Llorente, Ross, and myself, except such matters as were necessary to communicate to him." Thompson allowed as how Ross had frequently received funds from Madero's secret agent Felix Sommerfeld, but this money was to pay informants working under Ross's direction, not a bribe. "On July 18, I received a letter from Manuel Cuesta via Llorente, a copy of which is sent you attached hereto, requesting the removal from Douglas of Hebert. At the time and later I couldn't transfer him because no other agents were available. Barnes was assigned to Douglas when conditions were threatening and remained there for some time. While there a number of cases were gotten against neutrality violators, but aside from this, absolutely nothing has been accomplished by Hebert and I attribute the failure to secure prosecution of a number of persons there to his attitude toward the Mexican Government and its officials." Hebert was not diplomatic and was entirely too outspoken in support of the rebel cause. [US attorney for Arizona] Morrison requested that Hebert be transferred. [Agent Charles] Breniman replaced him. Since that time Hebert has remained in Douglas contrary to my instructions, there being no excuse for his remaining there." Only that morning had Thompson received a telegram from Hebert saying he had arrived in El Paso. "He was advised of your [Bielaski's] telegram in which you stated that if he did not take the next train he would be suspended and instructed him to make a full explanation concerning his stay there." Thompson enclosed letters and newspaper clippings and offered to provide anything else Bielaski required.[433] Thompson transferred Hebert to San Antonio, then to Del Rio.[434] A bitter Hebert telegraphed Chief Bielaski his resignation as of close of business on September 23, 1912.[435]

Significantly, Hebert had spoken with Cuesta in May 1912, at which time the consul enthusiastically described himself as a *vazquista*. And in July, Agent Barnes said he had received information that there was doubt about Cuesta's loyalty to the Mexican government, with the assertion he was a *vazquista*. Barnes, however, believed that Cuesta was loyal and was anxious to prevent the rebels from capturing Agua Prieta.[436]

There had also been suspicion regarding the relations between Consul Cuesta and A. A. Hopkins, who had become a deputy US marshal on April 5, 1912. (Hopkins usually translated his informants' reports and forwarded a copy to the Bureau.) The two appeared to be intimate friends, and since Cuesta's loyalty to Madero was suspect, it was feared Hopkins might have been suborned. Agent E. M. Blanford in El Paso had become concerned about their relations in connection with another case, and he wrote to US Consul Simpich in Agua Prieta requesting a detailed statement about the Cuesta-Hopkins matter. Simpich replied that State Department regulations restricted the sharing of official information with other Departments except through official channels. So, Blanford should make his request to the State Department and, if approved, Simpich would be happy to make a detailed statement. Blanford left the matter up to the

Chief.⁴³⁷ Disturbingly, Agent in Charge Thompson reported that "The Mexican consul [Manuel Cuesta] has openly declared himself as a 'Vasquista'[sic] and he seems to be directing the actions of Deputy Marshal Hopkins."⁴³⁸

Agent Blanford at Douglas wrote regarding employing an informant: "Luke Short, mounted Customs inspector, said he wouldn't help me secure information for Cuesta and that A. A. Hopkins would tell Cuesta everything he knows. Short also said Hopkins had received money from Cuesta [and] at same time was receiving salary as deputy US marshal." Short stated further that Cuesta had made the statement in the presence of two witnesses that Cuesta could put Hopkins in the penitentiary if he wished to do so. One of these witnesses, according to Short, told Hopkins about this statement of Cuesta's, whereupon Hopkins is alleged to have said, "What do you suppose I had better do, cut it out?" The other is alleged to have said to Hopkins, "Well, what is the matter with you, aren't you true blue to the cause you are serving?"—meaning the US government. Here the conversation between Hopkins and the witness of Cuesta's statement is alleged to have ended.

> I then related to Short the following incident that had come to my attention in connection with the relations existing between Hopkins and Cuesta. I had noticed a stranger, a Mexican, in conversation with Cuesta and Dr. José S. Saenz in the lobby of the Gadsden Hotel and was desirous of knowing his identity. I asked Hopkins to go to the hotel with me and see if he knew this man. Hopkins refused to go saying that he didn't want to see Cuesta as he didn't wish to cut the man in a public place. (Meaning that he did not wish to ignore him.) Short stated that this might be taken as Hopkins stated, that he did not wish to cut Cuesta, or it might be taken to mean that Hopkins is really afraid of Cuesta because he has the "goods" on Hopkins. Another time when in company with Hopkins

we ran unexpectedly upon Cuesta, Hopkins turned about face and retreated on the instant. Whether Cuesta knows something on Hopkins which Hopkins fears he will make public, I am unable to surmise. It may be that Hopkins simply wishes to avoid Cuesta as a result of Cuesta's recent confession of having used U. S. Govt. officials to secure information for the rebels. At any rate it will be seen that it is a difficult matter to select a trustworthy informant, not alone because the almost entire Mexican population is in sympathy with the Maderistas [sic—vazquistas] who are doing all the recruiting and smuggling, but because there seems to be some doubt as to which of the U. S. Govt officials with whom I am compelled to work are to be trusted. Short, however, suggested a man who will probably be given a trial.[439]

Agent Barnes said Hebert had told him Hopkins was employed by Consul Cuesta. Hopkins's attorney stated that indeed Hopkins had worked for Cuesta—but only for the month of March 1912, while he was a Douglas policeman and for which he received $100. Hebert subsequently told Barnes that Cuesta's exact words regarding Hopkins had been, "I can put the SOB in jail." Blanford interviewed T. B. Cunningham, formerly of the Thiel Detective Agency but currently a special agent of the Chino Copper Co., who was convinced Hopkins worked for Cuesta after becoming a deputy US marshal but could not prove it. Barnes investigated the allegations against Hopkins but said he was not too successful.[440]

Consul Manuel Cuesta was reassigned as consul in Baltimore, where on July 26, 1913, he gave a sworn deposition about his relations with Hopkins. He admitted using Hopkins as an informant for a few months at $100 per month, and admitted that he and Hopkins became friends, but stated categorically that when Hopkins was appointed as a deputy US marshal, Hopkins showed Cuesta his commission and said he must quit being Cuesta's informant. He denied paying Hopkins anything thereafter, although Hopkins did on occasion give Cuesta information and do him favors, but legitimately. Cuesta denied having said he could send Hopkins to jail.[441] Hopkins remained a deputy US marshal. As of January 1915, he was an Immigration inspector at Tucson.[442]

Hebert's replacement, Agent Breniman, arrived in Douglas on September 9, checked into the Gadsden Hotel, the local epicenter of intrigue, and began making the rounds of those persons providing intelligence. He started with American military and civilian officials, among them Deputy Marshal A. A. Hopkins. He became acquainted with Consul Cuesta, who offered his full assistance to the Bureau, as did Cuesta's secret agent Powell Roberts, who had previously worked in El Paso. Another Mexican government secret agent, L. L. Hall, was on his way from El Paso.[443] Breniman also met, among others, the Thiel Detective Agency manager, and Byron S. Butcher, a local journalist who provided occasional tips. Douglas was in an uproar because the rebels had demanded that Agua Prieta surrender. (This proved to be an empty threat.)[444] Lesser excitement was that two *vazquista* officers arrested back in July for neutrality violations and awaiting removal to El Paso for trial had sawed through the bars of the city jail and escaped.[445] Breniman did have some good news to report: that that section of the border was quiet, for the rebels were disorganized, lacked weapons and ammunition, and several of their leaders had deserted.[446]

The bad news was that the US military had caused a major flap. One of Consul Cuesta's men informed Agent Breniman that rebels Joaquín Esquer, Dr. Huerta, and Francisco Escandón were in Douglas at the shabby Hotel Mexico. Since the Bureau had no information on which to base a criminal complaint, Breniman passed the information along to US Consul Dye and to Colonel Guilfoyle commanding the 9th Cavalry stationed at Douglas. The War Department authorized Guilfoyle to arrest the trio. Two lieutenants and four or five enlisted men, along with Mexican secret agent Powell Roberts as interpreter, descended on the Hotel Mexico on the night of September 29 and thoroughly searched the place, but without results. Breniman acknowledged that he was there but insisted he took no part "personally or officially." For all he knew, the Mexicans might still be somewhere in Douglas. The hotel owner filed a complaint before the Justice of the Peace, charging assault with deadly weapons and forcible entry. Warrants were issued for the arrest of Consul Cuesta, his agent Powell Roberts, and the two lieutenants. The officers were not arrested but were requested to appear at a hearing set for October 2. The sheriff arrested Cuesta and Roberts, who were arraigned and posted a bond of $500 each. The local newspaper was stridently denouncing the army for conducting a search without a warrant.[447]

Consul Cuesta dropped a bombshell in an interview with the *Douglas Daily Dispatch* on February 20, 1913. He stated that he had never renounced his allegiance to Porfirio Díaz and had been actively aiding the revolutionary cause of Pascual Orozco and the *Científico* Party since his arrival in Douglas eighteenth months earlier. "The only obstacles I encountered in carrying on the revolutionary work in this city and vicinity were *The Dispatch* and C. D. Hebert of this city, formerly special agent for the Department of Justice. My every move and the cause thereof seemed to be anticipated by these two. With the exception of Mr. Hebert, I succeeded in deceiving every other American officer with whom I had dealings, and it was through our combined efforts that Hebert resigned from the Department of Justice. I succeeded in discrediting all his charge of [my] being a rebel, filed against me with the Department. However, against Hebert and *The Dispatch* I hold no malice, as they were right but at the time could offer no substantial proof of their charges ... He and the *Dispatch* were relentless in their efforts to run me to earth. They never knew how near they were to success. During the time of my consulship in this city I was able to secure much valuable information from any number of US officials, which resulted in the fact that the rebels were always fully informed of any move against them for violation of President Taft's proclamation on the neutrality laws and therefore there were practically no arrests on these charges made in the city of Douglas."[448] Consul

Cuesta's revelations vindicated Agent Hebert of collusion, but by then the embittered Hebert had resigned from the Bureau.[449]

As for Vázquez Gómez, his rebellion had been taken over by Pascual Orozco. Vázquez Gómez was a has-been who returned to his exile in the United States. He eventually did return to Mexico, dying in Mexico City in 1926.

Although the *magonistas* had dropped in the Bureau's priorities, this marginalized faction still merited some attention. In September 1911, Agent in Charge at San Antonio H. A. Thompson had dispatched Agent Hebert to Douglas, Arizona, to consult with Mexican Consul Torres. When they met at the upscale Gadsden Hotel, Torres said there was *magonista* activity at Pirtleville, a Hispanic settlement two miles away, where arms and ammunition were cached in a house, and that *magonistas* would attack a Mexican border town around September 16, Mexican Independence Day. Hebert followed up the lead, went to the house that night and found "about 200 old rifles of all kinds, about half of them are broke so that they could not be shot at all, and the others look as tho [sic] they were about worn out from use." Hebert's frustration increased when he endeavored to locate "a lot of rapid-fire guns stored somewhere around Douglas." Consul Torres claimed the guns had been shipped in from San Antonio but had no proof of any kind, "just some Old Peon's word for it." Agent Hebert spent a fruitless day running down that lead. He next rode horseback for fifteen miles along the border between Douglas and Naco trying to corroborate another claim by Consul Torres—the camp of a large group of well-armed revolutionists. He found nothing. These incidents illustrate the dead ends the BI often encountered, but the agency would have been remiss not to have followed up as many leads as its limited resources permitted. Hebert, on occasion, received information from Julio Martínez, a Mexican secret agent attached to Consul Torres and who had infiltrated the local *magonistas*. *Magonistas* along the Arizona border were remarkably quiet as of early 1912.

A trio of armed *magonistas* had been jailed at the town of Uvalde in South Texas. Hoping to get them to talk, Agent Hebert used Madero secret agent Teódulo Beltrán, arranging for him to be put in jail with the prisoners, who indeed talked freely. They were bound over to the grand jury charged with "enlisting and procuring others to enlist in a revolutionary movement against Mexico." Unable to post bond, they remained in jail.[450]

Agent Ganor in Los Angeles was still plowing through the trove of seized *magonista* papers and was trying to locate government witnesses for Flores Magón's forthcoming trial.[451] Enforcing neutrality was difficult in California. Agent Ganor reported from Los Angeles in March 1912, that a Mexican secret agent named Mancilla, sent from Mexico City, had called at the BI office to discuss revolutionary conditions in Los Angeles. But Ganor complained to the assistant US attorney that the Mexican officials "did not lend any assistance to this department and that they make reports to this office of conditions that are not true without making any investigations, and that if in the future they would make a more thorough investigation without hearsay, would make less work for this department here."[452]

The Consul General of Mexico in San Francisco, Victor Lomelí, had been more accommodating. He had informed Agent Herrington that a schooner was to be loaded with munitions in San Francisco for rebels in Chiapas, in southern Mexico. Lomelí requested the Bureau's assistance in shadowing those involved and in watching the schooner. Herrington suggested that Lomelí take the matter up with his own government and, providing the Bureau authorized Herrington, he would be glad to assist in every way to prevent neutrality violations. Herrington continued to receive information about several more suspicious vessels, and he arranged for customs inspectors to maintain surveillance. The Mexican consul continued to keep Herrington appraised of steamers leaving San Francisco for Mexico.[453]

Chapter 7: Unprecedented Intelligence Cooperation

Initially, Vázquez Gómez's ally, General Pascual Orozco took over the rebel movement against President Madero. Orozco had been Madero's principal commander in 1911 but had become disillusioned with Madero as president, reportedly because he had been given only a minor military post. Orozco had hoped to become Minister of War, but Madero had made him merely commander of irregular *maderista* cavalry in the state of Chihuahua. For this reason, Orozco, while outwardly maintaining loyalty to the Madero regime, had covertly supported General Reyes's bid for power in 1911.[454] In early February 1912, the *maderista* garrison in Ciudad Juárez mutinied. The government called on Orozco to use his prestige to quell the uprising, which he did. But scattered anti-Madero uprisings, some of them ostensibly *vazquista*, occurred in Chihuahua; these bands coalesced into a force of some 1,700, menacing Ciudad Juárez. After only token resistance by the Madero garrison, rebels occupied that town on February 27.

Desperate to build support, Emilio Vázquez Gómez wrote to Orozco, laying out his rationale for rebellion.[455] Orozco replied to Vázquez Gómez and asked him to come to Juárez to proclaim himself provisional president. (The Bureau obtained a copy of the letter, and had it photographed.)[456] Additional contingents soon swelled the insurgent force to some 4,000, and rebel chieftains called on Orozco to be their leader. The rebel cause received a huge boost on March 1, when Orozco publicly disavowed Madero. On March 3, he formally joined the rebel cause, assumed leadership, and dispatched a crestfallen Vázquez Gómez back to San Antonio. Further evidencing the propensity of politically "out" factions to unite against whoever was "in," the Bureau obtained and translated a letter from General Emiliano Zapata to Paulino Martínez, head of the *vazquista* junta in El Paso, urging him to cooperate with Orozco, as they and Zapata were "fighting for the same sacred cause."[457]

Although President Madero downplayed the loss of Ciudad Juárez, the fact was that Orozco controlled the largest port of entry on the border, and in short order gained control of the entire state of Chihuahua. American mercenaries, notably Sam Dreben and Tracy Richardson, soon joined him. While Richardson most certainly took whatever side paid the most at any given time, Dreben's true loyalties may not have been with Orozco. According to BI reports later that summer, Dreben "had been employed by Somelfelt [sic] to blow up bridges south of Juárez." It is highly unlikely that Sommerfeld, who was unforgiving in cases of loyalty breaches, would have rehired Dreben after working for the Orozco faction. More likely is the scenario that his old friend Sam worked for him throughout the Orozco rebellion as a spy, gathering intelligence and supporting the Madero administration.[458]

As Porfirio Díaz had complained about *maderistas* receiving aid and comfort in the United States, now President Madero made the same complaint about *orozquistas*. Like preceding revolutionary movements, Orozco depended on the United States for munitions and supplies. Conservative Mexicans considered Orozco a much stronger leader than Vázquez Gómez and gave him their political and financial support. This support, coupled with Orozco's popularity in Chihuahua, made the insurgents feel they had a reasonable chance of toppling Madero. They prepared to fight their way down the central rail line to Mexico City. One big problem was the lack of fire discipline among the rebels, who used up ammunition at an astounding rate. To succeed, Orozco would have to amass an enormous quantity of munitions in a very short time. His hope that the United States would grant the *orozquistas* belligerent status was a pipedream; worse, President Taft dealt the rebellion a devastating blow on March 16, when he lifted the arms embargo for the Madero government.[459] The *orozquistas* were reduced to having to smuggle munitions.

Most of the smuggling occurred through El Paso, for that city was Orozco's lifeline. As one historian put it, "The United States' strict enforcement of its neutrality laws would have a profound effect on the Orozquista movement."[460] Madero informants and operatives focused on the major hardware firms, Shelton-Payne and its competitor, Krakauer, Zork & Moye. The Krakauer company provided most of the ammunition for Orozco. The firm set up a system whereby a Mexican customer from Juárez would present an order for, say, "a pound of nails." This was a code for 1,000 cartridges. It was then up to the customer to smuggle the ammunition over to Juárez. The cost of the ammunition was debited from the $300,000 the *orozquistas* had reportedly deposited with the firm. Abraham Molina's informants swarmed around Krakauer, not only monitoring shipments in and out of the warehouse but shadowing every customer who purchased arms and ammunition. An indignant Julius Krakauer wrote to Senator A. B. Fall: "We state without fear of contradiction, that the Departments looking after the interests of the United States on the border, are absolutely controlled by the Mexican Consul at this point and his satellites."[461] Not surprisingly, the Krakauer family were most reluctant to cooperate with the federal authorities. There was no lack of persons, both Hispanics and Anglos, eager to smuggle ammunition across the Rio Grande.[462]

The Bureau's man on the spot in El Paso was L. E. Ross, one of the most effective agents on the border. Ross employed techniques that would become standard in the Bureau's repertoire: listening devices and "black bag" jobs. Ross installed a dictaphone in the house of an informant while he sweltered in the attic trying to overhear a conversation between his informants and the notorious mercenary, Sam Dreben. The results were disappointing. On another occasion, he and two informants burgled the home of veteran plotter Victor Ochoa at 2 a.m. and secured important papers.[463] Together with his *maderista* counterpart, Abraham Molina, Ross was instrumental in interdicting Orozco's supplies as he had done with those of Vázquez Gómez.

Ross received intelligence from a number of sources. Henry C. Kramp, local manager of the Thiel Detective Agency, sent his operatives' reports to the Madero government, the Mexico Northwestern Railway, and the Bureau of Investigation. He insisted, however, on sending the Bureau's copies directly to its San Antonio field office, fearing leaks in the BI's El Paso office and elsewhere along the border.[464] The San Antonio office then telegraphed the relevant information to Ross. He also received information from former BI Agents John W. Vann and Samuel Geck, the latter now proprietor of a rooming house. Geck routinely made the rounds of saloons, plazas, freight stations, etc., supplying low-level intelligence.[465] A much more valuable source was Felix Sommerfeld, Madero's man on the border, who consulted frequently with Ross.[466]

Ross also enlisted two men who proved to be by far his most effective informants—Maurice L. Gresh and Virgil L. Snyder. Snyder managed the local branch of the Western Detective Agency. Posing as corrupt private detectives, they proved exceedingly adept at infiltrating the *orozquista* smuggling network, even enduring a third-degree session in the rebels' Juárez headquarters in order to establish their bona fides. Agent Ross solidified their credibility by arranging for the army to permit the pair to smuggle ammunition across the river. The head of the *orozquistas* in El Paso, Victor Ochoa, repeatedly came up with imaginative schemes, such as blowing up the Mexican consulate with Sommerfeld and Consul Enrique C. Llorente in it, or planning a raid on the county jail to liberate *orozquista* prisoners. These schemes invariably failed because they were entrusted to his loyal subordinate—Maurice L. Gresh.[467]

Realizing the importance of El Paso, the Madero regime spared no expense to shut down Orozco's supply lifeline, spending lavishly for clandestine work.[468] Heading the Madero intelligence network were Consul Llorente and Felix Sommerfeld, who met daily in the consul's office to formulate strategy. Abraham Molina, who had been appointed by the *maderista* governor of Chihuahua, Abraham González, supervised day-to-day operations. He was an effective but mercenary spymaster.

Working directly under Molina was W. Powell Roberts, formerly a veteran local police sergeant who was well respected and spoke Spanish fluently. Another American, Lee L. Hall, functioned as Roberts's deputy. Roberts operated a network of agents and informers from a downtown office, numbering between twenty and eighty, paid between $2 and $4 per day. Roberts was tasked with cooperating fully with Agent Ross and with Charles H. Webster, a Texas Ranger detailed for neutrality enforcement. But Ross complained that "when this arrangement was first put into effect I arranged for close cooperation with the various forces at work. I have been unable to secure this from Roberts. Neither Roberts nor any of the men under him have done anything worthwhile since they have been working."[469]

Consul Llorente, who used the 1899 extradition treaty to good effect, also provided the Bureau with unprecedented—and crucial—financial support for employing informants and mercenaries, who flooded El Paso. Agent Ross could almost literally write his own ticket for his financial needs, and he was determined to stop munitions smuggling by any means necessary, which included giving free rein to Madero's intelligence agents. The pattern was for Mexican informants and agents, paid for by Llorente but often working under the direction of Ross, to saturate the city. The intelligence gathered was transmitted to Ross, who arranged for the Customs Service, the US marshal, the military, the Texas Rangers, or local and county officers to make the arrests for neutrality violations.

Mexican intelligence activities soon produced outrage among the citizenry, especially because armed Madero operatives searched passengers, including women, on the streetcars at the United States end of the two international bridges. Although Ross publicly approved of this as a necessary evil, the mayor and the sheriff indignantly ordered their men to arrest any searcher who was not an officer of the United States. American soldiers took over at the bridges, searching only men. But armed Madero agents were still in evidence.[470] As Agent Barnes, who went to El Paso to coordinate Ross's activities, admitted: "Strictly speaking, Madero men have no specific authority to carry arms except as comity is extended by local officers. They are assisting this Department and have not been elsewhere molested for carrying arms."[471]

Never in the history of the United States had a foreign intelligence service been permitted to operate as blatantly as that of Madero in 1912 against the *orozquistas*. Ross's superior, Agent in Charge H. A. Thompson in San Antonio, informed the Chief that "the Mexican secret service agents, both at El Paso and at San Antonio, have aided us materially in the investigation of neutrality matters, and it is only just fair to state that if it had not been for them and their co-work, it would have been next to impossible for us to have accomplished the results thus far obtained."[472]

Nevertheless, Orozco got off to an impressive start, dominating the state of Chihuahua and advancing down the central trail line. He defeated the Federal army in a major battle on March 24-25 at Rellano, near the Durango state line. The defeat was so crushing that the Federal commanding general, who was Madero's Minister of War, blew his brains out rather than return to Mexico City in disgrace. But Orozco had used up most of his 5,000,000 cartridges, and with US supply lines curtailed, his advance on Mexico City stalled.

Smuggling through El Paso being interdicted, the *orozquistas* developed new smuggling techniques and routes. Colonel Cástulo Herrera, the rebels' quartermaster, employing the alias of "George Valencia," went to Albuquerque, New Mexico, in May, and arranged with a local hardware store to ship 49,000 cartridges in barrels marked "limes" and "nails" by express to Deming, New Mexico. The shipment went from there by wagon thirty miles south to Columbus and into Mexico on June 1.[473]

But Orozco desperately needed huge quantities of ammunition. New Orleans seemed the place to acquire them, for the city had a booming traffic in arms. In fact, there were so many munitions deals going on despite the President's proclamation that it would be tedious to attempt to describe them in detail. Therefore, a few examples suffice.

Agent Billups Harris was interested in keeping track of Central American plotting as it involved the neutrality laws. He was focused on notorious mercenaries such as Lee Christmas, who was preparing to charter a vessel, the *Hornet*, for an expedition to overthrow the government of Honduras.[474] But Harris was also keeping an eye on Mexican exile plotters. He met at the office of the Mexican consul with Ernesto Fernández, "Chief of the Mexican Secret Service," who told him that *vazquista* Delio Moreno Cantón had been living in a boarding house at 3203 Esplanade Avenue and had been using the aliases of "Antonio Ortíz" and "Daniel or Samuel Morgan." Several other conservative Mexicans, among them Juan Peón del Valle, were in the city busily trying to organize an expedition; one of them, Gonzalo Enrile, had been living for some time on Howard Avenue under the name of "Rodríguez." There was said to be 200 rifles, one Gatling gun, and 40,000 rounds of ammunition stashed at the A. Baldwin & Co. hardware firm. Unfortunately, the Mexican consul and his secret agent Juan Leets were "not on confidential terms" with Fernández, and their various activities further confused the situation.

To add to Agent Harris' frustration, he could learn nothing from Mexican secret agent Juan Leets, who was one of the unsavory characters frequently encountered in the Mexican Revolution. His headquarters were at 1227 St. Charles Avenue, and he was described as "a Russian who figures here as a Madero secret service man. He is also connected with the Nicaragua troubles. He is considered one of the most dangerous and treacherous men here. He was a political refugee from Nicaragua and made his way to San Antonio and secured a place as waiter in a Mexican restaurant; while so employed he met Francisco Madero and gained his confidence. He tipped off Delio Moreno Cantón who was former governor of Yucatán a bitter opponent of Madero who was here to secure arms and was under indictment at El Paso for violation [of the] neutrality laws at a time when the marshal here was trying to arrest [Moreno] Cantón."[475] To establish his bona fides, Leets showed Harris his commission signed by the Mexican Minister of Foreign Affairs on February 12, 1912. Leets was suspected, however, of also working for Honduran exiles. His movements were also being covered by detectives working for the consul of Guatemala, who claimed to have information that Leets was plotting against that government.[476]

An ambitious *orozquista* operation had begun on April 17, when Orozco and his secretary Gonzalo Enrile delivered at Chihuahua to Salvador Rojas Vertíz, who had formerly owned and operated the keno games in Juárez, a check for 40,000 pesos, to be cashed in El Paso.[477] Since Rojas Vertíz could not speak English, he was provided with an interpreter, Manuel M. Miranda, a merchant originally from Mexico City who had been selling supplies to Orozco's army. The pair traveled to El Paso where Rojas Vertíz cashed the check at the First National Bank, receiving $19,700. Through a subpoena duces tecum, the Bureau later learned that there "were various other checks and drafts given by these people in large amounts, none of them less than $20,000, and some running into $100,000."[478] The Mexicans set out for New Orleans, traveling by rail.

They registered at the St. Charles Hotel under assumed names—Alberto Rojas (Rojas Vertíz) and J. J. Clark (Miranda). They later moved to the Grunewald Hotel, registering as A. Montero and M. M. Rodríguez, respectively, and occupying room 720. Rojas Vertíz sent Miranda out to visit the hardware stores, for he wanted to purchase 500,000 rounds of rifle ammunition.

The manager of A. Baldwin & Co., a leading hardware firm, subsequently stated that about June 1912, a man came into his office, told him his name was Clark, and said he wished to make a deal for 500 rifles and a large number of cartridges. The manager told him his name did not harmonize with his nationality, as he appeared to be a Mexican. "Clark" then left and went to Stauffer, Eshleman & Co. hardware firm where he negotiated the purchase of munitions. Agent Harris called at Stauffer and interviewed the manager. He said Miranda, alias Clark, bought $12,000 worth of arms and ammunition from him, and that this shipment contained about 600 carbines. The manager said he saw Salvador Rojas Vertíz give Miranda, alias Clark, the money for these goods.[479]

The Mexicans closed a deal with Stauffer, Eshleman for 600 Winchester carbines and 160,000 cartridges, paying $11,178 in cash. After waiting a week for the munitions to arrive by steamer from New York, Miranda paid the crew $100 to unload them at night. Arrangements had been made with the Pelican Box Factory to store the munitions and repackage them as "machinery." Forty 6-foot by 4-foot by 4-foot wooden boxes were constructed and filled with the smaller ammunition boxes containing the 160,000 cartridges. Awaiting repackaging were 510 carbines. The goods were loaded into two boxcars and covered with lumber, their destination being the fictitious "White Rose Mining Company" in Animas, New Mexico, near the border.

The Mexicans bribed an Illinois Central Railroad clerk to have the cars moved from the Pelican factory so the railroad would lose track of them. The ploy failed, for railroad officials learned of it. The munitions were then returned to the Stauffer, Eshleman warehouse, Agent Harris being convinced that the hardware firm meant to aid the Mexicans in shipping them secretly. The Chief instructed Harris to give this matter the closest possible attention and be sure to furnish him information in time to stop shipments at the border or at some point before leaving the country, even authorizing the temporary employment of an informant. This was welcome, for the agent also had to watch for large shipments of munitions coming by sea from New York consigned to the arms brokers Stauffer and A. Baldwin & Co., presumably also intended for the *orozquistas*.

Harris's problems increased, for he had only a couple of watchmen to keep track of the Stauffer, Eshleman munitions, as well as the shipments arriving by sea. But there was only so much a single Bureau agent could do in this cat-and-mouse game of moving munitions around to avoid detection.[480] The affair took a new turn when the broker, Maurice Conners, Agent Harris's principal informant in New Orleans, showed him a letter from General Orozco to the effect that the ubiquitous Mexican government operative, Juan Leets, was also a secret agent for Orozco. Conners said he had excellent reasons for believing that Leets was aiding the Honduras crowd of exiles and mercenaries, and that they were aiding Leets in his work for Orozco. Harris stated that Leets was aiding the Mexican revolutionists even though he was employed by the Mexican Government. Conners, who was "perhaps closer to the revolutionary agents here than anyone else," was helping them ship out the munitions and had agreed to advise Harris of developments.[481]

With the Bureau and Madero agents on their trail, the Mexicans had changed their plans. They decided to make another purchase; this time Remington cartridges from A. Baldwin & Co., paying a surcharge for secrecy to William Fitzpatrick, manager of the arms department. They intended to dispatch this ammunition in steamer trunks to El Paso by railway express.[482] And they were thinking big—they purchased forty trunks. The initial shipment was six trunks wrapped in burlap, each containing 4,000 rounds and weighing 240 pounds.

The operation unraveled. Rojas Vertíz instructed Miranda to return to El Paso and continue on to Orozco's headquarters for instructions. But upon arrival at El Paso, Miranda learned that Rojas Vertíz had arranged for his arrest at Juárez on a charge that he had embezzled $2,700 of the arms deal money. Miranda was also disgruntled because his commission was only $1,500. In a decidedly hostile mood, Miranda informed L. L. Hall of the Madero intelligence service about the whole affair. The Bureau learned of all this from Miranda's El Paso partner in crime, one T. C. Cabney, an erstwhile *vazquista* and *orozquista* who was also a BI informant. When the six trunks arrived in El Paso, Bureau agents seized them, arrested Ignacio López, the *orozquista* waiting to receive them, and made plans to confiscate the 54,000 rounds still in New Orleans.

This proved difficult. Fearing arrest, Rojas Vertíz fled to Mexico, turning over the ammunition in New Orleans to a broker named Carlos Martínez. The latter left the ammunition with A. Baldwin & Co. to sell. Rojas Vertíz later sent Ignacio López to New Orleans to arrange shipment of the ammunition to El Paso. Martínez instructed Baldwin to turn the ammunition over to López, who arranged with the Western Transfer & Storage Co. in El Paso for the receipt and storage of the goods. López then claimed ownership, declaring that he did not intend to smuggle the ammunition, but was trying either to sell or pawn it.[483]

Rojas Vertíz made his way back to El Paso but was apprehended and charged with conspiracy to export munitions to Mexico. He was bound over to the federal grand jury and was indicted in October 1912. Unable to post a stiff $3,500 bond, he was remanded to jail. His trial resulted in a hung jury. Miranda was not prosecuted because of the information he had furnished regarding Rojas Vertíz.[484]

Rojas Vertíz and Miranda bitterly disputed ownership of the munitions. The former colleagues spent a significant sum of $3,000 on lawyers. Rojas Vertíz desperately wanted to secure the weaponry for beleaguered General Orozco, who after all, had paid for it in the first place. The Mexican consul, working through Miranda, wanted to get possession of the munitions and ship them to the Madero government. Miranda's suit was dismissed, adding to the consul's apprehension, especially since Miranda, nothing daunted by losing his suit, now threatened to ship the goods to the rebels.[485] As it turned out, Miranda succeeded in selling the 600 rifles and 160,000 cartridges to the Mexican consul in New Orleans, who had the goods shipped to his colleague in El Paso, where they were stored in the Shelton-Payne hardware store.[486] These munitions would now be the El Paso field office's problem.

The overworked Agent Harris had to deal in July with a new player in the New Orleans arms scene. The newcomer was the most exotic figure yet—a millionaire Mexican bullfighter, no less.[487] Vicente Segura y Martínez had inherited a fortune, had built himself a bullring, but had become bored. He was described as being "about five feet ten inches. Weight one hundred seventy or eighty. About thirty years. Clean shaven. Large brown eyes, black hair, light olive complexion. Clear-cut regular features, good dresser. Striking athletic figure and carriage. Likely [to] use own name. Well known as bullfighter and millionaire. Is Mexican but speaks good English. Likely [to] have woman with him."[488]

Segura was in New Orleans on behalf of the *científico* faction to acquire munitions for the planned rebellion against President Madero by General Félix Díaz, Porfirio's nephew. Segura and an associate named Juan Cumplido, who owned a ranch in New Mexico near El Paso, checked into the Grunewald Hotel and spent much time with Fitzpatrick, head of the arms department at A. Baldwin & Co., which in itself caused Agent Harris to watch them. Harris conferred with the Mexican consul, whose attitude was not reassuring. It turned out that the consul and Cumplido had seen each other several times, and "it seemed to agent that the consul's attitude is uncertain and that he took too much [sic] pains to establish the belief that Segura and Cumplido are only tourists. He stated that they, or Cumplido, had assured him that they were going to Japan."[489]

However, Harris's informant Conners, "who has provided good information in the past," reported receiving a proposition from Mexicans, one of them Cumplido, who were preparing an expedition against the Madero government. They had plenty of money—Conners said Cumplido had $200,000 in a New Orleans bank—and proposed to land the expedition on the Gulf coast, then move against Mexico City. Conners said a "friend" had been offered a contract to load the munitions on a vessel, and the friend had asked Conners to ask Agent Harris if the US government would allow him as a reward one-third the value of the munitions on the boat, totaling about $60,000. The friend would load the boat, then furnish all details of the expedition so it could be captured. Conners said the friend would want to be arrested along with the others to preserve his cover. The friend would not take the contract unless some arrangement could be made. Conners was certain the munitions would come from A. Baldwin & Co. and said the "friend" was none other than Fitzpatrick, the arms manager at Baldwin.

The bullfighter, Segura, was clearly in over his head in dealing with people for whom treachery was an ordinary business practice. Conners and Fitzpatrick discussed plans to acquire a vessel for the expedition, for which Cumplido's crowd was going to pay $10,000. Conners told Agent Harris that if Fitzpatrick did not let him in on this deal, he would learn the facts, advise the agent, and petition the government for a reward as an informant. Fitzpatrick told Conners that Segura had ensconced himself with a woman at the Arcadia Apartments and Cumplido had left New Orleans, and that the munitions deal was off, but Conners believed this was a ruse to cut him out of the deal. He understood that the arms would come from New York by sea in a couple of weeks.[490]

The Mexican consul was most anxious to learn what Segura was up to, and he wanted to employ the Burns Detective Agency to plant a dictograph in Segura's apartment. At the consul's request, Harris accompanied him to talk with the Burns manager. Harris suggested getting the janitor to install the dictagraph as soon as possible. Since Burns had no Spanish-speaking operator available to listen in, the consul lent his clerk to the enterprise. To the frustration of the Burns operative, Segura never left the apartment, and the clerk proved unsuited for the operation. Since the instrument could not be secreted in the apartment, the Burns operative decided to install it on the wall outside the apartment on a pole by the window. This proved unsatisfactory because of the noise from passing cars. So much for technology. Harris in his reports was quite careful to stress that everything was done at the consul's insistence.[491]

Segura decided to place in broker Conners's hands the entire matter of getting the expedition away. This would entail secretly removing the arms and ammunition from Baldwin's warehouse to two small schooners which would transfer the material at sea to the schooner, *Dantzler*, which Segura had purchased. Conners said he was going to receive $10,000 from Segura and offered to give Agent Harris half. The Bureau agent played along, agreeing as a corrupt federal officer to accept the $5,000. A greatly relieved Conners admitted he would never have agreed to assist Segura without being sure Harris would be in on the deal. Harris prudently informed the Chief in detail, adding that "the only way to catch expedition is by some agreement with Conners, who of course will receive pay from other side. Please advise." The Chief wired: "Make necessary arrangement with Conners."[492] Conners, incidentally, planned to abscond with several wagon loads of munitions while transferring the shipment to the docks, as further compensation for his invaluable services. As matters developed, Segura put everything on hold until conditions on Mexico's Gulf coast were satisfactory.[493]

Another player in all this intrigue was none other than the notorious mercenary Sam Dreben, who registered at the St. Charles Hotel using the alias of "Lakowski." Dreben had penetrated another prospective expedition, one involving a group that wanted to separate Yucatán from the rest of Mexico. His plan was to miss the boat if and when the expedition departed, notify the Mexican authorities, and have the filibusters arrested as soon as they touched Mexican soil.[494] Dreben had ostensibly been working as a machine gunner for the *orozquistas*, but since Orozco's rebellion was collapsing, the mercenary had no intention of going down with the ship. He therefore publicly had switched allegiances and appeared now as an agent of the Madero government.

For lack of ammunition, especially artillery ammunition, Orozco was steadily driven back into Chihuahua by a Federal field force under General Victoriano Huerta.[495] Defeated, Orozco evacuated Juárez, which Huerta occupied on August 21. The crucial battle that Orozco had lost was the battle of El Paso.

Orozco's last stand was at Ojinaga, across from Presidio, Texas. Madero's forces captured the town on September 15, and the *orozquistas* fled across the river to Presidio and scattered. Orozco remained at large, sheltered by sympathizers in the Big Bend. His father, Colonel Pascual

Orozco, Sr., was not so fortunate. The army apprehended him, turned him over to the US marshal, who had him conveyed to El Paso, where in April he had been indicted for conspiracy to export munitions.[496] On October 18, Orozco Sr. and two associates were tried, found "not guilty," and released. Agent in Charge Thompson was outraged: "In this case the Government made up a strong case, the jury had no doubt been reached, at least this is the opinion of the United States Attorney, Judge, and ourselves. It was found that the jury had been in communication with noted revolutionists, in spite of every effort made by ourselves to prevent this thing being done. The sentiment here has been very much against us on account of the Senate investigation committee (a subcommittee charged with investigating American involvement in the revolution) who have been using their efforts to discredit our witnesses no doubt for the purpose of bringing about intervention."[497]

Orozco Sr. was immediately rearrested on a Mexican extradition warrant; the old forty-day incarceration ploy. He was returned to the county jail. Orozco shared a cell with other revolutionary figures, and the Bureau was most interested in learning what they were up to. Therefore, technology was employed. An agent concealed a dictograph wire from Orozco's cell to the jailer's quarters. The dictograph worked well, but since the cell was unlighted, Orozco and his companions retired early. Nothing of value was overheard. Orozco Sr. was released when the Madero government failed to substantiate its charges against him.[498] He, of course, resumed plotting.

Agent in Charge Thompson arranged with Mexican Federal army officers for them to expel as undesirables across the international bridges and into the arms of the waiting BI those for whom it had warrants outstanding. With the Orozco rebellion rapidly disintegrating, Agent in Charge Thompson advised that: "We'll have only our regular force of agents, as the Mexican government is taking out of service all their men and reducing expenses, so that in the future we will have to rely upon our own resources to secure information to cover this movement. This will make it extremely difficult for the reason that heretofore we have been able to call upon them at any time for a Mexican whom we could place at a designated point to furnish information for us and this has helped up materially in preventing the exportation at El Paso."[499]

Agent Ross had been quite effective against the *orozquistas*. He earned high praise from Agent in Charge Thompson, who planned to send him to assist the BI agent investigating neutrality violations in Douglas, Arizona: "My purpose in sending Ross there is the fact that he is familiar with the Spanish language and is known to most of the Mexican informants along the border and [is] in their confidence and can secure more information for us than nearly any other Agent now available for this work."[500]

Unfortunately, Ross did not confine his efforts solely to Bureau work. Evidence mounted that Ross and Abraham Molina were selling some of the munitions seized. The El Paso field office overflowed at times with confiscated rifles and some 30,000 rounds of ammunition. Some of this mysteriously disappeared.[501] Ross claimed that some malefactor had broken in and stolen the items, although there was no indication of forced entry. What sank Ross was his selling 100 rifles that he discovered in the course of his investigations. There were canceled checks from both Krakauer, Zork and Moye, as well as Shelton Payne paid to Ross for rifles. His only defense was that he considered the rifles abandoned property. Disgruntled Agent Curley D. Hebert was instrumental in gathering evidence of Ross's nefarious activities. And as the Chief put it, Ross "was himself committing offenses similar to or worse than those which he was charging and assisting in the prosecution of others for." The Bureau suspended Ross; then the Attorney General had him fired in September.[502]

Ross promptly went to work as an agent for Consul Llorente, who no doubt appreciated Ross's neutrality expertise.[503] He then became an operative of the Western Detective Agency managed by his former informant, Virgil L. Snyder. Snyder did not confine himself to investigations. He, Ross, C. P. Pitman, and R. F. Atkinson planned a daring robbery of a high-stakes poker game in the McCoy Hotel. On the night of January 13, 1913, Ross and Atkinson donned masks and relieved the high rollers of $4,300 in cash and diamonds. Atkinson, however, lost his nerve and had informed the police, who instructed him to proceed with the robbery. The police were waiting for Ross as he left the hotel with the plunder. The best his attorney could argue was that Ross was conducting an undercover investigation, and that the cash and jewels in his possession when he was arrested had been placed there by enemies while he slept. Although this was a ludicrous defense, the trial ended in a hung jury. Snyder and Pitman were indicted, but they were not convicted.[504] Interestingly, memories may have faded, or the vetting process had not improved, for Snyder became a BI agent on September 10, 1918.

The Bureau struggled under the handicap imposed by Judge Maxey's ruling that merely transporting munitions between two locations in the United States did not constitute smuggling. Having only to prosecute neutrality law violators that had been caught *in flagranti* affected some twenty-five pending federal cases in El Paso. All prisoners charged with neutrality violations were arraigned and released on their own recognizance on October 7, except those charged with conspiracy to violate these laws whose cases were already set for trial. The government appealed Maxey's ruling to the Supreme Court but, pending the outcome, the Bureau was crippled. Agents and other US officials on the border were instructed merely to seize munitions but not to arrest anyone attempting to smuggle them. Once again, the Bureau had to accommodate itself to drastic change.

While zealously combatting *orozquista* violations of the law, the Bureau had proceeded "with all deliberate speed" in gathering evidence of violations by *maderistas*.[505] Since the US recognized Madero as president of Mexico, the Bureau moved slowly against the flagrant *maderista* violations of the law. Not until it was obvious that Orozco was losing, did the US government take action.

Sommerfeld and Llorente openly violated the neutrality laws by recruiting, a practice that had the approval of President Madero himself.[506] Volunteers presented themselves at the Mexican consulate, and Llorente arranged to get them across the border. Llorente also hired mercenaries to cripple Orozco by blowing up railroad bridges between Ciudad Juárez and the city of Chihuahua. These commando operations failed; the mercenaries would spend a week or so in the Chihuahuan desert, then return with harrowing tales of encounters with *orozquistas* which had prevented them from carrying out their mission.

Agent Ross reported in June that Llorente had sent a four-man team of saboteurs into Mexico. Bielaski wired: "Take no action except secure full information and forward there. Be careful to give all evidence on which statements based."[507] Attorney General Wickersham wrote to the Secretary of State that the US attorney's report indicated that whatever recruiting and enlisting had occurred was under the direction of Llorente. Wickersham advised the DOJ representatives on the border to take no action until further instructions but to gather and report fully the facts.[508] Wickersham later wrote to the Secretary that Agent C. D. Hebert had reported that General Giuseppe Garibaldi was recruiting in Arizona with help from Llorente. Wickersham stated, "I am somewhat in doubt as to what steps to take, in view of the fact that the action seemed to be at the instance and for the benefit of the established Government of Mexico," adding that "the Department is bringing to the Mexican Government's attention the apparently improper undertaking and the connection therewith of Consul Llorente, with the object of inducing the Mexican Government to desist, and to have its agents desist."[509] The State Department in July requested the Madero government to stop Consul Llorente's recruiting activities forthwith. The Madero administration replied that Mexico had been scrupulously observing the neutrality laws. The *orozquistas* were now of course eager to assist the Bureau in gathering evidence of *maderista* neutrality violations.

Sabotage matters came to a head when the Bureau had Emile Charpentier, one of the mercenaries whom Llorente had hired to blow up bridges, arrested for neutrality violations. He proved unable to post a $1,500 bond, and Llorente refused to post it for him. A furious Charpentier took his story to the press, accusing Llorente of contracting with Charpentier and other mercenaries and then refusing to pay them. Secretary of State Philander Knox ordered a special investigation of Llorente, and the Bureau took affidavits from men whom Llorente's minions had enlisted, as well from a man who was offered a bribe to commit perjury. The government charged the saboteurs—Emile Charpentier, R. H. G. McDonald, J. H. "Jack" Noonan alias A. Monahan, and D. J. Mahoney—with conspiracy to violate the neutrality laws.[510] The jury acquitted them.

The government hesitated to charge Llorente with the same offense. A warrant for his arrest would not be issued until February 5, 1913. Interestingly, the US Attorney ordered that it not be served pending further investigation. However, the US Commissioner in El Paso, angry at being overruled, appointed a special officer to serve the warrant. Llorente, though, had learned of the warrant and fled to Ciudad Juárez. Not until the April 1914 term of court did the government bring the Llorente case to trial, and present the mercenaries as key witnesses against him. But presiding judge Waller T. Burns, of *reyista* trial fame, ruled that Llorente had been indicted under the wrong section of the Federal Penal Code—enlisting men for foreign service instead of for organizing an armed expedition. The case was dismissed on April 14, 1916.[511]

Agent in Charge Thompson at San Antonio had focused on ferreting out arms caches in that city. He wrote in May: "Munitions are stored in many places here; some because of close watch haven't been able to move it. These places are being covered by Mexican informants employed by the Mexican Government, but their information is very unsatisfactory, and especially so now when there is so much disorganization among their officers." He needed his own informants.[512]

The Bureau's budget for informants was woefully inadequate, but some intelligence came from the assistant police chief, Andrés [Santos] Coy, who had been an informant dating back to the BI's pre-1910 campaign against the *magonistas*.

And private detective John Mahan offered to assist the Bureau at San Antonio, saying he was no longer working for the Mexican government because Consul General Esteva had dismissed all of his agents in San Antonio and El Paso, claiming the reason was that the Mexican government was short of funds. Agent Lancaster took Mahan on as an informant.[513]

But the Bureau suffered a considerable blow on August 19, 1912, when Lancaster resigned because he had been appointed chief of police in San Antonio.[514] Fred Lancaster provided a new tone to the police department. A rigid law enforcement officer, Lancaster looked the part. A photo shows him with dark, closely cropped hair and mustache in formal police uniform and cap, looking confidently into the camera.[515] Through his tenure as police chief from 1912 to 1918, Lancaster provided intelligence to his former Bureau colleagues, but it was hardly the same as his being one of the few experienced agents knowledgeable about the border.

Figure 30 Fred Hill Lancaster, El Paso Herald, September 13, 1912.

Thompson's woes continued. He wired the Chief in October: "Every effort possible being made here by persons under indictment and others in sympathy with the rebel cause to discredit all government officers connected to neutrality investigations. They are having these persons taken before Senate Committee and examined evidently for this purpose also for the purpose of showing use of Mexican informants in connection therewith. Information just obtained by me is that rebels are recruiting men at Marathon. No agent available [to] assign to this investigation. With present force this division impossible to keep up with movements unless furnished additional men. Heretofore have been compelled use these Mexican informants account having no men our own. Advise action desire taken."[516]

To Thompson's relief, the Chief not only authorized the use of several informants, of course keeping expenses as low as possible, but he also dispatched two more agents to San Antonio. But they were rookies—H. A. Palmer and Eli Murray Blanford. The latter was born in Bewleyville, Kentucky, on July 24, 1883, and graduated in 1912 from Georgetown University with a law degree.[517] Palmer and Blanford took the oath of office and received their equipment in Washington, DC, then took the train to San Antonio. Furthermore, the attorney general himself authorized the hiring of a stenographer for that office at a salary not exceeding $70 per month. (He was actually hired for $75.)[518] These were most welcome developments. Blanford worked out of El Paso, dealing primarily with ammunition smugglers. He soon became the Agent in Charge there.

The Bureau was also investigating *orozquista* activity in New York City. From his headquarters at 916-920 Park Row Building, one of Division Superintendent William Offley's responsibilities was to monitor the traffic in munitions. Offley, on occasion, was unaccountably slow on the uptake. The Chief notified him that Agent Lancaster in San Antonio had learned of a deal for 1,000 rifles and 270,000 rounds reportedly involving Manuel Garza Aldape and F. A. Chapa. The munitions were to come from New Brighton, Connecticut.[519] Offley assigned special Agent Scully to "learn the name of the arms company in New Brighton, proceed there, and cover any shipment." Charles Joseph Scully, a New Yorker of

Figure 31 *William Offley. Source: FBI.gov.*

Irish descent, who started with the BI in 1910, traveled to New Haven, Connecticut and interviewed the president of Winchester Arms Co. He said that no such order had been placed with Winchester. After further investigation on the ground, Scully reported that he "was unable to locate any arms company at New Brighton, Staten Island, or at New Britain, Conn. There is [sic] however factories of this nature at Norwich and Meridian, Conn."[520] Surely, Offley could have determined that there was no New Brighton in Connecticut by simply consulting a map!

Offley personally directed a major operation trying to locate *orozquistas* Braulio Hernández, Manuel Luján, Juan Prieto, and Rafael Campa, all of whom had reportedly been staying at the Waldorf-Astoria hotel. Offley assigned nine agents to the case.[521] Assisting them was special informant Harvey J. Phillips, who gathered intelligence on arms dealers in New York City.[522] Phillips and the agents repeatedly checked the hotels and apartment houses suspicious Mexicans were known to frequent. They located Luján, Prieto and Campa, and shadowed them, hoping they would communicate with Braulio Hernández.[523]

The Chief was particularly anxious to apprehend Hernández, who had been a fervent *maderista* in the struggle against Porfirio Díaz, then after Madero's triumph was secretary of state in Chihuahua under Governor Abraham González. Becoming disillusioned with Madero, Hernández in 1912 led a *vazquista* uprising in that state. He then joined Orozco's rebellion. Hernández was under indictment in El Paso for neutrality violations, and there was an arrest warrant for him out of San Antonio.[524] Madero's attorney Sherburne Hopkins and Phillips conferred with Superintendent Offley about Hernández but without result. The search for Hernández extended to Agent C. R. Ambrose in Washington, DC, whom the Chief assigned to locate the fugitive. Ambrose checked at the post office for correspondence addressed to Hernández and interviewed Sherburne Hopkins to secure his description: "About 30, medium height, dark complexion, gray eyes, clean shaven, pock marked face; talks very much and excitedly; well-educated and speaks English fluently."[525]

The BI's efforts finally paid off, for Hernández was apprehended in Washington. Agent Craft escorted him without incident to El Paso, where on April 24 he was turned over to the deputy US marshal to await trial. Hernández's bond was set at $1,000, which he was unable to post. It was anticipated that the *orozquistas* would bail him out. Braulio Hernández, Cástulo Herrera, Pascual Orozco, Sr., E. H. Dean, and Jesús de la Torre were indicted at the April 1912 term of the court in El Paso, charged with conspiracy to violate the President' proclamation. When they were tried in October, Braulio Hernández, Cástulo Herrera, and Pascual Orozco, Sr. were acquitted. A furious Agent in Charge Thompson declared that the prosecution had a strong case which was lost because of jury-tampering.[526]

Last, and certainly least, the Bureau investigated the *magonistas*, whom Agent James Ganor was monitoring from Los Angeles. Ganor was overwhelmed. The US attorney wrote to the attorney general that Ganor was the sole BI agent there, and, "It is a physical impossibility for Mr. Ganor to do one-third of the work assigned to him, and the result is not only that Mr. Ganor is taxed beyond his powers of endurance but in addition thereto many important matters of necessity are not attended to. In addition to the work assigned to Mr. Ganor by this office, he is constantly in receipt of telegrams and letters from various officers and departments of the Government, calling for immediate action on his part, many times involving trips to a considerable distance from the city of Los Angeles, with the result, oftentimes, that he is compelled to abandon some important matter engaging his attention...." The US attorney requested that an additional BI agent be assigned to Los Angeles. The attorney general cited the Bureau's limited appropriation in denying the request.[527]

Ganor informed the Chief that he was still working on the mass of *magonista* papers seized in June 1911. An assistant US attorney helped Ganor prepare the Flores Magón case for trial, scheduled for April 18.

Mexican consul Dr. Francisco Martínez Baca had provided an interpreter and translator to assist Ganor in this task. But increasingly, Ganor's efforts focused on reports of a new campaign by *magonistas* and IWW militants to invade Baja California. Weakening the Madero government's ability to counter this movement was the growing unpopularity of Consul Martínez Baca. A committee of twenty Mexicans called on the consul demanding that he resign; the meeting became so raucous that the police had to be called. Furthermore, several thousand Mexicans signed a petition demanding Martínez Baca's resignation. Together with a *maderista* secret agent sent from Mexico City, Ganor visited several places in "Sonora Town," as the Mexican settlement in Los Angeles was called, and observed fiery speeches against the consul. The upshot was that anti-Madero feeling was growing. However, reports that the IWW had invaded Baja California were false. This was fortunate, for Ganor visited Tijuana as a guest of the Mexican consul and learned that the garrison there numbered a mere 255 men. Ganor was still trying to locate witnesses in the Flores Magón case and learned that many were now in jail in Mexico, prisoners of the Madero government.[528]

Ganor's relations with Madero's officials were cordial. Teodoro Frezieres (the secret agent who accompanied Ganor in visiting the Mexican settlement in Los Angles) whom Ganor referred to as the "Chief secret agent for the Mexican Government," had called at the Bureau office and said he had been sent to Los Angeles by the Mexican government to assist in matters pertaining to the present troubles in Baja California. "He also brought with him two men to assist. Agent informed Mr. Frezieres he needed no assistants at the present time but would assist them at any time as they have no knowledge of the neutrality laws, nor do they speak English."[529] Ganor needed competent informants, and he requested authorization to hire two. The Chief replied that if it were absolutely necessary, Ganor could hire the Anglo informant he asked for at $2.50 per day not exceeding ten days.[530]

Frezieres also informed Ganor that the two Mexican agents were tasked with surveilling Mexican citizens suspected of furnishing money for Orozco. Suspects were Alberto Terrazas and his father, General Luis Terrazas, the former Chihuahua oligarch, who were living in Long Beach. One J. Mancelas, a member of the *orozquista* junta in Los Angeles, had attended the meetings of the Terrazas and other wealthy exiles. Ganor mentioned that Mancelas was a Bureau informant and "a very important government witness." According to Mancelas, the exiles hoped to foment revolution in Baja California to weaken the Madero forces for Orozco's benefit.[531] Unfortunately for the exiles, Orozco was already losing.

When the trial of Ricardo and Enrique Flores Magón, Librado Rivera, and Anselmo Figueroa finally got underway in June there was no lack of drama. Several hundred Mexicans, "wobblies" (IWW members), and anarchists displaying red badges thronged the halls of the courthouse. A number of government witnesses were threatened, and Ganor found it necessary to call on the US marshal for assistance. The marshal deployed a force of officers in the courthouse to protect the witnesses and keep order. Fifty policemen guarded the courthouse and searched Mexicans and anarchists. The marshal, a deputy marshal, and five plainclothes officers patrolled the corridors, for a bailiff had told Ganor that several jurors feared violence from protestors in the corridors. Ganor testified at the trial and identified all the letters and documents he had seized in the raid on PLM headquarters; these were introduced as evidence. Ganor was asked to assist in transporting the defendants from the county jail to and from the federal building. On June 25, the defendants were each found guilty on four counts and were sentenced to twenty-three months at the McNeil Island federal penitentiary.

After sentence was passed, the turbulent crowd swarmed into the street, and about 500 protestors arrived at the jail a few minutes after the defendants were delivered inside. A Mexican struck a policeman, and a free-for-all ensued. The police used their clubs and called headquarters for reinforcements. When the police finally reestablished order, they had arrested eighteen of the rioters. Since he knew many Mexicans and was an eyewitness to the affray, the US attorney asked Ganor to assist as much as possible in these cases. And since the *magonistas* and wobblies openly declared their intention to continue with revolutionary work, Ganor hoped to keep in touch with the leaders of the new junta.[532]

A month later, partisans of Vázquez Gómez and Orozco made impassioned speeches in "Sonora Town," to some 400 Mexicans, wobblies, and anarchists. The crowd attacked two policemen with clubs and stones, knocking them down and attempting to trample them. The policemen opened fire to save their lives. A riot call went out to the central police station, and scores of officers rushed to the scene. Six rioters were critically wounded, and one, Leonídes Gutiérrez, was killed. What made the dead rioter noteworthy was that Gutiérrez had gained police attention in Los Angeles and at El Paso in 1909 as being one of the group of Mexican anarchists which was organized to kill Presidents Taft and Porfirio Díaz when they met on neutral territory at El Paso. Recently, he had been identified with IWW speakers at the Mexican settlement in Los Angeles.[533]

Ganor continued to attend meetings of Orozco and Flores Magón supporters, at which money was collected for the cause. "Agent has from time to time informed Mexican Consul and Secret Agents of Mexican Government who the parties are that are most active in this movement and that it would be well for them to keep in touch with their movements. They seem to rely entirely upon Department of Justice and make very little effort if any to assist."[534]

Agent Ganor was anxious to conclude some unfinished business: "Received information that Antonio de P. Araujo, a fugitive from justice, who has been hiding in Canada since June 1911, under indictment for violating the neutrality laws along with Magón et al. came to this city and is in hiding. It is not advisable for Agent to go to certain places to look for him as I am too well known among the Mexicans and his associates, and especially by him. In May 1911, I had him placed under arrest at Calexico, California. I was placed in jail with Araujo and he made a confession to me. US Attorney informed me the evidence secured was not sufficient to hold him. A few days later other matters came up when I arrested Magon and raided the Junta and secured evidence that caused their conviction. Araujo was secretary of this organization and the only one to get away. He has been writing very dangerous articles in the Mexican papers and inciting the Mexican people toward the revolution. Spent the day in various places trying to locate him. Notified Mexican consul and he agreed to assist in locating Araujo. I telegraphed Chief: 'Am reliably informed Antonio de P. Araujo, fugitive from justice connected with Magon et al. who were sentenced to McNeil violation neutrality laws is hiding in this city. Indictment has been found against him and if apprehended will be able to convict. Be necessary to use an informant to assist agent few days rate three dollars per day in apprehending his whereabouts.' Advise." Chief telegraphed back: "Authorized employ informant as requested."[535] A disappointed Ganor soon reported that he had used an informant to try to locate Araujo but, "This city has a population of 40,000 Mexicans in [the] Mexican settlements, and most of them are in sympathy with the rebel cause, which makes it very hard to locate Araujo."[536]

Ganor had his own complaints about Mexican government agents. Agent Ross in El Paso had wired that Orozco quartermaster Cástulo Herrera, who had jumped a $2,000 bond, and Manuel Mascarenas were wanted in El Paso, and if they were in Los Angeles to have them arrested and notify him. A Mexican government secret agent had called at Ganor's home at 2 a.m. and told him he had located Herrera in Venice, California. Ganor immediately dressed and searched by automobile for Herrera until 6 a.m. He resumed the search later that day into the afternoon, to no avail. After making inquiries, he leaned that the information was only hearsay, and although the Mexican agent claimed to know Herrera by sight, he did not. Ganor informed the Mexican consul that "I was at his service at any and all times to assist in matters of violation of neutrality laws, but I was very much disgusted with the way his officers handle a case, giving out information to newspapers and making false reports which make it necessary for this Department to run down without results."[537] To Ganor's presumed subsequent rage, a week later Mexican secret agents phoned him at 1 a.m. and claimed they were certain they had located Cástulo Herrera this time. Ganor searched in Boyle Heights until 7 a.m. The party located turned out not to be Herrera. And Ganor was still searching for Araujo, who "dresses well for a Mexican."[538]

The Mexican consul advised Ganor that he had had Manuel Mascarenas arrested. Ganor asked the police to hold Mascarenas until papers arrived from El Paso. The US attorney's office in Los Angeles contacted their colleagues in El Paso, who wired that "Manuel Mascarenas was not indicted by grand jury. Turn him loose." Mascarenas was released on habeas corpus proceedings.[539]

Agent Ganor reported that some time ago he had called Consul Baz and his secretary into the office and informed them confidentially that small boats which did not need to clear with the Customs Service were carrying arms and ammunition into Mexican waters. Baz said he had at his disposal two American secret agents at El Paso working under the direction of Felix Sommerfeld, and he sent for them. Ganor briefed the agents on the situation and assured the consul that he and his informant would cooperate in every way. The consul and his agents did likewise.

But, Ganor wired, "At no time from that day have they ever come to this office to receive information or to give same. I called them up by phone from time to time when they promised to assist, and instead of assisting, I am reliably informed, and have reasons to believe, and almost know positively they have been working with parties connected with the revolution instead of assisting their own government. Consul even went so far as to report to his government that the facts I gave him were nothing less than a story. It can be proven by me and by others that guns and ammunition have been shipped into Mexico, and it seems to me that with the knowledge they have had, they have given certain information to newspapers and to others who are operating with the Orozco faction. Mr. Baz has been told by me from time to time certain important facts relating to the good of his government and he has at no time paid any heed to same. I have reason to believe that at the present time more guns and ammunition are being shipped out of Los Angeles, California than at any time during the recent trouble in Lower California, Mexico, when the [Flores] Magons were arrested and convicted for violation of the neutrality laws. I know and have met all parties connected with the shipment of ammunition by water to Mexico. The Consul and secret agents have been given their names, boat, etc., and at no time have assisted. I have reasons to believe that when this information was given to them, they transferred the information to others connected with the Orozco revolution and have received a fair compensation for same."[540] Ganor "notified [the] Mexican consul in El Paso of conditions in his department. He is sending an official here who will arrive tomorrow."[541]

This was further evidence that throughout the revolution many persons reported to more than one master.

Chapter 8: Chasing Schooners

President Francisco Madero could take considerable satisfaction as the year 1913 opened—Generals Bernardo Reyes and Félix Díaz had led unsuccessful rebellions and were now safely confined in separate prisons in Mexico City. Díaz had launched his rebellion in October 1912, as Emilio Vázquez Gómez continued to plot but posed no real military threat. Crucially, in the strategic city of Veracruz, the principal port in Mexico, he seized control of the city, then waited for the rest of the county to rise in rebellion. Nothing happened, and a disconsolate Díaz was captured and whisked off to prison in Mexico City.[542] General Pascual Orozco's rebellion likewise had failed, and Orozco was a fugitive. True, General Emiliano Zapata was still leading an agrarian uprising, but it was landlocked, and largely confined to the state of Morelos. In the aftermath of a free and democratic election in the fall of 1911, the United States had recognized Madero as the legitimate president of Mexico.

Yet, even as Madero seemed to be consolidating his regime, he was being undermined. For one thing, Madero's popularity was declining because he proved unable to solve the nation's problems in short order; disenchantment set in. For another, some generals in the Federal army were still smarting from the humiliation of having been defeated by what they perceived as the armed rabble that had elevated Madero to power in 1911. Thirdly, Madero naïvely had permitted Reyes and Félix Díaz to receive a stream of visitors in prison. The result was plotting by disaffected officers, *reyistas*, and *felicistas*. They concluded that the reason Reyes, Orozco, and Félix Díaz had failed to topple Madero was because their rebellions had originated away from Mexico City, giving Madero time to react. Therefore, the way to get rid of him was by orchestrating a carefully planned coup d'état in the capital.

One of the most perceptive observers of the coup and the resulting bloodshed, known as the *Decena Trágica* for the ten days during which downtown Mexico City was devastated, was the urbane Harry Berliner. The son of a tailor, Berliner was born in New York City on November 17, 1872. He served during the Spanish-American War in Cuba as a sergeant in the 202nd New York Volunteer Infantry, being discharged in 1899 at Savannah, Georgia. He arrived January 1902 in Mexico City from San Francisco, as a mining engineer, a partner in the firm of Berliner & Lapum, and more recently as the general manager for W. A. Parker, "a typewriter magnate," representing the Oliver Typewriter Company in Mexico.[543] Blessed with an engaging personality, Berliner developed a wide circle of influential friends and acquaintances, both foreigners and Mexicans, among them General Felix Díaz. Despite Berliner's jovial personality, he habitually carried a sidearm, an understandable precaution in the chaos of 1913. He used it on at least one occasion. "I yanked out Betsey [his revolver] and turned round [sic] and saw a big snot nosed kid laughing [the kid had thrown a rock at his head]. I fired one shot right over his head, believe me it was no time, and there was no kid in sight."[544]

Figure 32 *Harry Berliner in Mexico City, ca. 1913. Courtesy of Kristin Rounds.*

General Manuel Mondragón, who had the considerable advantage of not being in prison, was a prime mover in the coup, which involved suborning units of the army. Partisans of Félix Díaz and

Bernardo Reyes liberated them on February 9, 1913, and a rebel column marched on the national palace to storm it and seize Madero.⁵⁴⁵ A mounted General Bernardo Reyes rode triumphantly at the head of the column. Loyalist troops laid down a barrage of machine gun fire. Reyes had the distinction of being the first man killed in the attack. He literally was riddled. As Harry Berliner memorably described it, "Down went General Reyes, punctured so full of holes that they had to run baby ribbons through him to hold him together in order to lay him out and make him look natural."⁵⁴⁶ Since Reyes was dead, the case against him was dismissed at the 1914 spring term of the federal court in Brownsville.⁵⁴⁷

Although the rebels were repulsed, the loyalist general defending the palace was wounded. His replacement was General Victoriano Huerta, who hated Madero. A panicked Félix Díaz took refuge in the Ciudadela, an arsenal downtown. The coup had failed, but for the next ten days the business district of Mexico City was devastated by intense fighting, including artillery barrages, between rebels and loyalist troops. Huerta had the means to crush the rebels but instead joined with Félix Díaz to create the impression that Madero had totally lost control. US Ambassador Henry Lane Wilson used Harry Berliner to carry messages to and from Huerta and Félix Díaz. This raises the question why use Berliner, ostensibly a civilian not attached to the embassy, when a number of male staffers were available at the embassy.⁵⁴⁸ Berliner also commandeered automobiles and reportedly conveyed many families to safety, a feat which the American Embassy on March 4, 1913, acknowledged by presenting him a gold watch inscribed "for valor, fidelity, and prudence."⁵⁴⁹ In what was not the finest hour in American diplomacy, Ambassador Wilson, who despised Madero, invited the two generals to confer in the embassy, in effect reaching a division of the spoils: Huerta to be provisional president and Félix Díaz to appoint the cabinet.

Madero and the vice president, José María Pino Suárez, were held under guard in the national palace and were forced to resign.⁵⁵⁰ Huerta wired President Taft on February 18: "I have the honor to inform you that

I have overthrown this Government; the forces are with me and from now on peace and prosperity will reign. Your obedient servant, Victoriano Huerta, Commander in Chief."[551] There ensued a farce to comply, technically, with the Constitution; with the president and vice president having resigned, foreign minister Pedro Lascuráin became acting president. His sole cabinet appointment was General Huerta. After being in office for an hour, Lascuráin resigned, and Huerta became the provisional president.[552]

On the night of February 22, as Madero and Pino Suárez were being transferred to the prison of the Federal District, their military escort under Major Francisco Cárdenas shot them. (Cárdenas later claimed he received orders from Generals Huerta and Aureliano Blanquet to do so.)[553] The official version, which few believed, was that their supporters had tried to rescue them, and in the ensuing fire fight they unfortunately had been killed.[554] Huerta would soon thereafter neatly dispose of his coconspirator Félix Díaz by sending him off as special ambassador to Japan. The wily Huerta was the new strongman of Mexico.

A distraction was tiresome Emilio Vázquez Gómez, who was still trying to be relevant. He travelled through El Paso and installed himself at the hamlet of Palomas, Chihuahua, on the New Mexico border. Agent in Charge Thompson contemptuously called him "a physical and moral coward." Vázquez Gómez issued a manifesto at Palomas on February 15, 1913, proclaiming himself provisional president and urging other revolutionary factions to unite under his leadership. None did. He left Palomas on March 31, refused to give the press an interview in El Paso, and returned to San Antonio to sulk.[555]

Much of the Mexican (and American) public was repulsed by the overthrow and killing of Madero, who was now a martyr. Huerta was denounced as "The Usurper." Like Ambassador Wilson, however, Consul Luther Ellsworth believed Huerta to be the rightful president of Mexico.[556] The United States withheld diplomatic recognition of the Huerta regime, calling it merely the "de facto government." The United States did permit arms shipments to Huerta under license. Madero's supporters, virtually overnight, found themselves in the political wilderness, and many fled to the United States.

Huerta enjoyed the support of conservative elements, the Church, and the Federal army. Among his subordinate generals was Pascual Orozco, whom Huerta had defeated in 1912. Orozco's most recent biographer states that: "As for whether Orozco was a principled military hero and political reformer or was instead a sellout to the oligarchy, a politically ambitious traitor to the revolution and an eager ally of a brutal assassin and dictator, the record reflects that, at various times, Pascual Orozco was all of those things."557 Pascual Orozco, Sr., also strongly supported Huerta. The dictator dispatched Orozco Sr. to interview Zapata and persuade him to acknowledge Huerta. Zapata had the elder Orozco shot.

Huerta's enemies began organizing as the erstwhile avengers of Madero and of the constitutional government. In Sonora, state troops under leaders such as Álvaro Obregón (a future president of Mexico) began fighting against Huerta forces. In Chihuahua, small guerrilla bands likewise took the field against Huerta. But the individual who seized the opportunity was Venustiano Carranza, a professional politician who had been a senator under Porfirio Díaz, had supported Madero in 1911, and who was currently *maderista* governor of Coahuila. After initially announcing his support for Huerta, Carranza immediately reversed course and placed himself at the head of the nascent opposition.558 He issued the obligatory revolutionary manifesto,

Figure 33 *Venustiano Carranza, 1888.* Courtesy Library of Congress Prints and Photographs Division.

the *Plan de Guadalupe*, on March 26, 1913. Carranza shrewdly avoided the mistake that Madero had made in 1910 by declaring himself provisional president, thus being at least theoretically bound by the Constitution. Instead, Carranza proclaimed himself the "First Chief" of the Constitutionalist Army (which barely existed and whose very name was good public relations.) The powers of the "First Chief" were whatever Carranza wanted them to be.

Huerta demanded that governors and other officials immediately recognize his regime. Reaction among northern governors varied. The governor of Sonora, José María Maytorena, urged his fellow citizens to fight the Usurper, then departed to the safety of Tucson. He did, however, retain his official title as governor of Sonora until July 1915. The staunchly *maderista* governor of Chihuahua, Abraham González, defied Huerta, was arrested and executed by the military.

As with previous revolutionary factions, the Constitutionalists, or *carrancistas*, were largely dependent on whatever munitions and supplies they could obtain in the United States. What differentiated them from other revolutionary factions was their organization. They quickly established a junta in practically every town and city near or directly on the American border. An office was maintained in the cities and larger towns, headed by the Constitutionalist "consul," or commercial agent.[559]

Whereas up to now the revolution had been centered mainly in Chihuahua, the Constitutionalist movement spanned the entire northern tier of states, and the traffic in munitions took a monumental leap. This would be a major test of the Bureau's ability to enforce the neutrality laws. But the

Figure 34 Keystone View Company, Lining up new recruits for the Revolution, 1914. Courtesy Library of Congress Prints and Photographs Division.

Bureau's figurative hands were tied. As conditions along the border had again become threatening in January, Judge Maxey's ruling made it extremely difficult to enforce neutrality. Since it would be some time before the Supreme Court addressed the government's appeal, all Bureau agents and other US officers on the border were instructed to seize munitions and other articles of war, but not to arrest the party taking them over. US Commissioners along the border hesitated to issue warrants to apprehend those persons. The Chief notified agents in March, however, that the Department's instructions regarding suspension of service process in neutrality cases was revoked, and informed them that all such process should be executed on any persons found within their districts.[560]

Huerta's partisans quickly seized most of the border towns, but the Constitutionalists lost no time in organizing to regain control of the border.

Figure 35 Sonora, Yaqui Indians, enlisted in the Mexican Army, being transported by box cars. Courtesy Library of Congress Prints and Photographs Division.

The Matamoros garrison, for example, mutinied on February 17, 1913 and seized the town in the name of Félix Díaz, quickly shifting their allegiance to Huerta.[561] The Constitutionalists made no attempt to recapture Matamoros for more than three months, confining their campaign to the interior of the states of Tamaulipas and Nuevo León. Special Agent Robert L. Barnes could report on April 5 that there was nothing much to report. About all that was going on was the distribution of circulars announcing that the Huerta government wanted men for the army. Potential enlistees would receive $1.50 per day and some compensation for their expenses in Mexico where they would be regularly enlisted, thus not violating the neutrality laws.[562] As prevailed throughout the Mexican Revolution, raw recruits received a rifle, some ammunition, and were thrown into battle. *Carrancistas* and *huertistas* competed in recruiting cannon fodder.[563]

Both the Huerta government and the Constitutionalists maintained consuls in Brownsville. The Constitutionalists soon organized a smuggling network. Special Agent Barnes went to Matamoros in April to obtain details about a seizure there of 15,000 30-30 rounds.[564] More importantly, Constitutionalists obtained the sinews of war by using fishing boats, which were not subject to customs inspections, slipping down the coast from Galveston to the small port of Velasco between Galveston and Corpus Christi.[565] The volume of armament increased substantially during the spring. A Bureau agent in New York City reported in May an alleged shipment of $200,000 of ordnance supplies on the steamship *Honduras* destined for Velasco.[566] A Huerta government agent (and Bureau informant), one Fredrick H. Keller, was dispatched from Eagle Pass to cover the unloading of the *Honduras*. He advised that the firm of Ullman, Stern and Krause was preparing to unload a 300,000-round shipment at Galveston for points on the border, especially Shelton-Payne in El Paso and Ullman's store in Brownsville. He was instructed to cover this movement until a Bureau agent could be assigned.[567]

There matters stood until June 3, 1913, when Constitutionalist General Lucio Blanco led 1,400 of his troops in a surprise attack against the 400-man garrison and seized Matamoros.[568] Attorney F. W. Shepard, representing the Mexican government, conferred with General James

Parker and secured permission for seventeen officers and ninety solders of the defeated garrison to come to the US side of the river to prevent their being slaughtered by the Constitutionalists. General Parker was reluctant to accept them because of the cost of feeding the group. Shepard then agreed that the Mexican government would pay. Customs official George J. Head received the contract, at 50 cents per head per day.[569]

As the Constitutionalists expanded their campaign down the Gulf coast of Mexico, the munitions floodgates opened. Shipments from New York were consigned to Constitutionalist Consul Juan T. Burns in Galveston. He, in turn, supervised a supply line by sea down the coast to Tampico using a Galveston firm, the Pearce Forwarding Company owned by W. C. Beers and O. A. Seagraves. Schooners were chartered and cleared for Havana but sailed directly for the vicinity of Tampico to deliver their cargoes.[570]

The most intriguing figure in all this was a certain Herbert Janvrin Browne. Born on October 3, 1861, in Fremont, New Hampshire, he spent most of his adult life in Washington, DC.[571] City directories listed him in 1887 as a clerk, in 1896 as a correspondent, and in 1898 as a correspondent for the *New York Journal*. Referring to the 1906 riot in Brownsville by black soldiers, a newspaper article in 1908 described Browne as "the detective upon whose report the president's recent message to congress on the Brownsville incident was based, conferred with the president today."[572] Between 1906 and 1910, Browne invested in mining ventures in Cuba. He still lived in Washington in 1913, and in 1914 operated for a time out of the Hotel Galvez in Galveston. He received the bills of lading for munitions from Consul Burns, chartered the schooners, and arranged for their loading.[573] He was ostensibly a Constitutionalist agent but insinuated that he had formerly been a Secret Service agent and was influential in Washington. The Collector of Customs in Galveston stated that Browne arrived bearing letters of recommendation from Secretary of State William Jennings Bryan, Acting Secretary of the Treasury C. S. Hamlin, and John Lind, a special representative in Mexico of President Wilson. Browne gave the impression that he was acting in a quasi-official capacity.

Reinforcing this impression was the fact that when the schooner captains were fined on their return to Galveston for having filed false clearances, claiming they had put into Tampico due to "stress of weather," Browne somehow got the fines remitted.[574] Significantly, as Secretary Hamlin telegraphed the Collector of Customs at Galveston on May 30, 1914: "In view of the fact that Browne's actions appear to have received official approval, it is doubtful if any case could be made against him for conspiracy to defraud the United States in connection with his securing the bills of lading for Havana, Cuba with the intention of proceeding to Tampico."[575]

There was, however, skullduggery at sea, as the Bureau subsequently learned.[576] The schooners *Emily P. Wright* and *Grampus* were both wrecked off Padre Island near the Mexican border under suspicious circumstances, touching off a fire storm of litigation over whether the wrecks were deliberate, how much of the cargo could have been salvaged, how much was actually salvaged, and its disposition. There were, for instance, allegations that the captain of the *Grampus* was paid $500 to beach his vessel.[577] Special Agent Barnes, for one, was convinced that the vessels had been deliberately wrecked so that their cargoes of munitions could be salvaged by O. A. Seagraves acting in collusion with Browne, "it being their idea that by so doing they would realize a greater financial profit than they would be putting through the deal as contracted and delivering the cargo to the Constitutionalist Government."[578]

But Browne allegedly was involved in yet an additional layer of intrigue, one that reflected the growing rift among Constitutionalist leaders. When in 1916 Agent George W. Lillard interviewed Charles A. Douglas, the Washington attorney for the *carrancistas*, about Browne, Lillard reported that Douglas told him confidentially that "Browne was at one time employed by the Carranza Government to look after the shipment of ammunition etc. for that faction; that during the time he was supposed to be acting in the capacity he was suspected for furnishing to the Villa faction munitions of war, but that they were never able to get any direct evidence of his duplicity; there, however, remains a question as to his honesty in his dealings with them. Douglas would not state that he believed Browne was mixed up in a conspiracy to get munitions to the Villa faction but led me to believe, by the manner in which he spoke, that the suspects it. He stated that there were three vessels sunk under very suspicious circumstances, which were carrying munitions to the Carranza faction, which caused a loss of about $125,000 to the carrancistas. Shortly thereafter, Douglas being unable to make the trip, he sent Mr. Leckie [on October 14, 1914] to make an investigation of the circumstances in the sinking of vessels. As a result of this investigation, Browne was discharged, and Douglas has not known much of him since."[579]

Attorney A. E. L. Leckie of the firm of Leckie, Cox, and Kratz, with offices in the Southern Building, Washington, DC, acted for Douglas, investigating the *Grampus* case, among others. Assisted by Seagraves, Leckie learned that the Pearce Forwarding Company had contracted to salvage the schooner's cargo: Pearce would receive 75% and the Carranza government 25%. Salvage operations recovered thousands of corroded cartridges which Pearce Forwarding polished up and sold on the open market to several buyers, including the National Arms Company of New Orleans. Some of these worthless cartridges were consigned to Constitutionalists in Sonora, who indignantly refused to accept them.[580] As of July 1915, Pearce Forwarding was salvaging the munitions from the *Emily P. Wright* under a contract with the *carrancistas*, who were to receive 25% of the salvaged ammunition as their share. But Juan T. Burns, the consul in Galveston, refused to accept the salvaged cartridges as being damaged and unfit.[581]

Chief Bielaski ordered in 1916 that Special Agent Barnes conduct a comprehensive investigation of the affair of the schooners. Barnes sent him a PERSONAL AND CONFIDENTIAL report. Attorney Leckie had learned that there was a discrepancy of 3,204 cases between the amount of ammunition shipped for distribution by Browne for the *carrancistas*, as shown by invoices furnished Leckie, and the amount of ammunition actually disposed of by Browne through shipment on the *Sunshine, Hatteras, Grampus, Emily P. Wright and Lillian B*, plus one rail shipment to El Paso. Leckie sent Chief Bielaski copies of the reports and exhibits he made to Charles A. Douglas regarding the *Grampus* and the *Emily P. Wright*. He recommended a DOJ investigation of the whole complex affair.[582] The investigation brought to light the foregoing account.

Special Agent Barnes also took measures to monitor the arms traffic through Brownsville. He managed to place informants in local hardware stores, but noted that it was next to impossible to secure satisfactory results in neutrality matters at Brownsville because of the friendly feeling between government officers, particularly the customs officers, and the *carrancistas*. The Deputy Collector of Customs, J. A. Maltby, appeared as a defense witness when a Constitutionalist arms smuggler was on trial. Some customs inspectors were reluctant to act against the Constitutionalists because they had been reprimanded by their superiors for doing so.[583] And the police chief in Brownsville, Ralph J. Tucker, had represented General Lucio Blanco in many of his confiscated cattle deals and was very friendly toward him.[584] Then there were the opportunists; besides being a customs official, George B. Head was the captain of a Texas National Guard company in Brownsville. He informed Special Agent Barnes that one of his men planned to sell the unit's rifles to a Constitutionalist agent that night. Barnes, a deputy US marshal, and a customs inspector kept watch, but nothing happened.[585] Captain Head himself would provide the Constitutionalists with considerable Texas National Guard property.[586]

Barnes wrote that some people in Brownsville seemed to have the idea that since the Huerta government had not been recognized, the neutrality laws were not applicable. He could not understand how some fairly intelligent people gave credence to such an erroneous opinion, unless it was because of the laxity with which the neutrality laws had been enforced there. Dr. Agustín Garza González, the *carrancista* consul, provided the money to purchase ammunition. Charles More, manager of the Brownsville Hardware Co., secured the ammunition for one Amado Stevens and assisted him in crossing it.[587] Barnes believed filing a criminal complaint against them would aid the Bureau in securing information because some persons were afraid to talk, not believing that the US was actually going to prosecute neutrality violations.[588]

Although Assistant US Attorney W. C. Staver was reluctant to prosecute those involved in the Amado Stevens smuggling conspiracy,[589] Agent in Charge Thompson instructed Barnes to file charges regardless of what Staver said.[590] Barnes had considerable evidence against Stevens, who had appeared in a locally produced film showing him and Macedonio García at General Blanco's headquarters. Stevens himself told Barnes that Blanco had offered him a captain's commission, which Stevens had rejected because he was a US citizen.[591]

Barnes filed complaints with the US commissioner against Charles More and Dr. Agustín Garza González, charging conspiracy to export munitions. Both defendants were bound over to the grand jury and bond was set at $2,000 each. Remarkably, R. B. Creager, the Collector of Customs, not only represented the defendants at the hearing but he and a Dr. Dougherty went bond for More, while Macedonio J. García and Charles More went bond for the consul.[592] According to Barnes, Collector Creager "told the commissioner I was without authority to file the complaints, to have become very angry and cussed things out in general, none of which appears to me to be quite in line with his official duties as Collector of Customs. It is rather an unfortunate state of affairs that exists here, in that politics appears to have been injected into Mexican revolutionary matters in this vicinity. People on one side will give information against a political enemy in order to 'get even' and at the same time fail to give information against one of their number. For this reason, the situation is rather delicate, and information is made even more difficult to secure by the fact that in the minds of most of the people, the

Huerta Government is in unusual disfavor."[593] Not surprisingly, Barnes vigorously protested Collector Creager's actions.[594]

Barnes later conferred with the consul, Dr. Garza González, and advised him that any information he could provide about ammunition smuggling by *huertistas* would be investigated and vigorously prosecuted if the evidence warranted. He took this action because of the President's announcement on July 21, 1913, that no more permits for the export of ammunition would be issued to the Huerta government, and to guard against giving the impression that the American government was taking sides in the controversy. "As stated in previous reports, the sentiment here is largely in favor the of the constitutionalists and if convictions are to be secured it is absolutely necessary that nothing be done to create the impression that one side or the other is being favored. I am guarding against this very carefully."[595]

Helpfully, Deputy US Marshal Eli Peoples told Barnes that in the future he would pay particular attention to ammunition smuggling, "as he had not heretofore given much attention to such matters."[596] By contrast, the army was much more helpful. Barnes reported that Captain Kirby Walker, commanding a cavalry unit at McAllen, detailed an officer and four men "to do secret work in cooperation with this office."[597]

Nowhere did the Bureau face more convoluted intrigues than in New Orleans. The arms traffic encompassed not just Mexico but Central America, and various factions and brokers were continually maneuvering to acquire the shipments arriving frequently by sea from New York City. To illustrate the situation, we will concentrate on two lots of munitions; first, those that the bullfighter Vicente Segura purchased from A. Baldwin & Co.

Returning from his leave of absence at Mobile, at informant Conners's suggestion, Agent Billups Harris registered at the Grunewald as "B. Hunt" and so wired to the Chief. Persons interested in launching the Segura expedition knew Harris was out of town on leave, and would probably know when he returned to the boarding house where he lived.

Harris called Conners, who came to his room and said the Segura expedition was about to start. Conners tried to arrange with Harris a reward as a government informant and made several propositions about taking part of the arms and ammunition, and dividing the proceeds with Harris. Conners said he would start the expedition, per his agreement with Segura, but only if Harris kept him out of future developments. Harris had already agreed to this as instructed by the Chief.

Conners did not know where Segura was, having received instructions indirectly to start the expedition. The broker said he had to make some money out of the deal to compensate him for his time and expenses—Segura had not sent him any money for a long time, either to cover the cost of getting out the expedition or to reimburse him for paying the crew of the *Dantzler*.

Conners so frightened two of those involved in the expedition—William Fitzpatrick and Edward J. Riley—that they agreed to meet in his office and tell Agent Harris what they knew of Segura's plans. Fitzpatrick had conducted Baldwin's arms department until January 1 and was now a hardware broker with an office in the Whitney Central Bank Building. He admitted selling the munitions the previous July to Segura, whom he said he first knew as J. Vincento [sic]. Fitzpatrick told Harris that Segura paid with drafts from Mexico City for approximately $118,000 and that he took Segura to the New Orleans National Bank, of which Albert Baldwin was president and Gus Baldwin, a member of A[lbert]. Baldwin & Co., was a director. Fitzpatrick said Baldwin's store manager, Waldo M. Pitkin, also knew of the transaction. The sale was strictly cash in advance, and it was the largest sale Baldwin had made; the profit was about $30,000. Fitzpatrick claimed Albert Baldwin knew the merchandise was for an expedition.[598]

Edward J. Riley, proprietor of an automobile repair shop, told Agent Harris that he had contracted to transport the munitions to a schooner for $20 per truckload per day. He had obtained large cardboard boxes to contain the munitions packed in small boxes. Riley said he would testify that when he learned the hauling was to be done secretly and the materiel was intended for a military expedition, he reneged on the contract. Agent Harris was skeptical.[599]

Harris's two watchmen reported on December 31 that Baldwin had loaded the merchandise into two boxcars, and had them sent to the New Basin Canal. Conners said he was going to remove a truckload (200 cases—200,000 rounds) of ammunition from the cars as his payment for what Segura owed him for handling the affair. Conners could not be dissuaded, and Harris said he could not stop him without attracting publicity. Later, Conners helped himself to another truckload of 200,000 rounds. He promised he would take no more. As Harris suspected, Riley was still working with Conners to haul what was left in the cars: some 1,300 Winchester carbines; more than 2,000,000 30-30 rounds; four Gatling guns; a mass of equipment and supplies, down to a duplicator for printing circulars; and, several colors of silk cloth for flags. Agent Harris instructed his watchmen to prevent any further attempt to remove the boxcars' contents, and he arranged for a revenue cutter to intercept the expedition.

Conners said he would assist in every way to make the case against Baldwin and Segura. Harris thought it advisable to seize the arms and ammunition in the boxcars and make a conspiracy case against Baldwin and Segura. The agent conferred with an assistant US attorney, omitting Conners's role because of his assistance: Conners told Harris he would tell the truth about Baldwin and Segura and induce Fitzpatrick to do likewise. The US attorney said Fitzpatrick agreed to testify that Baldwin knew what Segura planned to do with the arms and ammunition when he sold them to Segura, and Riley would testify about his contract with Baldwin. Also, Baldwin's manager, Waldo M. Pitkin, could testify as to Segura's written order to have the materiel moved into the two boxcars. But in order to proceed on conspiracy charges, it was necessary for Agent Harris to request instructions from headquarters.

Harris wired the Chief, adding that Segura was now said to be in Houston, Galveston, or San Antonio. Bielaski replied that if the US Attorney believed Harris had sufficient information on which to base a conspiracy charge, or the reasonable expectation of obtaining it after seizing the munitions, to take immediate action. Harris was to confer with the US attorney and inform the Chief as to what action would be taken. The US attorney said there was sufficient information for a conspiracy charge against Baldwin and Segura, and that he would present the charge to the grand jury. But he said there was no law under which the arms and ammunition could be seized. This dismayed Harris, who felt that the seizure was of the greatest importance. Despite the agent's best efforts, the US attorney refused to act. Harris appealed to Bielaski, but the Chief advised against seizure.

Conners had his employee, "Ed Hill" (whose real name was Hillary Nugent), direct the railroad to move the two boxcars to the United Warehouse, where the munitions would be stored in Hill's name pending developments. Agent Harris was unhappy with the US attorney's refusal to allow the seizure of the munitions in the United Warehouse because there existed the danger of the munitions, packed in small boxes, being shipped secretly from the large warehouse that covered a block and had numerous exits. This could occur even though the warehouse was being watched, to say nothing of the expense of watching the warehouse indefinitely.

Conners was now willing to testify that he knew Segura and also knew that Segura had a large shipment of arms and ammunition in Baldwin's warehouse; that Fitzpatrick had advised him that Segura's purchase was over $100,000; that he had introduced Riley to Segura before knowing that the merchandise was munitions; and that Segura told him he was going to ship the materiel to Mexico but that he could not ship it because of conditions in Mexico.[600] The "conditions in Mexico" were that General Félix Díaz's 1912 rebellion had fizzled out before Segura's munitions could reach him. Conners told Harris that he did not know where Segura was, but had received word that a friend of Segura's wanted Conners to ship by rail to the border the arms and ammunition from Baldwin's now in the United Warehouse.[601]

Worn down by all these byzantine intrigues, Agent Harris asked the Chief for permission to go to Washington and consult with him. The Chief agreed.[602] After the conference, Harris learned that the munitions were moved again, this time to the ramshackle warehouse of "Ed Hill" two blocks from the New Basin.[603]

Agents G. Raymond Matthews and J. P. Farmer replaced Agent Harris at New Orleans. Matthews attended the trial of Baldwin and Segura for neutrality violations. Segura had fled to Cuba, but testifying for the prosecution against A. Baldwin were Fitzpatrick, Riley, Pitkin, and Conners. The defense emphasized Albert Baldwin's standing as a prominent New Orleans businessman and bank president who was unaware that the munitions were destined for Mexico. Baldwin was acquitted.[604] Once again, the Bureau had developed a solid case only to have the jury return a verdict of "not guilty."

The munitions still at Meridian figuratively reared their ugly heads in April 1913. Numa Carrie, to whom they had originally been consigned, claimed ownership, disputing W. H. Hall of Hall's Transfer Co., where the munitions were stored. Carrie said he had worked for Luis Pérez who represented Delio Moreno Cantón back during the Reyes conspiracy in 1911. Since neither Pérez, Moreno Cantón, nor any of their associates had ever paid him for his services nor reimbursed him for the money he had expended looking after the merchandise, he was now negotiating with several *vazquistas* in New Orleans opposed to the new Huerta government to sell them these arms, as well as any future consignments they might want him to purchase.[605] Although Huerta was the new strongman of Mexico, Emilio Vázquez Gómez and his followers still operated under the illusion that Vázquez Gómez was a contender.

Further complicating an already convoluted situation, Hall wrote Agent Matthews that all he wanted was to be reimbursed for storing the munitions; Carrie had written to Hall that he had a buyer for the goods and would remove them shortly. The BI agent met with Carrie, who had decided that the *vazquistas* were losers and had aligned himself with the Huerta regime. In fact, the Huerta consul in New Orleans, Dr. Plutarco Ornelas, had hired Carrie at $4 per day plus expenses to maintain general surveillance over the Segura arms and ammunition, and the movements of several *vazquistas* recently arrived from Havana. Carrie believed Consul Ornelas was making a strenuous effort to obtain the arms and ammunition which Carrie had stored with Hall's Transfer Co., and Carrie planned to "work the 'Greaser' for everything in sight."[606] Numa Carrie's attorney attached the munitions stored in Hall's stable in Meridian to satisfy Carrie's claim for services rendered and money disbursed in safeguarding that consignment.

Yet another player entered the already crowded munitions stage—a Mexican calling himself Paul, or Pablo Northey, who purchased the Baldwin arms stored in Hillary Nugent's warehouse in New Orleans. Northey currently occupied room 676 of the St. Charles Hotel. The house detective accompanied Agent Matthews to look around Northey's room for anything that might reveal his real name, but Northey was in, and the idea was temporarily abandoned.[607] The St. Charles Hotel people checked out Northey with the local Hibernia Bank and Trust Co., and were told he was a man of considerable wealth and that his checks were good. Huerta consul Dr. Plutarco Ornelas said Pablo Northey was supposed to be a son "of one José Neight or Knight, a West Indian octoroon, who appeared in Mexico City about fifty years ago and acquired immense wealth by developing the gas plants in that and adjacent cities. Neight or Knight had two sons, one a dark swarthy fellow, the other a fair skinned, light or sandy-haired lad; it is the latter who Dr. Ornelas believed to have assumed the name of Pablo Northey, the friend and agent of Vicente Segura."[608] Northey, through his attorney, had the assessed value of the munitions reduced, and paid a tax of $13,518 with a check drawn on the Hibernia Bank.[609]

Agent Matthews encountered the same frustration that had plagued Agent Harris: keeping the players straight. When Matthews called at the office of William H. Byrnes, Northey's lawyer with offices in the Canal-Louisiana Bank Building, who should he find in Byrnes's private office but Maurice D. Conners, Paul Northey, and William Fitzpatrick, late of A. Baldwin & Co., huddled in conversation. Besides the Segura arms, Northey had delivered to the Importers' Warehouse another consignment of wire, shovels, axes, and so forth. The original markings on the packages had been removed. Northey and his friends claimed the goods were part of the Vicente Segura purchase made from Baldwin while Fitzpatrick was employed there.

Northey, whose family was in Mexico City, said he was a British subject and had purchased the goods on speculation and that newspapers with their comments on his movements would prevent his doing further business in Mexico. Later, in the lobby of the St. Charles, the agent saw Carrie inquire for Northey and go to Northey's room. Soon Edward J. Riley, intimate friend and associate of both William Fitzpatrick and Maurice D. Conners, did likewise. Riley, we recall, had contracted to transport Segura's munitions to the docks. Carrie said he was no longer working for the Huerta consul.[610]

The New Orleans field office had Northey and his acquisitions under surveillance, as well as the steamship *Sonora* owned by the Otis Manufacturing Co. of New Orleans, long suspected of handling shipments of arms and ammunition to Mexican ports.[611] Agent Farmer reported that Northey had taken out $60,000 of insurance on his munitions at the Importers' Warehouse, and that a dispute had arisen between Northey and attorney Pierre D. Olivier concerning the attorney's charge for legal services. Evidently, Northey, fearing that he might be indicted by a federal grand jury because of his manipulation of the Segura arms and ammunition, retained Olivier to defend him in the event of an indictment. Northey did so at the suggestion of William H. Byrnes, Jr., his legal adviser, who believed at the time that he would become an assistant US attorney and, therefore, could not defend Northey. Byrnes was now trying to adjust the matter of compensation between his friend, Olivier, and his client, Northey. Northey said he was corresponding with Remington Arms Co. to have them purchase the Segura munitions.[612]

Agent Matthews reported in May that Paul Northey, purchaser of the Vicente Segura arms and ammunition now stored in Importers' Warehouse, was enroute to Mexico City via Key West and Havana.[613] Matthews interviewed Byrnes and Olivier, the attorneys who had handled transferring ownership of the Segura arms to Paul Northey. They stated that Segura transferred ownership of his munitions to Paul Northey at Havana on April 10, 1913, and that they had seen the original deed. Segura had needed to go outside the US to make the transfer for fear of arrest. His friend, attorney Maurice Conners, was trying to arrange the sale of these arms to Remington. Matthews learned from what he considered a reliable source that Paul Northey was well known in Mexico City as a friend of Félix Díaz and Segura. When Northey left New Orleans, he went to Cuba where he was to meet Segura and return to Mexico with him.[614]

Reporting on the situation in New Orleans, Matthews stated with satisfaction: "Agent has things in such shape that he is confident the factions cannot do much that will not immediately be reported to Agent. With the limited men and informants shall do the best possible and keep other matters moving as they come in. Agent is using J. L. Mott a few hours each day. He knows most of these Mexicans by sight and being a man who does not drink has been invaluable to Agent on several occasions. It is arranged now so that no informants come to the office which is constantly watched but report by mail and get their orders by mail."[615] Matthews, incidentally, cleared up the allegations of munitions being shipped in piano boxes and tomato cans. He had investigated and determined that these were simply more of the rumors and false reports constantly swirling around in New Orleans.[616]

Matthews now had to deal with Ernesto Fernández y Arteaga, Carranza's representative in New Orleans. Raúl and Julio Madero, the martyred President Madero's brothers, were to help Fernández y Arteaga conduct the New Orleans junta, but they would not arrive as soon as expected. "It seems that these younger brothers of Madero became involved in a sporting house brawl in San Antonio and that Julio is in the Santa Rosa infirmary suffering with a severe fracture of the skull."[617]

Matthews learned of a meeting in the office of Honduras consul Albert J. Olivier between the consul, Richard Sussman, former consul of Nicaragua, Carranza's representative, Ernesto Fernández y Arteaga, "General" Gabe Conrad, the well-known soldier of fortune, and Camilo Arriaga, an engineer. Arriaga, incidentally, had once been a fervent *magonista*, but had traded ideological purity for personal advancement— he was now a wealthy *carrancista*.[618] The purpose of the meeting was to plan the purchase and transportation of munitions from New Orleans or some other point on the Gulf coast to Mexico. Nothing definite was agreed and participants intended to reconvene shortly. Matthews was also advised that Pablo Northey was back in town, at the Monteleone Hotel. The register showed that Northey was in room 458 while Camilo Arriaga occupied 457 immediately opposite. Further, the agent learned that Northey, Fernández y Arteaga, and Arriaga held a private meeting at which Northey told Fernández y Arteaga that the Félix Díaz cause was lost, and he came here only to see Fernández about selling the Baldwin munitions in the Importers' Warehouse to the Carranza faction.[619]

Northey and Arriaga left the Monteleone surreptitiously. Northey went to the BI field office saying his home was in Mexico City, that he was interested in mahogany, and came to New Orleans to purchase the arms as a speculation. Northey said he had known Segura since childhood, and that at present Segura was in Havana where Northey expected to meet him shortly. Maurice Conners called on Matthews, saying that he had gone to Havana to meet Segura, and was present when Segura transferred the arms to Northey. Conners, Northey, and Arriaga had left Havana together; the idea was to get these arms off Segura's hands. Currently, the Camilo Arriaga and Fernández y Arteaga families lived with Pablo Northey in an apartment house at 1319-1321 Carondelet Street.[620]

Matthews learned of trouble brewing between Paul Northey and Maurice Conners about money due Conners for services rendered and money disbursed for Northey's munitions in the Importers' Warehouse. Conners indeed filed suit against Northey, attaching the goods, and claiming Northey had paid him only $300 of the promised $1,000, and the US marshal took custody of the *Dantzler*. The agent also reported that Fitzpatrick believed Northey was now the real owner of the *Dantzler*. Northey and friends went to examine the vessel, whereupon Northey and Conners engaged in a heated altercation regarding ownership of the schooner. Conners called the cops, and Northey was arrested for disturbing the peace. Arriaga later told Matthews that the plan was for Northey to get the two boxcars of Segura arms and the *Dantzler*, and go to Havana. Northey was currently in Havana arranging for Segura to return to New Orleans for trial.[621]

Matthews received an arrest warrant for Vicente Segura as a defendant in the case of US vs. Lucio Blanco et al. conspiracy to smuggle munitions. The bullfighter, who was now a Constitutionalist, was long gone from New Orleans, popping up in Brownsville busily arranging the smuggling of arms from Brownsville to his colleagues in Matamoros.[622] Segura evolved from bullfighter to arms procurer; by 1915, he was a general in the Constitutionalist army.

Pablo Northey, Camilo Arriaga, Maurice D. Conners, William J. Byrnes, Jr., Gus Lemley the attorney for A. Baldwin & Co., and P. Olivier entered into an agreement by which the *Dantzler* would be released from the US marshal's custody. Northey was to vest the title of the boat in the names of Gus Lemley and a friend of Olivier's, who would then try to sell the vessel as soon as possible, using the proceeds to settle with Byrnes, Olivier, Riley and the others who held claims against Northey. But regarding the lien on the arms and ammunition in the Importers' Warehouse, Northey wanted this merchandise released, whereas Byrnes, Olivier and Riley wanted to know what price the *Dantzler* would bring before releasing their claims.[623]

Further complicating the situation, there were rumblings of discontent in the New Orleans field office. Matthews informed the Chief that Agent Billups Harris gave as informants only the names of newspaper men upon whose information Matthews did not place much faith, as they wanted too much in the way of exclusive stories. Therefore, Matthews listed a number of businessmen and officials upon whom he depended for reliable information, together with many clerks and employees occupying confidential positions with railroads, brokers, and business houses.[624] Disagreements among the agents became a crisis. J. L. Mott, who had been an informer for Matthews, was now working for the Huerta government, and he wrote a letter to Arturo M. Elías, Inspector of Mexican Consulates, recounting what he claimed was the inside story: Several months earlier, Agent James P. Farmer wrote to the assistant chief of the BI, Albert H. Pike, charging Matthews with being disagreeable, unpopular, etc. Matthews had recently learned of the letter and decided to teach Farmer a lesson by writing a letter—never meant to be sent— for Farmer to see, reviewing Farmer's drunken sprees in the red-light district, his inability to do his assigned tasks, and mentioning the designs of Agent Harris and Maurice Conners on the munitions stored in Hall's Transfer Company at Meridian, and in which $1,000 was to change hands.

Farmer discovered the letter as Matthews had intended, but instead of serving as a warning, it infuriated him. Farmer stormed off to headquarters with copies of Matthews' letter, taking care to send Harris a copy and doing everything in his power to discredit Matthews. Harris reappeared in New Orleans and immediately tried to squelch the story going the rounds of his complicity with Conners regarding the Meridian munitions. Harris, Conners, and Fitzpatrick got together and tried to discredit Matthews. Mott left it up to Consul Elías whether or not to pass all this on to Agent in Charge Thompson in San Antonio. Elías did so, happily causing problems for the Bureau, and Thompson sent the Chief a copy of Mott's explosive letter.[625]

Chief Bielaski dealt with this mess by replacing everybody in New Orleans with a new agent. Forrest Currier Pendleton became a BI agent on April 18, 1912, at age thirty-one, two years the Chief's senior. Born in Northport, Maine, the Pendletons moved to Boston, where Forrest grew up. He moved to Washington, DC in 1905, and worked as a bookbinder in the Government Printing Office.[626] A. Bruce Bielaski, the future Chief, worked in the same department and the two likely met at that time. Just like Bielaski, Pendleton studied law while working for the government. He was admitted to the Washington bar in 1908, the same year as Bielaski.[627] While Bielaski joined the initial cadre of the Bureau of Investigation, Pendleton remained in the Government Printing Office and rose through the ranks of the Washington bookbinders' union, becoming its secretary in 1911.[628] After Bielaski became the new Chief in 1912, he quickly convinced Pendleton to join the force. Pendleton's initial assignment was to the Kansas City field office investigating violations of the Mann Act.[629] He transferred to New Orleans on August 13, 1913, and ran that field office capably until resigning in 1920 to open a private security firm.[630] In New Orleans he also met his wife, Leah Marie Louise Adams, with whom he had a son and a daughter. After Leah died, he remarried in 1936. Pendleton would live in New Orleans for the rest of his life where his son Forrest Jr. continued running his detective agency. He died in 1969 at the age of 88.[631]

Figure 36 Forrest Currier Pendleton, Passport Photo, 1921

Pendleton's first assignment was the Baldwin munitions stored at the Importers' Warehouse. Through the attorney for Baldwin, Gus Lemley, the agent learned that the 2,168 cases of ammunition and 156 cases of rifles would be shipped to the Winchester Repeating Arms Co. in New Haven. Another source corroborated the information and advised Pendleton that it was quite probable there was some scheme underway whereby the munitions would be exchanged for another supply of war materiel, as the Mexican interests who negotiated the Baldwin armament had been very active lately. It was said that Pablo Northey, now a confidential agent of the Constitutionalists, had been in New Haven recently. Pendleton visited the Importers' Warehouse, and personally inspected the boxes of munitions. Informant James O'Donnell was watching the warehouse, and if munitions were moved, Pendleton would immediately know the details and advise headquarters.[632]

Pendleton conferred with the US Attorney and attorney Lemley regarding the shipping of the munitions in the Baldwin case to Winchester. Lemley stated that the title to these goods had been in Pablo Northey's name, but that Northey transferred his title to Baldwin & Co., which sold the munitions to Winchester. Lemley wished to report this matter so there would be no complications when the same were shipped. He said the arms would be sent on a Morgan Line steamer billed through to Hartford via New York, and he offered to furnish Pendleton the bill of lading. In April 1914, Agent Pendleton reported that although Lemley was on record as the sole owner of the *Dantzler*, allegedly Vicente Segura was the owner of the vessel.[633]

The Huerta operative, J. L. Mott, representing his consul, asked the US attorney whether he would stop the removal of the munitions from the warehouse. That official refused to give Mott any information, and advised Pendleton that he saw no way whereby he could interfere with the removal of the merchandise. Informant James O'Donnell covered the nighttime loading of the Morgan Line steamer in August.[634] So finally ended the intricate saga of the Vicente Segura munitions.[635]

Chief Bielaski telegraphed Pendleton that the State Department had advised that the President on July 21, 1913, had withdrawn permits for munitions shipments to the Huerta government including, especially, certain shipments in New Orleans consigned for Veracruz. Pendleton was to cooperate in preventing unauthorized exportations.

Former informant J. L. Mott boldly appeared at the BI field office to collect his back pay, and upon leaving casually inquired about customs officials at Gulfport and Biloxi. Pendleton stated that Mott worked for the Huerta consul, and was possibly thinking of assisting in getting out an expedition. Pendleton went to Biloxi to get some reliable party to monitor the situation there.[636] Perhaps not coincidentally, Pendleton learned from city editor of the *Times-Democrat* that A. Baldwin & Co., had sent out telegrams to every arms dealer in the country for quotations on three or four million rounds for immediate delivery to New Orleans. The editor stressed that this information was strictly confidential, and that he would pass along any further information. Among Pendleton's other sources were Conners and Riley, who were certainly well informed, and they agreed to keep Pendleton abreast of neutrality matters. Conners later announced that he had sold the *Dantzler* to A. Baldwin & Co. who were handling the matter for Pablo Northey; Conners believed the boat would be used in filibustering expeditions.[637]

Pendleton reported in November that substantial quantities of rifles and small arms ammunition were stored at the warehouses of Stauffer, Eshleman & Co. and A. Baldwin & Co. The weaponry had been arriving in small shipments. Matters were quiet in New Orleans at the present; the parties interested in getting out munitions for Mexico were awaiting President Wilson's decision in connection with the lifting of embargo on munitions to Mexico.[638]

Pendleton detailed informant O'Donnell to contact some Stauffer, Eshleman employee to get inside information about their warehouse. The assistant warehouse man assured O'Donnell that he would check on munitions on hand and report. He said he personally counted 4,500 cases.

Since ammunition usually ran 1,000 rounds to the case, Pendleton observed that the 4,500,000 rounds stored there would seem in indicate that they were not intended solely for local trade. Pendleton visited the firm's offices but was not cordially received by the manager, who grumbled that he had already been caused considerable trouble by Bureau agents, and he felt certain they had all the information needed concerning his firm. Pendleton kept the Stauffer warehouse under close surveillance, as they now housed most of the ammunition in New Orleans.[639]

The agent also learned that the notorious three-masted power schooner *Dantzler* cleared from New Orleans on December 30 in ballast for Gulfport to load lumber. E. F. Fremont, a noted filibuster, was captain of the boat, which had a crew of four. Pendleton's information strongly indicated that boat's destination was Veracruz or some other Mexican port. Those interested in the schooner were aware that informant O'Donnell had her under surveillance. Pendleton received word from Maurice Conners that the plan was to load lumber at Gulfport as a blind and proceed to Chandeleur Island at night, and take on arms and ammunition.

There was certainly no lack of ammunition in New Orleans. Besides the impressive amounts on hand, steamers kept arriving with new shipments. On December 30, for instance, the steamship *Comus* from New York brought 610 cases consigned to A. Baldwin & Co.[640] In the months to come, the arms traffic would become even more intense.

Chapter 9: Federals vs Locals on The Border

Securing the border and preventing the Huerta regime from using US supplies for their effort turned out to be a tough order to execute. Border communities benefitted greatly from the civil war across the border. Local businessmen, politicians, crooks of all shades, and even law enforcement generally disliked the influence of "Washington" in their backyards. The BI agents along the Texas, New Mexico, Arizona, and California border had to contend with unexpected obstacles, lack of resources, and a seemingly unending flood of munitions inundating the border states. The financing and organization of the arms and munitions epidemic originated in New York.

The New York field office was concerned primarily with monitoring arms shipments, some of them rather intricate. Besides the usual persons of interest such as Francis Bannerman and Ed Maurer, new players appeared in the persons of José B. Ratner and his brother Abraham, wealthy Russians who had lived in Mexico for years and owned the Tampico News Company, a mercantile firm with stores in Tampico and Mexico City. Belying the firm's innocuous name, the Ratners were also arms dealers whom President Madero had deported in 1912 as "pernicious foreigners." When Huerta seized power, the Ratners became some of Huerta's closest advisors and made impressive profits as the dictator's official munitions purchasers in the United States.[641] The Ratners worked through the New York commission merchants, H. M. Marquardt & Co., that in July 1913, secured Treasury Department authorization to ship 10,000 Winchester carbines and 8,000,000 cartridges to the Tampico News Company for delivery to Huerta's Secretary of War and Marine. During that month, Marquardt actually shipped 6,550 carbines and 4,000,000 cartridges.[642] The United States prohibited further arms permits for the Huerta government on July 21.

Bureau informant Harvey J. Phillips gathered intelligence on arms dealers in New York City, conferring frequently with BI agents.[643] *Carrancistas* had established an office at 115 Broadway. Reportedly, the Maderos had organized a company, eponymously called Madero Bros. under the laws of New York, with Rafael Hernández as attorney. They would use New York as their base for shipping munitions to Carranza because of Bureau agents' activity in New Orleans. Reportedly, the utmost secrecy was maintained in connection with the company's operation; not even the telephone number was known to the public. Agent G. Raymond Matthews in New Orleans learned all this from Francisco R. Villavicencio, former Mexican vice-consul in London and Liverpool, who passed through New Orleans enroute to join Carranza.[644] He operated in Eagle Pass and Piedras Negras in July 1913 as a secret agent for the Constitutionalists.[645]

An ominous development at Laredo in February 1913, was the arrival of persons from San Antonio who were planning an attack on Nuevo Laredo.[646] Alarmed, Thompson dispatched Agent Barnes to investigate. The newcomers proved to be the usual suspects—conservative Mexicans who had participated in the Reyes, Vázquez Gómez, and Orozco conspiracies—Andrés Garza Galán, Nicanor Valdés, his nephew Lauro Rodríguez, Crisoforo Caballero, Pascual Orozco Sr., and his secretary Indalecio Ballesteros (the one-time Bureau informant). All these individuals consulted frequently with the Webb County sheriff, Amador Sánchez of Reyes conspiracy fame, who housed them in the courthouse.

An independent but sympathetic plotter was C. F. Z. Caracristi, who in 1911 had suborned the Mexican consul in El Paso for the *maderistas*. He claimed he had been gathering information in Mexico City for Senator A. B. Fall of New Mexico for use by the Senate Investigating Committee. Caracristi stated that on October 18, 1912, Madero operatives Felix

Sommerfeld and Santiago González Casavantes had entered his hotel room, seized sixty typed pages of his notes, had him arrested, robbed of $1,200, imprisoned, hustled to Nuevo Laredo, and deported on October 25, 1912, as a "pernicious foreigner." Caracristi arrived penniless in Laredo but moved into the upscale Hamilton Hotel, dressed well, and had plenty of money despite having no apparent means of support. He boasted that the was a friend and business associate of General Félix Díaz, which probably explains his income; he was on the scene to protect the interests of Díaz, Huerta's partner in crime.[647]

Several American officials besides Sheriff Sánchez reportedly assisted the plotters—Collector of Customs James J. Haines, Deputy US Marshal A. J. Barthelow, Deputy Sheriff Apolonio García, and Sam McKenzie, one of the customs inspectors at the bridge, who was a former Webb County deputy sheriff and a known henchman of Sheriff Sánchez. Conversely, the military cooperated surreptitiously with the Bureau. Colonel Brewer, commander of Fort McIntosh, assigned a soldier in civilian clothes to a hotel to apprehend anyone calling for the baggage of two of the new arrivals—Pascual Orozco Sr. and Indalecio Ballesteros, who had registered under assumed names. Agent Barnes, with the hotel proprietor's consent, had already examined their luggage and had discovered incriminating documents, which he seized and sent to headquarters.[648]

The *huertista* plotters in Laredo did their work well—they were driven across the bridge in an automobile on February 15, and captured Nuevo Laredo without shots fired.[649] They effected this coup by suborning many of the federal officers in the garrison. Those who swore allegiance to the Huerta government remained in their present positions while those who refused were arrested. The plotters appointed their own Huerta consul in Laredo. Sheriff Sánchez crossed frequently to Nuevo Laredo and played a prominent role in reorganizing local government under the new regime. On February 23, a "Revolutionary Junta" was proclaimed in Nuevo Laredo, which included Andrés Garza Galán as Political Director and J. Cantú Cárdenas as General Secretary.⁶⁵⁰

Agent Barnes interviewed Sheriff Sánchez, who said Garza Galán was his friend, and that he was glad he had seized Nuevo Laredo, but this would in no way prevent his doing his duty as sheriff. This was true, for his duty now was to combat attempts by *carrancistas* to recapture Nuevo Laredo and zealously assist the Bureau in enforcing the neutrality laws. The Constitutionalists returned the compliment by burning down several buildings on the sheriff's ranch. Deputy US Marshal A. J. Barthelow, like Sánchez, was now vigorously enforcing neutrality, as were Huerta agents Antonio Magnón, Manuel M. Miranda, and former deputy US marshal Frederick H. Keller (who was also informing the Bureau).⁶⁵¹

Agent Thompson notified Barnes that a complaint had been filed against Andrés Garza Galán, Nicanor Valdés, Pascual Orozco, Sr., Juan Garza Galán, Indalecio Ballesteros, and Gustavo Caso, charging them with conspiracy to set on foot a military expedition. He sent a certified copy of the complaint and a warrant for their arrest. Several defendants managed to cross the bridge to Nuevo Laredo on February 15; others were apprehended. Since it was inadvisable to confine them in Sheriff Sánchez's jail for obvious reasons, Barnes asked Colonel Brewer to hold them in Fort McIntosh. The colonel was most reluctant to do so because he had no authority, but even when the War Department granted such authority, the colonel was still reluctant. It seems that back during the Reyes affair the *reyistas* confined at the fort had gobbled up $150 worth of rations, for which the Department of Justice had never reimbursed the army.⁶⁵²

Constitutionalists in Laredo had every intention of recapturing Nuevo Laredo. Under the leadership of Leocadio Fierros and Emeterio Flores, a former *maderista* and proprietor of the newspaper *El Progreso*, they were recruiting, bringing in ammunition, and attempting to get the men and munitions across the river to their colleagues.⁶⁵³ Encouraging them was the overwhelming support for Carranza among the residents of Laredo.

A new Bureau agent, Webster Spates, was assigned to Laredo. He was born in Poolesville, Maryland, on March 7, 1884, into a devout Catholic family. The tall, slender, blue-eyed Spates earned a law degree from Georgetown University. He became a BI special agent on August 23, 1913, resigning on November 1, 1919, to become a special assistant to the attorney general.[654] Spates quickly learned what he was up against in Laredo: "I find it very difficult to accomplish much at this place as a great majority of the Federal Officers of this Government are in sympathy with the rebel forces of Mexico and it is very difficult indeed to get any cooperation through these officials. In fact, I have been told on several occasions since I have been here that some of these officials, especially in the Immigration Service, have actually assisted in getting munitions of war across the river. Of course, this is hearsay, nevertheless it has a bad effect and makes it hard for the Department to accomplish as much as it might otherwise."[655] Spates recounted that once he had found neither Customs nor Immigration officers on duty at the international bridge. He respectfully suggested that the Department try to have the military on continual bridge duty, "as I find this to be, after a thorough study of the situation here, the only way to accomplish a strict enforcement of the neutrality laws here."[656]

A few weeks later Spates wrote: "After investigating, I find local political conditions in Laredo and vicinity have so shaped themselves that they affect the Mexico situation on this part of the border in that the local political factions assist at least in sympathy and influence the corresponding factions in Mexico. These conditions obtain chiefly among the Mexicans, very few Americans [Anglos] being mixed up in the affair. While most Americans here may have their individual opinions regarding Mexican affairs, they do not carry their sympathies into action leading to any violations of the law. The Mexicans, however, do not stop at anything to assist their respective factions, especially if they are reasonably sure their acts of assistance will not be found out by US officers here. Mexicans here are in it mainly for the money…. Each faction immediately opposes federal officers who arrest colleagues. All local newspapers, both Spanish and English, are enlisted in the cause to make the vilifications as strong as possible and to further prejudice the general public against federal officers.... We have to investigate, since allegations by factions are prejudicial."[657]

The Bureau agent tried to investigate both Constitutionalists and *huertistas*, all the time conscious that each faction was trying to manipulate him against the other.[658] Anyone crossing to Nuevo Laredo needed a pass signed by Sheriff Sánchez. Spates spent much of his time watching him, "for under the circumstances I can hardly make inquiries of anyone here as it is very hard to know whom you can trust."[659]

In terms of neutrality prosecutions, the federal grand jury's report in November was most discouraging. Most of Spates's investigations had been of Constitutionalist sympathizers, but the grand jury failed to indict any Constitutionalist, instead returning three indictments of Huerta government operatives, charging them with being spies. The foreman stated that there were fifteen to eighteen Huerta spies in Laredo, and it was the unanimous opinion of the grand jury that the "troubles, difficulties, strife and conditions" resulted entirely from the operations of the Huerta agents. The jury hoped the Department of Justice would remove them. The grand jury's one-sided report reflected not only public opinion, which strongly favored the Constitutionalists, but also the fact that the foreman, rancher Tom Coleman, had been purchasing large numbers of confiscated cattle from the Constitutionalists.[660] Spates inquired of the Chief whether the Bureau could prevent secret agents of the Mexican government from operating on American soil. The Chief replied: "I know of no legal way in which we can prevent these men from carrying on their work so long as they conduct themselves in a regular and proper manner."[661]

The Del Rio section of the border proved to be less of a challenge for the local BI agents to secure. The Constitutionalists occupied Las Vacas (today Ciudad Acuña) opposite Del Rio and installed José Garza as their consul in Del Rio. Garza had been working with a prominent local dentist, Dr. F. M. Rose, who had a contract with the *carrancistas* to deliver weaponry to them in exchange for confiscated cattle. Garza was charged with conspiracy to violate the neutrality laws, but at his examining trial the two important government witnesses took the Fifth Amendment. Carranza's principal representative in Del Rio was the talented Teódulo R. Beltrán. The Huerta consul repeatedly protested to Agent Breniman and other federal officers against Beltrán, alleging nefarious activities against the Huerta regime, but Beltrán was careful not overtly to violate the neutrality laws, whether consulting with the Constitutionalist junta in San Antonio or in Del Rio, or on his trips to Eagle Pass.[662] But sometimes Beltrán had serious setbacks, as when on May 17 the army seized 50,000 rounds at the express office consigned by Shelton-Payne in El Paso to one "V. Davila," in all probability a fictitious name.[663] The local Constitutionalist paymaster, Severo Fuentes, kept his money in the First National Bank at Del Rio, prompting the Huerta consul further to protest Fuentes's frequent trips back and forth across the river. Inspector of Mexican Consulates Arturo M. Elías sent an operative, Fred D. Thompson, to Del Rio to secure evidence of neutrality violations. Thompson was a former deputy US marshal who had been a Bureau informant. Now he not only worked for Elías at Del Rio, Laredo, and Eagle Pass but continued to be a Bureau informant.[664]

At Del Rio a majority of residents supported Carranza, and there was a lot of recruiting going on. But as Agent Thomas "Todd" Monroe Daniel noted, the only way to secure evidence was to have a Mexican who was unknown be approached and enlisted. Daniel spoke with the Huerta consul who said a good man would be sent out from San Antonio to get recruited and inform the Bureau. Daniel also received authorization to employ one Joe Patton as an informant for a few days at $3 per day—keeping expenses as low as possible. When Daniel telegraphed Agent Barnes that Patton was to "make a proposition by which he hopes to be taken in with them," Barnes warned about entrapment: "It will not be permissible for your informant to induce the parties you have under investigation to commit a crime which they would not otherwise voluntarily commit."665

Daniel surmised that ammunition was unloaded at one of the numerous railroad sidings between Del Rio and Langtry, taken to the river and crossed.666 There was also an easier method—Daniel's informer Patton said it was common knowledge that if the soldiers "were given a little bonus there was no trouble at all in taking it [ammunition] straight across on the ferry."667

Eagle Pass saw the most intense Constitutionalist activity. The small Huerta garrison across the river at Piedras Negras hurriedly evacuated that town in late February to the forces of Jesús Carranza, the brother of First Chief Venustiano Carranza.668 The First Chief established his headquarters in the Piedras Negras customs house. Consul Luther Ellsworth complained of the Constitutionalists' blatant violations of the neutrality laws. And he denounced their execution of ex-Federal judge Joaquín Cantú Cárdenas, whom Ellsworth knew personally and esteemed highly. Cantú Cárdenas was one of the thirty-eight *vazquistas* indicted in San Antonio, and he was later general secretary of the *huertista* city government in Nuevo Laredo. Constitutionalists had captured him and four others on the outskirts of Nuevo Laredo and transported them to Piedras Negras. On the night of March 24, Cantú Cárdenas and the others were taken from jail, put on a special military train, and several miles down the line were taken off and unceremoniously shot.669 Consul Ellsworth suggested that Spanish-speaking BI agents be sent to assist the army in enforcing neutrality.670 None were available.

Chief Bielaski sent Agent Charles Edward Breniman to Eagle Pass to monitor the situation.671 Breniman, born on August 16, 1870, in Jasper, Iowa, became a peace officer in 1894 as a deputy US marshal in St. Louis. He later worked for the St. Louis police department. He became a Secret Service agent in 1907, then in 1908 was transferred to the newly established Bureau of Investigation. He figured prominently in several important cases, among them the 1910 bombing of the *Los Angeles Times* building. Breniman retired from the BI in 1925 to become chief special agent of the Pullman Company, retiring from that position in 1944. He died on April 15, 1960. His son, John Brennan, was also a BI agent.[672]

As elsewhere along the border, Breniman had to contend with public opinion regarding the arms traffic. He conferred daily with federal, state, county, and local officers, as well as businessmen, and explained that "Conspiracies are rare here. A common expression of even well-meaning people living along the border, but who do not consider all phases of the situation, is to let the Mexicans have all the ammunition they want so long as they are willing to pay for it, but as a rule this does not take the form of assisting them to get it so long as it constitutes a violation of the laws."[673]

Breniman received complaints from the Huerta consul general that the *carrancistas* had appointed a consul in Eagle Pass and were flying the Mexican flag above his office. Teódulo R. Beltrán, the Constitutionalist operative, complained that *huertista* spies had been placed at the international bridge to denounce *carrancista* sympathizers. Besides complaining, Beltrán provided Breniman with valuable information.[674] Beltrán, incidentally, had a temper that prompted him on May 14 to engage in a shootout on the streets of Piedras Negras against another prominent *carrancista*, Alfredo Breceda, wounding the latter in the foot.[675]

The *carrancista* consul signed bills of lading for export to Mexico, and one of the first orders of business was to acquire the arms and ammunition needed for the swelling number of volunteers streaming into Piedras Negras. The task was made easier because US Commissioner Bonnet in Eagle Pass was a strong *carrancista* sympathizer and had close business ties with people in Piedras Negras. He was prone to dismiss smuggling charges. As Agent Breniman reported, "There is unanimous opinion among federal and military officers here that Bonnet is not in sympathy with the government's policy concerning munitions smuggling and neutrality law enforcement....We do not believe there is any element of dishonesty on the part of the Commissioner in his official capacity but rather one of self-preservation in a business way and a pronounced desire that the present revolution in Mexico as represented by Governor Carranza shall win out."[676]

Breniman reported in April that the situation was satisfactory except for Consul Ellsworth, who complained that the neutrality laws were being openly violated around Eagle Pass. When Breniman asked the consul to explain, it turned out that Ellsworth referred to Constitutionalists who came from other border towns through American territory to Eagle Pass, and crossed to Piedras Negras to confer with Carranza. "Consul believes such persons should not be allowed to return to the United States."[677] Ellsworth protested specifically about Teódulo Beltrán, who worked closely with Constitutionalist Consul L. M. Gutiérrez, and Ellsworth helpfully provided a list of *carrancista* officers in Ciudad Porfirio Díaz and Piedras Negras. Ellsworth also telephoned the deputy US marshal that Beltrán had taken $18,000 from Eagle Pass to San Antonio to buy arms for Carranza. On the other hand, however, Agent Barnes mentioned that Beltrán had furnished the government valuable information about the *huertistas*.[678]

Consul Ellsworth complained about the lack of cooperation he was receiving from the army and the Bureau, citing his neutrality work from 1908 to 1911 and suggesting that he be reappointed to that position. While acknowledging his past contribution, the State Department on May 8 informed Ellsworth that the army and the Bureau "would seem to be sufficient for the needs of the situation" and instructed him to confine himself to his regular consular duties.[679] But Ellsworth could not contain himself: "Pardon me for again calling the attention of the [State] Department to the fact that Federal Officers, the majority of them, stationed in the American Border, are firmly convinced that the 'Department of State' does not desire alertness in Neutrality matters at the present time, or it would have advised the other Departments that the present easygoing methods employed to prevent Violations of the Neutrality Laws were not satisfactory."[680] He continued to report on revolutionary developments. Regarding Ellsworth's complaints, the Attorney General informed the Secretary of State that the Bureau had as many men on the border as the appropriation would permit and that, in cooperation with US marshals and Treasury agents, the necessary service was being fairly well performed.[681]

Despite Agent Breniman's rather optimistic reports concerning Eagle Pass, there was a growing traffic in munitions. He advised that there were eight to ten local firms dealing in ammunition. The agent's plan was not to interfere with an occasional small shipment of guns and ammunition when consigned to bona fide dealers, but he reported that dealers had been gradually increasing their shipments.[682] The First National Bank of San Antonio forwarded to Eagle Pass $40,000 to an unidentified party, presumably for revolutionary purposes. The army on May 1 stopped an automobile near Eagle Pass and seized 10,000 rounds. The ammunition had been sold by the prominent Houston firm, Peden Iron & Steel Co., to the Border Hardware Company, a recently established Constitutionalist front company.[683] Breniman seized at the express office on May 30 and June 2, two complete Marlin machines for reloading 30-30 cartridges consigned to Juan B. García, local merchant and purchasing agent for the *carrancistas*. A Bureau agent went to Hartford, Connecticut, and learned at the Marlin Arms Co. that García had previously been purchasing weaponry from Marlin.[684] Breniman had 6,000 cartridges seized at the express office, a machine gun, and 4,500 cartridges marked "dry goods" seized at the depot. Customs inspectors on the river seized 5,000 rounds and two machine guns. The army was taking custody of all munitions confiscated.[685] The Constitutionalists did not confine their purchases to armament, however. Breniman seized at the depot boxes containing 1,000 khaki uniforms consigned to Juan B. García. Consul Ellsworth immediately pointed out that these were identical to the uniforms of Constitutionalists in Piedras Negras. On Chief Bielaski's instructions, Breniman filed a complaint against García for the reloading outfits and the uniforms. García was duly arrested, claimed he had not ordered the reloading machines, and was released on a $500 bond.[686]

The García case brought up again the problem of US Commissioner Bonnet, who was not a qualified person because of personal business interests to preside at a hearing in which ammunition smuggling and other violations of the neutrality laws were charged. Bonnet was a customs broker, whose business depended entirely on maintaining friendly relations with the Constitutionalists at Eagle Pass and elsewhere on the border. Bonnet made daily visits to Piedras Negras to consult with the rebels. Breniman emphasized that "as there are cases of neutrality pending before the Commissioner, we believe this matter should be given immediate attention."[687] Predictably, Commissioner Bonnet dismissed the case and ordered García released from custody.[688] To Breniman's great relief, Charles W. Hartup, a justice of the peace formerly in the Customs Service, became the new US Commissioner in late July.[689]

Breniman by no means confined his activities to Eagle Pass. On one occasion he accompanied a cavalry detachment to scout the river ten miles northwest of town. On another, he and two mounted customs inspectors staked out a river crossing for three nights.[690] Although Breniman and other officers were certain on many occasions that specified individuals were smuggling ammunition, the evidence was not enough to support prosecution. One reason was because local dealers were increasingly hostile to federal officers seeking information that would incriminate their clients.[691]

The Constitutionalists also had printed in the United States fiat currency which they tried to smuggle through Eagle Pass. The army seized five million pesos' worth.[692] Several revolutionary factions printed such currency, whose value, of course, depended on how well the faction was doing on the battlefield.

Yet, the stark fact facing the Constitutionalists at Eagle Pass was that they could not amass enough munitions to risk a major battle.

Desperate, they were disguising their shipments, marking them in every conceivable fashion to avoid detection. One technique, as had been done in El Paso, was to have Mexican women cross the international bridge carrying concealed ammunition. Since there were no female inspectors on duty this was effective, but only limited quantities of ammunition were involved. Several times, Constitutionalist tried unsuccessfully to ship trunks with ammunition from San Antonio to Eagle Pass. These were seized and F. R. Villavicencio, a well-known Constitutionalist, was arrested.[693] Another smuggling technique was to conceal ammunition in barrels supposedly containing beer or lard, the munitions being purchased in San Antonio from the Praeger Hardware Co. The Southern Pacific Railroad yardmaster in Eagle Pass was paid to have a boxcar with sixty-seven barrels of "beer" containing two disassembled machine guns and between 50,000 and 100,000 rounds shunted across the river to Piedras Negras on the night of August 27.[694]

The Federal army had launched an offensive to recapture the state of Coahuila, and the small *carrancista* garrison at Piedras Negras offered little resistance. Federals occupied Piedras Negras on October 7. First Chief Carranza had evacuated his headquarters, and because the United States prohibited him from passing through American territory, he and his entourage made a lengthy and difficult horseback journey westward to the state of Sonora, where Constitutionalist forces were having considerable success.

The Huerta consul in San Antonio instructed the general in command at Piedras Negras to deliver to the Bureau the Constitutionalist documents he had seized. Disappointingly, when an Immigration inspector translated them, they were found to contain little of value.[695] The mere fact that the San Antonio field office had to get an Immigration inspector to translate documents illustrates the Bureau's continuing problem—an inability to have documents translated in a timely manner by its own translators.

The hotbed of revolutionary and counter-revolutionary activity remained San Antonio, the site of continuous plotting and conspiracy from the beginning of the Mexican Revolution. Huerta's seizure of power resulted in all kinds of Conservative sympathizers eagerly assisting the Bureau in enforcing the neutrality laws. The San Antonio field office had to try to sift out fact from a deluge of rumor, misinformation, and disinformation. Francisco A. Chapa, the local drug store owner and influential supporter of the Texas governor, called at the office and volunteered information. Consul Luther Ellsworth advised that Constitutionalists were using American railroads to transport officers and men to border localities. The consul urgently requested that Agent in Charge Thompson immediately notify Chief Bielaski. Huerta consul general J. A. Fernández (who was one of those indicted) chimed in with a report that Carranza agents were using a local employment agency to recruit men and send them to the border. Marshall Hicks, the prominent attorney who had represented Sheriff Amador Sánchez, now represented the Huerta regime and supplied information against the Constitutionalists. *Huertistas* reported that the Constitutionalists had had an important planning meeting at the Menger Hotel. The dictator's followers were particularly concerned about the activities of Teódulo R. Beltrán, owner and operator of the Alamo Safe and Lock Company. He had been one of Madero's most enthusiastic supporters, and now he not only conferred with First Chief Carranza but also purchased armament in San Antonio and arranged for automobiles to convey the supplies to the border.[696] But the Bureau office also received information about the *huertistas* from Constitutionalist agents Sam Dreben and Felix Sommerfeld.[697]

In the midst of trying to keep abreast of what the warring Mexican factions were doing, the Bureau received some heartening news in May. Chief Bielaski wired that the Supreme Court reversed Judge Maxey in the Chávez case on May 8, ruling that shipment intended for Mexico and seized before actually crossing into Mexico constituted a violation of the law, and that personal carriage of prohibited articles came within the meaning of the word "shipment." Bielaski instructed agents to act in all cases of attempted exportation, and in addition to seizing munitions of war, to arrest the parties involved. Agents were to notify all US officials to be on the lookout for this kind of shipments.[698] The Bureau was fully back in business.

An intriguing development in San Antonio was the Huerta consul showing Agent Barnes a cablegram from Francisco León de la Barra, Huerta's Minister of Foreign Affairs, stating that Constitutionalists, acting through Clyde Shenan [sic] and Francis Barneman [sic-Francis Bannerman] "one or both of whom are located at 501 Broadway, New York City," had purchased 50,000 Mauser rifles in Germany and had placed with the Remington Arms Co. of New York an order for a quantify of cartridges. The Mausers were in Hamburg, ready to be shipped to some point along the Gulf of Mexico. The German government had confiscated the arms at one time, but efforts were being made to secure a permit to send the shipment through the US. Apparently, these rifles were part of a purchase made by Madero while President of Mexico. Consul Fernández advised that he would probably be notified as soon as this shipment was moved. Barnes suggested that the New York field office investigate.[699] Fernández advised in June that the steamship *Las Antillas* of the Morgan Line would arrive in New Orleans with the cargo of munitions Madero had bought in Germany and was being shipped via New York to New Orleans for distribution. Additionally, an informant at Laredo reported that the Constitutionalists had purchased two three-inch fieldpieces from Bannerman in New York.[700]

By June 1913, there was considerable revolutionary activity along the border, and the Bureau was overwhelmed. Agent in Charge Thompson pointed out that he had only three men to cover the border from Yuma, Arizona, to Brownsville, including Agent Daniel.[701]

Given the limited number of agents, the Bureau had to rely heavily on Mexican informants. For example, Francisco A. Chapa, ever willing to assist the Bureau against the Constitutionalists, introduced Agent Daniel to Gregorio Cortez, recently released from the penitentiary and an Hispanic folk hero because he had killed two Texas sheriffs in 1901. Cortez "says he is constantly approached by Constitutionalists trying to persuade him to enlist and solicit others to enlist in their cause and go to Mexico. He promised to get the names of some of these parties."[702]

Thompson urgently requested additional personnel, pointing out that the number of cases they could add to the criminal docket in San Antonio would amply justify the expenditure. He also stated that there was reluctance along the border to provide information to the Bureau regarding violators of the law, given the overwhelming sympathy for Carranza and his followers.[703] By August, however, Thompson reported the border being relatively quiet. Further indicating how the United States influenced the Mexican Revolution, both factions awaited developments in Washington; they anticipated permission to export munitions or to receive some form of diplomatic recognition. But as the factions realized it unlikely that permission to export would be granted, they resumed the arms traffic with renewed effort.[704]

Chapa was eager to provide Agent Daniel with additional information against the Constitutionalists, saying their headquarters were at 912 West Houston Street, and that J. A. Martínez, alias J. M. Morton, a wealthy Mexican living in a suite at the St. Anthony Hotel, was purchasing munitions from the Peden Iron & Steel Co. and sending them by automobile to Brownsville and Laredo for General Lucio Blanco's Constitutionalist army in Tamaulipas.[705] Agent in Charge Thompson arranged to have the Peden Company report all munitions sales to private individuals and deliveries to private residences.[706] In addition, the Chief authorized Thompson to employ two informants for a few days at reasonable compensation to cover shipments. Informant C. P. [F?] Swigelson covered freight houses and hardware firms. On one occasion, he located an arms cache and accompanied Thompson and two city detectives in a raid resulting in the confiscation of 11,500 Winchester 30-

30 cartridges being packed in lard barrels. Four Mexicans were arrested. Informant J.W. Sanders covered the movements of persons of interest such as Felix Sommerfeld, staying at the Hutchins Hotel.[707]

Thompson had both informants cover Mexican laborers that the Contreras Labor Agency was sending by rail to Laredo. Informant Sanders searched many of these men, finding some carrying ammunition. Thompson telegraphed Webster Spates in Laredo that about forty were going in one shipment and had been enlisted for service in Mexico. The Bureau was doing its best to gather sufficient evidence for prosecution.[708] Sadly, Agent Barnes interviewed an American businessman who had recently returned from Monclova, Coahuila, who had seen a group of Mexican laborers just arrived from the United States being forced into the Huerta army and their earnings taken from them.[709] Until more agents were assigned to border duty, the Bureau continued to rely on informants such as lawman Charles F. Stevens and newspaper reporter H. B. Yelvington.[710]

Thompson reported on the surge of revolutionary activity: "This office is continually in receipt of various reports of efforts to export munitions from nearly every point along the border. Never since taking charge of this office has there been such a general effort to violate the Joint Resolution of Congress and the President's proclamation. It is wholly impossible to cover all of these points with the forces at the command of this office and we have only endeavored to cover the most important places. At present we have no agent in the District of Arizona and New Mexico, the entire border of these two States being left uncovered by the Bureau of Investigation. A number of these places are covered by the army, but it is essential that someone be assigned to this border to keep them informed of the movements of these people. The US attorney fully supports this office's efforts to prevent violation of the neutrality laws and realizes the grave necessity of more men."[711] Chief Bielaski inquired whether it was essential for an additional agent for work in Arizona and New Mexico. Thompson replied that he preferred to hear from Agent

Breniman, who was currently investigating in Calexico, California, upon Breniman's return to Arizona.[712] The Chief later inquired about assigning an agent at Eagle Pass, as the army had requested. Thompson replied that it was not necessary to keep an agent there permanently, but it was advisable to have an agent cover both Eagle Pass and Del Rio, which he considered just as important as Eagle Pass.[713]

A major change in US policy toward Huerta on July 21, 1913, directly affected the Bureau. The Chief telegraphed: "Department of State advises President has withdrawn all permission for shipment Munitions of War to Mexican Federal Government, including especially certain shipments through Laredo consigned Nuevo Laredo and El Paso consigned Juárez. Advise Special Agents these points and cooperate in preventing unauthorized exportation."[714]

This change affected a *huertista* operation. Consul General J. A. Fernández wrote to Agent in Charge Thompson on September 8 asking if the Bureau would permit his receiving 1,000 horses purchased in Texas since July for the Huerta government. The horses would be received during September and concentrated and cared for in a suitable location, perhaps Uvalde, Texas, until the US granted an export permit. Thompson checked with the US attorney and with Chief Bielaski, who wired: "Make no arrests parties or detention horses without specific authority but advise this office of developments so that arrests and detention may be made if deemed advisable."[715]

Mexicans in San Antonio purchased three second-hand automobiles which, together with cans of motor oil filled with ammunition, were sent by rail to Eagle Pass consigned to the firm of Trueba & Pardo. The idea was to cross the vehicles to Piedras Negras where machine guns would be mounted on them for action in Coahuila. Thompson received orders from the Chief to prevent the exportation of the automobiles, and the army seized them at Eagle Pass.[716] Interestingly, US Marshal John H. Rogers, who originally notified Agent in Charge Thompson, believed the operation was a Constitutionalist scheme. When

Bureau agents investigated, they concluded that it had been a *huertista* operation, formulated as the Federal army prepared to capture Piedras Negras from the Constitutionalists. Agent Barnes wired that the firm of Trueba & Pardo were known Huerta sympathizers. Moreover, Thompson interviewed the seller of the automobiles and Manuel M. Miranda (who had purchased ammunition in New Orleans for Orozco in 1912), now a Huerta operative who knew the buyers and who was present at the purchase.[717] Unfortunately, Miranda was so sleazy that Barnes hesitated to subpoena him as a material witness, noting that "This man's character is such that to put him on the witness stand would have a tendency to prejudice the jury against the Government's case."[718]

Constitutionalists continued to smuggle ammunition from San Antonio. The US marshal and one of his deputies seized at a railroad depot four barrels billed as sugar and salt shipped by Francisco R. Villavicencio to one Anastacio M. Plata at Webb, a small station near Laredo. Three barrels contained 8,600 30-30 rounds packed with sacks of salt surrounding the ammunition, which was in the center of the barrel, to prevent noise and make the weight about the same as an ordinary barrel of sugar or salt. The fourth held sixteen Winchester rifle breeches and barrels, cushioned by granulated sugar. The pair were charged with conspiracy to export and released on bond: $500 for Villavicencio and $2,000 for Plata. Villavicencio, residing at 240 Belden Avenue in San Antonio, was already under bond for appearance before the grand jury at Del Rio, charged with a similar offense at Eagle Pass. Villavicencio was indicted on December 20, 1913.[719] We will encounter him again.

After the frenetic activity El Paso had witnessed during the Orozco rebellion, the year 1913 opened on a surprisingly quiet note. The local chief of the Madero intelligence service, Lee L. Hall, stated there was virtually no arms smuggling. Things were so quiet, in fact, that Hall's entire network was eliminated on February 1. Hall, who had worked in the Mexican Secret Service since start of the Orozco rebellion, arranged to work as chief of security for a mining company.[720]

General Huerta's seizure of power changed all that. *Huertistas* occupied Ciudad Juárez after only token resistance. Hall informed the Bureau field office that he had been asked to take charge of intelligence work in El Paso for the Huerta regime and had accepted.[721] Hall worked for whoever paid him, while others such as Victor Ochoa tacked with the prevailing political winds.[722] Huerta's coup resulted in Consul Enrique Llorente being replaced by a new consul in the person of Miguel E. Diebold, who had been in the consular service for fourteen years, part of that time on the border. The United States government did not recognize Diebold as the legitimate Mexican consul; technically, Enrique C. Llorente remained the de jure consul.[723] Diebold had his work cut out for him because the residents of El Paso strongly supported Carranza. As Agent Breniman noted, "This includes state officers who have been active in suppressing arms smuggling and other neutrality violations; have stated they will not assist federal officers in arresting anyone smuggling against the present government."[724]

As the El Paso field office tried to adjust to the new situation, one of its priorities was keeping track of Mexican exiles. Chief Bielaski advised that Francisco "Pancho" Villa merited close coverage. Villa, who had figured prominently in the Madero rebellion, had served under General Huerta in 1912 in the campaign against Orozco. Huerta despised Villa and had him sentenced to death by a drumhead court martial. President Madero learned of this and, at the last minute, countermanded the order, fueling Huerta's hatred of Madero. Villa was taken to prison in Mexico City for trial but managed to escape and make his way to El Paso, where he had been living quietly since January. Villa announced, however, that he would take the field against Huerta.[725]

The local BI office learned nothing of his plans, which included purchasing weapons in El Paso. The agents were surprised when informed that Villa and eight followers had quietly crossed into Mexico on the night of March 6.[726] Villa would build the largest revolutionary army in the struggle against Huerta. As had happened with Madero and General

Reyes, the Bureau proved unable to maintain surveillance on an important person of interest.

Getting a handle on the arms traffic was of immediate concern, however. The Bureau concentrated on the firm of Krakauer, Zork & Moye as the principal violator of neutrality. The test came when the case of the United States v. Robert, Julius, and Adolph Krakauer, Cástulo Herrera, and Victor Ochoa was tried before Judge Maxey in April.[727] The defense moved for a directed verdict of acquittal for Adolph and Julius Krakauer and Cástulo Herrera. Maxey granted the motion. Although disappointed, the government was confident it had solid cases against Robert Krakauer and Victor Ochoa, but because El Pasoans disliked such neutrality cases, as well as Consul Llorente, former Special Agent Louis Ross, Abraham Molina and others whom the defense attorneys contemptuously referred to as "Mexican spies," the jury deliberated for a whole of fifteen minutes before returning a verdict of "not guilty." Adding insult to injury from the Bureau's position, Judge Maxey dismissed cases against nineteen other defendants accused of neutrality violations on the ground that it was virtually impossible to secure convictions.[728]

The result of these devastating defeats was that the arms traffic boomed, with Krakauer and Shelton-Payne increasing their shipments to points along the border in Texas and Arizona. The Bureau's intelligence-gathering was severely handicapped by public support for the Constitutionalists, who quickly established a junta in El Paso and began recruiting. One of the recruits was Abe Molina, former Madero spymaster, who became a Constitutionalist secret agent and established ties with leaders such as José María Maytorena, the titular governor of Sonora. Molina was, however, a double agent, working for Huerta consul Miguel Diebold. The consul had no illusions about Molina, describing him as "a man of little education, very shrewd, and in my opinion having little conscience. He has no political allegiance, nor does he care about politics, having no other aim than that of serving whoever pays him best, whether as a smuggler, a recruiter, or a secret agent."[729]

American supporters of the Constitutionalists at a more important level included Washington attorney Sherburne Hopkins, who had represented Madero. He now represented Venustiano Carranza, utilizing the alias of "F. González Gante," and later the "Royal Gold Mining Co." in his correspondence with the First Chief. Hopkins worked closely with Carranza representative Ignacio Pesqueira lobbying to secure diplomatic recognition of the Constitutionalists as belligerents and getting the arms embargo lifted.[730]

On July 21, 1913, the United States halted munitions shipments to the de facto Huerta government, thus leveling the playing field. Now *huertistas*, as well as *carrancistas*, had to rely on smuggling. Constitutionalist smugglers had a considerable advantage. Regardless of the evidence the Bureau developed, public opinion favored the Constitutionalists, as was reflected in the federal grand jury's refusal in October 1913, to indict eleven individuals accused of neutrality violations. The Bureau did receive some assistance from the army, however. Soldiers in civilian attire were deployed to help maintain surveillance over freight depots, pawn shops, and the major hardware stores.[731]

But like prospectors panning for gold, the agents occasionally hit pay dirt while sifting through tons of gravel. Gustavo Padrés, paymaster for the Constitutionalist rebels in Sonora, on June 20 phoned from Douglas and ordered 448,000 7-millimeter and 30-30 cartridges from Shelton-Payne. A few days later, he appeared in person and made a down payment, followed by a second payment on July 12, when he directed that the boxcar containing the ammunition coming from Winchester through Galveston be turned over to Powell Roberts, former Madero secret agent now working for the Constitutionalists. The authorities surprised Roberts supervising a gang of Mexicans busily transferring the munitions from the boxcar to a gondola, and covering the shipment with coal. Roberts was arrested, as was Padrés in Douglas. The cartridges were hauled off to Fort Bliss for safekeeping as evidence. Roberts and Padrés were indicted but secured a continuance, confident that by the time their case came to trial, witnesses would have vanished—and even if there were witnesses, the jury would be sympathetic.⁷³²

The Bureau in El Paso spent much of its time having to follow worthless leads, many of them provided by volunteer Constitutionalist operatives lurking around Krakauer, Zork & Moye and Shelton-Payne.⁷³³ But the Bureau also had an effective, and unlikely, informant in the person of John Killian Wren, born on July 1, 1875. Wren had worked for the Madera Company in Madera, Chihuahua, in 1912, was part Ute, was fluent in Spanish, interpreted for the Bureau, and proved to be an effective investigator. He became a Bureau of Investigation agent in 1916 and resigned in 1932. He died in El Paso in 1942.⁷³⁴

Figure 37 John Killian Wren, Clay Family Tree. Source: Ancestry.com.

Adding to Constitutionalists' confidence, their colleagues in Chihuahua were winning. Pancho Villa's command, the Division of the North, had become formidable—by June, the *huertistas* controlled little more than the city of Chihuahua and Ciudad Juárez—and Villa was advancing on both prizes. In this increasingly tense atmosphere, some El Pasoans worked both sides of the street—at Western Union two Hispanic brothers were telegraphers: one passed intelligence to the Constitutionalists, the other to the *huertistas*.⁷³⁵ The Huerta garrison in Ciudad Juárez desperately tried to shore up its defenses by purchasing 1,000 rolls of barbed wire from Krakauer, Zork & Moye for entanglements. The firm then sold to the *carrancistas* every pair of wire-cutters in stock.⁷³⁶ Business was business, after all.

The blow fell on November 15, 1913, when Pancho Villa used a variation of the Trojan horse stratagem. He captured a freight train traveling from Juárez to Chihuahua, loaded 1,500 troops on it, telegraphed Juárez that the train was having to return, and when in rolled into the Juárez station at 1:30 a.m., his troops poured out and captured the town before the Huerta garrison knew what had hit them. This feat won Villa international fame. The Bureau now had to deal with the new set of Juárez officials: *villistas*.

The Bureau faced a daunting challenge in Arizona. Unlike New Mexico, whose only real port of entry was Columbus, Arizona had three: Nogales, Douglas, and Naco. Like New Mexico, there was only the invisible international boundary, making Arizona a paradise for smugglers, especially in Nogales, where the boundary ran down the middle of the street. Gathering intelligence against Constitutionalists was problematic because public opinion overwhelmingly favored that faction. The US attorney for Arizona urgently requested a BI agent.

Agent Blanford received that unenviable assignment.[737] Arriving at Douglas, he noted that: "To obtain the inside information relative to any activity, the use of an informant seems almost indispensable. I am advised that it will require a Mexican and am also advised that a trustworthy Mexican is very hard to find."[738] He employed Carlos Herminio Echegaray, who was recommended as capable and trustworthy, at $4 per day. When Blanford had remonstrated that this was excessive, Echegaray pointed out that to get any information it would be necessary to deal with the rebel leaders, who were rather affluent and were fond of treating and being treated. Echegaray would have to spend money to ingratiate himself with them. Blanford gave Echegaray a trial but asked headquarters to be advised at once if the rate of pay was considered excessive. As matters developed, within a month Blanford had to dismiss Echegaray, who through no fault of his own had been unable to penetrate the Constitutionalist junta.[739] Thereafter, Blanford relied heavily on reports from Deputy US Marshal A. A. Hopkins, who was fluent in Spanish and ran his own informants, and on intelligence from Byron Butcher, a reporter for the *Douglas Daily Dispatch* who was well-versed in Mexican affairs.

In a separate operation, the US army tapped the Federal telegraph wire at Nogales, Sonora.[740]

Agent Blanford reported that Roberto Pesqueira, a congressman from Sonora, arrived in Douglas on March 9 and held a meeting in his office for a select few, so it would be very difficult to get an informant into this junta meeting. Pesqueira was reported to be enroute to California. The deputy Collector of Customs informed Blanford that there were 50,000 rounds stored in Douglas consigned to Manuel Cuesta, the former Madero consul with *vazquista* sympathies. The customs office was watching the ammunition, thinking perhaps Cuesta might make an effort to get it across the border. It was learned later that the consignment was originally some 83,000 rounds, shipped to Douglas during the Madero administration. Cuesta had crossed about 33,000 cartridges on permits from Washington to the de facto Huerta government prior to July 21, 1913.[741]

Blanford received little help from Consul Cuesta. Although Cuesta knew Blanford to be a Bureau agent, he refused to meet with him. The consul, in fact, was doing little to help the Huerta cause. He was such a pariah among the citizenry that he and his clerk were refused service in a local restaurant.[742]

With regard to recruiting, the Constitutionalists instructed volunteers to cross into Mexico before they were recruited. The *huertistas*, growing more desperate, recruited on the American side of the border. Blanford's initial strategy at Douglas was to have a Constitutionalist sympathizer approach a Huerta recruiter ostensibly to volunteer, but really to learn how recruiting worked.[743] The agent then came up with a better plan. He enlisted "the aid of one faction in securing evidence on the other" by collaborating with Roberto Pesqueira, the leader of the local Constitutionalists, who enthusiastically agreed to provide all possible assistance by having men present themselves to *huertista* recruiters. Blanford stated that "The matter will have to be handled cautiously as the parties involved know they are being watched and are taking every precaution to prevent what we are trying to bring about."[744]

Constitutionalists along the Arizona border were confident from the very beginning, for the Federal army was demoralized. The garrison at Agua Prieta under General Pedro Ojeda, for example, made no attempt to send out patrols because it was split—a little over half were loyal to Huerta and rest were deserting and joining the rebels. One hundred fifty with their weapons deserted in a single night. And hundreds in Douglas were eager to participate in the struggle. Mass meetings denouncing the Usurper were the order of the day.[745]

Among the Constitutionalist chieftains was the former Agua Prieta police chief, Plutarco Elías Calles (a future president of Mexico). He was believed to be hiding in Douglas, and a warrant was issued for his arrest for neutrality violations, based on his letter to a Sonoran colleague seized from a courier captured by a patrol of the 9th US Cavalry. Calles, though, managed to slip across the line and in short order raised a force of some 200 rebels. What was left of the Federal garrison at Agua Prieta—500 men—was withdrawn to the state capital, Hermosillo, and on March 12 Calles triumphantly occupied Agua Prieta at the head of some 450 fighters.[746]

The Federal forces on the Arizona border continued to crumble. Commanding the *huertistas* in Nogales was Colonel Emilio Kosterlitzky, a larger-than-life figure. He was a Russian, born in Moscow on November 16,

Figure 38 Colonel Emilio Kosterlitzky, his wife Francisca, and two daughters in Los Angeles as exiles from the Mexican Revolution, 1914. Source: Creative Commons.

1853, and attended a military college in St. Petersburg in 1867. He emigrated to Mexico via London and enlisted in the Mexican army on May 1, 1873, as a private. Rising through the ranks, he became known as the flamboyant colonel of units of constabulary.[747] At Nogales, Kosterlitzky resisted an attack by the commander of state troops, Colonel Álvaro Obregón (another future president of Mexico) for twelve hours then fled with his men across the line and surrendered to the US army on March 13, 1913. Kosterlitzky and the other officers were paroled after close to a year in detention. He settled in Los Angeles in 1914, where he continued to be involved in Mexican politics and became an informant for the BI.[748]

Constitutionalists now occupied Douglas and Nogales and were well on their way to controlling the entire Arizona border. However, Calles's attack on Naco, Sonora, on March 14 proved to be a disaster—the rebels suffered heavy casualties and fled in panic.[749] Obregón then took charge, and on March 25 captured Naco. Although they were losing, the *huertistas* gamely struggled on. In desperation, the Huerta government authorized its consul in Tucson to offer a reward of ten percent of the value of all munitions seized to anyone giving information leading to the seizure.[750]

Blanford did his best to monitor the arms going to the Constitutionalists. He traveled to Tucson in June and interviewed the managers of the Albert Steinfeld & Company, who "made no claim of being 'lily whites,' but argued that the percentage of profit was too small to run the risk of having to defend a government prosecution."[751] Nevertheless, the firm had been indicted for having in April handled a shipment of 20,000 30-30 cartridges sent from Connecticut whose destination was Sonora, in violation of the President's proclamation. The indictment, however, was quashed on demurrer and dismissed.[752] Others were bolder. George Barker Clark and J. H. "Jack" Noonan openly worked for the Constitutionalists in smuggling munitions. Clark, "a Yale graduate and the discredited member of a formerly rich Eastern family" and brother of the head sales manager for Remington Arms, took a

Constitutionalist order for 1,000,000 7-millimeter cartridges, 500,000 30-30 rounds, several 80-millimeter field pieces, and a sizeable consignment of artillery ammunition. Reportedly this shipment, except the cannon, was smuggled across the border at Nogales on June 25 consigned as blasting powder and went south that night on a special train. Shepherding this operation were Clark and his leader, Jack Noonan.[753] Noonan, born in Troy, New York, had been in the Yukon gold rush and had belonged to Madero's "foreign legion" in 1911. The following year he was a mercenary who had worked for Madero consul Llorente in El Paso during the Orozco rebellion, one of a team hired to blow up bridges on the railroad south of Ciudad Juárez.

Noonan played a prominent role in a most audacious Constitutionalist operation. It began in Los Angeles, where Constitutionalist agents Ramón P. De Negri and Colonel Santiago Camberos, an officer interested in aviation, joined with two Los Angeles residents, Manuel Bauche Alcalde and his brother Joaquín, quickly commissioned as a captain, to acquire an airplane for the cause. The group was financed by the Sonoran Constitutionalists headed by Ignacio L. Pesqueira, interim governor in the absence of José María Maytorena, now living in Tucson. The group in Los Angeles were especially quick off the mark. Carranza had promulgated his Plan de Guadalupe on March 26, 1913; by the end of April, Camberos and the Bauche Alcalde brothers had contacted the American aviation pioneer Glenn L. Martin, who in 1912 had built an airplane factory (which through a series of mergers became the Lockheed Martin Company of today) and purchased from him a Martin Pusher biplane with a 75-horsepower Curtiss engine. The airplane could carry up to 150 pounds of bombs. At the same time, they hired twenty-seven-year-old French aviator Didier Masson, a company instructor, as a mercenary to fly the plane. They reportedly spent $5,000 for the airplane and an allotment of $750 for equipment costs. Masson was to receive a salary of $300 per month, $50 per flight for sorties flown in Mexico, and at least $250 for every bombing sortie flown.[754] The problem of course was how to get the aircraft, disassembled in five large crates, across the border. The first stage was easy—ship the crates by Wells Fargo Express on the Southern Pacific to Tucson consigned to one Tom Dean at the town of Sahuarita, twenty-five miles south of the city. "Tom Dean" was Thomas J. Dean, an Australian aviator who was to be Didier Masson's mechanic.[755]

On the evening of May 6, however, the Mexican consul in Tucson, Alejandro Ainslie, his clerk, and two Huerta operatives appeared at the office of Deputy US Marshal L. D. Johnson and informed him that an airplane was being shipped from Los Angeles to Dean at Sahuarita and was to be taken to Mexico for use in warfare. To corroborate his story, Ainslie produced several pages of what he said was evidence gathered by a Burns Agency detective in Los Angeles. Ainslie asked Johnson to seize the airplane. Deputy Johnson put in a call to US Marshal Charles A. Overlock at Phoenix for instructions and in the meantime went to the Wells Fargo office and saw the five crates. The clerk told him the shipment was indeed for T. Dean at Sahuarita. Johnson instructed the clerk not to let the shipment leave until he had consulted with Marshal Overlock. The clerk demanded a written order, which Johnson gave him. The marshal told Johnson to do nothing until he had consulted with the US. Attorney J. E. Morrison. Morrison said not to seize the crates. But about midnight a policeman phoned Deputy Johnson a message from the US attorney instructing him to seize the crates after all. Johnson rushed to the Wells Fargo office, only to be told that T. Dean had signed for the crates and had removed them in a wagon an hour earlier. As Johnson put it, "So not having anything to go on and knowing it would be like looking for a needle in a haystack I immediately telegraphed US marshal that shipment had been removed."[756] It apparently did not occur to Johnson that it might be a good idea to investigate Tom Dean at Sahuarita.

There matters stood until the next morning, when Huerta consul Ainslie went to Johnson's office and said he thought he knew where the crates were, and he again asked the deputy to seize them. Johnson notified the marshal, who instructed him to hire an auto, go out and if Ainslie's information proved correct, seize the shipment. Johnson asked Sheriff John Nelson of Pima County to assign a deputy to accompany him, which the sheriff did. Johnson also told the sheriff he needed a man to guard the crates, and the sheriff recommended one Rube Hopkins, who was lounging on the courthouse steps at the time. Deputy Johnson already knew Hopkins as a competent chauffeur "and being the only man available at the time I took him along as guard." A hired chauffeur drove Johnson, Hopkins, and one of the Huerta operatives to Sahuarita, where they learned the shipment had not passed through. They then proceeded some thirty-five miles southwest of Tucson to the Chesterfield Mining Company camp. About a hundred yards from the camp, they came across a wagon stuck in a rut. It contained the five crates. And standing beside the driver of the wagon and two helpers was another Pima County deputy sheriff, José Escobosa. Johnson said he asked Escobosa what he was doing there, to which Escobosa replied that the wagon driver had hired him to help him up the hill. Johnson informed Escobosa that he was seizing the crates; Escobosa raised no objection. Escobosa's presence was significant. He was not just an ordinary deputy sheriff—he was a wealthy rancher and Constitutionalist sympathizer who had a deputy sheriff's commission. Consul Ainslie was convinced that Escobosa, Tucson real estate dealer Enrique V. Anaya, and José María Maytorena were at the head of Constitutionalist activity there.[757]

At this point the owner of the crates arrived and said his name was Didier Masson and wanted to know by what authority Johnson had seized his property.[758] Johnson identified himself, told Masson he had orders to seize the crates, and did so. He placed Rube Hopkins on guard, returned to Tucson, and reported to the US marshal and US attorney by telegraph.

Not until May 19 did Marshal Overlock, who had originally been uncertain whether an airplane was a munition of war, think it advisable to haul the crates back to Tucson. He instructed Johnson to get bids from the different transfer companies, explaining that "Deputy Johnson secured the bids but about the time he had the figures he also heard that the airplane and man who was in charge had been taken out of the country, and as yet I have been unable to obtain the truth as to whether this man Hopkins, who was in charge, was bought, or volunteered, or was forced to cross the line into Mexico."[759] The crates and Hopkins had disappeared on May 15.

An assistant US attorney in Los Angeles had wired the US marshal to arrest Masson and his assistant, Captain Joaquín Bauche Alcalde, as well as Hopkins, Escobosa, Tom Dean, and Richard W. Graeme, a chauffeur. When interviewed by a newspaper reporter, Rube Hopkins claimed that he had been overpowered by *carrancista* agents and carried by them across the line into Mexico. Rather than face possible charges of bribery, he decided to remain in Mexico and join the Constitutionalist army at Nogales, Sonora, and was commissioned as a major![760]

The superintendent of the mine where the crates had been left stated that no federal or state officers had been there during the eight days the crates had been there, but on several occasions, automobiles had come and the occupants had conversed with Hopkins, who told the superintendent on one occasion that they had offered him $250 to let them take the crates away. One of these men was in all probability Jack Noonan, suspected of being the prime mover in the airplane caper.[761]

Agent Breniman interviewed Noonan about the airplane, but he was "quite reticent on the subject." The crates were crossed into Agua Prieta from Douglas on the night of May 18, and transported from there by rail to Hermosillo, where the airplane was reassembled.[762] To appease the American government, Colonel Camberos was ostensibly made the scapegoat in the affair. The American consul in Hermosillo reported that Constitutionalist provisional governor of Sonora, Ignacio L. Pesqueira, "has caused arrest and degradation of Colonel Camberos for taking part in securing airplane across the line. Claims he does not approve of said action. Claims he has respect for laws of our country so is punishing said Colonel."[763]

Agent Breniman investigated the airplane case, interviewing a number of individuals.[764] Among them was reporter Byron Butcher who said he was in Agua Prieta soon after the airplane arrived there and saw the persons who arrived with it. The only ones he was acquainted with were Rube Hopkins and R. W. Graeme. Butcher said the entire party lined up together and had their picture taken. Breniman eagerly requested that he obtain that photo, which Butcher promised to try to do. He also asked that his name not be used in connection with the case.[765]

The Chief wired Breniman that E. V. Anaya and José Escobosa had been indicted in Los Angeles in the airplane case. They were said to be Tucson. Los Angeles officers wanted Agent Breniman to apprehend them because of information that if Tucson authorities learned the men were wanted, they would be warned. If apprehended, Breniman was to advise the US Attorney at Los Angeles by wire and confer with the US Attorney in Arizona. Breniman duly carried out these instructions, accompanying Deputy Johnson in arresting Escobosa and Anaya on October 2 and placing them in the county jail. Enrique V. Anaya, formerly an interpreter in the federal court in Tucson, was now the Constitutionalist commercial agent, or "consul," in Tucson and directed the juntas in Tucson, Douglas, and Nogales. Escobosa was his brother-in-law.[766] The attorney for Anaya and other Constitutionalists was none other than the US Commissioner at Tucson. So, the defendants were arraigned before the US Commissioner at Benson and were released on a $5,000 bond.[767]

Agent John M. Bowen, in charge of the Los Angeles field office, dealt with several of the other defendants. One was Richard W. Graeme, who was tracked down in Seattle and returned to Los Angeles.[768] He was charged with neutrality violation for having driven the crates across from Douglas in a truck.[769] He confessed his role, arguing that he was merely a tool and could not be convicted on the evidence the government possessed and should be released on his own recognizance. The US Attorney at Los Angeles agreed, and Graeme thereafter became a Bureau informer.[770] Captain Joaquín Bauche Alcalde was arrested in Los Angeles by Agent

Bowen on a tip from the Huerta consul at Mexicali.[771] Bauche Alcalde readily admitted his role in the airplane affair and charmingly asked Agent Bowen to inquire of Bureau headquarters if he could be permitted to return to Mexico upon his promise to return to Los Angeles when his case came to trial. Bowen reported: "I gave him no encouragement, but to show his good faith he claimed that a Mexican of the Revolutionary party was in this city trying to purchase 100,000 rounds of ammunition; he would inform me when they were purchased and just where they would be shipped so that a seizure could be made and the Mexican apprehended. I kept in the office a good part of the day as he promised to communicate with me later but up to 5:30 p. m. he had not communicated."[772] However, Bauche Alcalde was released from the county jail on his own recognizance.

Bowen's efforts were appreciated by the Huerta government. He wired that "Mexican consul came to office, presented me with a letter from Mexican Government's Department of Foreign Relations thanking me for 'the valuable and efficient assistance you have rendered in the various matters and affairs placed in your hands by the Consulate, aiding us at all times in our labors.' Consul Manuel Piña y Cuevas also expressed his personal thanks."[773]

The principal defendant, Didier Masson, was safely in Mexico testing the smuggled airplane, being joined by Dean and Joaquín Bauche Alcalde. The Constitutionalists christened the airplane *Sonora* and soon put it to good use. Constitutionalist General Álvaro Obregón was advancing on the Huerta-held port of Guaymas, and he was anxious to use his newly acquired airpower. With Masson piloting the airplane and Bauche Alcalde as bombardier, on May 10 [sic], 1913, they carried out "the first aerial attack on surface warships under combat conditions in aviation history."[774] They dropped improvised bombs on Huerta gunboats blockading the Guaymas harbor. The bombs caused no visible damage but did scare the hell out of the crews and caused the gunboats hurriedly to evacuate the bay. So, it was a victory after all.

Captain Joaquín Bauche Alcalde indeed returned to Los Angeles and at his arraignment on September 20 pleaded "not guilty" to enlisting for service under a foreign power. His counsel asked for a reduction in his client's bail. Through an arrangement with the court, the matter of bail was left open for a few days to let the defendant obtain bonds in any amount up to $5,000.[775] Constitutionalist sympathizers supplied the bail.

Except for the airplane smuggling scheme, revolutionary activity was at a low ebb in California. Agent Isaac F. Lamoreaux at Los Angeles did investigate press reports that Constitutionalists were engaged in enlisting. The Mexican consul also investigated these newspaper stories and found them to be fake news. He agreed to furnish Agent Lamoreaux with three copies of the weekly *Regeneración*, marking those articles he felt needed attention. Lamoreaux sent two copies of the Chief, retaining one for the field office's files.[776]

Agent John M. Bowen was stationed in the Los Angeles field office. Born in Boston on September 10, 1881, he worked as secretary to a Massachusetts congressman while studying for the bar. In January 1911, he graduated from Georgetown University law school, among the first in what became the FBI tradition of special agents being lawyers. Bowen mainly worked white slavery cases before being assigned to neutrality enforcement. His photograph shows a grim, gimlet-eyed special agent eager to fight crime. By 1915, though, Bowen became tired of fighting crime; he resigned from the BI for more lucrative work as a Los Angeles attorney in private practice.

He went to Calexico in August 1913 where he conferred with the Mexican consul. He also visited several ranches and spoke with the managers, who unanimously asked for a troop of cavalry as a precaution, for Constitutionalists were reportedly enlisting men for an attack against Mexicali.[777] But the recruiting effort soon fell apart. Governor of Sonora José María Maytorena had dispatched one Robert D. Fisher, lately of Tucson, to Calexico and Mexicali to supervise enlistment and hopefully invade Baja California. Joining Fisher in this endeavor was Rodolfo

Gallego, who had a ranch near Mexicali. When the Huerta authorities in Baja California attempted to arrest them, Fisher and Gallego fled back to the United States. Agent Bowen learned that Fisher and Gallego had had a falling out because Gallego had not been able to collect his share of the money Fisher had raised from Constitutionalist sympathizers.[778]

The newly hired Agent C. E. Breniman replaced Bowen at Calexico and accompanied Customs and Immigration officers on trips of inspection along the border. Born in Jasper, Iowa in 1870, of a Swiss immigrant father and German-American mother, Charles (Charly) Edward Breniman (originally the family name in Europe had been Broennimann), was active in Republican politics in Iowa, where he served as county treasurer from 1898-1907.[779] He seemed to have been a popular resident of the town. The local paper congratulated the thirty-five-year-old businessman upon buying the local Commercial Bank of Audubon in 1905, stating that he was well suited for the career move into banking as he had "a very large acquaintance, is popular, [and] has excellent judgment." Breniman promised to serve out his term as county treasurer.[780] In 1908, Breniman moved to Shoshoni, Wyoming, where he invested in copper mines, and was elected state representative.[781] He joined the BI in 1913 and moved first to El Paso, then San Antonio.[782] In 1916, Breniman married Helen Hine in Houston. The couple moved back to Wyoming in 1917, where Breniman owned a sizable ranch.[783] He returned to San Antonio in 1919 as Division Superintendent.[784] He served in the Justice Department for fifty years until retirement and died in Fort Collins, Colorado in April 1960.

Breniman advised Agent in Charge Thompson that a troop of cavalry had arrived to reassure the locals. Breniman also conferred at Mexicali with the leading Huerta officials: the governor of Baja California and, more importantly in light of future developments, Major Esteban Cantú, commanding the Federal troops at Mexicali and vicinity. In sum, Breniman stated that no important neutrality violations had occurred, and he was returning to his station in Arizona. Thompson advised the Chief that the Huerta government's report of revolutionary activity at

Mexicali had been greatly exaggerated, as were a great many other *huertista* reports reaching the Bureau and other government agencies.[785]

Some of the arms smuggling the Bureau had to contend with involved local lawmen. The Collector of Customs at Nogales reported in late July that some peace officers sympathized with the Sonora rebels, adding that the Nogales town marshal had recently been apprehended in the act of assisting them in stealing arms and ammunition from army headquarters at Nogales. The marshal was being held to await the action of the federal grand jury.[786]

The real concern was that during the summer and fall of 1913 a flood of munitions shipped from El Paso inundated the Arizona border. The Constitutionalist junta in Douglas, whose head was the wealthy and prominent Francisco Elías, secured enormous amounts of cartridges. As of September, Douglas merchants had received 1,200,000 7-millimeter and 30-30 rounds just since June. The Douglas Hardware Company alone sold between 700,000 and 1,000,000 cartridges. The Douglas junta smuggled a total of some 3,000,000 rounds, spending money lavishly to bribe American soldiers and to purchase a fleet of automobiles to transport the contraband across the invisible border. Elías frankly told Deputy Marshal Hopkins that between $3,000 and $4,000 had been paid to soldiers of the 9th Cavalry to let ammunition pass.

But the government struck back. Agent Breniman and Deputy Marshal Hopkins inspected more than 10,000 freight bills at the Douglas railroad depot to obtain positive evidence of arms trafficking. Agent in Charge Thompson reported from Douglas on October 2 that a wave of arrests of ammunition dealers had virtually stopped the traffic there. Some dealers had even returned munitions to the consignor. The federal grand jury in Phoenix followed up by indicting forty firms and individuals in Douglas, Tucson, Bisbee, and Patagonia, Arizona, and Krakauer and Shelton-Payne in El Paso.[787]

This triumph proved short-lived. When the cases came to trial in Phoenix in December, Federal Judge W. H. Sawtelle sustained demurrers in all munitions cases where conspiracy was not charged on the ground that the mere shipment from one point in the US to another US point with Mexico as the destination did not constitute a violation of the 1912 Joint Resolution. Only the conspiracy cases against dealers Phelps-Dodge, Douglas Hardware, Shelton-Payne, Wright Wilson, W. F. Fisher, and L. D. McCartney went to trial.[788] But the court ruled that the government was not allowed to show the shipment or receipt of munitions by the defendants, or the movement of munitions in any manner. In the first conspiracy case, that of Fisher, the court sustained a defense motion to instruct the jury to render a verdict of "not guilty." The US attorney then threw in the towel, asking that the cases against the other defendants be dismissed. Two Constitutionalist smugglers who had pleaded guilty and had turned state's evidence and had testified for the government were fined $200 each, and released with a stern warning that if they smuggled again, they faced prison. The court commended the US attorney for endeavoring to prosecute and suppress the arms traffic. Accepting defeat, the government decided not to appeal the judge's ruling. Additionally, the Attorney General's office ordered those confiscated munitions be returned to their owners.[789]

Once again, the Bureau's months of intensive investigation had resulted in a crushing defeat in court. A disheartened Agent in Charge Thompson reported that "We were very much astonished at the action of the court in this case in directing a verdict of 'not guilty' as we had been advised that an exceptionally good case had been made out. Presuming that this matter will be covered in a report of the United States attorney for the District of Arizona, no further effort has been made to obtain additional information."[790]

Chapter 10: California Intrigues

R**EVOLUTIONARY INTRIGUES IN CALIFORNIA INVOLVED** the split between Carranza, still heading the Constitutionalists, and Villa. A major complication was a situation that had developed on the California border with Mexico. On September 3, 1914, José María Maytorena, by the authority of his ally General Francisco Villa, "Commander of the Northern Army of the Revolution," appointed Baltazar Avilés, then a judge in Guaymas, Sonora, to the position of governor of the Northern District of Lower California. Illustrating the split, Carranza had appointed David Zárate as mayor of Ensenada, the capital of Baja California, but Villa had sent M. Vela to take his place since Villa no longer recognized Carranza as First Chief.[791]

Avilés assumed the duties of the position. However, Colonel Esteban Cantú, the leftover Huerta commander, remained in power. Cantú's headquarters were at Mexicali, while Avilés maintained his headquarters at Ensenada. There was mounting friction between the two men, culminating in Avilés fleeing to California on December 1, 1914, claiming he did so to prevent Cantú from performing acts of violence against him. Furthermore, he claimed that Villa had ordered him to reestablish his position by force of arms. In doing do, Avilés ran afoul of the neutrality laws.[792] He became the major figure in one of the Bureau's most complex cases.

Complicating the Baltazar Avilés case was the involvement of the California-Mexico Land and Cattle Company. The Secretary of State had received a telegram from a supposedly reliable person in El Centro that the Huerta government in Baja California had notified a syndicate of capitalists holding in the Colorado River delta a substantial concession of land dating back to Porfirio Díaz, that they had to pay more taxes. Unwilling to do so, the syndicate arranged with the distinguished Boer General Benjamin J. Viljoen, who had been Madero's military adviser during the initial phase of the Mexican Revolution, and Colonel Enrique Anaya, whom we last saw in connection with the Arizona airplane smuggling case, to recruit a filibustering expedition to protect the syndicate's interests. Chief Bielaski instructed Agent F. P. Webster at Los Angeles to proceed immediately to Calexico to investigate whether the neutrality laws had been violated.

Webster interviewed an Immigration inspector who said that the California-Mexico Company, incorporated in 1902, owned substantial property on both sides of the border. The Huerta government had levied new taxes on the C-M Company because it was exporting cattle into the United States without paying the export tax, and this was the source of the dispute. Headquarters of the C-M ranch were located about 100 feet on the American side of the invisible border approximately a mile from Mexicali, which was just across the border from Calexico, California. The ranch manager, Walter Bowker, had recently been seen in the company of Anaya and Jack Noonan, also of airplane smuggling fame. Their presence could only mean trouble.

Figure 39 Baltazar Avilés. Source: Creative Commons.

Colonel Anaya, armed with a credential from Venustiano Carranza, demanded that Colonel Esteban Cantú, commanding the Federal garrison at Mexicali, surrender the town to him. Cantú refused, claiming the credential was issued to Anaya on December 4, 1913, when Carranza was not president of Mexico, but he expressed a willingness to comply if proper credentials were presented. Cantú, however, had no intention of relinquishing power. When General Miguel Ruelas, commissioned by the defeated Huerta army to oversee the disbanding of Cantú's forces, arrived, Ruelas was also rebuffed. (The Bureau, incidentally, had been tracking Ruelas and his party all the way from Galveston.)⁷⁹³ Colonel Cantú as military governor proceeded to consolidate his regime, appointing his own consular agent at Calexico to represent the "Government of Lower California."⁷⁹⁴

Still trying to assert his authority, Anaya camped with about sixty men, mostly Mexicans, across from the C-M ranch house and claimed he was awaiting Carranza's instructions. On August 25, 1914, Colonel Cantú ordered Anaya and his men away from Mexicali. Anaya's response was to launch an attack against Mexicali that night. It did not go well. After firing several hundred shots, most of Anaya's men threw down their weapons and sprinted for the border. The US army captured five armed Mexicans. In the aftermath of this fiasco, an Immigration inspector pointed out Jack Noonan to Agent Webster. Noonan bought a ticket for Tucson and boarded the train. Webster reported that "Noonan talked freely before going, giving the impression to the people in Calexico that he was going away for the purpose of organizing troops for the purpose of returning to take the city of Mexicali."⁷⁹⁵

Figure 40 Colonel Esteban Cantú Jiménez.
Source: Creative Commons.

Agent Webster crossed to Mexicali, and through an interpreter interviewed Colonel Cantú. The colonel said that after the hostilities he examined Anaya's camp, finding rifles, ammunition, equipment, and foodstuffs. He took Webster to see for himself. Further, he stated that prior to the engagement, he had seen Anaya and his men entering and leaving the C-M ranch house and using C-M horses, saddles, and blankets, and that he had seen Anaya, Noonan, and Walter Bowker together on the Mexican side of the boundary in front of the C-M ranch house. Cantú also produced two men who had been Anaya's prisoners but had escaped; he assured Webster they would testify for the government in any neutrality case. The colonel also showed Webster captured boxes of cartridges marked Dyas & Company, Los Angeles and E. J. Irwin, El Centro, California. Webster intended to follow these leads. When the agent interviewed the proprietor of the livery stable in Calexico, he was told that Jack Noonan had commanded Anaya's motley force. The proprietor of the Calexico Hotel stated that Noonan had been a registered guest August 7 to 30, and had often had Anaya and other men in his room, sometimes talking and using the typewriter all night.

At El Centro, Webster learned that Anaya had been organizing there, and indeed some twenty-five to thirty armed men had left in the direction of Mexicali. The proprietor of the Imperial Valley Hardware Company told the agent that a man answering Jack Noonan's description had tried to buy 10,000 rounds from him, but the sale had not been concluded. The owner of the Broadway Hotel said Anaya had told him he had been appointed Governor of Lower California and was going to capture Mexicali. The proprietor added that on August 27, two days after Anaya's fiasco of an attack on Mexicali, about fifty Mexicans came to the hotel to see Anaya and his colleagues; about noon they held a meeting in a vacant lot, where the men were paid off in pesos. Then Jack Noonan left with Anaya and Anaya's brother-in-law José Escobosa, the wealthy Arizona rancher and sometime deputy sheriff who had also figured in the airplane case. Hardworking Agent Webster next interviewed the agent at the SP depot and learned that E. J. Irwin had received 6,000 30-30 cartridges, delivered to his ranch house just outside El Centro. Irwin also owned the El Centro Meat Market, where he received a suspicious box possibly containing rifles.

Webster's next interview produced important results. E. F. Howe, owner of the local newspaper, admitted that he had sent the telegram to the Secretary of State denouncing the California-Mexico Company's having enlisted Enrique Anaya to capture Mexicali. Howe wanted his name to be kept secret, as in his position he could not afford to antagonize people in the Imperial Valley. He also mentioned that the manager of the Delta Implement Company at El Centro told him Walter Bowker of the C-M ranch had bought a number of saddles from him, which he delivered personally, and on Bowker's order, turned over to Anaya's men. Howe further stated that General Viljoen stopped at the Oregon Hotel and conferred with Anaya shortly before the attack on Mexicali. To Webster's disappointment, the local Western Union manager refused to let him see copies of the many telegrams Anaya, Noonan, and Viljoen had sent.[796]

Frank Reading, formerly president and general manager of Delta Implement Company of the Imperial Valley at El Centro told local BI officer Dave Gershon that on August 26, 1914, Walter Bowker came to his store and bought all canteens and saddles in stock, plus some bridles. Bowker said the deal was not to be charged to the C-M ranch. Bowker said he would pay in cash and instructed that the goods be delivered to a ranch house on the Mexican side of the international line. When Reading took them there, several armed Mexicans challenged him at the line. He told them the goods were for Bowker, so they let him pass, but he was again challenged a few yards from the ranch house. Bowker made no attempt to pay, so Reading charged the goods to the C-M ranch account. (Bowker personally paid the $177.30 on May 24, 1915). Gershon and Reading checked Reading's books, which corroborated Reading's account. He said the books at his Calexico store would also corroborate his account.[797]

Matters became even clearer when Agent Webster spoke in Los Angeles with Robert Lincoln Hall, a prominent arms dealer who had formerly lived in Mexico, and who had an office at 1103 Garland Building, 760 South Broadway, Los Angeles, cable address "Make good," Phone F 5462.[798] Hall was a representative of the Constitutionalist (*carrancista*) government.[799] He stated that he had called on Harry Chandler, one of the principal owners of the C-M ranch, and Chandler made no attempt to deny that the C-M syndicate backed Anaya and his men, giving them what aid the C-M could in helping Anaya to capture Mexicali. According to Hall, Chandler said he had given Walter Bowker, manager of the C-M ranch, instructions to assist Anaya and his men in any way he could to enable Anaya to take Mexicali, and that the C-M expected to receive protection from Anaya should he succeed. Chandler also told Hall that the C-M had put up $1,000 to aid Anaya in organizing his men and purchasing ammunition. Hall also reported the rumor that Anaya had skipped town after getting what he could out of the C-M people.[800]

US Attorney at Los Angeles, Albert Schoonover, was surprisingly reluctant to prosecute Anaya and Noonan for conspiracy. Agent John M. Bowen recalled having conversed with Schoonover regarding some neutrality cases, and the Anaya case might have been one of them. After hearing what Bowen had to say, "Schoonover dismissed the matter by saying in effect that those fellows are patriots and fighting for their country." Reporting this to the Chief, Agent Blanford added: "Mr. Bowen further stated that he received such poor support, generally, in neutrality matters that he was very much discouraged in his work along that line. This I think is the explanation of the manner in which the Anaya case was handled."[801]

If US attorney Schoonover had been less than enthusiastic in prosecuting the Anaya case, he was even less enthusiastic now, for interjecting Harry Chandler into the Anaya affair elevated matters to a whole new level. Harry Chandler was one of the wealthiest men in America, a renowned philanthropist. Working as general manager for the *Los Angeles Times* in the late 1880s, the 30-year-old Chandler, whose first wife had died two years earlier, married Marian Otis, the daughter of General Harrison Gray Otis, the owner of the Times-Mirror Company, which owned the *Los Angeles Times*. Chandler and his wife had six children together, and the couple also raised two children from his first marriage. When Harrison Otis died in 1917, Chandler became the publisher of the *Los Angeles Times*, and a principal rival of William Randolph Hearst and his newspaper empire, also based in California.

Harry Chandler was a tireless entrepreneur and one of the leading citizens of Los Angeles. The publisher and philanthropist was directly involved with helping found the Los Angeles Coliseum, several hotels, the Douglas Aircraft Company, Trans World Airlines, and the Los Angeles Art Association. His business empire spanned corporations in the oil, shipping, real estate, and banking industries. As a real estate investor, Chandler developed most of San Fernando Valley and Hollywood Hills. The famous white Hollywood sign in the hills was Chandler's advertisement for his real estate development. He died of a heart attack in 1944.[802] Important for this story is the fact that he and his father-in-law were also the principal stockholders in the California-Mexico Company, of which W. K. Bowker was manager and General B. J. Viljoen assistant manager.[803] This was no longer just another Mexican Revolution conspiracy.

Agent in Charge Bowen conferred with Webster in Los Angeles, reviewing Webster's investigation. Bowen also contacted broker R. L. Hall, who was also investigating the Anaya matter. Hall gave Bowen "the following code, which is used by the Carranza Agents throughout the country. It consists of the letters of the alphabet with corresponding letter of the alphabet, which is used as the code. It is as follows: A-M, B-T, C-V, and so on."[804] Cooperation between Hall and the Bureau continued in San Diego, where he and Webster focused on reports that anti-Carranza insurgents were being organized.[805]

Hall asserted he had definitely learned that representatives of General Pancho Villa had recently been in San Diego "recruiting Mexicans for the purpose of going over the line into Mexico at Tijuana and Tecate to have the garrison at those places and at Ensenada, the capital of Lower California, turned over to representatives of Villa."[806] He stated he had located two Mexican recruits who had been promised $10 per day with a $50 bonus if they would cross the line at Tecate and join the garrison there. Hall reiterated that he had several informants who could give valuable information. Lastly, Hall stated that he was cooperating with the army at

Fort Rosecrans at San Diego. Agent in Charge Bowen instructed Webster to follow up these leads. Webster interviewed Hall's informant, businessman P. W. Garey, and arranged with San Diego police chief J. Keno Wilson to have a detective pick up two Mexicans who claimed to have been enlisted, so Webster could interrogate them.[807]

He also spoke with I. Mateos, whom Carranza had just appointed as consul in San Diego. Mateos, a veteran of sixteen years in the consular service, said he had made many enemies among the other Constitutionalists who had been working for Carranza in expectation of appointment to the office Mateos now held. Because of the Carranza-Villa animosity, Consul Mateos put no faith in anyone, and believed only the information he himself had gathered. This, he told Webster, implicated former *huertistas* and *orozquistas* such as Enrique de la Sierra and Baltazar Avilés, who now supported Villa and were organizing for another attempt to seize Baja California.

Webster was trying to develop his own informants. He went to the detention camp the army maintained at Fort Rosecrans for Federal soldiers who had fled to the United States after being defeated in Arizona. The officer commanding the camp was amenable, providing he received authorization from higher headquarters. The army's Western Department headquarters agreed to let Webster have a prisoner if he would pay for his maintenance. Webster of course had to secure Bielaski's approval. While awaiting the Chief's reply, Webster interviewed Colonel Emilio Kosterlitzky, one of the paroled Mexican officers. The Russian, no doubt with a bit of pride, said he had received letters "from leaders of all factions offering him a position as general." Kosterlitzky claimed never to have talked to other Mexicans on the street for fear someone would think he was conspiring to break his parole. Webster did receive the Chief's approval to employ a prisoner as an informer at $2 per day, but by then the army had closed the detention camp and the prisoners had scattered.

At Carranza Consul Mateos's request, Webster called at his office and received further news of the situation in Baja California. The consul stated that a *villista* colonel, one of those plotting in San Diego, had recently passed through Tijuana and forced the customs officials there to give up 9,000 pesos, alleging that Carranza was no longer to be recognized. The colonel said he had orders from Villa himself to seize the customs revenue and that Villa would give the orders hereafter. Mateos had gone to Tijuana and learned that the report was true. Regarding the American syndicate, Webster called on the chief of detectives in San Diego whose informant alleged that the plotters in San Diego were motivated not so much by factional allegiance as by the hope of obtaining the C-M syndicate's lands if there were a change of government in Baja California.[808]

Plotting continued apace. Deputy US Marshal F. G. Thompson at San Diego telephoned Bowen at Los Angeles concerning Baltazar Avilés, who was at Tijuana with several hundred troops trying to force the Tijuana garrison to switch sides from Carranza to Villa. The garrison resisted, and a battle was expected momentarily. Avilés was crossing to San Diego daily to recruit. Thompson suggested that a Bureau agent be dispatched forthwith. Bowen briefed US Attorney Schoonover, but the latter believed it would be extremely difficult to convict Avilés of violating neutrality by recruiting because Mexicans would be reluctant to admit they had been recruited in the United States. Bowen contacted his *carrancista* informant R. L. Hall, who promised to try to find men willing to testify.[809]

The Bureau in California now had to keep track of the increasingly complex situation in Baja California: the high-profile owners of the American syndicate trying to retain their concession and property; Carranza and Villa partisans at daggers drawn and battling for control; Colonel Cantú determined to retain power and playing Carranza and Villa off against each other; and, neutrality violations all over the place.

Deputy US Marshal Thompson at San Diego informed Webster about Baltazar Avilés. When Avilés had tried to bring the military under his civil control, Colonel Cantú, commanding at Mexicali and Colonel

Justino Mendieta, commanding at Tijuana, had deposed him. Attempting to regain his authority, Avilés was recruiting men and was stockpiling ammunition at his house in San Diego to take the territory by force. The army raided Avilés's house at 151 24th Street, but the reported 175 rifles, several sacks of ammunition, eight to fifteen boxes of dynamite, and twenty saddles had been removed to an unknown location. The rumor was that Avilés was depending on Villa for assistance, but if that were not forthcoming, he would invade the territory on his own.[810] The Carranza consul at Calexico, Fernando Serrano, reiterated that Avilés was violating the neutrality laws, but Blanford was skeptical, "having been impressed at various times in the past with the proneness of Mexican Consuls generally to exaggerate situations and oftentimes with the express purpose of hiding their own operations."[811] Blanford asked Immigration Inspector George W. Webb at Calexico to check out the consul's claims. Webb replied that all he had heard were the consul's unverified allegations. Blanford decided that for the time being there was insufficient justification for sending an agent to Calexico.[812]

Shortly thereafter, however, Webster learned that indeed a representative of Avilés had purchased arms at the Tufts-Lyons Sporting Goods House in Los Angeles. He followed up this lead by calling on the Carranza consul, who said there were two men in town recruiting for Avilés. The consul refused to disclose their names, stating cynically that "it would be for the benefit of the Carranza faction should Avilés and Cantú demolish each other and their men." The consul finally—and grudgingly—gave their names: Manuel G. Brassell and Juan N. Fernández. They were Los Angeles residents who had been around Mexicali, El Centro, and San Diego during the preceding month, and both would figure prominently in the Avilés affair. The Los Angeles police department obligingly arrested the pair on suspicion, so that through an interpreter Webster could interrogate them. They stoutly maintained that their only connection with Avilés concerned a lawsuit over land in

Mexico. As Webster sagely observed, "It's plain Brassell and Fernández know a lot about Avilés which they don't care to tell."[813]

Webster promptly went to San Diego, where he gained further insight in the matter from José F. Costillo and Luis Rivas Isais. The agent had them taken to the Immigration office, where they agreed to tell what they knew. Through an immigration interpreter, Costillo gave a lengthy statement about Avilés's attempts to mount an expedition against Baja California and about the C-M Company's involvement, a statement which merely confirmed many facts already known.[814]

Blanford had Webster assemble José F. Costillo, Luis Rivas Isais, Manuel Brassell, and Juan N. Fernández at the field office, where Webster interrogated them through an interpreter in the presence of Blanford and the assistant US attorney. Brassell and Fernández admitted that Costillo's allegations were true, and that letters and telegrams between Avilés and Gerónimo Sandoval on the one hand, and Brassell on the other, concerned recruitment for a military expedition. Brassell produced a memorandum book containing, in Gerónimo Sandoval's handwriting, the address of the Tufts-Lyons Company, where Sandoval had instructed him to pick up ammunition for the proposed expedition. On the advice of the assistant US attorney, Blanford filed a criminal complaint against Baltazar Avilés, Gerónimo Sandoval, Francisco Ayón, Ignacio Díaz de León, Ventura Palacios, all of San Diego, W. K. Bowker, manager of the C-M Land and Cattle Company, of Calexico, and Charles Guzmán, of Los Angeles, charging conspiracy to set on foot a military expedition.[815]

An additional piece of the puzzle came from arms dealer R. L. Hall, who advised that there were telegrams from defendant Charles Guzmán to a certain Count Wilhelm von Hardenberg at Los Angeles. Von Hardenberg, according to Hall, was a soldier of fortune, and he had told Hall that he "had in mind getting some arms and ammunition for Avilés."[816] Several days later the Count appeared at the BI office with R. L. Hall and stated that Charles Guzmán had approached him about purchasing ammunition. Von Hardenberg had then gone to San Diego and met with Baltazar Avilés, who informed him that he had all the ammunition he needed. The Count delivered to the Bureau the letter and telegram he had received from Guzmán.[817]

A major development in the investigation was Webster's obtaining search warrants for the residences of Baltazar Avilés, Francisco Ayón, and Gerónimo Sandoval in San Diego on the grounds that arms and ammunition were being secreted in them. Accompanied by plainclothes detectives, Webster found nothing at Ayón or Sandoval's homes, but at that of Avilés on February 5 he hit paydirt. Webster found only a handful of firearms, but he seized Baltazar Avilés's personal correspondence file. Furthermore, he arranged with the local Western Union manager to receive a list of all telegrams between Avilés, Sandoval, Ayón, and Bowker, and the dates sent, so Webster could apply for a subpoena duces tecum.[818]

Avilés's personal correspondence established a connection between Avilés and General B. J. Viljoen, the assistant manager of the C-M Company. Accordingly, a criminal complaint was filed against Viljoen on February 8. This enabled Blanford to consult with the assistant US attorney to propose offering Viljoen a deal if he agreed to turn state's evidence and testify about the C-M Company's connection with Avilés. The US attorney said he would be willing to dismiss the case against Viljoen if the latter testified to all the facts in his possession. Adolph Danziger, the attorney for Viljoen and the other conspirators, informed Blanford, however, that Viljoen would not consider turning state's evidence because he would undoubtedly be stripped of his stock in the C-M Company. Viljoen could not afford such a monetary loss. Attorney Danziger threw out a tantalizing bit of information by telling Blanford that he knew of one man in the conspiracy who would plead guilty or turn state's evidence and tell all he knew about the C-M Company if the case against him were dismissed. Danziger refused to name him.[819]

Blanford, attorney Danziger, and Mrs. Avilés went to the county jail, where Blanford interviewed Baltazar Avilés, with Danziger and Gerónimo Sandoval interpreting. After considerable hesitation and deliberation, Avilés agreed to plead guilty to the charge against him. Regarding Harry Chandler's connection with the conspiracy, Avilés stated that about mid-December 1914, B. J. Viljoen telegraphed Avilés asking him to come to Los Angeles. Avilés conferred in the Van Nuys Hotel with Viljoen and Harry Chandler. They discussed the means and methods of Avilés reestablishing himself as governor of Baja California, and their discussion involved recruiting and the acquisition of weapons. Avilés solicited the C-M Company's assistance. Chandler promised to help, but said he would have to consider how much assistance he could lend. "By this it was construed by Agent to mean that Chandler would have to be guided by the action of the board of directors as to the amount of money the C-M Co. would furnish."[820] The meeting ended with the understanding that Chandler would help to an extent to be determined in the future. On December 22 or 23, Avilés met with Viljoen and Sandoval. Viljoen said $5,000 had been agreed upon, and he gave Avilés the money. Avilés gave a receipt specifically stating that the money was to be used to assist him in regaining his position as governor. Avilés said this receipt was in his personal correspondence file, being unaware that Agent Webster had already seized the file, which was being translated.[821] As soon as he received the money, Avilés had gone to San Diego where he purchased an automobile and began planning his strategy. Avilés admitted that Manuel Brassell, Juan N. Fernández, and José F. Costillo had worked for him as recruiters, and that their salaries came from the $5,000, as he was absolutely without other funds.

Avilés further stated that he had directed Sandoval and Ayón to go to Los Angeles and try to get from Harry Chandler another $8,000, to be used to buy the garrison of Tijuana commanded by Colonel Justino Mendieta, for negotiations were already underway for Mendieta to deliver the town. Sandoval and Ayón explained their mission to attorney Danziger. The latter stated that he personally tried to secure the $8,000 from Chandler, who refused, saying Avilés had assured him that the $5,000 would be sufficient. Avilés also said that Viljoen, who said he was acting for Chandler, offered the use of a C-M boat to transport munitions, recruits, and supplies from San Pedro, San Diego, and other points along the California coast to the Coronado Islands, about fifty miles off the coast, to be used as a base of operations against Baja California. Avilés ended by reiterating that he would plead guilty, and if called on, would testify to the above facts.[822]

Attorney Danziger called at the field office and said the man he had suggested might plead guilty was none other than Baltazar Avilés. He wanted to know what kind of deal the government was prepared to give Avilés to secure a guilty plea. Blanford said he would have to consult with the US attorney. Danziger suggested that he and Blanford proceed to San Diego, where he would try to persuade Avilés that the best thing for him was to plead guilty. Blanford indeed conferred with the assistant US attorney regarding Danziger's proposition and was told that the value of a guilty plea by Avilés was to secure a statement from him implicating Harry Chandler. He advised Blanford to go to San Diego and see Avilés concerning this matter, but to make no promises or threats; to state to Avilés that by pleading guilty and forcing the government to conduct a trial, he would be more likely to receive clemency from the court in passing sentence, as a plea of guilty was always taken into consideration under these circumstances by the court; that if Avilés were willing to plead guilty, to get his story as to the connection of Chandler and any others who had not been named, and further, to assure Avilés that if he later decided to go to trial, his statement would not be used against him.[823]

The next significant development in what Chief Bielaski considered "a very important case" occurred when the federal grand jury in Los Angeles on February 19, 1915, heard testimony, including that from attorney Danziger and from Blanford, who recounted the admissions Baltazar Avilés and Gerónimo Sandoval had made to him. The grand jury returned an indictment against Harry Chandler, B. J. Viljoen, W. K. Bowker, Charles Guzmán, Baltazar Avilés, Gerónimo Sandoval, and Francisco Ayón. Ventura Palacio [Palacios] and Ignacio Díaz de León, who were included in the criminal complaint before the US Commissioner, were not indicted. When the defendants were arraigned, Avilés, Sandoval, and Ayón, not having attorneys, requested a delay to secure advice of counsel and plead to the indictment. Charles Guzmán, through his attorney, also asked for a delay. Harry Chandler, B. J. Viljoen, and W. K. Bowker, represented by their attorneys Oscar Lawler and William J. Hunsaker, were granted until March 29 to plead to the indictment. The defendants' bail was set at $3,000 each.[824]

Attorney Danziger was not included in the criminal complaint but, fearing possible arrest, had telephoned his friend Harry Chandler to be prepared to furnish bail for him in such an event. Chandler had refused. When Chandler was arrested on the indictment, he had stated to the press that his indictment was the result of efforts by a certain attorney in Los Angeles to blackmail him. The arrests made national news.[825] While no names were cited, Danziger knew, as did many others familiar with the facts, that he was the attorney to whom Chandler referred. Blanford informed Chief Bielaski that "the case is being prosecuted in the most satisfactory manner possible; I am convinced of the guilt of all parties concerned in this case as defendants but having had experience in such cases I have reason to fear that we will be unable to secure a conviction, which will naturally cause us to put forth stronger efforts to overcome this handicap. Danziger is himself an important witness in this case and it is hoped his goodwill may be maintained until the case is disposed of."[826]

Blanford reported that he had again interrogated through an interpreter Avilés and Sandoval in the county jail. They were no longer represented by Adolph Danziger, having replaced him with another attorney. Benjamin Viljoen also dispensed with Danziger's services, whereupon Danziger announced that his relations with Viljoen were no longer covered by attorney-client privilege, and he was prepared to testify against Viljoen and to provide documentation of interest to the Bureau. Danziger regaled Blanford at great length about his dealings with Avilés and Viljoen: Around January 1, 1915, Avilés had tried to borrow $8,000 from the C-M Company through Viljoen to buy the town of Tijuana from Colonel Mendieta, commanding the garrison. The attorney also related that Viljoen had urged Avilés to come to Los Angeles in connection with the libel suit Avilés instituted against J. F. Mauricio, editor of the newspaper La Prensa, for publishing an article alleging C-M had bribed Avilés with $30,000. Danziger also produced a crude map showing San Diego, the Coronado Islands, Ensenada and Tijuana, Baja California, explaining that the map indicated that San Diego and the Coronado Islands were to be used as shipping points and bases of supplies, respectively, for operations against Ensenada, Tijuana and other Baja California points.[827]

Regarding Avilés, Blanford reported: "Avilés was somewhat inclined to recede from his former position and declared that he did not wish to plead guilty to recruiting men on the American side. Avilés explained that the money he obtained from Harry Chandler through B. J. Viljoen, while intended to be used to reestablish himself in Lower California as governor, was in the nature of a loan and not a contribution [a distinction without a difference]. I made no further effort to persuade Avilés and Sandoval to adhere to their former position, but it's believed when the time comes, they'll plead guilty and turn state's evidence."[828] Danziger, incidentally, billed the Bureau $25 for "services rendered" in connection with the interrogation. Chief Bielaski disallowed the bill.[829]

Attorney Danziger, now eager to assist the Bureau, said that defense attorneys Oscar Lawler and others believed the government would drop the Chandler matter by letting time pass. Danziger expressed his fears in a letter to the Department of Justice.[830] He charged that the defendants were also warned that material witnesses Brassell and Costillo were going to leave the country and that it would be best for him to get a sworn statement from them in the case of Avilés vs La Prensa for libel. He had also heard that after Avilés entered his plea he would flee to Mexico. Blanford informed the assistant US attorney, and suggested that when the witnesses were first called, they be held in jail as material witnesses until the date of the trial. If any of these witnesses were offered money to leave the United States, they would be gone in a flash. Manuel Brassell called and informed Webster that José Costillo expected to leave for Sonora and did not know when he would return to the United States. The US attorney said he would get an order from the judge to hold Costillo in jail as a material witness until the trial.[831] Brassell, a tall, slender Hispanic who spoke very good English, would figure prominently in the Avilés case. He stated that he was a native of Chihuahua and had come to the US with his father, a Frenchman whom informant Kosterlitzky knew well. Brassell said, he and his brother Frank Brassell had become naturalized American citizens.[832]

Shedding further light on the Avilés matter was the latest batch of confiscated and translated papers from Avilés's file, including his personal code, and a self-serving letter from Harry Chandler to Viljoen dated on November 10, 1914:

> I've just read the infamous lies *La Prensa* published signed by a number of people in Mexicali. The statement about the C-M Company is a complete lie. We have no quarrel with Col. Cantú, and this has no bearing on lies about the C-M Company. You personally know of your own knowledge that the Company has never since you became an owner in the company and associated with the management paid one dollar of bribe money to Governor Avilés or any other Mexican official. In fact, since the company was organized in 1902, we have never yet been guilty of bribing any officer of the Mexican Government, local or national, to the extent of one dollar. We have always made it a rule to support loyally whatever regime of Governor is in charge of affairs in Lower California. We supported the Díaz Government, then the Madero Government, then the Huerta Government, and then when Col. Anaya came, representing himself as having

been appointed by Carranza and that his appointment had been approved by Villa, we were loyally preparing to support him. And now that Governor Avilés appears to have the powers of the Mexican Government behind him, we are determined to support him. We've invested heavily in the property, in taxes, duties, etc. with one exception — of bringing across cattle last April or May without a permit. This was done because of the unsettled conditions and because different officers offered to bring the cattle across upon the payment of only very small proportion of the exportation duty charged by other officers. We'd been advised by the Huerta government that the duties would be entirely remitted and that instructions had been sent to local authorities at Mexicali. We're now ready to pay whatever those in authority decide what's right. This infamous, lying statement to the effect that we have paid Governor Avilés $30,000 gold is just like a lot of their lies that have been put out from time to time about our company and our operations. Signers of this document, being Mexicans, are beyond the reach of US law, but I am endeavoring to have the publisher of this paper prosecuted for criminal libel. I feel that in justice to Governor Avilés we should, if possible to do so, bring about criminal prosecution against a newspaper which would print and circulate such infamous statements against an officer that, insofar as we have been able to see, is patriotically doing his duty.

Another interesting letter was from Avilés to Viljoen on December 27, 1914, acknowledging receipt from Viljoen of $5,000 as a loan for a six-months' term at five percent per annum for the purpose of reorganizing and reestablishing the government of Baja California for the Conventionist government of interim President Eulalio Gutiérrez by order and appointment of Avilés by General Villa and Governor Maytorena. The loan could be paid back sooner if Avilés chose.

Yet another noteworthy letter was from Viljoen to Avilés on December 29, 1914:

> I hope you have succeeded to make all the necessary arrangements. I hope you will act with great care so as not to violate any neutrality law; at the same time when you start act quick to not start anything and then delay; your success will depend upon the rapid way you go to work; accomplish your object before your opponents are aware of what is happening. But be well prepared when you strike; don't forget that after you have started it will be too late to turn back, so *cuidado*. I suggest that you have some hand bombs, this you may need very much, especially in taking the Cuartel [headquarters] or other buildings which may be occupied by the other side. I will be glad to hear from [you] often. Don't forget to let the wires be cut by some *compañeros* between Ensenada and Tijuana, and on the night of the assault on Mexicali let someone destroy the wires inside the town so they can't get reports out. You should have friends use dynamite in Mexicali when the attack starts. Please destroy this letter.[833]

A new element was interjected into the Avilés saga: witness intimidation. Material witnesses Manuel Brassell and Juan Fernández said they were walking near the Los Angeles post office on the night of March 26 when they spotted Avilés and Ayón following them. They claimed Avilés berated them for ratting him out and offered them money from the roll of bills he carried. They refused, Brassell saying it was money Avilés had gotten from Chandler and Bowker. Avilés then drew a pistol. Brassell told him he was not afraid, and to put the pistol up. Avilés did. The group walked to the door of a nearby church, and Avilés again offered them money not to testify, and he was again refused. Furious, Avilés intimated that Brassell and Fernández might not be around when the case came to trial. Brassell and Fernández reported the incident to Blanford, who had Brassell bring a couple of witnesses to the BI office, Brassell acting as interpreter and Blanford taking their statements. The US attorney filed a criminal complaint charging Avilés and Ayón with attempting to bribe and intimidate government witnesses. They were arrested, but were released on their own recognizance. Brassell also brought to the office three men whom he had recruited for Avilés in El Centro. Each of them gave a statement.

The Bureau continued to gather evidence for a hearing on the Avilés case, which had been postponed until April 5. But on April 5, only Charles Guzmán appeared, and he pled "not guilty." The judge was in San Diego at the time, so the hearing was postponed. At the hearing on April 28, Avilés, Ayón, and Sandoval pled "not guilty." Chandler, Bowker, and Viljoen were given until May 17 to enter their plea.[834]

The Bureau's new ally, attorney Danziger, called Webster to his office to impart additional information about the case. Danziger said Francisco Ayón had brought Avilés to his office. Avilés told Danziger he wanted him to be his attorney, but due to other facts was unable to employ him. Avilés said that it was Chandler who had put up the bail for Avilés, Ayón, and Sandoval. Danziger showed Avilés certain telegrams and letters he had concerning the case, and a few days later Danziger found them missing. He believed someone had stolen them, although it was possible, he had just misplaced them. In any case, Danziger had copies of everything. Danziger also complained that he was being shadowed, and he "stated that Chandler and his lawyer who is representing him claim that they will hang this matter up in the courts until the next administration and will then have it dropped as they think a Republican party will be in control of the next administration."[835]

Manuel Brassell produced a chauffeur who stated that Brassell and others had hired him to make a number of trips between December 14 and 31 between El Centro and Calexico, Imperial, Heber, Brawley, the C-M ranch and other places for the Avilés expedition. The chauffeur corroborated many of Brassell's statements to the Bureau. And munitions dealer R. L. Hall stated that he had recently purchased 400 30-30 rifles and sixty cases of ammunition from W. K. Bowker, munitions that had been cached at the C-M ranch for the Avilés expedition. Hall had had an agent at the ranch to handle these arms and he could produce the agent as a witness in the Avilés case.[836] Chief Bielaski, worried about a case as sensitive as one involving a personage such as Harry Chandler, traveled to Los Angeles in July.[837] We may speculate that besides meeting with Agent Blanford, Bielaski conferred with the reluctant US attorney Schoonover.

Additional bribery attempts further complicated the Avilés case. The lawyers for Chandler and the other defendants delivered to the assistant US attorney a letter ostensibly from Brassell and Fernández to one Manuel L. Velarde at Los Angeles on May 10, 1915, offering for $2,000 to retract their testimony before the grand jury and depart for Mexico prior to the Avilés trial. The US attorney had instructed Brassell and Fernández to take any bribe money offered and immediately report the matter to him, but above all, not to sign any paper.[838] Their signatures were on the letter. Blanford was told to see Brassell and Fernández and get their story. Brassell told Blanford in the US attorney's presence that Ed V. Vega, another witness in the Avilés case, had delivered to Fernández a note from Manuel Velarde asking the pair to call on him. They met Velarde at the Hollenbeck Hotel. Velarde told them Chandler had commissioned him to make them a proposition, showed them the letter, and requested that they sign it. Since they received no money, they said they would think the matter over. Several days later, Velarde met with them again and said payment had been arranged.

Handling that transaction would be none other than John M. Bowen, the former BI agent in charge at Los Angeles. Bowen had been disillusioned by the lack of support he received in neutrality cases from US attorney Schoonover, and he had recently resigned for a more lucrative private law practice with the firm of Oscar Lawler and W J. Hunsaker, attorneys for Avilés and Chandler.[839]

Bowen quizzed Brassell and Fernández at his office about government witnesses, whether the Bureau was going to take Brassell and Fernández to Calexico to secure additional witnesses, and other matters. Brassell insisted that they had come solely to discuss the proposed bribe. Since they still saw no cash, they refused to sign the letter. Brassell informed Blanford and the US attorney that both his and Fernández's signatures were forgeries, and produced twenty receipts for dues from August 1908 to August 1913 in a fraternal order in Nogales bearing his genuine signature. The Bureau also had the memorandum book Brassell had delivered, and in which he had signed his name. In sum, Brassell's and Fernández's signatures on the letter were a forgery. Evidently, the Avilés defense team had made a clumsy attempt to discredit the two government witnesses.

But Brassell, the government's key witness, was hardly the most reputable of citizens. Bowen informed Webster that witnesses Manuel Brassell and Juan Fernández were nothing but crooks. He had done a background investigation, and before the trial was over, would make the government swear out a white slave case against Brassell. Bowen also stated, "that the men which [sic] Brassell and Fernández and others allege to have been recruited in the Imperial Valley were never in the Imperial Valley, and that they will prove an alibi for all men alleged to have been recruited by Brassell and others for Avilés." On entering Bowen's office, Webster found Juan Córdova, one of the government's witnesses in this case, waiting to be interviewed. "Agent is of the opinion that all witnesses in this case are being interviewed by Bowen, and thereby ascertaining what they will testify to when this case is tried."[840]

To the Bureau's discomfiture, former Agent in Charge Bowen's assertion that he would make the government file a white slave case against Brassell was not an empty threat. Brassell had previously been associated with a prostitute named Anita Carrillo, and Bowen intimated that Brassell had recently taken her across state lines—from San Diego to El Paso—in violation of the Mann Act to ply her trade. A worried Blanford contacted Agent C. E. Breniman in El Paso to investigate Carrillo's activities and interview her regarding her connection with Brassell. Blanford enclosed a photograph of Carrillo.[841]

Tending to support Bowen's characterization of Manuel Brassell as a crook was R. L. Hall's account of a failed military expedition. According to Hall, Carranza officer Eduardo Casillas wanted to lead an expedition against Colonel Esteban Cantú at Mexicali. Casillas secured the services of Manuel Brassell, whom he appointed second in command and tasked with organizing and setting on foot the expedition. Brassell induced one Flavio Sandoval, a *carrancista* sympathizer, to finance the venture to the tune of $1,310 in cash, delivered to R. L. Hall, and a promissory note for $1,500 due in three months, in return for which Sandoval would get control of Mexicali. Brassell, Juan Fernández, and Ed V. Vega, all witnesses in the Avilés case, made the rounds of towns in the Imperial Valley of California, apparently to put the plan into operation. Hall produced receipts Brassell had signed in May for expenses and for purchasing 100 30-30 carbines and 10,000 rounds of ammunition, as well as canteens and other equipment. "Hall stated that the entire purchase amounted to $3,100; that it is his opinion that the plan will never be carried out, and that Brassell is simply working the scheme to get some easy money."[842]

A worried Blanford interrogated Brassell about Hall's claim that Brassell, Fernández, and Vega were organizing a Carranza force in the vicinity of Calexico to invade Baja California. Brassell was noncommittal but did not deny the truth of the report, stating he knew where the Bureau got the information, and mentioned R. L. Hall as the source. Evidently, Brassell and Hall had had a falling out over money, and Brassell claimed that Hall was really the man behind the failed expedition. Brassell put the

Bureau in a bind. The US attorney admonished Brassell, but Blanford stated that "it is not desired at this time to institute any proceedings involving Brassell, Fernández, and Vega as they are important witnesses in the Avilés case."[843]

While all this scheming was going on, Harry Chandler and W. K. Bowker on May 24, 1915, entered pleas of "not guilty." B. J. Viljoen was given until May 27 to plead because he was recovering from an operation. Blanford speculated that the case would probably be set for trial in July.[844]

Blanford advised Webster to hire an informant in Los Angeles, and send him to Calexico if conditions made it necessary. "Agent contacted Fred Boden, who speaks Spanish and who has worked for Carranza and Villa along the border and who is familiar with Mexicans, to work on this matter. He said he'd accept $4/day and expenses to go to Mexicali."[845] Boden reported from Calexico that Antonio León Grajeda, ex-Consul General for Huerta at San Francisco, was now working for Colonel Cantú at Mexicali. Francisco Siqueiros, editor of *La Libertad* printed in San Bernardino, was in constant communication with Manuel García in Calexico. Enrique de la Sierra, manager of the Calexico Meat Market, was the former Huerta consul at San Diego, El Paso, and Calexico. De la Sierra received all his mail through Box 623 at Calexico.[846]

An encouraging sign from the government's point of view was that Webster, with Manuel Brassell interpreting, spoke with defendant Gerónimo Sandoval, who said he would be willing to turn state's evidence in return for immunity. Blanford referred the matter to the US attorney, who asked Blanford to have Sandoval make a statement and to assure Sandoval that it would not be used against him provided the government, after hearing his statement, did not wish to dismiss the case against him. Sandoval, however, decided to do nothing until he had spoken with a Los Angeles attorney who was a friend of his. Nevertheless, Webster was sent to San Diego to obtain a sworn statement from Sandoval and to promise him immunity. Sandoval failed to appear to meet with Webster and the assistant US attorney as promised, whereupon the attorney declared he would not try to obtain Sandoval as a government witness, and would let him remain a defendant.[847]

The Avilés case was set for trial on November 23, 1915.

A major problem for the government was that its witnesses, mainly Mexicans, were scattered in various towns in Southern California. The US attorney wanted Webster to track down and interview each witness and obtain a statement as to what each would testify. Regardless of how unsavory Manuel Brassell might be, the Bureau had to continue to rely on him. Webster, after losing track of Brassell, ran into him on the street at Los Angeles and took him to the US marshal's office, where Deputy Marshal Fenton G. Thompson served a subpoena on him. At the US attorney's request, "Not knowing the addresses of many of the Mexican witnesses in this case, Agent instructed Brassell to accompany Thompson in serving the subpoenas and would pay him for this time as the Marshal stated he has no fund out of which to pay him."[848] Webster informed Chief Bielaski that "most of the parties subpoenaed are Mexicans and Thompson not being able to locate same as they change their residence so often. If witnesses are re-interviewed, it will entail the expense of an interpreter who speaks Spanish."[849] Bielaski instructed him to interview each witness and obtain a statement as to what each would testify.[850]

Webster reported from San Diego that Gerónimo Sandoval had just returned from Los Angeles, and while there had allegedly learned that Chandler and others had paid Manuel Brassell not to testify in this case. Webster phoned Blanford recommending immediate action due to Brassell's failure to appear to testify before the grand jury in the intimidation of a witness case of Avilés and Ayón.[851]

Brassell called at the Bureau office with a translation of an article just published in *El Correo Mexicano*, of Los Angeles. In it, Avilés defendant Ignacio Díaz de León, styling himself "colonel," bitterly attacked Brassell as a spy interested only in the money he made by falsely denouncing to the authorities his fellow Mexicans. An indignant Brassell sued the newspaper's editors for libel, and a week later they published a retraction, stating that only Díaz de León was to blame.[852]

Another incident of alleged bribery involved Severino Rodríguez, one of the witnesses in the pending intimidation case against Avilés for having tried to bribe and to threaten Brassell. Rodríguez stated that he was invited to attorney Bowen's office, where Bowen and another lawyer questioned him through an interpreter. Rodríguez alleged that Bowen gave him $2 and promised him $45 per month, provided he would deny he had witnessed Avilés offer Brassell money on the street or draw a pistol. According to Rodríguez, Bowen had him sign a statement to that effect, and told him he would see him later. Another witness, Juan Córdova, was later seen in Bowen's office.[853]

The government's most important witness, Manuel Brassell, was currently in El Paso, and when the US marshal's office notified him to appear in Los Angeles on September 21, 1915, to testify before the grand jury, Brassell said he lacked the money to make the trip. He next wrote from Las Vegas, New Mexico, explaining that he had not gone to Los Angeles as instructed for lack of funds. Blanford informed Brassell that another subpoena would be served on him at Las Vegas, and stressed that Brassell must absolutely be in Los Angeles on November 23 for the trial. He would receive a witness fee and mileage reimbursement from the government.[854]

An interesting development in the process of locating and serving subpoenas on government witnesses occurred when Webster traveled to Tijuana and interviewed rancher Pedro Badillo, who said that about January 24, 1915, Adolph Danziger introduced himself on the street and announced that Baltazar Avilés had sent him to discuss purchasing the Tijuana garrison. Badillo, it turned out, had been negotiating for Avilés with the garrison commander, Colonel Mendieta, for some time before Danziger's appearance. Badillo said Danziger drove him to Avilés's residence in San Diego. Enroute, Danziger informed Badillo that he would have to obtain an inventory of all arms and ammunition in the

Tijuana garrison before General Viljoen and the Company he represented would be willing to pay Colonel Mendieta $8,000 to turn the garrison over to Avilés. Badillo said he asked Danziger what company, and the attorney replied that "it was the California-Mexico Land and Cattle Co. composed of [Harrison Gray] Otis and Harry Chandler, and that the latter would not put up the money unless an inventory was obtained." Badillo pointed out that trying to conduct such an inventory was suicidal. "Danziger informed Badillo that the people he represented knew they could only obtain the garrison through Avilés."

At the residence of Avilés, Badillo asked Avilés if he had instructed Danziger to have Badillo count the munitions in the garrison. Avilés said he had not, and Danziger denied ever having made such a suggestion to Badillo. "Badillo stated upon Aviles learning from him in Danziger's presence that Danziger had informed him who was to pay for the garrison, Chandler, Viljoen and others, he became angry and asked Danziger what he meant by implicating the men whom he was to obtain the money from, and ordered Danziger to leave his house, cursing him as he went." Badillo asserted that if Avilés had not been arrested, Colonel Mendieta would have accepted the proposition. Webster commented that "Badillo appears to be a little frightened about answering the subpoena which was served upon him as he is inclined to believe the Government might desire to prosecute him for what part [he] took in the matter. Agent assured him that the Government only desires him as a witness and that no harm will come to him while on American territory. Agent will interview Badillo again upon his arrival in Los Angeles when he answers the subpoena, as Agent is of the opinion that he did not care to talk freely while on Mexican territory. Badillo will favor the Government as he is very anxious to see several of the defendants convicted."[855]

When Webster interviewed an Immigration inspector at San Isidro, across the boundary from Tijuana, he learned that Pedro Badillo had confided in him Avilés's attempt to purchase the Tijuana garrison, adding that Badillo was to receive $2,000 extra as his commission if he put the deal through. Badillo had offered the inspector $1,000 of this commission if he helped Badillo negotiate the matter. The inspector said he told Badillo he wanted no part of the affair, and he wrote to his superior in Los Angeles detailing the incident.[856]

At Calexico, Webster had been trying to secure from Western Union copies of the many telegrams sent and received by Bowker, Anaya, and Noonan, among others. The local manager refused to comply unless he had authorization from his superior in Los Angeles. That individual informed Webster that the only way he would obtain the copies was by legal proceedings. Webster conferred with US Attorney Schoonover and began the paperwork for a subpoena duces tecum. Later, the San Diego manager confidentially showed Webster twenty-nine telegrams that had passed through his office between December 15, 1914, and February 15, 1915, between several of those prominent in the Avilés affair. Because the telegrams were in Spanish, Webster did not copy them, but suggested that they be obtained through a subpoena duces tecum.[857]

Offsetting this gain, District Judge Oscar Trippet had the Avilés case continued. Trippet ordered the government to supply the defendants with a bill of particulars.

The Avilés case was now scheduled for trial on May 16, 1916.

Blanford informed Chief Bielaski of this setback, saying the defense had requested this order for the express purpose of causing delay. Blanford also notified Manuel Brassell that he need not be at Los Angeles on November 23.[858]

A most interesting slant on the Avilés case came from former Agent in Charge Bowen. Referring to the Anaya-Noonan expedition against Mexicali in September 1914, he told Webster that the Anaya matter was never presented by the US attorney although the BI had developed a very strong case against Anaya, Bowker, Chandler and others, and that it was much stronger than the present case against Avilés, Chandler et al. Therefore, Bowen was confident that the government would never secure a conviction in the Avilés case.[859] Blanford sent the

Anaya-Noonan file over to the assistant US attorney, M. G. Gallaher, pointing out that Harry Chandler and Walter Bowker, defendants in the Avilés case, were also implicated in the Anaya conspiracy, for which a fairly good case could be made. He asked whether Gallaher intended to take any action.[860]

Blanford informed the US attorney in January 1916, that Colonel Justino Mendieta, commander of the Tijuana garrison under Cantú when Avilés had negotiated with him to purchase the garrison for $8,000, was in Los Angeles. The US attorney issued a subpoena for Mendieta's apprehension as a witness in the forthcoming Avilés trial. Bureau informant Colonel Kosterlitzky accompanied Mendieta to the field office, where Mendieta spoke with the US attorney and acknowledged the $8,000 proposition negotiated through Pedro Badillo. Mendieta was about to leave for Cuba where he planned to go into business, but was quite willing to return and testify in the Avilés case.[861]

Blanford referred to Bielaski's letter of January 24 concerning Anaya and Noonan. Shortly after receiving it, Blanford spoke with attorney John M. Bowen, who said he did not recall the conversation with Webster about Anaya referred to in Webster's report and Bielaski's letter. Blanford presented the case to assistant US attorney M. G. Gallaher, leaving the file with him. Blanford asked Gallaher his opinion several times but had received no response so far, which had delayed Blanford's responding to Bielaski's letter. Gallaher was not connected with the US attorney's office when the case was first presented. "As he has shown a disposition to handle the neutrality violations rather vigorously, I anticipated that he would take this case up either separately or if possible, in connection with the Baltasar Aviles case. I shall advise you as soon as Mr. Gallaher has reached a decision."[862]

Manuel G. Brassell wrote to Blanford on March 8, from 1504 East Overland St., El Paso. He had recently been in Mexico as far south as Aguascalientes. On the trip, he met his friend Fernández at Santa Rosalía (now Camargo), Chihuahua. Brassell wrote: "Should you need me to assist you in any way call on me. I will be glad to do so at all times. With regards to Mr. Webster and yourself."[863] Blanford wrote back saying that the Avilés trial was now set for May and "your presence here at that time will be desired." He added that the deputy US marshal wanted Brassell to assist him in locating the other witnesses since they would have to be subpoenaed again. Blanford asked Brassell to keep him advised of his whereabouts.[864]

Blanford reported that "As this case is not due to come up until May 16 and not having been advised of any arrangement whereby the case was not to be tried on that date as scheduled, I interviewed Asst. US Attorney Gallaher, who is handling the case. He said the attorney for Viljoen said Viljoen is still physically unable to stand trial; that Gallaher took the position that he did not care to bring the defendant into court on a stretcher and try him; that he also preferred to try all defendants in this case at the same time as in that event they would have to tell the same story, should they take the stand in their own behalf, whereas if defendants were tried separately each could tell a story to suit his own case; that Gallaher consulted with Oscar Lawler, principal attorney for the defense, and Lawler stated it was perfectly agreeable with him for the case to go over until next term; that when US Attorney Albert Schoonover, who is now in Washington in connection with the Government's oil land suits, was recently in Los Angeles he took the matter of the trial of this case and ventured the opinion that in the present state of relations between US and Mexico it was not advisable to try the Avilés case and would be better to try the [Flores] Magón case instead. (The Magón case as is probably known, is a case against Enrique and Ricardo Flores Magón and W. C. Owen for sending through the mails matter printed in *Regeneración* tending to incite murder, assassination and arson); that it is virtually settled that the Aviles case will not be tried on May 16 but will be reset for trial during the next term of court."[865] Gallaher moved to continue Avilés's trial from May 16 until next term of court which opened in July, on account of illness of defendant Viljoen.[866]

Agent Breniman at Tucson wired Barnes at San Antonio that "[Eliseo] Arredondo, Mexican Ambassador [sic], telegraphed E. V. Anaya, Tucson last night for list refugee political offenders this locality. Anaya pretends publicly to be neutral, but I have positive information is in communication with Mexican [Carranza] consul Nogales and planning assist recruiting." Breniman transmitted this message to special employee William Neunhoffer at Nogales, instructing him to advise American Consul Simpich and the military.[867]

After yet another continuance, the Avilés trial was set for September 12, 1916.

The point worth stressing is that each time the Avilés case was continued, the Bureau was ordered to locate the numerous witnesses and have subpoenas served on them. This was a daunting task, as the following examples illustrate.

US attorney Schoonover asked the BI field office to furnish him with names and whereabouts of witnesses in the Avilés case so subpoenas could be served on them. Blanford went through the office files and reported on the whereabouts of numerous witnesses, adding that where the present whereabouts of witnesses were doubtful, they would be looked up.[868] He felt it advisable to secure the services of witness Manuel Brassell to locate other witnesses in this case.[869] Webster informed Gershon at San Diego that subpoenas were being issued and forwarded to the deputy US marshal there for service for Pedro Badillo, Luis Rivas Isais, Pedro Martínez, José Costillo, Frank G. Kiessig, Archie Aldrich, J. M. Wood, and F. A. Bennett. Should these parties not be readily located by the marshal, Gershon was to assist in ascertaining their whereabouts so that subpoenas could be served.[870]

Still engaged in the thankless task of trying to track down witnesses, Webster checked with the post office for information about other witnesses' change of address.[871] None of them was known as a caller at General Delivery. Webster went to 107 South Utah St. where Manuel Brassell's brother lived. The Mexican family at this address had been living there for the past nine months and knew no one named Brassell.[872] He also learned that witness Count Wilhelm von Hardenberg was no longer residing at the Crown Hill Apartments. He was said to be living at an apartment house on Olive Street. Webster hired Martínez, who tracked down a number of people. One was in prison somewhere else in California, seven others he could not contact, while one was said to have worked for the Mexican secret service and disappeared.[873]

Dave Gershon reported from San Diego that per Webster's letter of August 1, he interviewed Deputy Marshal W. C. Carse, who said he had all the witnesses located except Pedro Badillo, José Costillo, and W. Sherman Bacon. Gershon located Bacon at 1230 Broadway, and personally served him with a subpoena. Gershon planned to locate the other two witnesses the next day when he went to Tijuana. He did indeed locate Pedro Badillo, a rancher in Mexico who seldom crossed the border. Gershon found him in a pool hall in Tijuana with the assistance of William Dato, chief of police at the racetrack (and Colonel Esteban Cantú's brother-in-law.) In Dato's presence, Gershon asked Badillo if he would accept service of a subpoena to appear in US court in Los Angeles. Badillo replied that it made no difference to him whether he was subpoenaed in Mexico or in the US, and that he would accept service, so Gerson personally served him with the subpoena. He was now trying to locate José Costillo.[874]

Blanford wrote to Gershon at San Diego: "I notice in your reports that you have personally served subpoenas on Pedro Badillo and W. Sherman Bacon. As to you not being able to make valid returns on these subpoenas, I advise you that it would be best to have the deputy marshal serve these subpoenas as then there will be no question raised if these witnesses do not appear at the proper time as to the propriety of the service on these subpoenas. Therefore, please see that the proper service is made on these subpoenas."[875]

Deputy US Marshal Walton informed Webster that he had been unable to locate Count Wilhelm von Hardenberg to serve a subpoena on him. He was not at the Angelo Apartments, nor at Flower Street as previously reported. Webster would try to locate him. Webster received a letter from J. M. West, city marshal at Needles, California: "I have no record of Timoteo Córdova."[876]

Porfirio Brassell, Manuel's brother, called at the Los Angeles field office and said he had not heard from Manuel for three or four months. The last time he heard, Manuel was in Albuquerque. Porfirio was leaving for El Paso to visit their sister, Amelia Aguirre, 1304 East Overland St., and said he would inform the office if he located Manuel. Webster suggested that Agent in Charge Barnes have the proper officer make a further effort to locate Manuel before Porfirio saw him, as Porfirio worked for the *Los Angeles Times*, which was owned by Harry Chandler and his father-in-law Harrison Gray Otis, and in all probability was going to Texas to look for his brother to prevent him from coming to Los Angeles to testify in this case. Webster said he would not be surprised if Porfirio Brassell had received instructions from his employers to keep Manuel from coming to Los Angeles to testify.[877]

US Attorney Schoonover informed Webster that attorney Tom L. Johnson, who had obtained José F. Costillo's release when the latter was being held in county jail as a material witness in this case, supposedly knew Costillo's whereabouts. Webster called at the office of the attorney, who said the last time he had heard from Costillo was by mail about three weeks earlier, and at that time Costillo was in San Diego.[878]

Gershon at San Diego was still trying to locate witnesses José F. Costillo, Ramón Sánchez, and Frank Núñez whom Deputy Marshal Carse had been unable to find. Webster did locate Luis Rivas Isais in Los Angeles and asked him if he knew Costillo's whereabouts. Rivas said Costillo had returned from Arizona four or five weeks earlier. He met Costillo on Main Street in Los Angeles but did not know where Costillo resided or where he worked. He suggested contacting Detective Rice of the Los Angeles police department who knew Costillo and might know where he was. Isais was positive that Costillo was not in San Diego or Tijuana. Roberto Farfán, one of Governor Cantú's henchmen, promised to help locate Costillo and Sánchez.[879]

Deputy Marshal Carse returned from the Imperial Valley and advised Gershon that in addition to José F. Costillo, he had been unable to locate Frank Núñez and Ramón Sánchez. Gershon had been conducting a thorough search for Costillo and had not been able to locate him. He would do everything possible to locate these witnesses so they could be served with subpoenas.[880] Gershon proceeded to El Centro to try to locate witnesses Ramón Sánchez and José F. Costillo so the marshal could serve subpoenas on them. He located Sánchez at the Fourth Street Hotel; Sánchez said the marshal could serve him there. Gershon asked Sánchez if he knew Costillo. He said, "No."[881] But then Blanford wired Gershon that Costillo had left Los Angeles on June 13, 1916, to work for the Imperial Irrigation District, of which C. R. Rockwood was chief engineer, at Calexico. Blanford understood that Costillo was sent across the border to work but believed Gershon could easily arrange with Rockwood to have him recalled to this side of border, where the subpoena could be served on him.[882] At Calexico, the paymaster of the Imperial Irrigation District and Gershon went over payrolls very thoroughly but failed to find José P. Costillo's name for June, July, or August. The paymaster was positive Costillo was not employed by them at present.[883]

With Deputy Sheriff Henry González acting as interpreter, Gershon made a thorough search for Costillo both in Calexico and Mexicali, but was unable to find anyone who even knew such a man. He interviewed all the Mexican officials in Mexicali and many Mexicans in Calexico, but was unable to secure any information whatever about Costillo.[884]

A thoroughly frustrated Gershon next tried San Diego, using two Mexican informants, but they reported that no one knew Costillo's whereabouts. Gershon again hunted up witness Luis Rivas Isais, who said he had heard nothing but thought Costillo was in Los Angeles. He said Costillo was a clerk and would hardly be found doing any kind of manual labor. Rivas Isais was going to Los Angeles shortly and would do what he could to locate Costillo. He speculated that since Costillo was an important witness, perhaps Avilés was paying him to hide out until after the trial. Gershon gave Rivas Isais Blanford's address and told him to call on Blanford when he arrived in Los Angeles. He promised to do so.[885]

Webster hoped witness Timoteo Córdova might shed light on Costillo's whereabouts, but he learned that Córdova was said to be in the state penitentiary at Florence, Arizona. Webster contacted the warden, stating that he understood that Timoteo Córdova was an inmate, and if so, to please inform him when Córdova would be released. Webster also asked the warden to learn from Córdova the whereabouts of his brother Juan Córdova. Webster needed this information as soon as possible, enclosing a self-addressed envelope requiring no postage. Warden S. M. Sims replied that Timoteo Córdova, convict No. 4823, was serving a sentence of from one to five years for burglary in the first degree, from August 14, 1916, and "we are unable to foretell his release." At least Gershon was able to provide a description of Costillo.[886]

Agent Webster wrote to witness Juan N. Fernández, Colonia 6 Abajo, in Jiménez, Chihuahua (300 miles south of El Paso), saying he understood Fernández had communicated with Ed. V. Vega and informed Vega he was willing to go to El Paso to be served with a subpoena to testify in Avilés case. Webster assured Fernández that money for transportation would be arranged through Agent E. B. Stone in El Paso, who would also instruct the US marshal to advance Fernández $3 per day witness fee. Webster requested an immediate reply, as the Avilés trial was set for September 12. Should Fernández have sufficient funds, he was to proceed at once to El Paso and be served with a subpoena by the marshal in the post office building. Webster informed Stone, emphasizing that US attorney Schoonover was very anxious to have Fernández appear as a witness.[887]

In a further effort to locate Manuel Brassell, whom Bradford described as "an indispensable witness," he dispatched the following telegrams: To Agent Stone at El Paso, "Please again inquire 304 East

Overland whereabouts Manuel Brassell. Suggest covering mail as may be attempting concealment. Answer."; and to local officer George C. Taylor at Albuquerque, "Please again interview F. G. Brassell reference whereabout brother Manuel. Suggest covering mail as may be endeavoring to conceal whereabouts. Answer." Blanford received the following on August 31 from Agent Stone: "In interview with Mrs. Aguirre, 304 Overland Street, she states Brassell is now in Globe, Arizona, working as insurance agent, or was there last week. He is in communication with his brother in Albuquerque all the time who in turn corresponds with Mrs. Aguirre who is sister to both. Post Office address in Globe is General Delivery. Name of insurance company for whom he works is unknown. Would suggest Agent Barnes have further investigations made at Albuquerque and Globe assisting you." From local officer Taylor: "Brassell out of town. Wife insists knows nothing brother whereabouts. Will request Postmaster cover mail." As result of information contained in Agent Stone's telegram, Blanford dispatched the following: "To Local Officer Shaffer, Globe, Arizona. Desire locate Manuel Brassell witness case here. Said be Globe working as insurance agent probably Kansas City Life Insurance Co. Address General Delivery. Please locate and wire me. Important. Do not allow Brassell know looking for him. Also advise if Deputy Marshal at Globe."[888] Blanford took this matter up directly with local officer Shaffer instead of through Agent in Charge Barnes in order to facilitate matters. Blanford wired local officer Taylor in Albuquerque that he was wiring Barnes to authorize Taylor to spare no time nor expense in locating Brassell.[889]

Agent T. E. Campbell at Kansas City, Missouri, reported that Blanford had wired him to secure from the Kansas City Life Insurance Company the address of Brassell, the company's agent in Arizona. Campbell went to Rialto Building where the life insurance's offices were located, and learned that the company did not have the exact address; that he was addressed c/o O. J. Durand, Albuquerque, who had charge of agents in that field. Campbell was told that Brassell could be located through Durand. He so wired Blanford. Blanford noted that Durand was the general agent for New Mexico and Arizona. The Company wired to Durand that the Bureau was trying to locate Brassell and instructed him to assist. Blanford wired local officer Taylor at Albuquerque that he believed Durand and Manuel Brassell's brother were both attempting to conceal his whereabouts.[890]

Blanford cast his net for witnesses even farther. Colonel Kosterlitzky advised Blanford in July that he had received a letter from Colonel Justino Mendieta, one of the witnesses in this case, stating that Mendieta left Havana on May 28 for Oaxaca in Mexico.[891] Kosterlitzky advised that Colonel Justino Mendieta's address in Havana was "En Lista" (General Delivery) and that he went from Havana to Salina Cruz, Mexico, and from there to city of Oaxaca. Kosterlitzky said Mendieta had a brother, Ismael Mendieta, in Oaxaca, and he would furnish the brother's address. If US attorney approved, Blanford planned to send a telegram to Ismael Mendieta requesting him to communicate with his brother advising Justino that his presence was desired in Los Angeles on September 12. With the authorization of US attorney Schoonover and his assistant Gallaher, Blanford wired Ismael Mendieta at Marquesada 139, Oaxaca, Oaxaca, Mexico, asking him to advise his brother Colonel Justino Mendieta that his presence was desired in Los Angeles on September 12 to testify in the Avilés case. All expenses were guaranteed, and Justino was to come at once. If Justino could come, he was to answer a collect phone call.[892]

Given the trial of the Avilés case was imminent, Harry Chandler applied to the court for a continuance because of an operation he had on August 23, and on account of the alleged necessity for another operation within a few days to relieve a serious condition in the nasal cavity on one side of his face. The eye, ear, nose, and throat specialist who was treating him, as well as another physician, took the stand at a hearing and testified that it would be detrimental to Chandler's health to require him to be confined for a period of two or three weeks, as would be necessary in the trial of this case. US attorney Schoonover had a physician of his own selection examine Chandler and reported the condition as outlined by Chandler's physician did exist and stated that danger to Chandler's health by forcing a trial at this time was appreciable. The doctor confirmed that if Chandler were a patient of his he would much prefer that he be not subjected to an ordeal requiring the attention and nervous strain necessitated by a trial beginning September 12. He agreed that the patient's health should be much improved in the ordinary course of treatment within fifty or ninety days.

The Avilés case was continued until November 14, 1916.

Agent Stone wired from El Paso that Juan N. Fernández from Jiménez had reported to him, and was served by the deputy marshal, who would have transportation ready for him. Fernández said he would leave for Los Angeles on the Southern Pacific the following day. Blanford wired Stone that case was continued because of the illness of the two defendants Chandler and Viljoen. Fernández was to render an itemized bill of expenses between Jiménez in El Paso and return if he desired to return, and to forward the bill to Blanford. Stone was to have Fernández keep Blanford advised of his whereabouts so he could be instructed whether or not report in November. Fernández wanted funds in order to return to Jiménez, and Blanford ordered that they be furnished. Fernández wrote from El Paso that Agent in Charge Barnes gave him $15 which only covered his return trip. His expense bill was $59, and he wanted the rest. Blanford wired Barnes that Fernández would be reimbursed provided he submitted an itemized bill. Blanford sent $20, and when he received authority from Washington would forward the remainder. But being a government witness, at least in this case, had a cost: Fernández, back home at Jiménez, wrote concerning his expense account. He justified his expenses, saying he had a small grocery store and had to close it during his trip. When he returned, he found he had been robbed of everything.[893]

Blanford wired local officer Taylor in Albuquerque that the case had been continued until November 14 because of illness of two defendants, and if Brassell were located, to admonish him to keep Blanford advised of his whereabouts. Blanford also wired Ismael Mendieta to advise his bother Justino that his presence in Los Angeles was not desired until November 14 because of the continuance.[894]

Colonel Justino Mendieta wrote from his exile in Havana both to the Bureau and to his comrade Kosterlitzky that he was willing to testify against Avilés. He was informed that the case had been postponed until November 14, when his presence in Los Angeles would be desired, and directing him to keep the Bureau office advised of his address so he could be notified whether or not to appear.[895]

Pedro Badillo, who was not notified in time of the continuance, responded to the subpoena. Blanford interviewed him. Badillo said on January 19, 1915, he and wife had dined with Avilés at a restaurant in San Diego. Avilés brought up the subject of purchasing the Tijuana garrison from the commanding officer, Colonel Justino Mendieta. On January 21, he saw Avilés at the latter's house, and Avilés said he would give Mendieta $8,000 and Badillo $2,000 for consummating the deal. He saw Mendieta in Tijuana on January 23, and put the proposition to him. Mendieta told him to get the $10,000, which they would split 50-50, and Mendieta would retain the garrison. Adolph Danziger, whom Badillo did not know before that, approached him in Tijuana on January 24, 1915, telling him that he had come with Avilés, who remained on the US side, as a representative of Avilés and Viljoen and of the Otis and Chandler's C-M ranch. He said he wanted to check up on men and equipment in the garrison, and complete arrangements for the transfer of Colonel Mendieta. Badillo declined to go with Danziger to Mendieta and refused to acknowledge even that he had any business transactions with either Avilés or Mendieta, not knowing Danziger or what trap might have been laid for him. At Danziger's suggestion, Badillo went to the US side where Danziger had left Avilés in a car and found that Avilés had returned to his San Diego home. He went with Danziger to Avilés's home and when Avilés learned that Danziger had told Badillo that Viljoen and the C-M ranch were behind him in this deal, Avilés became furious and denounced Danziger very bitterly. Prior to his talk with Danziger, Avilés had merely told him that Avilés was not furnishing the money to buy the garrison, but was backed by parties in Los Angeles. Based upon the conversation, Badillo gathered that Avilés had sent Danziger to Tijuana in order that he might be assured that everything was arranged and that the garrison would be surrendered on payment of $10,000. On January 21, Avilés gave Badillo a letter to Mendieta which Avilés sealed in his presence after having read it to him hurriedly. Badillo took the letter, but desiring to know its full contents, opened and read it, but did not give it to Mendieta as it potentially implicated him as the originator of the idea, and the chief conspirator. Badillo still had the letter, which he turned over to Blanford. Badillo stated that this was his only connection with the transaction in question.

Blanford quoted the letter, which was in Spanish, and was translated by Kosterlitzky: "San Diego, Jan 21, 1915, Lt. Col. Justino Mendieta, Tijuana. On various occasions Pedro Badillo had made me propositions in your name, tending to deliver to me the arms you have at this place and that you would retreat with your force, under the only condition that Mr. Badillo place at your disposal the sum of eight thousand dollars, all this under the highest reserve. For my part I see no inconvenience in accepting this proposition but on condition that you will acknowledge by writing the delivery of said sum, for you must understand that otherwise we could not effect this operation. Awaiting your reply so as to place at the disposal of Mr. Badillo or you direct if you so prefer the sum mentioned, I am, Yours truly [signed] B. Avilés." The original letter and envelope were marked for identification by Badillo who wrote his name on the back of each.[896]

To Blanford's great relief, he received a break with one witness, at last. Manuel Brassell telegraphed: "If you want me, I am in Phoenix." Blanford wired back to Brassell telling him the trial had been postponed until November 14 and instructing him to leave his address with the US marshal so a subpoena could be served. Blanford advised Schoonover and Gallaher that Brassell had reported. Since the insurance supervisor, Durand, and Brassell's brother were trying to conceal Brassell's movements, Schoonover decided to subpoena Brassell before grand jury on September 11 and interrogate him regarding the case. Disturbingly, Brassell failed to appear. Blanford wired the US marshal in Phoenix asking whether a subpoena had been served. US Marshal J. Dillon replied that Brassell was served by his deputy on receipt of a wire from the US attorney. Brassell showed Dillon a wire stating it was not necessary for him to appear. Blanford also received a telegram from local officer Taylor at Albuquerque stating that he had just been advised positively that Manuel G. Brassell was at Ajo, Arizona, remaining indefinitely and glad to testify. Brassell wrote from Sonora, Arizona, on October 3, that he would be working there for a couple of weeks. If his presence was required, to notify him and forward transportation. Blanford notified US marshal that Brassell was in Sonora.[897]

But the Avilés case took still another turn. One of the defense attorneys, W. J. Hunsaker, filed an affidavit to the effect that he was engaged in a case set for trial in Superior Court, Los Angeles County, on November 13, 1916, which would require about three weeks for trial, and requested that the Avilés case be continued. The Court, over the strenuous objections of the US Attorney, granted the continuance.[898]

The Avilés case was continued until December 5, 1916.

Given this latest continuance, Blanford conferred with Gallaher on how best to notify witnesses of that fact and secure their presence in Los Angeles on December 5. Blanford duly prepared a list of witnesses with the addresses at which they were recently served. Gallaher suggested that new subpoenas be issued and served at once. He informed Gershon that the trial was again postponed, and that the defense had subpoenaed from San Diego witnesses David Zárate and Luis D. Cach. Gershon was to interview these witnesses and learn what they would testify. Blanford was convinced these witnesses were subpoenaed in order to impeach Manuel G. Brassell, the government's chief witness.[899]

Gershon called on Luis G. Cach, formerly a justice of the peace at Ensenada, who said he did not understand why he had been subpoenaed, since he knew nothing about case or about Brassell. He knew Avilés only by sight, having met him but once after Avilés's arrival in Baja California, and could be classed as being absolutely opposed to Avilés and his activities. Gershon also interviewed David Zárate at his office in the Central Mortgage Building. Zárate said he did not know why he was subpoenaed, as he knew nothing about the case and was not friendly toward Avilés. Zárate declared that he did not know Manuel Brassell, and had never heard of him before. Zárate was formerly mayor of Ensenada and was acting governor of the Northern District of Baja California when Avilés arrived with his commission from Villa as governor; it was he who turned the government over to Avilés. Zárate was of the opinion that he was subpoenaed by the defense to testify that Avilés was at the time of his arrest in the above-entitled matter, the legally appointed governor of Baja California.[900]

Deputy Marshal Carse at San Diego informed the US marshal that Frank Núñez, for whom a subpoena was issued, was really Frank Snee, who was now in jail at Yuma for horse stealing. Another report states that "Frank Snee" was an alias for Frank Valencia.[901] Schoonover stated that Snee was not an important witness, and "it would not be good policy to subpoena him in view of the fact that he is a horse thief." But Schoonover suggested that he be interviewed about his knowledge of the case, after which it would be decided whether to subpoena him. Brassell had employed Snee and his car when Brassell was recruiting men in El Centro for the Avilés expedition.[902] Gershon later reported that Snee, who had been in the county jail in Yuma, had been convicted and sent to the Arizona State Prison at Florence for three years for cattle rustling.[903]

Also, a subpoena was issued for chauffeur W. Sherman Bacon at 4213 Montgomery Street, Oakland. Blanford suggested that Webster interview him as Bacon might be able to add something to his former statement, with which Webster was familiar.[904]

While Bureau agents continued to assemble the government's witnesses, the Avilés defense team moved for yet another continuance. This time, the reason was that certain oil cases in which Harry Chandler's attorneys Hunsaker and Lawler were presenting before a judge in Portland were set for trial on November 15, and that trial would last an estimated six weeks. Moreover, attorney Hunsaker stated that Chandler had been operated on two or three times for his sinus condition since he had last appeared in court for a continuance. The continuance was granted.[905]

The Avilés case was continued until January 30, 1917.

Once again Juan N. Fernández arrived in El Paso from Jiménez in compliance with a subpoena, planning to leave next day for Los Angeles. Blanford wired Stone that the case was continued from December 5, 1916, to January 30, 1917. A new subpoena was not required. Fernández would be reimbursed when the case came to trial. Fernández told Stone in El Paso that he had come from Jiménez to El Paso before being notified of the continuance. He had left Jiménez on November 7 to be at the Avilés trial on December 5. He had left early because *villistas* had captured Jiménez—all mail, telegraph, and railroad communication with Jiménez had been discontinued. He had to go from Jiménez to Torreón on a burro, from Torreón to Laredo, thence to El Paso, where he contacted Agent Stone. He planned to return to Jiménez at once. Blanford had Stone checking on whether Fernández came solely as a witness or had other business, and was claiming reimbursement as a witness. Blanford asked headquarters to determine whether Fernández's expenses should be reimbursed. Fernández said he saw Brassell in El Paso and that Brassell had not received notice of continuance mailed to him at Sonora, Arizona. Blanford asked Stone to notify Brassell of the continuance. Fernández stated that as communications with Jiménez had been discontinued at present, he could be reached through Frank Mariscal, Box 260, El Paso.[906]

While discussing the Avilés case with Schoonover, the latter suggested to Blanford the advisability of dismissing the case against General B. J. Viljoen provided Viljoen turned state's evidence. Blanford asked Kosterlitzky to feel Viljoen out. Kosterlitzky later reported that he had learned that Viljoen was at La Mesa, New Mexico, where he had a ranch.[907] The matter became moot when Viljoen died in La Mesa on January 13, 1917.

Perhaps the most striking development in the Avilés case occurred when Assistant Attorney General Charles Warren suggested that the BI employ an informant to surveille Harry Chandler. Chief Bielaski authorized Blanford "to employ someone temporarily in the capacity of informant for the purpose of covering the movements of Mr. Harry Chandler." Such "employment to be at lowest practicable figure and to be discontinued promptly when the necessity for it is no longer apparent."[908] After consulting with Schoonover, Blanford employed a certain "C. G. Varcos," apparently an alias for Charles George Varcoe, a civil engineer and a Los Angeles city inspector, at $3 per day plus expenses. Why Varcoe was hired is unclear; perhaps to maintain plausible deniability if something went wrong. Varcos began work on November 16, the date on which another Chandler case would be tried in State court, Department 14. That trial was for a civil suit instituted by E. [?] T. Earl against the *Los Angeles Times* and Chandler for libel.[909] Informant Varcos reported that Chandler was in his office all day. The civil case in which Chandler was a defendant was continued to November 20. Varcos covered Chandler's movements from November 19 through 25, although on November 23, on a motion from the plaintiff's attorney, Chandler's name was stricken from the complaint, as it was shown that he had nothing to do with the editorial policy of the paper, the basis of the suit being an alleged libel contained in a *Times* editorial.[910] Interestingly, the Bureau continued the surveillance by Varcos of Harry Chandler from November 26 to 30. Varcos also supplied the license plate number of Chandler's car.[911]

Varcos was again employed beginning on January 4, 1917, at the rate of $3.50 per diem to investigate the venire of seventy-five men from which the jury in the Avilés trial would be drawn. This action was taken on the recommendation of US Attorney Schoonover.[912] Varcos reported not only about the venire for Harry Chandler's trial but also about the attorneys for the defense.[913]

Another development occurred in El Paso with the appearance of Agent Gus T. "Buster" Jones. A former Texas Ranger, Jones would have a distinguished career in the Bureau. His initial assignment was the Avilés case. After several tries, he was finally able to interview W. D. Greet, the County Clerk of El Paso and a former El Paso police captain. Greet said he had been subpoenaed by the defense to impeach and testify to the character of Manuel G. Brassell. Greet said he greatly regretted being subpoenaed, that in all his experience as an officer he had never appeared as a witness against the government, but that if he were placed on the witness stand, he would have to testify that Brassell's character was very bad while he lived in El Paso. Greet based his opinion on the fact that the man had a long police record in El Paso, and on the personal experience he had had with Brassell.[914]

Carlos Minck, formerly employed as an informant for the El Paso office, told Agent E. B. Stone that he had met Manuel Brassell in the Uncle Sam saloon on South El Paso St. and had quite a talk with him. Brassell said he had no intention of going to Los Angeles as a government witness in the Avilés trial. Stone would try to interview Brassell, if he could be located in El Paso, and ascertain whether or not he had been served with a subpoena to appear at Los Angeles, and if so, whether or not he intended to answer the subpoena. Minck said Brassell informed him that he only expected to be in El Paso for a couple of days, and Stone felt it was quite likely that if Brassell talked this way to Minck about not wanting to go to Los Angeles, his sister in El Paso would endeavor to conceal his whereabouts from the BI in the event she was interviewed in any effort to locate him. Stone stated that this matter would be handled with proper care, and every effort would be made to locate Brassell and determine his intentions.⁹¹⁵

A greatly relieved Blanford learned from Agent Stone in El Paso that Brassell had called at that office by arrangement, and that Stone felt satisfied after interviewing him, that Brassell fully intended to appear at Los Angeles on behalf of the government on January 26. Stone noted that his manner and conversation throughout the interview were most friendly, and Brassell advised he was living at the present with his sister, Amelia Aguirre, at 130 East Overland St., and he intended to remain there until time for him to leave for Los Angeles. Stone also spoke with witness Juan Fernández, who had decided not to return to Jiménez, and was employed at El Modelo clothing store. Fernández said he had not yet been served with any subpoena but was ready to appear as a witness in Los Angeles for the trial. His El Paso address was 916 South Kansas Street.⁹¹⁶

As it happened, the Avilés case would not be tried on January 30, 1917, after all, because no judge was available: Judge Trippett had been disqualified because of his connection with defendants; and Judge Bledsoe was engaged in the trial of oil land suits. The first date on which a visiting judge could be secured was March 19, on which date the trial would be set. New subpoenas were issued for witnesses to appear.⁹¹⁷

The Avilés case was continued until March 19, 1917.

Manuel Brassell came to Los Angeles and was advised that the case had been continued until March 19, and was served with a new subpoena for that date. Webster conferred with Blanford, Schoonover, and Brassell reviewing the evidence in the Avilés case in Brassell's possession. Brassell said he had certain original telegrams in his suitcase in El Paso in connection with the case. Blanford wired Agent Stone to see Porfirio Brassell, 220 San Jacinto St., the Twenty-Five Cent Auto Service, and secure those papers, in two folders in a suitcase at 1304 East Overland St. and mail them to Blanford.⁹¹⁸

Webster went over his own files because Schoonover wanted Webster and Blanford to make a brief of this case setting forth the chronology and what each witness would testify.⁹¹⁹

Blanford hired Brassell temporarily to locate witnesses Frank Núñez, Ignacio Díaz de León, and José F. Costillo. Brassell assured Blanford that he had not been trying to evade a subpoena when Blanford had found it difficult to locate him on one occasion. Brassell reiterated his former statement that if he should be approached by anyone representing the defense with an offer of a bribe, he would immediately notify the field office. He stated further that he expected to go from Los Angeles to Ray, Arizona, but did not know how long he would be there; he could be reached through his brother, F. G. Brassell, 508 West Copper Ave., Albuquerque. Brassell reported that Díaz de León could be located about five or six o'clock any afternoon at San Román's restaurant on Spring St., Los Angeles; that the best information he was able to obtain concerning José F. Costillo was that he was in Mexicali, Baja California, or somewhere in the Imperial Valley; that Costillo told him the last time Brassell was in Los Angeles several months ago, that he was going to work as a carpenter's helper on a school building in Mexicali. Costillo had friends and relatives in Calexico and should not be difficult to locate there. Frank Núñez was known to José Ramírez or to Mrs. Ramírez, José's mother, at the beach town of Hueneme, three miles west of Oxnard, California. Núñez was also well known in Santa Paula and El Centro and Calexico. Blanford prepared a voucher and forwarded it to BI headquarters for $4 for Brassell's two days' work endeavoring to locate these witnesses.⁹²⁰

At the direction of Schoonover, Blanford prepared a summary of the case.⁹²¹ Besides preparing the summary, Blanford was still trying to track down witnesses. The postmaster at Oxnard knew nothing about Frank Núñez's whereabouts. The postmaster at Hueneme reported that he did not know Frank Núñez, but that his friend José Ramírez was in El Paso and that Núñez's mother, Mrs. Maese, lived in Hueneme. Agent Rathbun at San Francisco wired that witness W. Sherman Bacon, 1853 38ᵗʰ Ave.,

East Oakland, had been served with a subpoena there and would like several days' notice, if possible, before starting for Los Angeles.

José F. Costillo at Calexico contacted the field office, stating he had heard he was wanted as a witness. Costillo asked just when he would be needed, so that he could make arrangements; he intended to leave shortly for Ensenada and did not know when to come. Blanford notified him to be in Los Angeles on March 19, and to notify Blanford how he could be reached in Ensenada. Gershon served Costillo with a subpoena at Calexico, and Costillo said he would be in Los Angeles on March 16 per instructions in the subpoena. Witness Ed V. Vega, working as a clerk in the shoe department of the Boston Store in Chicago, advised Blanford of his whereabouts. He was subpoenaed.[922] The Bureau's heroic effort to keep up with the witnesses, something akin to herding cats, resulted in subpoenas for a number of persons.[923]

Schoonover informed Agent Webster that William J. Hunsaker, representing Chandler and others for the defense, had pneumonia, and other attorneys in the case would make a motion to have this case postponed yet again. Schoonover also informed Webster that after reviewing the case, he would decide whether to subpoena José M. Maytorena, M. G. Gallaher and Ed Holderness.[924]

The Avilés case was continued until May 8, 1917.

Blanford wired witness Justino Mendieta at Havana and Ed. V. Vega at Chicago advising them of this latest continuance. Schoonover said he would notify the rest of the witnesses. On March 8, Blanford received a letter from Manuel G. Brassell from Chillicothe, Illinois, stating that he was leaving for El Paso and requesting that he be notified as to whether he was needed on March 16. He was notified that he was not, and a subpoena for his appearance on May 8 was issued.[925] John Wren at El Paso tried to locate witness Francisco Núñez but learned he was not there. Manuel Brassell called at the El Paso office and stated that Núñez was in the Imperial Valley.[926]

The assistant attorney general responded to Schoonover's request of April 18, and enclosed the original letter from Adolph Danziger to the Attorney General dated March 15, 1916. "The affidavit of Harry Chandler referred to in the memorandum accompanying this Department's letter of August 8, 1916, was brought to the attention of the Department by Schoonover's letter of July 15, 1916, enclosing a copy of the indictment and other records among which was the copy of said affidavit. The original should be on file in the District Court with this defendant's motion for a bill of Particulars."[927]

At request of Assistant US Attorney Robert O'Connor, Blanford wired the Chief: "James Nourse now with International News Service, Washington, took statement from Harry Chandler, defendant Avilés case, which was published *Los Angeles Examiner* February 20, 1915, Section one, page 4. Please have Nourse interviewed and wire whether or not he has independent recollection taking said statement and also whether Chandler made any additional statements to him other than as published."[928] Bielaski replied: "Telegram received. Unable to get copy *Examiner*. Nourse states owing to friendly relations between Chandler and editor *Examiner* did not ask Chandler for facts. Requested Chandler submit statement for publication in *Examiner*. Nourse wrote short story but does not recall full particulars article but does recall article he wrote so much changed he would hardly recognize it."[929]

Bielaski instructed Agent George W. Lillard at Washington to try to secure a copy of the *Los Angeles Examiner* for February 20, 1916, and interview James Nourse. Lillard checked with the local *Examiner* office, but they did not have the issue. He tried the Library of Congress, but they did not have a copy, either. Lillard then called on Nourse and questioned him about the article. Norse stated that he learned of Chandler's arrest about the time he was assigned to see Chandler regarding an article for publication in *Examiner*. Norse added that the relations between Chandler and General Otis, editor and owner of the *Los Angeles Times* respectively, and the editor of the *Examiner* were of such a friendly nature that he deemed it advisable not to question Chandler about the facts leading up to his arrest, but requested Chandler to submit a statement for publication in the *Examiner*. Nourse stated that he returned to the office after having seen Chandler and wrote a short story about Chandler's arrest, and then went home. On following morning, he saw an article which appeared in the *Examiner* but said that he could hardly recognize it as being the one which he had written, as it had been materially changed by the editor. Nourse said he did not believe that Chandler talked to him about any of the facts involved in this case. The Chief wired: "James R. Nourse has been served with forthwith subpoena. Advises unable testify to anything of value to Government. Advise whether he shall proceed Los Angeles." Blanford replied that the US Attorney wanted Nourse to proceed to Los Angeles. The Chief wired Blanford that Nourse was leaving immediately.[930]

Former informer F. C. Boden, who was now a special employee, learned that Pablo Coronel, wanted as a witness in this case, was either in Globe or Miami, Arizona. Webster wired the postmasters at Miami and Globe asking for any information about Coronel. The Miami postmaster replied that he had mail in the post office for Pablo Coronel, who was in town. The postmaster intended to notify local officers and asked for instructions if Coronel were to be apprehended. Webster conferred with Assistant US Attorney Robert O'Connor, who was now handling the Avilés case, and O'Connor suggested that a subpoena be issued but that the postmaster be notified not to advise Coronel that he was wanted. Webster had a stenographer in the US attorney's office issue a telegraphic subpoena for Coronel, and Webster wired instructions to the postmaster.[931]

In the midst of lining up the witnesses, the Bureau continued to build a case against Avilés. The US attorney was anxious to prove that Avilés had a certain pamphlet printed, a pamphlet which was among his personal files the Bureau had seized. Among other things, the pamphlet allegedly stated that Avilés was acting on instructions from Francisco Villa.[932] Agent C. L. Keep at San Diego received instructions to ascertain who published for Baltazar Avilés or Francisco Ayón in the latter part of 1914 *Acontecimientos que se desarroyaron durante la administración del señor Baltazar Avilés jefe político del Distrito Norte de la Baja California*. Agent Keep was to secure the names of a witness, or witnesses, who could testify that Avilés or Ayón or Gerónimo Sandoval requested, or was connected with its publication. Keep interviewed William. H. Buck, who said his company had printed the pamphlet. Buck said both Avilés and Ayón had arranged for the printing, and that they made the first deposit on January 4, 1915; 1,000 pamphlets were printed. Both Avilés and Ayón read the proof and made corrections, and Gerónimo Sandoval accompanied them at all times. The pamphlets were delivered to Avilés and Ayón. Buck was told that should he be subpoenaed, he should take to Los Angeles with him his office records of this transaction.[933]

Blanford and O'Connor went over the testimony of a number of the most important witnesses. O'Connor suggested that Manuel G. Brassell be sent to Calexico and El Centro to try to secure more witnesses who were recruited by Brassell, Fernández, and others for Avilés's force. Accordingly, Brassell was given transportation and Pullman accommodations to Calexico on a Transportation Request and $10 in cash for expenses. Brassell wired from Calexico that he had located a certain Moreno, and he asked for a subpoena. Also, José F. Costillo was located a hundred miles south Mexicali, and his date of return was uncertain. Brassell asked if he should proceed by automobile for Costillo. He expected to locate additional witnesses and planned to return soon to Los Angeles. Blanford wired Brassell that a deputy marshal with subpoenas would be in Calexico the next day. Brassell was to meet him at the Immigration station. As for witness Costillo, Brassell was to write him a letter, hire an automobile to pick up Costillo—but not go himself—and send Blanford the bill for the automobile hire. Brassell wired to have two one-way railroad tickets from Calexico to Los Angeles for witnesses. He would pick them up at the Immigration station. Blanford sent him the government Transportation Requests.[934]

Immigration Inspector in Charge A. A. Musgrave at Calexico wired that the Mexican driver had to go thirty miles further than agreed, and wanted $15 extra. Costillo wanted a $3 daily witness fee, mileage from Calexico to Los Angeles, and $20: the fare from Mexicali to the work camp in Baja California. Blanford replied guaranteeing these terms, and he gave instructions for Costillo to proceed to Los Angeles immediately. Blanford's answer was based on authority from Schoonover and O'Connor.[935]

Gershon wired from Calexico that Immigration Inspector Beck advised that witness José Costillo, who was now in Mexicali, had promised to come over the border the previous evening and be furnished transportation and expenses to Los Angeles. Ten minutes before the train left, he sent word that he could not go because he had no clothes. Beck and Gershon crossed to Mexicali and found Costillo after a two-hour search of Chinese holes-in-the-wall dives. Costillo said he would not go unless he were furnished with a pair of shoes, a pair of pants, and expenses in advance. Gershon humored Costillo, telling him if he would agree to come over the line, Gershon would provide him with clothes and money so he could go to Los Angeles all dressed up. Gershon's impression from Costillo's manner was that he would try to get clothes, expense money, and transportation, and then would probably leave the train at the first stop and re-cross into Mexico. Gershon wired Blanford describing the situation, saying he was trying to induce Costillo to cross over from Mexicali. "He promised to come at 3 o'clock. If he comes, I think I had better hold him and bring him to Los Angeles so as to be sure he will be there." Blanford replied: "Get Costillo here. If necessary, bring him." About 3:30 P. M. Costillo came across the line to the Immigration office. Gershon immediately put him in an automobile and took him to El Centro, where he bought him a pair of pants and a pair of shoes. The troublesome witness remained in Gershon's close custody until they arrived at Los Angeles on May 15. Gershon took Costillo to the federal building and delivered him to the US marshal, instructing the marshal to deduct from Costillo's witness fee and mileage $15 that Gershon had paid for his transportation and clothes.[936]

Manuel Brassell stated that defense witness Victor G. Rojas told him that Pablo Coronel took Rojas to former Agent J. M. Bowen's office and that Bowen promised to pay him something for his time to testify about Brassell at the trial. Brassell also said that on the day before he went to Calexico, May 9, Rojas told him he had met Bowen on the street and Bowen told him that he wanted him to appear at the trial. Rojas said he knew nothing about the case and had not told Bowen that he knew anything. Bowen told Rojas if he did not appear he might make it embarrassing for him. Rojas thought the defense wanted him to testify as to Brassell's reputation for truth and veracity. Rojas gave Brassell an introduction to Juan Cisneros and his brother, the latter's first name unknown to Brassell, being in partnership with Rojas; that this brother told Brassell that Coronel took him to Bowen's office and that Bowen gave him three dollars and also gave his brother some money, the amount of which he did not know.[937]

D. R. Crawford at El Centro wrote to Assistant US Attorney Moody that Blanford had asked him to make certain investigations. One involved a letter stating that Frank Reading had sold saddles to W. B. Bowker across the line. Crawford was also to check with the family of one A. J. Snee, a notary public who had done a lot of work for Mexicans, and who said he paid out the money and had enough data in his possession to convict. Perhaps the family had his papers, although there was nothing to connect Snee with the Avilés matter. Later, at Calexico, Crawford received a phone call from O'Connor to return to Calexico and interview two deputy sheriffs as to what they knew regarding the employment of Nicholas Zogg as a recruiting agent by Bowker. They knew nothing; Crawford took the auto stage back to San Diego.[938]

Assistant US attorney O'Connor sent Agent Webster and deputy US marshal Bassett to the Jonathan Club in Los Angeles with a subpoena to have the Club produce at once in court their register, it being alleged by Nicholas Senn Zogg that he had stayed at the Club in August 1914 under name of J. H. Winkleman. A clerk checked their register, which showed that a J. J. Winkleman stopped there for eight days in August 1914 and was introduced to the Club by P. T. Griffith, a member, who paid $51.70 for Wilkleman's eight-day stay. A two-weeks' membership card was issued to Winkleman on July 30, 1914. Webster also called on Corridor H. Putnam, whose office was 701 Haas Bldg. Zogg alleged Putnam knew him and knew what Zogg was doing in Los Angeles the latter part of 1914. Putnam told Webster that one J. H. Winkleman came to his office and volunteered to give him some information regarding magnesite property Putnam was interested in at Magdalena Bay, Baja California. Winkleman also had Putnam cash a $10 check on a Brawley, California, bank, which was later returned marked, "No funds." Winkleman later called on Putnam and tried to explain why there had been no funds. According to Putnam, "This man known as Winkleman stated that General Otis and Mr. Harry Chandler put funds in a bank at Brawley for him, as he was organizing a revolution against Baja California for Otis and Chandler. Putnam stated that he later learned that Winkleman's correct name was Nick Senn Zogg." Webster called at the reported residence of Ernest Lightfoot, $144\frac{1}{2}$ S. Grand Ave., it being alleged that Lightfoot's mother had letters belonging to Nick Senn Zogg. O'Connor wanted them, if possible, in order to substantiate Zogg's allegations. But the postman told Webster that he had never delivered mail there for Ernest Lightfoot or anyone by that name. Webster and Bassett called at office of P. T. Griffith, 346 Wilcox Building, to interview him before a forthwith subpoena was served on him in this matter. The office was closed. Webster phoned and learned he was not at home.[939] At O'Connor's request, Kosterlitzky visited Ocean Park seeking information about Nick Senn Zogg, finding that he had registered at the Harold Apartments, 40 Westminster Ave., Ocean Park, on December 2, 1916, accompanied by his wife and daughter.[940]

Unfortunately, Nicolas Senn Zogg could not be used as a government witness. Back in June 1915, the attorney for Zogg, who was in jail charged in state court with passing worthless checks, came to the field office and said his client had information about the Avilés affair which he would give to the government in return for a promise of immunity. Since he knew nothing about Zogg, Blanford conferred with the assistant US attorney, who instructed him to promise Zogg immunity from prosecution and secure a statement from him. Blanford duly interviewed Zogg for two hours, "during which time he related a very remarkable story to the effect that a plan was formulated during the past year, or since March 4, 1914, to establish a republic in Lower California composed of three states, and that certain concessions were to be awarded to parties interested. Zogg named as persons interested in this scheme, himself, General Harrison Gray Otis, Harry Chandler, B. Avilés, and a slew of others. Zogg claims to have papers in his possession and to know the whereabouts of other papers to substantiate his story."[941] The assistant US attorney was focused on the Avilés case, and said once that had been resolved, he would get around to hearing what Zogg had to say. But he had Zogg's case in state court continued so Zogg would be available as a witness in the Avilés case. Blanford was instructed to get a statement from Zogg because a machine gunner, one B. L. Russell, aka Ralph Younger, claimed Zogg had introduced him to Harry Chandler, who hired him at $250 per month, and gave Zogg $250 as Zogg's salary in advance.[942] However, Zogg, who had been considered a probable witness in the Avilés case, was convicted in state court of passing a worthless check, and sentenced to three years in San Quentin. Agent Blanford observed that "this would seem to destroy the usefulness of this party as a witness."[943]

The Avilés case finally came to trial on May 8, 1917.

The trial was underway when Assistant US attorney O'Connor, who was presenting the government's case, asked Blanford to his home to confer with himself and Assistant US Attorney Moody. Among other things, they decided to try to introduce testimony connecting defendants

Chandler and Bowker with the previous expedition against Baja California headed by Enrique Anaya and reported by the Bureau under the title "In re Enrique V. Anaya et al." As a result, Blanford dispatched night letters: To H. B. Mock at Nogales, "Have Jack Noonan proceed Los Angeles immediately witness Avilés case testify relative Anaya incident."; to William Neunhoffer at Tucson, "Have Enrique Anaya proceed Los Angeles immediately witness Avilés case testify relative incident Calexico August 1914."; Mock replied, "Noonan recently went New York to join Roosevelt's proposed army. Present address unknown. Was in Washington May 13."; US Attorney Flynn at Tucson wired, "Enrique Anaya will leave today arrive Los Angeles No. 1 tomorrow morning."[944]

Blanford noted: "During the presentation of this case I have been in the courtroom a greater part of every day and all day during the presentation of the Government's side. With the exception of Adolph Danziger, the witnesses testified the fact that there were several convicts and ex-convicts on the list. Mr. Danziger claimed a loss of memory as to some very vital testimony to the effect that Harry Chandler had admitted to him paying $5,000 to Avilés which was used to defray the expenses of the recruiting operations and the negotiations for $8,000 to be used for the purchase of the garrison at Tijuana, which would have undoubtedly resulted in the acquittal of Mr. Chandler had the case finally gone to the jury. The Government was seriously handicapped by a Bill of Particulars ordered by Judge Trippet which circumscribed the introduction of testimony.

At the conclusion of the Government's case, the defense made the usual motion for an instructed verdict, etc. urging, among other grounds, that the indictment charged the hiring and retaining of men to go into Lower California to be enlisted in the service of the people of Lower California, while the proof showed that the men were hired for the service of the conspirators and against the people of Lower California, further urging that there was no Government of Lower California, but if there was any Government, it was the Government of the Northern

District of Lower California. The court, Judge Farrington presiding, at first denied the motion and compelled the defense to introduce their testimony. During the presentation of the testimony for the defense, the motion was again renewed and again denied. At the conclusion of the testimony, the court granted the motion on the legal ground that the indictment was fatally defective for the reasons above stated, whereupon *the case was dismissed*. In determining whether or not to represent the matter to the grand jury, "Assistant US Attorney Robert O'Connor tells me that he interviewed a number of the jurors and especially those upon whom he chiefly relied for favorable votes, among them being men who are known to be favorable to a strict maintenance of law, and was told that it was the consensus of opinion among the jurors that a verdict of 'not guilty' would have been voted eventually in view of the unreliable character of the Government's witnesses."[945]

Historian Lowell L. Blaisdell's account of the Avilés conspiracy and Harry Chandler's reported involvement focuses first on the government's flawed case that "possibly Avilés'[s] intrigues did not fall within the purview of the neutrality statutes!"[946] Section Ten of the Criminal Code, under which the government prosecuted the case, prohibited the organization of a military force to enter into the service of a "foreign prince" or "state," but Avilés was neither—he was aspiring to gain power. As for Section Thirteen, which prohibited recruitment to attack a "foreign prince" or "state, Avilés had recruited to regain his office as governor, not to attack Baja California or alter its sovereignty." Second, Blaisdell dismissed the government's witnesses as a bunch of lowlifes whose reputation had not even been investigated, and "the willingness of the Bureau of investigation's agents to assert that their sources lent weight to the possibility of Chandler's complicity, raised questions about the reliability of that organization." He concludes that "While the evidence suggested that Avilés had tried to organize a force to capture Mexicali, Chandler's connections therewith were not proved, nor even credibly asserted."

Blaisdell, however, wrote before the Bureau of Investigation's files were declassified. What those files demonstrate is that the Bureau did an outstanding job of building a case and keeping track of scattered witnesses through the repeated continuances. In an era before more sophisticated investigative techniques became standard procedure, the Bureau necessarily relied heavily on witness statements, and it had to work with the witnesses available. (As in more recent Mafia trials, many witnesses were disreputable.) Furthermore, the Bureau files show that Harry Chandler was indeed involved in the Avilés intrigue. And if the prosecution of the Avilés case was flawed, that was the responsibility of the US attorney, not of the Bureau of Investigation. Once again, the Bureau had done its job, only to have the government's case fail in the courts.

Chapter 11: Clash of the Titans

The Constitutionalist movement became unstoppable in the first half of 1914. On the Texas border alone, *huertistas* held only Ojinaga, Las Vacas (Ciudad Acuña), and Nuevo Laredo as of January 1, 1914, and Constitutionalist forces were advancing against all three towns. As of May 12, *huertistas* controlled no territory along that border.[947] Although Emiliano Zapata continued his independent rebellion against Huerta, it was the Constitutionalists who delivered devastating blows to the tottering Huerta regime. Under the leadership of First Chief Venustiano Carranza there developed three main Constitutionalist armies: commanded in the east by General Pablo González operating against the lower Texas border and the Gulf coast; in the center by General Pancho Villa driving down the central rail line from Ciudad Juárez; and, in the west by General Álvaro Obregón advancing down the Pacific coast. General Huerta's Federal army suffered not only defeats on the battlefield but plummeting morale, having to rely increasingly on reluctant conscripts.

On February 3, 1914, President Wilson lifted the arms embargo. This was a tremendous boost to the Constitutionalist cause, and once more, the result of the capable lobbyist Sherburne Hopkins. Carranza had paid Hopkins his usual retainer of $50,000, clearly a worthwhile investment. Wilson's action nullified much of the Bureau's work in gathering evidence, but it also greatly facilitated the agency's task by eliminating the necessity for suppressing arms smuggling. And in a sense, the United States delivered the *coup de grâce* against Huerta by cutting off his lifeline to Europe. On April 21, 1914, the United States navy bombarded and occupied the strategic port of Veracruz to prevent Huerta from receiving a shipload of munitions coming from Germany on the *Ypiranga*. Fortunately, the resulting crisis did not result in a war and was defused by mediation. By August, Huerta was finished. It was during the struggle against Huerta that Pancho Villa emerged as the most powerful general in Mexico. His 40,000-man-strong Division of the North won the most important battles and spearheaded the campaign, which became a race to see which Constitutionalist general reached Mexico City first, and was thus in a commanding position in a post-Huerta Mexico.

EL PASO

El Paso was Villa's lifeline. Having captured Juárez by his daring stratagem in November 1913, Villa established a Commercial Agency in Juárez headed by his brother Colonel Hipólito Villa. The Commercial Agency funneled to Villa's front lines the munitions and supplies obtained in the United States.

The key figure, however, was not Hipólito Villa but Lázaro de la Garza, whose financial acumen kept the Division of the North going.[948] De la Garza was one of the few outstanding civilians working for Pancho Villa. Working close to the general bore its risks. Villa had a habit of going into a rage, having the unfortunate culprit who was the object of his ire shot, and then tearfully regretting having done so—until the next time.

Lázaro de la Garza was born in Laredo, Texas, and had two brothers, José and Vidal. Vidal de la Garza, the scion of an old and well-known family that could trace their roots to Spain, was the manager of Madero family businesses in Parras, the town where the slain Mexican president, Francisco Madero, grew up. Lázaro de la Garza studied finance in Monterrey in the years leading up to the Revolution. While in Monterrey, he frequently visited his brother Vidal in Parras and, in the process got to know the family of the future president quite well. His closest friend was one of Francisco Madero's brothers, Emilio, who after Francisco's murder joined Villa's forces and rose to become a general. Leading up to the revolution, Lazaro worked closely with the Maderos trading cotton and mining products in the US and Europe. In the process, the business savvy Lázaro made quite a fortune, owning his own cotton gin and mining properties in and around San Pedro. The recession of 1907 reduced US demand for cotton and ore, and a severe drought in 1909 ruined harvests. When Francisco Madero challenged the dictator in 1910, Lázaro de la Garza headed Torreón's revolutionary junta.

After Villa took Torreón in the beginning of October 1913, the Maderos recommended de la Garza to head the infant administration of the Hacienda (Treasury) for the *División del Norte*. Together with Alberto, Alfonso, and Ernesto, three uncles of Francisco Madero who had started their own import business in New York in 1913, de la Garza took charge of purchasing supplies for Villa, first in El Paso, then after 1914 in New York. He worked out of the Madero office at 115 Broadway. He handled the finances of the Villa army and its illustrious general until the summer of 1915. While working on behalf of Pancho Villa, he was also one of Zach Cobb's most important informers in El Paso.[949] As a result of military successes and a well-oiled supply machine, Villa's army swelled to over 40,000 strong and became the largest insurgent army of its time in Mexico. The troops moved along rail lines, spearheaded by the repair train. It followed a fully equipped hospital train (before either the US or the German army had one), with a caboose for the general, and one for George Carothers, the Wilson administration's special envoy. The trains also included cars loaded with kitchen supplies, *soldaderas* (camp followers), and soldier families. Cattle cars transported the cavalry mounts with loads of alfalfa hay and grain between engagements. The trains also carried tankers with water for the soldiers and animals. Ammunition and artillery formed the rear of this modern, mobile army.

Everything changed with President Wilson's lifting of the arms embargo. Besides purchasing millions of cartridges for Villa, de la Garza arranged, for example, with firms in New York City for items such as 55,000 pairs of shoes, 2,000 suits of underwear, 25,000 khaki uniforms, 10,000 campaign hats, and 10,000 pairs of leggings. He also arranged for the sale of enormous quantities of loot, such as the entire cotton crop of the Laguna district around Torreón and thousands of head of confiscated cattle.[950] Supplying Villa was big business. De la Garza worked hand in hand with the Madero Bros. firm in New York, which organized exports of cotton and ore from Mexico.[951] In their employ in 1914 was the German intelligence agent Frederíco Stallforth, who a year later joined the Albert office and became one of the most important German agents in World War I.[952] Supporting de la Garza with arms purchases was the German intelligence agent Felix A. Sommerfeld. Sommerfeld through his association with Sherburne Hopkins initially coordinated arms purchases though Charles R. Flint[953] and Hans Tauscher.[954] As part of the German strategy to prevent arms and munition sales to Entente powers, Sommerfeld organized large munitions shipments from all major munitions manufacturers which offered 7-millimeter cartridges to Villa. By 1915, the Western Cartridge Company in Alton, Illinois, became the largest supplier, with Germany footing the bill when Villa was financially unable to pay. German military attaché Franz von Papen under the cover name of "James Manoil" placed the orders for Villa through Sommerfeld.[955]

As usual, a cloud of rumors and third-hand reports swirled around El Paso. Furthermore, the Constitutionalists engaged in disinformation. They supplied the press in early January with a sensational tale of having smuggled an airplane across the border west of Presidio, to be flown by an unidentified Argentine aviator. The local Bureau office investigated and concluded that this was but another instance of fake news.[956]

Huerta continued to lose. Villa on January 1 ordered an all-out attack against Ojinaga, across from Presidio, where the *huertistas* were making their last stand in Chihuahua. Impatient with his generals' failure to capture the town, Villa took personal command, and in one day, on January 11, captured the place.[957] Pascual Orozco, who had been fighting as a general under Huerta (who had defeated him in 1912), disappeared into the Big Bend region of Texas, but most of the other Federals and their families stampeded in panic across the Rio Grande, and were interned at Fort Bliss in El Paso.[958] There local *huertistas* did what they could, both in terms of acquiring ammunition and in recruiting. Bureau Agent Blanford and his informant, John Wren, spearheaded the investigation of these matters. They worked in cooperation with Hector Ramos, the head of Villa's intelligence network in El Paso. Ramos claimed to have twelve informants working for him, including Henry C. Kramp and Powell Roberts. Another Bureau source was the ubiquitous Felix Sommerfeld, who was Villa's purchasing agent in the United States.

Until the lifting of the arms embargo, the Bureau closely monitored Krakauer, Zork & Moye and Shelton-Payne, firms whose owners were most reluctant to provide the government with any information. Shelton-Payne, especially, was suspected of the clandestine sale of ammunition to Huerta operative Guillermo Porras. When interviewed by informant Wren, W. H. Shelton and his head clerk adamantly denied any sales. The clerk, however, told Sommerfeld in confidence that such was not the case. Detailed inspection of outgoing shipments at railroad and express facilities failed to detect any contraband.[959] Yet the BI office was informed that anyone wanting to engage in ammunition smuggling was assured that in case of apprehension, bond would be furnished, and a defense attorney employed. All that a smuggler had to fear was a prison sentence in the event of conviction which, as we have seen, was the government usually found problematic to secure.[960] But sometimes the acquisition of ammunition did not involve smuggling. Some 70,000 rounds of confiscated ammunition were stolen by a Quartermaster sergeant at Fort Bliss and sold to Huerta sympathizers.[961]

A further impediment to neutrality enforcement in El Paso was that, whether by accident or design, one Homan C. Myles, who had been serving on the federal grand jury, turned out to be a British subject. He was appointed as the British consul in March 1914. "The consequence of the discovery that a foreigner had been serving on a federal grand jury was that all of that jury's indictments had to be thrown out and the whole procedure gone through again, necessitating the kind of delays that delighted defense attorneys."[962]

With the lifting of the embargo, not only were military guards at the international bridges removed, but a flood of munitions poured across the border to Villa; an estimated 3,000,000 rounds, plus thousands of rifles. Additionally, on February 6 the Department of Justice ordered the immediate release of all munitions seized in Texas, New Mexico, and Arizona except those required as evidence in pending cases. Thus, another 1,000,000 rounds, several hundred rifles, and two machine guns being held at Fort Bliss were also released to Villa. The Chief instructed all agents to suspend munitions investigations. Consequently, the US attorney instructed the grand jury to return "no bill" in all such cases. These dramatic developments severely impacted the smuggling community.[963]

On another front, the BI field office was concerned with prosecuting Huerta consul Miguel E. Diebold and his associates for neutrality violations. Let's remember that Diebold et al. were indicted for enlisting and sending men to Eagle Pass to fight for Huerta. Diebold's defense was that he was merely repatriating destitute Mexican refugees, thus relieving the burden on El Paso taxpayers. In reality, he was engaged in getting *huertista* soldiers back into the battle. He collected Federal escapees from the internment camp at Fort Bliss as well as *huertistas* not in custody. Almost on a nightly basis, he was sending out by rail parties of ten to twenty Federal soldiers under the command of an officer to Eagle Pass and Laredo, areas still under Huerta control in early 1914. Agent Blanford reported that they "are not being armed and equipped on this side but it does appear men are being enlisted."[964] Blanford cooperated with Hector Ramos, Villa's intelligence chief, in arresting at the railroad depot groups of *huertistas* that Consul Diebold was sending out of the city.[965] And Special Agent Barnes at San Antonio asked Constitutionalists in El Paso to communicate with their colleagues at Eagle Pass as to whether the latter had been able to locate any witnesses to testify against Diebold.⁹⁶⁶

Blanford sent Chief Bielaski his file on Diebold and asked the Chief to "advise whether or not prosecution approved if evidence shows to satisfaction of Assistant District Attorney that Mexican Inspector of Consulates [is] engaged [in] enlisting, paying and sending men to join Federal army." The Chief's reply was "Most certainly."⁹⁶⁷

Consul Diebold complained bitterly to Agent Blanford and to Chief Bielaski that he was being shadowed and that his office was being subjected to organized spying. He decried "false reports" that the consulate was recruiting and organizing a military expedition. Bielaski informed Diebold that as long as those surveilling him did not violate the law, they could not be made to desist, and as long as Diebold did not violate federal law, the Bureau would take no action against him.⁹⁶⁸

Despite Diebold's disclaimer, the consulate was indeed organizing a military expedition. Some 250 recruits were transported downriver to Ysleta. However, the filibustering effort fell apart on the night of February 11. Only a handful managed to cross into Mexico and were immediately captured; the US army dispersed the remainder.⁹⁶⁹ Agent Blanford received valuable information about this affair from Carlos H. Echegaray, whom the agent had used as an informant in Douglas in 1913. Echegaray, a former *orozquista*, had been a member of the ill-fated military expedition and provided a detailed account. With Agent Blanford as his handler, Echegaray agreed to the dangerous move of allowing himself to be arrested and placed in the *huertista* internment camp at Fort Bliss to gather intelligence. After Blanford had him extracted, Echegaray continued to provide information despite suffering a serious beating at the hands of a prominent *huertista* sympathizer. Echegaray testified before the grand jury and would be a key witness against Consul Diebold. Evidently Blanford was not concerned with tradecraft, for he had Echegaray make his reports at the Bureau field office, which was just across the hall from the US Commissioner's office where individuals were continually being arraigned for neutrality violations.

Relying heavily on Echegaray's testimony, Blanford on March 8, after conferring with the assistant US attorney and the US Commissioner, filed a complaint against Consul General Miguel Diebold, Consul Enrique de la Sierra, Vice Consul Alfredo Margáin, and paymaster F. de J. Saldaña, charging them with "conspiring to hire and retain men to go beyond the limits or jurisdiction of the US to enlist in the service of a foreign people, to wit: the Federal or Huertista Army." Bond was set for Diebold and de la Sierra at $2,000 and Margáin and Saldaña at $1,000. The bonds were quickly posted.[970] The grand jury indicted Diebold, de la Sierra, Saldaña, and another consular official, F. Marmol.

Diebold's defense attorneys had secured a continuance of the case, and Agent Blanford was worried. He explained that if the Penal Code were used to file a criminal complaint for enlisting men for foreign service, it would be six months before the matter could be presented to the grand jury, and after an indictment was secured, a continuance was granted almost as a matter of course upon the application of the defendant, which meant another six months' delay. The experience of the US attorney in El Paso had been that after the lapse of a year, and sometimes longer, witnesses in neutrality cases had disappeared. Blanford and the assistant US attorney explored the possibility of the Immigration Service detaining suspects pending their deportation. The Immigration supervising inspector was agreeable to taking men into custody, but emphasized that any subsequent action would depend on examining the men from an Immigration standpoint and would not depend on whether they had violated the neutrality laws.[971]

The government had such a strong case that the defendants' attorneys proposed that two defendants would plead guilty if the charges were dropped against the other two. The US attorney was amenable to dismissing the charges against Saldaña and Marmol if Diebold and de la Sierra plead guilty. The day before the trial scheduled for April 15, the defense employed the usual tactic of requesting a continuance, which the judge granted. Witnesses were discharged on their own recognizance until the October term of court.

The government's star witness would not be testifying. Villa agents enticed Echegaray over to Juárez in June under a promise of safe conduct. They promptly arrested him as a spy; his execution a foregone conclusion. In a remarkable instance of callousness, Agent Blanford asked Constitutionalist agent Henry N. Gray to use his influence to have Echegaray's execution postponed until after the October term of the federal court so he could testify against Consul Diebold. To Blanford's undoubted disappointment, Gray informed him that Echegaray had already been shot.

When Diebold, de la Sierra, and Saldaña were tried at the October term of court their defense was that of merely repatriating destitute Mexican refugees. The jury returned a verdict of "not guilty."[972] Agent Blanford was understandably bitter, attributing the government's loss in a crucial and ironclad case to the loss through death of Echegaray and the absence of witnesses who could no longer be located. Had the witnesses present at the April term been present at the October term the case would easily have been won. He decried the defense attorneys' use of continuances to postpone trials until witnesses were no longer available.[973] Once again, the Bureau built an ironclad case only to have the government suffer defeat in the courts.

Blanford was concerned in another case because groups of men were departing El Paso by rail for Columbus. While gathering evidence, Blanford had to avoid being manipulated by his ally, Hector Ramos, who was eager to supply the Bureau with evidence, some of it questionable. For instance, Ramos provided two typewritten enlistment receipts allegedly signed by *huertista* operatives, explaining that the receipts had been thrown through the transom of his office door. Blanford conferred with the assistant US attorney, who agreed that this evidence was insufficient to warrant Ramos's request that those operatives be arrested.[974]

The Chief on October 30 ordered an immediate investigation of the happenings at Columbus.[975] Blanford dispatched Agent L. M. McCluer to Columbus and asked Ramos for any information he might have. Ramos replied that several old offenders were involved: William P. "Red" Stratton, the former Immigration inspector who had run guns for the *maderistas*, and R. H. G. McDonald, who had been one of Consul Llorente's saboteurs in 1912. In addition, Victor Ochoa, the former *orozquista* who was now a *carrancista*, had purchased with funds from the Carranza consul 111 cases of ammunition and nineteen boxes of small arms, plus saddles, bridles, stirrups, girths, canteens and so forth from the El Paso firm of Feldman & Company. This shipment was consigned to one Tandy Sanford at Columbus. José Orozco, Pascual's cousin, was to head the expedition, assisted by McDonald, Stratton, Fred Mendenhall, Tandy Sanford, and the numerous filibusters who had appeared in Columbus during the previous week.[976] McDonald and Mendenhall tried to recruit several 13th US Cavalry enlisted men stationed at Columbus as machine gunners in Mexico, at $85-90 per month.[977]

Everything when wrong for the plotters as matters developed. The destination of the boxcar loaded with ammunition had been changed several times to throw off suspicion, but the railroad delivered it to Columbus by mistake, and the army promptly posted an armed guard around the car. McDonald and several of the others fled when they heard that a government man had arrived to investigate. Agent McCluer interviewed Colonel Herbert Slocum, commanding the 13th Cavalry whose headquarters were in Columbus, the Deputy Collector of Customs, and the mayor. McCluer arranged with the constable and justice of the peace to have "all the Mexicans in town whom I desired, arrested on a charge of vagrancy, and to be given an opportunity to question them concerning their probable connection with the military expedition." He also arranged for Colonel Slocum and the Deputy Collector to participate in the interrogations if they so chose. The interrogations of the filibuster rank and file produced nothing significant, but Agent Blanford reported admiringly: "Agent desires to state that this bunch of Mexicans were without doubt the greatest aggregation of liars ever gathered under one roof. I expect to profit by the experience."[978]

McCluer returned to El Paso and interviewed Ernest Hughes, manager of the arms and ammunition department of Feldman & Company. Hughes, who had held a similar position at Shelton-Payne, was most reluctant to provide information, and did so only when McCluer pointed out the penalties for aiding and abetting the commission of a crime. Bureau agents in El Paso determined that the ill-fated expedition had been part of a general move by Carranza to offset Villa's strength in northern Mexico. The enterprise was not a failure, however; the army released the seized boxcar, and the munitions and supplies reached Douglas on December 1, consigned to *carrancista* General Benjamín Hill.

The irony in all this was that Victor Ochoa subsequently confided to Agent Breniman that the filibusters had planned to take the shipment that the Carranza consul had paid for, smuggle it across the border, sell it to the *villistas*, and split the profits.[979]

Ochoa, José Orozco, Constitutionalist soldier of fortune Emil Holmdahl, and *carrancista* consul Jorge Orozco were indicted on April 16, 1915,[980] for conspiring to begin a military expedition into Mexico.[981] Special Agent Barnes worried that owing to the difficulty in keeping the government's witnesses together and away from the influence of Victor Ochoa, it was very important that this case be tried at the April term of court.[982] But, as was usual in these matters, defense attorneys secured a continuance.

Ochoa actually had three cases pending against him in federal court: for enlisting men; for organizing a military expedition; and, jointly with Holmdahl for bribing government witnesses. Ochoa and his friends were betting that none of these cases would ever go to trial. The government decided to try the bribery case first, for it seemed open and shut. Ochoa secured a delay because the physician sent to Ochoa's house to examine him reported that he was "suffering from inflammation of the testicles from being kicked." The Bureau was most skeptical of the doctor's integrity. The prosecution presented a clear-cut and amply corroborated case, while the defense attacked the credibility of the government's Mexican witnesses and argued that the case was an attempt by the Villa faction to frame Ochoa and Holmdahl. The jury returned a verdict of "not guilty." Although the evidence was overwhelming, the jurors felt that the government's witnesses were as disreputable as the defendants, and they did not want to send a white man, Holmdahl, to the penitentiary on the testimony of Mexicans, but they could not acquit Holmdahl and convict Ochoa on the same evidence, so they decided to acquit them both. They hoped the government might convict them in some future case.[983]

Not until October 14, 1915, were Ochoa, Holmdahl, José Orozco, and former Carranza consul Jorge Orozco finally brought to trial for the abortive 1914 Columbus filibustering expedition. One of the conspirators, Fred Mendenhall, turned state's evidence, bolstering the government's overwhelming case. Defense attorneys attacked the government's witnesses on the ground that they had been paid by Villa agent Hector Ramos to testify against Ochoa and Holmdahl.[984] The jury deliberated for an hour, acquitted Jorge Orozco, but found Ochoa, Holmdahl, and José Orozco guilty. They were sentenced to eighteen months in Leavenworth.[985] This was the government's first major neutrality violation victory since the fall of 1911.[986]

Released on a bond of $7,500 each, Holmdahl and José Orozco served notice of appeal. As far as the Bureau was concerned, there were no hard feelings—on occasion 28-year-old Special Agent Stephen Lee Pinckney, based in the Houston field office, used Holmdahl as an interpreter in the county jail.[987] Holmdahl's sentence was affirmed by the Fifth Circuit Court of Appeals in January 1917, but he was granted a sixty-day respite to arrange his affairs before beginning his prison sentence. He mounted an impressive campaign for a presidential pardon, enlisting the support of a number of important people, and stressing his having helped the government by securing the names of important witnesses regarding

Huerta. The Bureau was assigned to investigate his application. After successive delays, on the day he was finally supposed to begin serving his sentence, July 13, 1917, Holmdahl received a presidential pardon and joined the US expeditionary forces in Europe.[988] José Orozco also appealed his conviction, which the Fifth Circuit upheld. He spent almost a year in the El Paso County jail before beginning to serve his prison sentence. He, too, received a pardon in May 1917, the Attorney General stating that Orozco had been punished enough. Victor Ochoa was not as fortunate; he did hard time in the federal penitentiary in Atlanta, not released until May 1919.[989]

Figure 41 Stephen Lee Pinckney, Yearbook Photo, University of Texas, 1912.

The El Paso field office also had to deal in 1914 with a situation in Santa Fe, New Mexico. General José Inés Salazar, whose checkered career included being a *magonista*, a *maderista*, again a *magonista*, a *reyista*, an *orozquista*, a *vazquista*, and currently a *huertista*, soon to be a *villista*, faced trial in Santa Fe for conspiracy to smuggle ammunition. Salazar's attorney was the flamboyant Elfego Baca, who had been an *orozquista* sympathizer in 1912. Agent Beckham described Baca as being "unscrupulous, would stoop to anything and stop at nothing." The Huerta regime had hired Baca to defend Salazar. The US attorney for New Mexico feared witness- and jury-tampering, and urgently requested BI agents from El Paso. Agent Blanford got the assignment.

Salazar was confined in the Santa Fe County jail, reportedly under pleasant conditions. The deputy US marshal who delivered him there had left instructions that only Salazar's lawyer could meet with him. However, a female inmate claimed he was allowed to have women prisoners sent to his cell to spend the night. And Salazar was also allowed to spend considerable time in the jail office, on several occasions being permitted to leave the jail with his lawyer and friends.[990] Salazar's trial began on May 11. As a bemused Blanford reported, the jailer had permitted anyone to speak with Salazar, and mixed in the procession of well-wishers were several jurors. The prosecution believed it had a cast-iron case. But one of the government's witnesses recanted his earlier statement; attorney Baca quickly put him on the stand as a defense witness. The jury was sequestered, under the supervision of two bailiffs. Blanford concentrated on the witnesses. During a noon recess, the Bureau agent followed three government witnesses who accompanied attorney Baca to a hotel bar, where they enjoyed a few drinks. They then went up to Baca's hotel room where, from an adjoining room Blanford heard them deep in conversation trying to get certain dates straight. On May 14, an all-Hispanic jury returned a verdict of "not guilty." US attorney S. Burkhart at Albuquerque wrote to Special Agent Barnes concerning *huertista* General Roque Gómez, who had been indicted together with Salazar. After Salazar's acquittal, the case against Gómez was dismissed as there was no chance to convict him on the facts developed in the Salazar case.[991]

Although acquitted of smuggling munitions, Salazar faced another trial, this time for perjury. The government charged that Salazar had lied when he swore to American officials that he had resigned from the Huerta army at Ojinaga five days before Villa's forces captured the town. The government maintained that, in fact, Salazar had crossed to Presidio, Texas, on January 10 with the rest of the *huertista* fugitives. Bureau agents began building a case. Salazar's trial was to begin in Santa Fe on November 30, 1914, but on the night of November 20, he escaped from jail under circumstances indicating that it had been an inside job orchestrated by Elfego Baca for a sizeable fee. (Salazar returned to Mexico, where he was killed on July 26, 1917.) Interestingly, the jury, after deliberating for eight hours, returned a verdict on December 9 of "not guilty" on the charge of perjury.[992]

Chapter 11: Clash of the Titans

Agents Blanford and Beckham began gathering evidence against Elfego Baca and his associates for conspiracy in the Salazar escape. Beckham employed an informant, and he even considered tapping the telephone line to Baca's residence and installing a dictograph in the saloon that Baca and his cronies frequented. The US marshal recommended an electrician for the job, but the US attorney squelched these initiatives as being both improper and risky. Chief Bielaski suggested that "steps be taken to secure all possible information concerning Baca's bank account and his deposits before and after Salazar's escape."[993]

Matters took a turn when on January 31, 1915, Baca shot and killed Celestino Otero, one of his fellow conspirators, on a street in El Paso. He pleaded self-defense and was placed under a $7,500 bond. Otero's widow alleged that her husband had gone to see Baca about collecting $1,000 for his role in the Salazar escape, and she named the seven others in the escape conspiracy. Bureau agents were seriously worried that Baca would have Mrs. Otero killed to prevent her from testifying. The Bureau had no safehouse in El Paso, lacked the manpower to protect Mrs. Otero, and the law did not permit hiring a member of a private detective agency as a bodyguard. Therefore, agents hid her temporarily with former BI Agent Samuel Geck, who now operated a rooming house. Geck fed and lodged her while the agents figured out what to do. It was suggested that she could be sent to Fort Bliss where the army could protect her, a suggestion the army quickly rejected. Another suggestion was to send her for safekeeping to the New Mexico state penitentiary at Santa Fe. Mrs. Otero willingly accepted the penitentiary option, and arrangements were hurriedly made for the warden to receive her without commitment papers and for Beckham to drive her from Geck's rooming those to the railroad depot. Beckham reported that a car had followed them, but he had managed to lose it. Mrs. Otero was hustled through the baggage area at the depot to avoid Baca and his henchmen, and installed in a Pullman. A deputy US marshal accompanied her safely to Santa Fe, and Special Agent

Pinckney interviewed her in the penitentiary, surely one of the oddest safehouses on record.[994]

Elfego Baca and his associates were indicted at Santa Fe on April 10, 1915, for conspiracy.[995] The Bureau was building a case against him, including securing telegrams by a subpoena duces tecum, and on occasion shadowing Baca. But on December 18, 1915, a jury acquitted everybody.[996] And on January 25, 1916, a jury in El Paso deliberated for twelve minutes before acquitting Baca for the killing of Celestino Otero.[997]

The US attorney for New Mexico, S. Burkhart, summed up the situation in the two cases of United States v. José Inés Salazar for perjury and United States v. Elfego Baca et al. for conspiracy to liberate Salazar from the Bernalillo County jail. The result in both of these cases was a verdict of "not guilty." Burkhart believed that in the perjury case, under the conditions in Santa Fe, the government could not have gotten a conviction although the case was strong. The jury was composed of nine Hispanics and three Anglos, "and Salazar is much of a hero amongst native people." In the Elfego Baca case, he felt the prosecution had presented a perfect case. That jury was composed entirely of Hispanics. In Burkhart's opinion, "there could have been no conviction if we had had a dozen witnesses who heard the conspiracy entered into. Notwithstanding the handicap under which we labored the jury was out about five hours. I desire in this case to commend very highly the services of Mr. Stephen L. Pinckney as Special Agent. He had the evidence prepared properly, and no one could have been of more assistance than he was. I hope hereafter when important cases are to be investigated in New Mexico, I shall have the benefit of Mr. Pinckney's assistance."[998]

SAN ANTONIO

Among new arrivals in San Antonio were the family of General Pascual Orozco. Like some other prominent revolutionary figures, Orozco sent his family to the United States for safety. The Bureau field office kept track of the family as they changed residences, for the agents hoped through them to apprehend Orozco, who was under indictment in El Paso. An Immigration inspector and a deputy US marshal assisted in this endeavor. The Bureau also had the post office establish a mail cover. As for Orozco, he reportedly was sighted in various locations, among them Mineral Wells, Texas. Agent Todd Daniel was sent there to investigate but without result. But Sam Belden, the Constitutionalist attorney in San Antonio, telephoned that Pascual Orozco had gone aboard the Mexican vessel *Zaragoza* at New Orleans on February 25. Barnes immediately wired Pendleton in New Orleans.[999]

Pendleton replied that, unfortunately, Orozco was said to have boarded the Huerta steamship *Zaragoza* in New Orleans ten days earlier on his way to Mexico City as a witness in the trial of General Salvador Mercado for dereliction of duty when the latter abandoned the city of Chihuahua.[1000] Pendleton tried to trace Orozco's movements while in New Orleans and interviewed reporter John Meehan, the *Times-Democrat*'s expert on Mexican and neutrality matters. Meehan said that about February 6, at a time when he was told Orozco was in town, several Mexicans registered at the Monteleone Hotel. He suspected that Orozco was in that party under an alias. Meehan said he had been able to glance into the room of the suspected Orozco and had seen him with two large guns and a sword. The reporter understood that Orozco was back in Mexico City and was confident that he had left New Orleans on the *Zaragoza*.[1001]

Neutrality cases produced varying results. Sam Dreben and Ernesto Meade Fierro pleaded guilty in federal court to conspiracy to export munitions and were each fined $500, which was not much of a deterrent. The cases against Joaquín Sepulveda and J. G. Hermosillo were dismissed, and those against Gustavo Espinoza, Alfredo Breceda, and Jesús Valdez Leal were continued because they had not yet been arrested. The case against Esteban S. Meza was continued at the request of his attorney. Francisco R. Villavicencio pleaded guilty to attempting to export munitions for the Constitutionalists and was fined $250, which was even less of a deterrent. Villavicencio had been a Madero agent working against Reyes and Vázquez Gómez and had managed to infiltrate those movements.[1002]

Most interestingly, Villavicencio called at the field office and said he was trying to locate former Special Agents H. A. Thompson and James Ganor, whom he wanted to employ to work for the Constitutionalists.[1003] He did indeed employ Thompson, who had been the agent in charge at San Antonio, presumably at a better salary than Thompson had received from the Bureau. Thompson provided the Constitutionalists with a wealth of knowledge about neutrality matters. Although Thompson was no longer a BI agent, his former colleagues had no qualms about working with him.[1004] It is not known whether Ganor also became a Constitutionalist agent, but as an attorney in private practice, he sometimes defended those accused of neutrality violations.

Villavicencio said he wanted to hire the former BI agents to investigate yet another attempt by Emilio Vázquez Gómez to be relevant. The usual dynamic involving the political "outs" was at work. At least three issues of a newspaper entitled, *Emiliano Zapata*, appeared in January. It was purportedly published in Dallas but was really published in San Antonio, and Vázquez Gómez was apparently the editor. He was trying forge an alliance with Zapata, which in itself was extremely problematic, and was allegedly receiving support from General Félix Díaz, who was trying to get back in the revolutionary game.[1005] The envisioned Vázquez Gómez-Zapata-Díaz alliance would presumably combat both the Huerta regime and the Constitutionalists, which meant it was risible.

There were remnants of the Vázquez Gómez conspiracy to be dealt with. Of prime importance was locating and interviewing government witnesses. An essential witness was Francisco Pérez, who had been a *vazquista* courier, and who was now at Hermosillo with Carranza, not dead as previously reported. He would return to San Antonio to testify.[1006] The other crucial witness was Dr. José Saenz, former Bureau informant against the *vazquistas*. According to Felix Sommerfeld, Dr. Saenz opposed the Constitutionalists and would not testify under any circumstances. But Constitutionalist agent T. R. Beltrán assured Barnes that M. García Vigil, who had conspired with Vázquez Gómez to set on foot a military expedition, was now a Constitutionalist sympathizer, and would willingly testify.[1007]

Something that caused considerable anxiety in government circles was the loyalty of Hispanics, who constituted most of the population along the border—were they loyal to the United States, or would they support Mexico in a crisis, such as the United States seizure of Veracruz on April 21? This question was particularly critical in San Antonio, where in April 1914, according to Special Agent Barnes, there were between 20,000 and 35,000 Mexican refugees.

Barnes conferred with the police chief and with the military at Fort Sam Houston about the situation, and detailed Agent Frederick Guy to watch the Huerta consulate. Guy witnessed able-bodied Mexican laborers headed for the consulate in groups of two or three. And Barnes received reports from different sources that a thousand or more Mexicans in San Antonio had registered for military service to defend their homeland in case of war. By contrast, the Constitutionalist consul issued a circular urging his fellow Constitutionalists to remain neutral.[1008] Longtime informant Charles F. Stevens acted as interpreter when Special Agent Barnes interviewed persons of interest.[1009]

Special Agent Barnes received an unusual offer of assistance. J. D. Petrocelli, local manager of the New York Detective Agency whose offices were in the Book Building where the Huerta consulate was located, informed Barnes that he had observed a number of well-dressed Mexicans in conference with Arturo M. Elías, the Huerta Inspector of Consulates, and suspected they were discussing revolutionary matters. As a matter of courtesy to the Bureau, Petrocelli offered to place a dictograph in Elías's office. Tempting as the offer was, Barnes turned it down because he thought it inappropriate to bug a foreign consul, especially since mediation between the US and Huerta was proceeding.[1010]

LAREDO

The situation in Laredo in early January left much to be desired. A quantity of ammunition had been seized, presumably intended for the Constitutionalists planning their forthcoming attack against Nuevo Laredo. Constitutionalist General Pablo González was considerably less effective than his fellow generals Pancho Villa and Álvaro Obregón; his frontal attack against Nuevo Laredo on January 1 was a disaster.[1011] Moreover, Colonel A. P. Blocksom, commander at Fort McIntosh, informed Special Agent Barnes that Mexicans were offering bounties and liberal pay to soldiers if they deserted. He asked that one or more BI agent be assigned to investigate. Barnes dispatched Agent Leverett Francis Englesby. Englesby was the only agent available, but he proved to be an unfortunate choice. Sixty years old, he could neither speak Spanish nor did he have any border experience. Born in Vermont, Englesby had worked as a lawyer in Washington, DC for the decade between 1900 and 1910, when he joined the BI.[1012] His assignments took him to Georgia and Florida where he worked exclusively on Mann Act cases. Thrown into the middle of Mexican revolutionary intrigue in Texas, Englesby was not only ill-prepared with respect to experience, he even lacked a typewriter for reports, and had to rent one at $4 per month. Englesby described himself as "being so new to this work."[1013] As his reports painfully demonstrated, he was in way over his head.

Englesby began, sensibly enough, by making the rounds of officialdom. He went to Fort McIntosh to see Colonel Blocksom in person because he feared leaks if he spoke on the telephone.[1014] The colonel was cooperative but disappointed, for Blocksom had requested "a man who could speak Spanish and so get close to the Mexicans as an English [sic] person could not."[1015] Randolph Robertson, clerk of the federal court, promised to help Englesby in any way he could. The assistant US attorney, the Immigration inspector in charge, and the deputy Collector of Customs likewise assured Englesby of support, as did the postmaster, although he was a fervent Constitutionalist sympathizer.

Englesby also called on an official who was not a strong Constitutionalist partisan—Sheriff Amador Sánchez. The agent reported that, "He received me very pleasantly, but I question if he will be helpful although I am certain he could be very useful if he so desired. He has the reputation of being very influential in all local politics and of having a large influence here. His reputation as I get it is very bad and if the story I am told is true, and I am told it could probably be proved, would make him amenable to the Mann Act."[1016] The BI agent also called at the Huerta consulate. Consul Ricardo S. Bravo, with the vice consul interpreting, promised to provide valuable information against the Constitutionalists.[1017] Regarding Colonel Blocksom's concerns about Carranza sympathizers trying to entice soldiers to desert, "before anything could be done to catch recruiters in the act, the matter became known, and the principals disappeared."[1018]

As for neutrality violations, Englesby wrote that it "seems the great majority of Laredo residents are strong Constitutionalist partisans and at all times ready to help break the neutrality laws where it will help that side."[1019] In the case of US v. Leocadio Fierros et al., the assistant US attorney said that "he had all the testimony needed before the grand jury, provided they had a normal grand jury, but if they had a prejudiced grand jury, he intimated further testimony would not avail," so unless otherwise instructed, Englesby would not investigate further.[1020] Since there was no evidence to connect anyone with the ownership of seized contraband, the assistant US attorney ordered the parties released.[1021]

Englesby reported he had been "trying to get a line on something tangible in regard to violations of the Neutrality Laws but while I am led to believe that there is much going on it seems very hard to get any tangible evidence thereof. I am of course handicapped by my lack of ability to understand or to speak Spanish, but of course that was understood before I came."[1022] And, "I am told that smuggling is going on but can get no tangible evidence of how or where or when."[1023] He said his information was that at San Ignacio a great deal of munitions smuggling was occurring, but his "information is however not such that I can place reliance upon it and as it is said to be a forty-mile ride by automobile and very expensive I have not gone down there. Another fact that keeps me from going is that the minute I should show up there I expect that everything would be quiet in that line and as I cannot speak the language, I feel rather helpless to cope with the situation."[1024]

Englesby reported at the end of January that the assistant US attorney had informed him that there was no reason to keep a Bureau agent in Laredo at the present time. Barnes mercifully recalled Englesby to San Antonio on February 4.[1025] Soon thereafter, the department assigned the agent to investigating German intrigue in New York.[1026] He settled in Florida after retirement in the 1920s, and eventually moved to Hawaii, where he died in 1934.[1027]

Nuevo Laredo remained in *huertista* hands until April 24, 1914, when General Pablo González finally managed to capture Monterrey. Within hours, the Huerta garrison evacuated Nuevo Laredo.

DEL RIO AND MARFA

On New Year's Day, 1914, Agent Todd Daniel in Del Rio reported on his investigation of a restaurant where Constitutionalist recruits were allegedly fed before being taken upriver to Langtry, from whence they crossed to a rebel encampment. The proprietor of the restaurant, Mrs. Francisco Aguirre, confirmed that she had been receiving meal tickets signed by Constitutionalist consul José Martínez Garza and stamped with the seal of the consulate. She produced a ledger with the names of those she had fed; 130 during December alone. Interestingly, although Agent Daniel copied the names, the ledger was turned over to the Huerta consul.

At Langtry, the military apprehended some of these recruits and brought them to Del Rio. Accompanied by the Huerta consul, Agent Daniel took Mrs. Aguirre to the jail, where she identified several of the prisoners. A complaint was filed against Constitutionalist consul Martínez Garza and nine recruits. The consul was arrested but released on his own recognizance to appear before the US Commissioner L. F. Garner. At the hearing, Daniel had to present the government's case because, by a mistake, the assistant US attorney failed to appear. The consul's bond was set at $500, those of the other defendants at $250. One of the recruits could not post bond and remained in jail, but was released when he agreed to turn state's evidence. Mrs. Aguirre agreed to testify at the trial.[1028]

Daniel had to make a quick trip to Marfa in response to a directive from the Chief to investigate reports that the *huertistas* in Ojinaga were receiving amounts of ammunition from Marfa concealed in provisions and alfalfa. By the time Daniel arrived, however, Villa had captured Ojinaga. Daniel displayed his grasp of the obvious by writing that, "It is not likely that the smuggling contemplated by the Federals will now materialize, they having been defeated by the Constitutionalists at Ojinaga. At any rate it is not likely to occur in the vicinity of Marfa."[1029] While in Marfa, Daniel encountered former Special Agent in Charge H. A. Thompson, now a Constitutionalist operative who had been investigating *huertista* smuggling. Thompson's superior, Felix Sommerfeld, arrived, and the pair left for Presidio to gather intelligence.[1030]

Daniel returned to Del Rio to concentrate on enlistment violations of neutrality. He tried to find a reliable Mexican to obtain the kind of information that was impossible for an official to obtain, since "There is hardly any way an agent can establish the fact of enlistment other than an admission on the part of one enlisted."[1031] Constitutionalist Consul José Martínez Garza was continuing to direct recruiting efforts but now was most careful not to be implicated. The consul relied on the overwhelmingly pro-Constitutionalist sentiment at Del Rio. In any case, a troop of US cavalry was stationed at Langtry, and recruitment virtually ceased.[1032]

BROWNSVILLE

Ammunition was being smuggled, as usual. The Bureau investigated Charles H. More, a wealthy partner in the Brownsville Hardware Co., for conspiring to export munitions.[1033] And at the international bridge, customs officers seized 3,000 rounds hidden behind the seat of a buggy; the driver escaped in the crowd.[1034]

More importantly, the army seized 30,000 rounds found on the bank of the Rio Grande, but US Commissioner W. J. Russell refused to accept a complaint against W. C. Craig, manager of the firm of Cafferelli Brothers, even though the ammunition boxes were marked "Cafferelli Brothers." A witness would swear that this ammunition came from a boxcar containing 467 cases of 30-30 and 7-millimeter ammunition consigned to Cafferelli. The boxcar still contained nearly 120,000 rounds, which the army also seized. Moreover, manager Craig had already received 329 boxes of ammunition from the same boxcar and refused to deliver them to the army for seizure. The US Commissioner asked Special Agent Barnes what the government wanted to do about the matter, adding that when Assistant US Attorney Staver came to prosecute the case, "there will be hell and no mistake." There were also artillery pieces on the way for Cafferelli. The commanding officer at Brownsville requested that a BI agent be sent to investigate.[1035] Agent Webster Spates, currently in Galveston working on munitions cases, got the assignment.

Spates found that it was the disreputable Manuel M. Miranda, whom we have encountered before, who had informed the army. He had followed the cart that took the first load of thirty cases from the boxcar to the riverbank about two miles from Brownsville, where they were covered with brush. But before Miranda could alert the army, someone alerted Cafferelli, and there was a frantic effort to unload the remainder of the ammunition. Sixty cases (1,500 rounds per case) of 7-millimeter were rushed to the grocery store of M. J. García, who was involved in the smuggling enterprise, and manager Craig had 329 cases hauled to the Cafferelli store before the army seized the rest.[1036] Cafferelli contacted Senator Morris Sheppard of Texas, urging him to use his good offices to have the 467 cases released. Sheppard contacted the Attorney General, who contacted Chief Bielaski, who had Spates report on the matter. Senator Sheppard was informed that the investigation was still ongoing.[1037]

US Attorney Lock McDaniel went to Brownsville and consulted with Spates. They decided to have warrants issued to search and seize the ammunition at Cafferelli and the García grocery store that could be identified as part of the suspicious shipment. This was done on February 3, and the army hauled the ammunition to the post. McDaniel suggested that no complaint be made, but that the evidence be presented to the grand jury.[1038] All this, of course, proved to be moot as a result of President Wilson lifting the arms embargo on February 3. Presumably the ammunition was eventually returned to Cafferelli.

NEW ORLEANS

Strange things happened in El Paso. One of the strangest was the shipment by rail on December 20, 1913, of 300,000 Winchester and Mauser cartridges consigned to the government of Guatemala via New Orleans. Agent Blanford notified the New Orleans field office that the shipment might be diverted "because it is almost unbelievable that a car of ammunition would be shipped to the Government of Guatemala from El Paso."[1039] The consignors, Shelton-Payne, had acknowledged that the Constitutionalists had purchased 78,000 of the cartridges. The boxcar reached New Orleans without incident, and Agent Pendleton's informant James O'Donnell closely covered its transshipment to Puerto Barrios by a United Fruit steamer.[1040] Adding to the suspicious nature of the transaction, none other than Sam Dreben was at the docks overseeing the loading on January 8, 1914. The steamship *Marowjine* stopped at no Mexican ports, its first port of call being Belize in British Honduras. In all probability, the arms were destined for an anti-Huerta faction headed by Manuel Castillo Brito, former *maderista* governor of Campeche, with whom Dreben was closely associated, and whom the Huerta government had unsuccessfully tried to have extradited from New Orleans on a spurious charge of murder. Munitions usually reached Castillo Brito from British Honduras and Guatemala.[1041]

Adding further to the suspicious nature of the affair, joining Sam Dreben at the wharf was T. M. Solomon, a businessman whose T. M. Solomon & Co. had a warehouse in New Orleans and who also operated in New York City. Solomon supervised the shipment in New Orleans. Pendleton described him as "a man who has been indirectly connected with Revolutionary parties in New Orleans for some time and was the bondsman for Governor [Castillo] Brito during his trouble and is a personal friend of Sam Dreben."[1042] Solomon subsequently received more weaponry at New Orleans, also consigned to the government of Guatemala. But Solomon was also doing business with rebels trying to overthrow that government. The Guatemalan consul in New Orleans reported that Solomon had sold 500 Mausers and ammunition to a rebel agent who was trying to raise the money to pay for the weapons, currently stored in Solomon's warehouse. The consul asked Pendleton to recommend a man to watch the warehouse. Pendleton introduced the consul to Frank Patton, a former deputy US marshal, whom the consul quickly hired. Pendleton, of course, instructed Patton to report any developments to him at the Bureau office.[1043]

Solomon was not solely involved in the arms traffic with Mexico and Central America.[1044] He also appeared in El Paso once again accompanied by Sam Dreben. Solomon was staying in Felix Sommerfeld's room at the Sheldon Hotel in Sommerfeld's absence. This time, Solomon was marketing cotton that Villa had confiscated, and was showing at his hotel samples of khaki uniforms he was trying to sell to the Constitutionalists. Working for him at the time was former BI informant John Wren, who said Solomon was known to be willing to turn almost any sort of deal for the money, and was leery of all government officers or men who had been connected with the government. Solomon knew that Wren had been a Bureau informant and would probably not tell him if he was working some ammunition deal, but Wren promised to keep Agent Blanford informed.[1045]

Back in New Orleans, Pendleton's attention was on keeping track of vessels that could be used to carry munitions. One was the auxiliary schooner *Margaret M. Ford*, which after being watched for three weeks sailed for Matanzas, Cuba in ballast with no attempt to smuggle arms. Another was the power boat *Fidget*, said to be bound for Brownsville. Pendleton believed she might be used for a filibustering expedition.[1046] But topping the list of suspect vessels was the notorious *Dantzler*, moored at Gulfport, Mississippi in January. The Chief had arranged for the revenue cutter *Winona*, to cover the schooner, which left for Cuba with a load of lumber. Although she was indeed carrying only lumber, the captain of the *Winona* suggested the *Dantzler* was used as a decoy to keep the *Winona* from surveilling other boats carrying contraband and operating farther up the Gulf coast. He did not think any arms were being taken directly from New Orleans.[1047]

In an ironic development, J. L. Mott, who had been one of Pendleton's informers but who now worked as an agent for the local Huerta consul, called at the field office to say he had learned that the *Dantzler* had taken on a load of arms at Gulfport two weeks earlier. Pendleton "thanked Mr. Mott for his information but if it is not more authentic than the information he had volunteered before, it will not be of much use. I learned that he had given this information to the newspapers before he came to the office."[1048] Mott also took Pendleton to the Mexican consulate to meet the consul, who was eager to cooperate with the Bureau in foiling Constitutionalist filibustering expeditions. The munitions cat-and-mouse game continued.

ARIZONA

Agent Breniman advised in January that customs officers and the military at Nogales had the export of ammunition well under control. At Douglas, though, Breniman was meeting arriving trains and checking incoming shipments, which were increasing. On occasion, he had an army officer wear civilian clothes and check shipments while Breniman discreetly remained in the background. He had the military guard a suspicious shipment, and the consignee promptly disclaimed any knowledge of it.[1049] But, Breniman complained, "I cannot handle such inspections as I would like because colored soldiers that are stationed here [9th Cavalry] cannot consistently be given authority to make inspections that safely could be entrusted to white soldiers."[1050] And, "Negro soldiers entirely undesirable for practical purposes."[1051] Breniman also surveyed the situation at Naco, where wagonloads of ammunition were coming from Douglas. He urged stricter examination of freight and of vehicles crossing to Naco, Sonora.[1052]

The main problem was in Tucson, where the major dealers, heartened by the government's devastating courtroom defeat the preceding year, were steadily increasing the amount of ammunition they were receiving. Dealers frankly admitted that there was great demand for 30-30 and 7-millimeter cartridges, and that it was reasonable to assume that ammunition was intended for export. But when ammunition left hardware stores in small quantities at a time, it was impossible to follow them to their destination. One hardware firm's policy for sales of more than 1,000 rounds was to deliver them in the original cases at the front door of their store, and what happened after that was not their concern. Dealers were reluctant to provide Breniman with data about the larger sales, saying that would not be fair to their customers. He warned them that their operations would sooner or later involve them in court, but they assumed that the demand for munitions in Mexico was legitimate trade, and that as long as they did not directly engage in export, they had nothing to fear.

Breniman stressed that the situation at Tucson demanded immediate action. No troops were stationed at Tucson to help, and a single BI agent could not succeed without the assistance of other federal officers. The Bureau agent, with the consent of the US attorney, devised a strategy. Whenever he felt that a business received an excessive amount of ammunition of the kind generally used in Mexico, he would bring an action before the US Commissioner against the person to whom the shipment was made. Regardless of the Commissioner's verdict, Breniman would hold the ammunition by subpoena duces tecum in the custody of the transportation company as evidence before the federal grand jury. While this procedure would likely not result in a conviction, at least it would act as a deterrent.[1053] While doubtless appreciating Breniman's frustration, Chief Bielaski squelched this strategy: "I have before me your report for the 6th instant, page 3, in which you submit your intentions to delay by legal process shipments of ammunition in cases which in view of the recent ruling of the United States court in Arizona may not result in a conviction. I do not believe this action is altogether advisable. I think you should be very careful not to institute proceedings of any kind in any case where a conviction seems improbable."[1054]

The Chief did authorize the employment of an informant for thirty days, with the usual stipulation, "at the lowest practicable terms." Breniman hired one G. Gardner as his informant at Douglas to ferret out ammunition exports. Gardner reported his findings every evening to Breniman at the latter's room in the Gadsden Hotel. The agent's other informer at Douglas was former Deputy US Marshal A. A. Hopkins. Initially, Breniman reported to Bielaski that he was not permitted to reveal this informant's name. Bielaski demanded the informant's name and admonished Breniman to observe this requirement carefully in the future. Breniman complied.[1055] Summing up, on January 30 Breniman wrote: "I am advised that at Agua Prieta, Naco, and Nogales, Sonora, all of which are located directly on the international line, there is headquarters established where at any time during the day or night persons bringing cartridges and guns find a ready market at profitable prices."[1056]

Four days later, the lifting of the arms embargo drastically altered the situation. Breniman dismissed informant Gardner, and could now concentrate on illegal recruiting. I.G. Levelier was the Constitutionalist commercial agent at Douglas. He wired the US attorney at Phoenix in March that *huertistas* were recruiting men and would probably soon cross the border. The US attorney instructed Breniman to follow up this lead. Breniman called on Levelier, who said he had become alarmed because of statements made by two *huertista* saboteurs executed near Cananea, Sonora, on March 17. They had confessed to burning several bridges on the Constitutionalist-controlled railroad between Nogales and Cananea. They admitted having been recruited in Douglas, and claimed *huertistas* were recruiting more men there. The American vice consul at Nogales, Sonora informed the Secretary of State that filibustering expeditions for robbery and the burning of railroad bridges in Sonora had been sent out from Douglas and that a band estimated at from 75 to 125 was operating between Nacozari and Moctezuma. Levelier referred Breniman to J. M. Moore, a Constitutionalist secret agent, who could provide only vague rumors as to recruiting. Breniman concluded that there was no recruiting going on in Douglas.[1057]

The lifting of the arms embargo also had a bearing on the resolution of the airplane smuggling case. Agent Bowen at Los Angeles still received information from Captain Joaquín Bauche Alcalde, one of the main defendants. True to his word, Bauche Alcalde had returned to await trial and was currently living in Bellflower, California. He was still working against the *huertistas*. Bowen broached the subject of Bauche

Alcalde's obtaining a copy of the Huerta consul's code. The captain readily agreed to try but was evidently unsuccessful.[1058]

Bowen also telephoned Bauche Alcalde in January and asked him about a shipment of 91,000 cartridges from Los Angeles to Tucson, reportedly for the *huertistas*. The captain informed Bowen that the ammunition had gone from the store of W. H. Hoegee & Co. in Los Angeles on December 26, 1913, to a box yard and was repackaged as "hardware." When Bowen interviewed Hoegee's general manager, the latter was most reluctant to talk.[1059] Bauche Alcalde suggested the consignor might have used the alias of "Bay" when the munitions went out on the Southern Pacific on December 31. It was later learned that the consignor was one Alberto Rael, who used the alias "A. Bay." The "hardware" went to the Mayhew Mining Co. at Mohawk, Arizona, a small station about 75 miles east of Yuma. The plan was for one Antonio Contreras, uncle of the Mayhew of Mayhew Mining, to transport the ammunition by wagon to the border, some seventy miles distant. Bowen informed Breniman, who was then at Nogales, and Breniman telegraphed the deputy US marshal at Tucson to cover the shipment and, hopefully, apprehend the consignee. Breniman himself immediately took the train to Tucson. His efforts to have the shipment held for his inspection were frustrated by railroad's delay in granting authorization. The ammunition presumably reached the border.[1060]

Manuel Bauche Alcalde, Captain Joaquín's brother, had been indicted in El Paso in connection with the airplane case. The brothers called at the BI field office asking for the date of their trial. The US attorney informed Agent Bowen that he was going to set the case at the end of the calendar for the current term in order to determine what action he would take pending the result of the US attorney for Arizona's application for a warrant of removal of defendants E. V. Anaya and José Escobosa to the district of Southern California for trial. Bowen, meanwhile, conferred with the local US attorney to prepare the Bauche

Alcalde case.[1061] This involved reviewing the copious documentation and lining up the witnesses.[1062]

Federal Judge William H. Sawtelle, who had dismissed the ammunition trafficking cases in 1913, presided over a hearing at Tucson on February 2 involving the extradition to California of Anaya and Escobosa. Breniman attended the hearing because he was most knowledgeable about the airplane case. Government-subpoenaed witnesses included Glenn L. Martin, R. W. Graeme, E. W. Coe, all of Los Angeles, US Marshal C. A. Overlock and Deputy US Marshal L. D. Johnson of Arizona. Glenn Martin testified to having sold the airplane to the Constitutionalists and to having received $4,000, paid through the First National Bank of Los Angeles. The bank's assistant cashier, W. E. Coe, testified to having paid the $4,000 to Santiago Camberos, and to having seen the same amount paid to Martin. Martin said he knew only by hearsay that the airplane was intended for exportation to Mexico. The US marshal and his deputy testified to the seizure of the airplane. R. W. Graeme, who according to his own statements assisted in smuggling the airplane, was testifying when court adjourned. The US attorney announced when it convened the next day, February 3, that in view of President Wilson's just having lifted the arms embargo, he needed to communicate with the Attorney General before proceeding with the hearing. During the adjournment, Breniman conferred with the US attorney and government witnesses, one of whom, R. W. Graeme, claimed that Anaya and his attorney had threatened him.

The upshot of the hearing was that the US attorney believed that Wilson's revoking the March 14, 1912, Proclamation establishing the embargo so weakened the government's case as to make it impossible to secure a conviction. On February 4, he presented a motion to withdraw the application for the warrant of removal, which the judge readily granted.[1063] Whether revocation of the President's Proclamation exempted from punishment those who had violated the Proclamation while it was in force, the Department of Justice was "inclined to the negative view of this proposition; that it believes that generally speaking no action should be taken in such cases where prosecutions have not been instituted; and that it will be governed largely, if not entirely, by the views of the various United States attorneys respecting the disposition of pending indictments."[1064] Since the Department of Justice had passed the buck down to the US attorneys, and since the attorney for Arizona believed it virtually impossible to secure a conviction in the airplane case, the defendants were home free.

The Bureau's perennial problem of suppressing recruiting became acute by September, when both Constitutionalists and *huertistas* were trying hard to increase their supply of cannon fodder. Mining in Arizona was in a slump, and miners, who were predominantly Hispanic, were being laid off at an alarming rate. Agent L. M. McCluer reported that an estimated 1,500 men had left Morenci, Metcalfe, and Clifton in the preceding six weeks. Agitators were haranguing the unemployed at mass meetings, making a fertile climate for enlistment.[1065]

At the State Department's request, the Bureau investigated whether some American citizens languishing in the Nogales, Sonora jail had actually been arrested on the United States side of the international boundary.[1066] Agent Breniman's investigation revealed plotting, double-dealing, and treachery. It seems one Thomas W. Carroway, an employee of the Nogales, Arizona, electric company, was approached by Carranza consul Julio Carranza with a proposition. The consul introduced Carroway to a Lt. Col. López Mendoza and to a Carranza agent, one Pedro Torres, who a offered him $200 to make an electrically detonated bomb to blow up a railroad bridge near Nogales in *villista* territory. Carroway accepted the assignment, went to a garage, obtained two harmless dead batteries containing no explosives, wrapped them up, and had two electric wires projecting to give the appearance of a bomb. As it happened, a certain Harry Carlson had participated in the meetings between the consul and Carroway. Carlson was a lowlife well known to law enforcement officers in Tucson and Nogales. He was working as a chauffeur in Nogales,

Arizona, but was in the pay of the mayor of Nogales, Sonora, a *villista* sympathizer. Carlson promptly reported the bomb plot to the mayor.

The Carranza consul and one J. R. McInerny drove out from Nogales and met Carlson, J. C. Wilson, and Carroway at a spot near the international boundary. Carroway claimed he remained with the consul in the auto until the others called him over to explain how to set the bomb to explode. While he did so, Wilson and McInerny went some distance away behind a hill where they had cached several sticks of dynamite, exploded the dynamite, returned, and reported that they had destroyed the bridge. In the meantime, Carlson had disappeared. He had alerted a waiting squad of *villista* soldiers. When he returned, the fake saboteurs piled into the auto, which would not start because Carlson had disabled it. Immediately, the soldiers appeared and covered the group with their rifles. Carroway, Wilson, and McInerny protested that they knew their rights and could not be arrested on the American side of the border. Unimpressed, the soldiers jabbed them with their rifles, bound them with ropes, and marched them across the border to Nogales, Sonora and jail.

The American consul in Nogales, Sonora demanded that there be no summary executions and that the hapless trio be tried in a civil, not a military, court. The mayor indicated that if the US government would proceed against Consul Carranza, Pedro Torres and other *carrancistas* involved in the affair, he would dismiss the charges and release the prisoners. Breniman and the American consul proceeded to the scene of the capture and determined to their satisfaction that it was indeed 200 yards on the United States side of the border. Breniman filed a criminal complaint before the US Commissioner in Tucson charging Consul Carranza, Pedro Torres, and four other *carrancistas* with violation of the neutrality laws. All were arrested. Harry Carlson testified before the Commissioner but there was no corroborating evidence, and his testimony was considered worthless. Carranza, Torres, and two others were discharged after the hearing. Agent Breniman related the facts to the US attorney, who agreed that the case should be presented to the grand jury then in session in Tucson. The grand jury indicted Julio Carranza, Pedro Torres, and Colonel López Mendoza. Torres was apprehended in Nogales, taken to Tucson, and jailed when he failed to post a $1,500 bond. Carranza and López Mendoza were not found and were sought as fugitives. The Bureau followed up leads that Julio Carranza was hiding in San Bernardino, California, but failed to locate him. Carranza subsequently obtained a position as a clerk in the custom house at Agua Prieta.[1067]

Despite the mayor's promise, the imprisoned Americans were not released, but were taken to Hermosillo, the capital of Sonora. Breniman was disappointed because their testimony would be needed at the trial of the *carrancistas*. The three Americans were finally released, however, on November 27, 1914, at Nogales, Sonora. They immediately dashed across the street to Nogales, Arizona. Breniman interviewed them, then had them taken to Tucson to be held under bond as witnesses. He reported that the case required no further investigation on his part, and that a trial would probably take place at the May 1915 term in Tucson.[1068]

In another matter, one José Macías strolled into the Bureau office in El Paso with an interesting tale. Macías said he was the *carrancista* agent in Naco, Arizona and supervised the crossing of arms and ammunition to *carrancista* General Benjamín Hill, who was defending the town of Naco, Sonora, against determined *villista* attacks. He said that the previous November he had met a certain C. Ramírez, an agent for Villa's ally governor Maytorena. Ramírez told Macías that he had given Macías's bother Federico, at that time a captain in Hill's forces, $1,000 to steal the breech blocks from Hill's sixteen howitzers and deliver them across the border. Federico had returned the $1,000 saying he wanted $3,000 for the job. Ramírez claimed he had given Federico the $3,000, but Federico told José that he had never received a cent. José Macías further stated that Villa's brother Hipólito and the El Paso *villista* Carlos Jáuregui later offered Federico $1,500 to steal the breech blocks. According to José, Federico rejected this proposition. José Macías described himself as a former *villista* who had gone over to the *carrancistas*, and alleged that Villa had ordered his execution if he ever returned to Mexico. Villa's intelligence chief in El Paso, Hector Ramos, had José Macías arrested and charged with fraud, but the grand jury returned "no bill" because Macías had merely failed to do what he promised to do.[1069]

Barnes telegraphed Agent W. W. Orme at the Gandolfo Hotel in Yuma to proceed to Naco and investigate alleged recruiting by General Benjamín Hill as reported by General Tasker Bliss.[1070] At Naco, Orme met with Lt. W. C. Bristol of General Bliss's staff, who stated that there had been complaints by both the Maytorena and Hill people that there had been recruiting on the American side, but that he knew of no specific instance of General Hill having recruited in violation of the neutrality laws, and as a matter of fact, it would be a difficult thing to prove, inasmuch as there was free coming and going across the line at all points outside of the military zone at Naco proper. It would be necessary for an agent to remain in Naco for some time in order to determine whether illegal recruiting was going on. But Barnes telegraphed Orme that unless matters at Naco were imperative, to proceed at once to San Antonio. Orme left by auto stage.[1071]

CALIFORNIA

Chief Bielaski was concerned as 1914 opened that there was an organized effort to secure munitions from Western cities. He sent a circular letter to agents in Portland, Seattle, San Francisco, Los Angeles, Denver, St. Louis, and Omaha instructing them to cover such movements by arranging with the leading hardware and department stores in their cities to advise the agents whenever there was a suspiciously large sale of arms and ammunition such as was used in Mexico.[1072] Once the arms embargo was lifted, Bielaski on February 8 rescinded his circular letter.

There was a scare in California following the American seizure of Veracruz on April 21 and the subsequent possibility of war with Mexico.

There was a large Hispanic population in the state, and rumors spread in June that militants planned a campaign of sabotage. For example, a Bureau informant in San Francisco reported that Mexican track workers on the Santa Fe railroad planned to sabotage the line, then go to Mexico and join their countrymen in fighting the US. The Chief had Bureau agents at San Francisco and Los Angeles conduct discreet inquiries. Agent Arthur M. Allen at San Francisco investigated the rumor that Mexicans planned to burn down cities using fuel oil. He called at the headquarters of the Standard Oil Company and interviewed a vice president, who stated that Mexicans had purchased no unusual quantities of naphtha or fuel oil. Agent in Charge Don S. Rathbun spoke with the chief special agent of the Southern Pacific, who discounted the rumors, as did his colleagues at the Santa Fe and Western Pacific railroads. Agent Bowen at Los Angeles also found no substance to these reports.[1073] Agent Webster at San Diego investigated rumors the army had learned of a plan to blow up public buildings in the event of war. He also spoke with the Immigration Inspector in Charge and with the deputy US marshal, both of whom felt that if there had been any sabotage conspiracy, the situation was now peaceful.[1074]

The agents at San Francisco were primarily concerned with surveilling vessels, such as the barque *Geneva*, suspected of transporting munitions to Mexico. The problem was that Rathbun's informant, one Knapp, got this information from his informant, Donald Schorb. Rathbun was not impressed with this third-hand hearsay, and the vessel was allowed to proceed.[1075] Rathbun received a letter from Bowen at Los Angeles quoting a proposition that one D. H. Armstrong of San Francisco had made to Constitutionalist consul Adolfo Carrillo at Los Angeles for reloading rifle shells; Carrillo had sent Armstrong's letter to Bowen. Armstrong offered to sign a contract to reload 30,000 "lubricated wire patched" rifle cartridges good as new per day for less than $28 per thousand, compared to the $50 per thousand currently being paid for new ammunition. He could deliver the special machinery in El Paso, or anywhere else, and could provide a competent manager to supervise the work at a salary of $300 per month. Armstrong hoped to sign the contract with the Constitutionalists as soon as possible.

Acting on Bowen's information, Allen called at army headquarters in San Francisco to learn about the proposed cartridges. The adjutant had never heard of them. Allen then called on Armstrong, passing himself off as an emissary of Carrillo's. Armstrong styled himself as representing the "National Projectile Works of Grand Rapids, Michigan." He allowed Allen to take away cartridges as samples showing that the wire patch and copper base, both being the features of this bullet, which could be applied to the nickel steel jacked bullet of the regular service ammunition. Armstrong explained that the machinery could be sent across the border as mining machinery, and that there was no lack of empty cartridge cases on Mexican battlefields. He gave Allen his business card and price list. The agent then returned to army headquarters and showed a sample to the adjutant, who was alarmed, viewing use of the bullet as cruel and inhumane. The adjutant sent the bullet to the ranking headquarters surgeon, who said it would cause terrible wounds. The major general commanding the Western Department denounced it as a flagrant violation of the Hague Convention on warfare. Allen turned over all of his documentation to the army. Evidently, nothing came of Armstrong's proposition.[1076]

Agent Bowen at Los Angeles reported a coup: "Found on C. A. Pacina, Mexican Immigration official, was a dial code used by the Mexican Secret Service men to communicate with their department, and this is now being used by the US Attorney and myself in working out the code messages sent by Pacina and another Mexican official to President Huerta, on the killing of Sánchez and Valencia, killed recently in Mexicali."[1077] He was referring to the shooting of these two American citizens by Mexican Immigration officers. Bowen was unable to secure the consul's code, but he obtained and sent to headquarters the code Constitutionalist agents used between El Paso and the West Coast.[1078]

More prosaically, Bowen investigated reports that the Huerta consul in Los Angeles was sending recruits to Mexico via San Diego. Each recruit was said to have been given a train ticket and $2. Bowen scored a notable success when he persuaded the consul's confidential clerk, Estelle Campbell, to become a Bureau informer. She not only confirmed that the consul was sending men to Mexico, but also that W. H. Hoegee & Co. was selling ammunition to *huertistas*. A jubilant Bowen telegraphed the Chief, who authorized the employment of Miss Campbell at $10 per week to secure codes and provide information about the consul's arms traffic. Bowen instructed Miss Campbell to keep him advised of everything that was done in the consulate. She was to report to him at least once a day and more often if necessary. Bowen emphasized that she would have to show results or else would not be paid. The results were disappointing. Campbell reported that the codes were locked up in a safe and she had been unable to copy them. As for recruiting, she reported that the consul had sent two men to San Diego. She kept trying to provide information, however, by inviting the consulate staff to dinner at her house. But evidently nothing significant resulted. Bowen also tried to learn of the consul's activities by securing copies of telegrams the consulate had sent and received.[1079]

Bowen took an active role in investigating the consul's recruiting activities. Acting on a tip from Constitutionalists, Bowen witnessed one Ignacio Palacios, secret agent for the consul, purchase train tickets to San Diego for three Mexicans, to whom he gave each a silver dollar, promising them more money upon arrival. Bowen, however, arranged for them to be arrested upon arrival and held for investigation for a few days. He conferred with the US attorney, who was willing to prosecute the Mexican consul, and Bowen redoubled his efforts to build a case. The Chief cautioned him to ensure that the evidence was satisfactory to the US Attorney before instituting any prosecution. The BI agent conferred with the US attorney, and they decided to have the three Mexicans released so that they could testify against the consul, because to prosecute him, there had to be sufficient evidence to preclude any doubt as to his complicity. Bowen also had another recruit, now his informant, brought to his office and instructed him to inquire among his friends to identify any others whom the consul had recruited, and to bring them to the BI office to be interviewed. Bowen's informant persuaded three other Mexicans to present themselves at the consulate for recruitment. They were unsuccessful, being told the consul was out of the office. The assistant US attorney at San Diego stated in June that he believed the evidence against the Huerta consul did not constitute an offense under the statute. In any case, the consul would be out of a job in a month, once the Huerta regime had collapsed.[1080]

NEW YORK

The most intriguing, and ultimately significant, munitions shipment from New York City was made by Leon Rasst, a notorious Russian émigré of most dubious character. Historian Michael C. Meyer identified Leon Rasst (often misspelled as Raast), as one of the financiers behind the arms of the German freighter *Ypiranga*, which triggered a US military intervention in Veracruz in 1914.[1081]

Rasst exemplifies the exotic characters that people our story, and thus merits discussion in some detail. Leon Moses Reichin (or Reichen, or Rychen) aka Leon Rasst, was born on July 17, 1866, in Homyel, Russia (today in Belarus). The Jewish family moved to St. Petersburg, Russia, around 1870, where his brother Josef (later José) was born in 1873. Leon would later use the more fashionable birthplace of St. Petersburg on various immigration forms. He left Russia sometime in the 1880s and appears on immigration records in Antwerp, Belgium, then Zurich, Switzerland.[1082] There he met and married his wife, Eliza (or Luise, Luisa, Elise). The couple had a daughter, Helen, in January 1896. In an apparently rushed departure, the Reichins shipped out to New York in February of that year. Upon arrival in Hoboken, customs inspectors could not help but notice the father's "bulging pockets," and searched him, while his wife and infant daughter went to a hotel. "Eighteen valuable gold watches were found in different parts of his clothing." With Leon Reichin arrested, customs inspectors went to the hotel and searched Mrs. Reichin and her luggage but found nothing. On a hunch, or maybe hearing a strange rattle in the crib, the inspectors searched the baby. "Lifting up the long white dress of the wee maiden [they] found concealed in a necessary part of [the] baby's clothing eighteen gold watches of great value."[1083] The Reichin family thus entered the United States for the first time, making their mark with ample publicity, as newspapers excitedly covered the gold timepieces concealed in their baby's diaper. Customs determined the value of the watches to be somewhere between $10,000 and $12,000 (around $250,000 to $300,000 in today's value) and fined Reichin $100 for the attempted smuggling, while also confiscating the watches.[1084] The episode would foreshadow Reichin's lifelong pursuit of petty crime, fraud, and miscellaneous crookedness.

The family moved to Puebla, Mexico, in short order. Reichin now changed his last name to Rasst, hoping to conceal his previous existence. The Swiss embassy in Mexico was not fooled. Apparently, the smuggled gold watches had not been Reichin's. The family had barely settled in their new community of Puebla under the alias, when the Swiss government in September 1898 applied to the Díaz administration for "Leon Rasst, ó [aka] Leon Moses Reichin" to be extradited on a charge of fraud committed in Zurich, Switzerland. The crime amounted to 20,000 Swiss francs, matching the customs agents' estimate of the value of the watches.[1085] The Mexican government refused to extradite the Russian immigrant on the ground that fraud was not covered as a cause for extradition, although the offense was punishable by penal servitude in Mexico.

That did not mean that Reichin aka Rasst would stay out of trouble in his newfound home. Far from it. In 1897 he was accused of robbery but beat the charges in court. In 1898, two trading companies

Rasst had founded, Rasst, Headen y Compañía in Puebla and A.M. Davis and Company in New York, sold anything from semi-precious stones to coffee and liquor through German merchants and New York middlemen. The first documented victims were clients who paid down money for "six [railroad] cars" of onyx, which were supposedly stored in Veracruz. According to court documents, the onyx was already sold to someone else.[1086] Rasst used the value of the onyx orders to borrow money from a Mexican bank and private investors. He used those funds to buy a liquor factory.

These wild international trading schemes quickly turned into several court cases involving Mexican, German, and American plaintiffs. The fraud not only revolved around onyx, but also 50,000 German Marks[1087] worth of coffee, for which Rasst received down payments from a company in Hamburg but never delivered, and at least five loans he did not repay worth 60,000 German Marks.[1088] Through a fraudulent bond scheme, Rasst had signed most of the loaned money over to his wife, then declared bankruptcy for his two front companies. Judge Francisco Pérez in Mexico City decided on July 9, 1898, that Rasst through his now defunct companies had cheated customers in Mexico, New York, and Hamburg, falsified documents, and "abused customers' trust." He was ordered to pay 10,000 pesos in gold and was sentenced to prison.[1089]

Rasst seemed to have only spent a few months in Belén, the notorious federal prison in Mexico City. The *El Paso Daily Herald* reported on January 6, 1899, that all but one charge against Rasst were dropped. "It is very likely," mused the paper, "that Rasst is a free man by this time."[1090] One would imagine that the Mexican government insisted on the 10,000-peso fine in gold. The paper claimed that Rasst was "the former Puebla banker."[1091] Of course, the international fraudster was not a respectable "former banker" or anything of the sort. At that point he was a convicted felon who had done time. And this was not the only brush with the law for Rasst. Fresh out of prison, in 1900, he was sued for fraud once more. This case was dismissed.[1092]

By the turn of the century, Rasst was involved in various businesses: textiles, liquor, money lending, international trade, and real estate. While in prison, another child was born, albeit not by his wife. The baby died only one year later.[1093] After returning to Puebla from his stint in Belén, the convicted felon recovered some of his reputation. In a history of the city of Puebla, Rasst appears in the first decade of the twentieth century as a respectable Jewish businessman who owned a textile mill with the Teutonic name, "La Prusia."[1094] The businessman also had another child in 1907, son Benjamin "Benno" Reichin Rasst Moses, this time with his wife.[1095] Rasst also acted as a broker for an investor in the Ferrocarríl de Capulac a Chachapa in 1909.

Without fail, fraud, illegal business schemes, and theft follow Rasst's ventures like a putrid smell. In a pattern that stretched through twenty-six lawsuits against career criminal activity between 1901 and 1913, Rasst would be a defendant eighteen times; business partners had been cheated, loans not repaid, and investors had lost property and shares.[1096] And, a second pattern seems to be that he now hired good legal representation, such as the elite member of the Spanish community of Puebla, Manuel Sánchez Gavito.[1097] Instead of serving more hard time, he beat most of his accusers. According to historian Andrew Paxman, the crooked dealings and high-powered legal representation paid off. In the first decade of the twentieth century Rasst owned "at least four rural estates, various Puebla City houses, and a hotel."[1098]

The illegal schemes Rasst devised in his criminal career also involved artificially, and, as it turned out, fraudulently, inflating his social stature. To that effect, he used the Russian government. By 1910, Rasst's letterhead represented him a "consular agent" for the Russian Empire in the city of Puebla. Of course, once more, he was nothing of the sort. Puebla's governor, Mucio Martínez, finally objected to Rasst's misrepresentations that went so far that he even affixed the "Imperial Russian coat of arms ... above his front door."[1099] The governor threw him in jail in October 1910, and apparently had the fraudster roughed up a bit. But here shines Rasst's brilliant career criminal mind: While in prison for impersonating a Russian diplomat, he convinced the Russian ambassador to Mexico, Alexandre Stalewsky, to come to his aid. The Russian government interceded and had Rasst released from prison.

Not content with just regaining his liberty, Rasst also wanted to continue the use of his fake diplomatic title. He apparently convinced the ambassador of his importance to Russian-Mexican commerce. Initially, the Russian government officially and categorically denied that the businessman ever received a diplomatic commission, but the Russian ambassador finally acquiesced to letting Rasst use the meaningless term "consular agent," since "a predecessor might have promised it and failed to complete the paperwork."[1100] Relentless in the pursuit of his accusers, Rasst even succeeded in having Governor Martínez publicly reprimanded, which reverberated all the way from Mexico to American newspapers. "In a message from Minister of Foreign Relations [Enrique] Creel, in which the minister says to the governor of the state that Rasst did not take the title of consul in bad faith, but that the accused man believed his appointment was legal. On this account, the minister urges that no steps be taken against Mr. Rasst."[1101]

Rasst would use his fake title for the rest of his career. He even added to the title as needed. MID Agent William Doyas reported in 1918 that Rasst "stated that he is a former Russian Consular Agent of Mexico" [not just Puebla].[1102] Bureau operative Harry Berliner, always perceptive when it came to judging people, wrote in 1918: "Rasst is a Russian Jew of the lowest type and is a very slippery customer. Agent is personally acquainted with him."[1103] It should

Figure 42 Harry Berliner. *Passport Photo, 1913.*

be noted that Berliner, himself Jewish, did not likely cast Rasst in a negative light based on antisemitism.

Rasst maneuvered through the early part of the Mexican Revolution more or less unscathed. He dabbled in any "get rich quick scheme" that came his way. Alleging to have lost property as a result of rebel attacks in 1912 gained him access to the Madero government to file a claim as a Russian citizen. The facts of the case should be taken with prejudice. Rasst's big chance for yet a new fraudulent scheme came in 1913, after Madero's overthrow. Most likely through the good offices of fellow Russian-Jewish immigrant and chief arms buyer for Victoriano Huerta, Abraham Ratner, Rasst agreed to arrange an arms shipment for the beleaguered dictator in the fall of 1913. Francisco Madero had expelled Ratner, who operated the Tampico News Agency, from Mexico in 1912 for arms trafficking in support of the Orozco rebels. The American military attaché in Mexico City could only confirm that someone was going to New York City to acquire a large shipment of arms, but he did not know who the individual was.

Traveling with his daughter, Helen, who as a baby was the unwitting accomplice in the gold watch smuggling episode, Rasst sailed from Veracruz to New York in November 1913 to make the arrangements, checking in at the upscale Park Avenue Hotel. In his US immigration records, Rasst raised his diplomatic status from lowly "consular agent" to "General Consul."[1104] He thus entered as an "important diplomat," and with a commission from Mexican president Huerta, as well as, according to historian Michael Meyer, ample cash. Rasst connected with Ratner. The latter had already acquired and stored a quantity of arms for Huerta in New York. Rasst and Ratner arranged for the firm of Marquard & Co, importers, to purchase twenty machine guns from Colt and to have all the munitions, which now totaled 500 tons, shipped to Russia.

On December 11, 1913, though, one Max Korngold, a former Bureau informant, wired President Wilson that Huerta agent Rasst was in New York arranging a shipment to Mexico via Europe to circumvent the arms embargo. Division Superintendent Offley immediately assigned Agent A. G. Adams to interview Kornberg and to investigate Rasst. By then, a representative of the Marquard Company had introduced Rasst to Charles Gans, president of the Gans Steamship Line, whose *Brinkburn* had sailed on December 7 for Odessa via Istanbul, its cargo marked "Rasst, Odessa, Russia." With the New York field office in high gear, Agent Charles J. Scully interviewed the general sales agent of Colt, who confirmed the machine gun order and revealed confidentially that he believed the guns were to be sent to Mexico. Consigned to Rasst on the *Brinkburn* were 10,000 cases of 30-30 and 4,000 cases of 7-millimeter ammunition, 500 cases of carbines (50 per case), and the twenty machine guns. The Gans Line valued the cargo at $607,000.[1105] Rasst planned to reach Odessa first and pay the cargo's $12,000 freight charge upon arrival, but instead sailed for Veracruz. Huerta had recalled Rasst to account for misappropriation of funds, and when the Russian landed at Veracruz he was arrested and escorted to Mexico City.

No one was there to pay the freight when the arms reached Odessa, so on Gans's order the captain refused to unload the cargo. Two weeks later, the Russian government, fearing the arms might be for revolutionists, impounded the cargo. A further two weeks later, Gans succeeded in having Russian diplomats in the United States intervene and secure the release of the cargo. It was transferred to the steamship *Pernau*, on February 5, 1914, headed for Hamburg because the steamship line's agents were chartered in Germany, and Gans believed he had a better chance of collecting the $12,000 freight charge in German courts.[1106] The *Pernau* arrived in Hamburg in early March and the arms were unloaded and stored.

Rasst, who had evidently explained himself satisfactorily to the Huerta regime about misappropriation of funds, paid the $12,000 through a German bank and had the cargo loaded on the Hamburg-America liner *Ypiranga*, destination Veracruz.[1107] Enroute the steamer stopped at Le Havre, where it took on 718 cases of artillery shells and 78 cases of cartridges; and while laying over at Havana, it loaded another 1,333 cases of cartridges.[1108] It was the impending arrival of the *Ypiranga* at Veracruz with this enormous cargo that motivated the United States to bombard and occupy the port on April 21, 1914, precipitating a major crisis with Mexico, which happily was resolved through diplomacy.

If the reason for the bombardment and occupation of Veracruz had been to prevent the landing of the *Ypiranga*, the operation was hopelessly bungled. The first mishap was that the *Ypiranga* was not at the docks when the marines landed. As long as the cargo remained on the German steamer, it could not legally be seized. Once unloaded, the arms would have been under the authority of the customs house. Seizing the customs house then would have brought the arms under the control of the Americans. The ownership question thus would be a dispute between Mexico and the U.S., not Germany and the U.S. The timing of the invasion, namely landing troops before the *Ypiranga* had discharged her cargo, botched the seizing of the arms. When she finally approached the harbor around 1:00 p.m., without having been notified of the American action, a US navy captain boarded the HAPAG steamer and ordered it to drop anchor and wait.[1109] Unaware that it was his ship that apparently caused the landing of marines on Mexican soil, the captain of the *Ypiranga*, Karl Bonath, cabled to the German naval cruiser SMS *Dresden*, anchored in Tampico, and requested instructions.[1110] Captain Erich Köhler of the *Dresden* had no idea about the U.S. interest in the *Ypiranga*, either. In the meantime, reacting to the developing crisis, Minister Paul von Hintze asked German naval authorities to provide a ship in case of war so that German citizens could be evacuated from Mexico.[1111] Captain Köhler of the *Dresden* therefore requisitioned the steamer *Ypiranga* for the German navy. All he knew was that the *Ypiranga* would be assigned to take on German and American refugees in Veracruz and Tampico, which she transported in the following days. For the services to the German navy, including the requisitioned steamer, *Ypiranga*, Captain Köhler personally received a letter of appreciation from President Wilson for his outstanding service during the crisis.[1112]

In charge of the *Ypiranga*'s cargo was Carl Heynen, the former German consul and shipping agent for HAPAG and North German Lloyd in Mexico, who appeared a year later as German spymaster Heinrich Albert's right-hand man in New York. He stood accused of circumventing American authorities by sending the *Ypiranga* and two other German freighters loaded with arms and munitions to Puerto Mexico to discharge their cargoes a week later. The cargoes filled several railroad trains that carried the arms and ammunition to the arsenal in Mexico City.[1113]

In a firestorm of public outcry over the botched intervention, Heynen was unfairly made the fall guy in the American press. William F. Buckley testified to the Senate Committee on Foreign Affairs in 1919, that apparently none other than Carl Heynen desperately tried to prevent the arms from falling into the hands of President Huerta. "...Carl Heynen ...called on the chief of port at Veracruz, Captain [Herman O.] Stickney, an unusually obtuse naval officer, and tried to get him to order him, Heynen, or even ask him, not to permit his boat to land the arms and ammunition in question, as Heynen was anxious for an excuse not to obey Huerta's orders, but this brilliant commander practically ordered Heynen out of his office."[1114] The *New York Times* seconded Buckley's claim, "Capt. C. Bonath of the *Ypiranga*, however, said: 'The possibility that our cargo might be landed at Puerto Mexico was not new to the Collector [Captain Stickney]. Before clearance to Puerto Mexico was granted to us, I asked him specifically: 'What would you do if I were compelled [by Huerta] to land these arms at Puerto Mexico?' To this he made no reply.'"[1115]

From his office in Veracruz, Heynen cabled to the HAPAG office in Hamburg, "...the Americans never gave any indication that unloading the arms and ammunition from the *Ypiranga* would not suit them."[1116] German Military Attaché von Papen seconded Heynen's assertion that the weapons would not have been unloaded if American authorities had voiced any reservations.[1117] On May 31, 1914, Heynen told a *New York*

Times reporter: "This is not a matter between the Washington and Berlin Governments, for there was no understanding that we should not land the *Ypiranga's* cargo elsewhere, the American Admiral commanding at Vera Cruz having said on April 22 that the ship was free to go where it pleased. We made all arrangements for landing at Puerto Mexico, and the German Government had nothing to do with the matter."[1118]

Starting with Barbara Tuchman in the *Zimmermann Telegram*,[1119] historians have used this episode as proof of the German government's support for Huerta and hostility against the American government. The facts tell a different story. Regardless, the munitions came too late to save Huerta, who went into exile in July. The United States would retain Veracruz until November as a means of influencing the Mexican Revolution.

There was a flurry of activity resulting from the American seizure of Veracruz. Chief Bielaski instructed Division Superintendent Offley on April 28 that "because of the complications existing between this government and the Huerta regime in Mexico and with a view especially to preventing any shipments of arms and ammunition manufactured and sold in this country from getting into the hands of Mexicans who may use them against our troops, I wish you would make arrangements with the Bannerman Company to keep you promptly advised of any shipments of arms and ammunition shipped to points along the border or sold or shipped elsewhere under circumstances which may create any suspicion as to the ultimate destination. The Winchester people voluntarily began sending statements to us a few days ago and I have written to the Remington and Colt Companies requesting similar data from them."[1120]

Offley assigned Agent C. J. Scully to contact Bannerman & Sons. The firm told Scully they were concerned whether their having shipped three Hotchkiss one-pounder cannon and 700 shells to Walker Brothers-Hancock Co. of Brownsville, Texas might be a violation of the law. It seems Bannerman had sent the wrong shells and Walker Brothers had requested they be exchanged for proper ones. The arms embargo for all

343

factions was lifted in May.¹¹²¹ Bannerman hesitated to do so. Scully conferred with Offley, who asked Bielaski's opinion. The Chief stated that Bannerman could forward the shells as legitimate commerce but should advise the Bureau when the transaction took place, as well as any other shipments to border points. It turned out that Walker Brothers could not return the wrong cannon shells to Bannerman for exchange because the US army had seized them.¹¹²²

It was not Bannerman but the Charles R. Flint & Co. of New York City which was supplying the bulk of ammunition to the Constitutionalists. Shipments sometimes went by rail to destinations such as El Paso, but most went by sea to Galveston. A snapshot of just the month of July 1914 reveals an image of the volume: Remington sent 300,000 rounds on July 14 via the Morgan Line steamer, *El Mundo*, consigned to Galveston; The Union Metallic Cartridge Company (Remington Arms Co.) reported that on July 18, 350,000 cartridges went to Shelton-Payne in El Paso and 450,000 to Galveston; on July 21, a Morgan Line ship carried 215,000 rounds for Shelton-Payne and 300,000 cartridges for Galveston; on the 25th, Morgan Line steamer *El Sol* transported 1,000,000 cartridges to Galveston; four days later, another 350,000 rounds left for the same destination; and, in August, Flint & Company handled 1,750,000 cartridges and twenty-six cases of rifles.¹¹²³

Lázaro de la Garza, who handled Villa's supply chain, placed an order with Remington Arms for 5,000,000 cartridges, 3,000,000 of them destined to El Paso, and the rest to some Gulf seaport.¹¹²⁴ Remington hesitated to make the shipment, seeking the government's permission. Chief Bielaski assured Remington that the shipment could proceed. Flint & Co. ordered de la Garza's cartridges, 3,000,000 going by sea to Galveston and paid for on delivery, and 2,000,000 by sea to Tampico. Remington kept the Bureau apprised of these and subsequent shipments.¹¹²⁵ These munitions would prove crucial in the next iteration of the Mexican Revolution.

CHAPTER 11: CLASH OF THE TITANS

After his forces had suffered a series of defeats, mainly at the hands of Pancho Villa, Huerta on July 15, 1914, submitted his letter of resignation to Congress and left for exile in Spain, courtesy of Captain Köhler and the SMS *Dresden*.

Huerta's defeat precipitated a vicious power struggle among the victorious Constitutionalist leaders. First Chief Carranza demanded obedience from his principal generals, Pablo González, Álvaro Obregón, and Pancho Villa, but the latter, whose Division of the North was the most powerful military force, increasingly adopted an independent attitude. Despite efforts at reconciliation, there was an open break between Carranza and Villa by September 1914. Constitutionalists would now be fighting each other, and individuals had to choose sides in this latest chapter of the revolution. The late President Francisco Madero's family supported Villa, his uncles in New York as buyers, and his brother, Emilio, as a general in the División del Norte. Felix Sommerfeld moved to New York in the summer of 1914, ostensibly to represent Villa's interests in the United States as an arms buyer and a diplomatic representative. In truth, German naval intelligence had re-assigned Sommerfeld to Karl Boy-Ed, the German naval attaché in New York to head Mexican missions during the World War. Sam Dreben worked for Sommerfeld in El Paso as a Villa agent. Enrique Llorente, working closely with Sommerfeld and Hopkins, represented Villa in Washington, where there was also a Carranza representative, Eliseo Arredondo. Informants Stevens and Thompson stayed with Carranza.[1126]

Those opposed to Carranza convened at the city of Aguascalientes and formed a government headed by General Eulalio Gutiérrez, chosen because he had no troops, and thus was acceptable to all. Gutiérrez was a figurehead; the real power was Pancho Villa, who commanded the Convention's army, consisting mainly of his Division of the North. Supporting Villa was governor of Sonora José María Maytorena, who now styled himself as a general. In the South, General Emiliano Zapata continued his independent rebellion centered in the State of Morelos; he likewise opposed Carranza and allied himself with Villa. First Chief Carranza shrewdly continued to use the designation, "Constitutionalist," for his faction while denouncing his enemies as "reactionaries." Crucially, Carranza retained the loyalty of generals Pablo González and Álvaro Obregón. Villistas and carrancistas battled each other with the same ferocity they had earlier directed against the Huerta administration.

The Wilson administration's position regarding this new round of civil war was to announce a posture of neutrality while waiting to see which faction prevailed. Once again, the Bureau had to rearrange its priorities, because by 1915 the Mexican Revolution reached a new level of intensity and complexity.

Conclusion

During the six years following its inception in 1908, the federal Bureau of Investigation made remarkable progress. The public perception was that the agency mainly enforced the Mann Act, but the Bureau also enforced the neutrality laws. In fact, the BI figuratively cut its intelligence eyeteeth enforcing the neutrality laws. Significant, but largely overlooked, were the first two leaders: Chief Stanley Finch who established the Bureau's organizational structure, and the youthful Chief A. Bruce Bielaski who guided the agency through a period of rapid expansion.

While enforcing the neutrality laws, mainly concerning the Mexican Revolution, the BI developed investigative techniques that

Figure 43 *Alexander Bruce Bielaski at his desk. Source: Findagrave.com.*

provided the agency with an intelligence capability. Working under US attorneys, the BI's mission was to develop evidence for cases to be tried in federal court. This involved using techniques such as mail covers, the subpoena duces tecum, Dictaphones, "black bag" jobs—and above all, HUMINT—informers. The great strength of the Bureau was that it was a nationwide organization. Leads could be followed up quickly because the telegraph enabled field offices to communicate with each other and with headquarters in Washington. The pattern, however, that evolved was for the Bureau to develop a seemingly airtight case, only for the government to lose it in court. This resulted from several factors: locals resenting the government's interference in profitable businesses such as the arms traffic; juries rejecting the testimony of the prosecution's Mexican witnesses; and, defense attorneys securing continuances so that by the time a case finally came to trial, important witnesses were nowhere to be found.

Neutrality enforcement, however, was not just the application of federal statutes. On occasion, the Bureau bowed to political pressure and amended or self-censored its reports. The agency also reflected US foreign policy. The Bureau slow-walked and dropped investigations of regimes and factions the US favored, while moving aggressively against those the US opposed. A prime example was the Bureau's unprecedented cooperation with the Mexican intelligence service during the Madero administration in 1912. Mexico provided badly needed finances and manpower, and the Bureau allowed Mexican agents to operate brazenly in the United States. Further evidence of the uneven application of the neutrality laws was the Bureau's aggressive attitude toward the anarchist Flores Magón faction, and the American socialists, anarchists, and militant organizations, such as the Industrial Workers of the World (IWW), who supported the *magonistas*.

Because of the way Mexican factions continuously merged and divided, the Bureau frequently had to shift investigative gears—yesterday's persons of interest were now allies. In this connection, any faction was eager to provide the Bureau with detrimental information about its enemies. BI agents constantly had to guard against being manipulated. They also had to sift through misinformation and disinformation, with "fake news" being the order of the day.

Besides being chronically underfunded, the Bureau lacked an effective surveillance capability. Maintaining surveillance on a prominent person of interest was a difficult enterprise, necessitating considerable manpower and equipment. The Bureau lacked both, and as for equipment, the field offices even lacked fundamental tools such as an automobile, a deficiency that would not be corrected until World War I. It was hardly surprising that the Bureau lost track of personages such as Generals Bernardo Reyes, Victoriano Huerta, and Félix Díaz.

This situation underscored another major problem for the Bureau: initially, few of its agents spoke Spanish or had any border experience. Thus, they had to rely on interpreters of varying ability and veracity. Compounding the problem, despite the BI repeatedly seizing masses of revolutionary documents, was the lack of agency personnel to translate these documents in a timely manner.

The Bureau routinely exchanged information with the Department of State, and especially with the US Army. Although by law the army was prohibited from enforcing civil law, on occasion, the military supplied personnel to assist a BI investigation. What did not figure prominently was the US Secret Service, tasked with protecting the President and chasing counterfeiters. We should note that in archival documents and newspapers articles of the period, the term "secret service" often did not refer to the US Secret Service at all. Confusing many an historian, "secret service" or "secret agent" were generic terms for those agents involved in intelligence work, often the special agents of the Bureau of Investigation.

The Bureau grew from a small office with limited resources in 1908, to become an effective national law enforcement agency by 1914. Its intelligence capabilities would soon include counterintelligence capabilities, particularly as the German menace developed in the run-up to America's entrance into World War I (1914-1917).

ENDNOTES

1. New York: Checkmark Books, 2000.
2. New Haven: Yale University Press, 2007.
3. New York: Simon and Schuster, 2022.
4. New York: Dutton, 1947.
5. The Story of the FBI, 10-12.
6. When J. Edgar Hoover became Director in 1924, he was only the sixth head of the Bureau of Investigation: Stanley Wellington Finch (July 26, 1908-April 29, 1912), Alexander Bruce Bielaski (April 30, 1912-February 9, 1919), William E. Allen (February 10, 1919-June 30, 1919), William J. Flynn (July 1, 1919-August 22, 1921), William J. Burns (August 21, 1921-May 10, 1924), J. Edgar Hoover (May 10, 1924-May 2, 1972).
7. New York: Random House, 1956.
8. Willard M. Oliver, *The Birth of the FBI: Teddy Roosevelt, the Secret Service, and the Fight Over America's Premier Law Enforcement Agency* (Lanham: Rowan & Littlefield, 2019), 261-263.
9. For example, the FBI's pursuit of civil rights leaders in the 1960s to the controversies surrounding the alleged involvement of Russia in the 2016 presidential elections and the subsequent firing of FBI Director James Comey.
10. Ronald Kessler, *The Bureau: The Secret History of the FBI* (New York: St. Martin's Press, 2002), 10.
11. Raymond J. Batvinis, *The Origins of FBI Counterintelligence* (Lawrence: University Press of Kansas, 2007), 1.
12. Kessler, *The Bureau*, 11.
13. Roy Emerson Curtis, "The Law of Hostile Military Expeditions as Applied by the United States," *The American Journal of International Law*, 8, (January, April 1914), 1-37, 224-256.
14. Hazen report, July 29, 1915, BI, roll 858.
15. "Purchasing Power Today of a US Dollar Transaction in the Past," Measuring Worth, 2023. www.measuringworth.com/ppowerus. Throughout the text there are US dollar and Mexican peso amounts quoted and mentioned. The value of the Mexican peso in that period was firmly linked to the value of the US dollar at fifty percent, i.e. 1,000 Mexican pesos during that period had a value of 500 US dollars. The 2023 value of 1,000 US dollars in 1910 was approximately 31,000 US dollars. This current value decreased throughout the decade 1910-1920. By 1920 the current value of 1,000 US dollars was approximately 15,000."
16. There are exceptions to the rule—e. g. Antonio López de Santa Anna, Francisco Vázquez de Coronado, Plutarco Elías Calles, Ricardo Flores Magón, etc.
17. Whitehead, FBI Story, 13, 17-18.; H. W. Brands, T. R. *The Last Romantic* (New York: Basic Books, 1997), 632-634.
18. Annual Report of the Attorney-General of the United States for the Year 1907, 2 vols. (Washington, DC: Government Printing Office, 1907), I:9-11.
19. Annual Report of the Attorney-General of the United States for the Year 1908 (Washington, DC: Government Printing Office, 1908), 27-29; Whitehead, FBI Story, 18-19.

20 See, for example, Finch to McNish, April 29, 1908, Letters sent by the Chief Examiner, BI, RG 65, NARA, hereinafter cited as CE.
21 The best account of the FBI's beginning is John R. Fox, Jr., "The Birth of the Federal Bureau of Investigation," Federal Bureau of Investigation website, July 2003 (www.fbi.gov/history/history-publications-reports/the-birth-of-the-federal-bureau-of-investigation.)
22 The chief forensic accountant.
23 Theoharis et al., The FBI, 3.
24 Attorney General, Annual Report, 1908, 7.
25 Garland Globe, January 30, 1909; Daily Press, January 21, 1909.
26 Finch asked for an appointment with J. Edgar Hoover in 1934. Largely forgotten for his service as Chief of the BI, he felt that he had to introduce himself to as the "'Grand-Daddy' of the Division of Investigation." Whether Director Hoover ever received the former chief remains unknown. T. D. Quinn to Director Hoover, December 19, 1934, Personnel file of Bruce A. Bielaski, file 62-HQ-26902-3, courtesy John Fox.
27 Theoharis et al., The FBI, 325-326.
28 Theoharis et al., The FBI, 241.
29 Finch to Bank, April 28, 1910. Finch informed the Savage Arms Company that their automatic pistol tended to jam, and most bureau agents preferred a revolver. Finch to Savage Arms Company, November 3, 1910, CE.
30 Finch to Munson, July 20, 1910, CE.
31 Finch to National Dictograph Company, October 6, 1910, CE.
32 Oliver, Birth of the FBI, 174-175. Some other early special agents are listed in Hoover to Dick, March 10, 1949, Alexander Bruce Bielaski file, Federal Bureau of Investigation, Washington, DC
33 Minneapolis Journal, December 22, 1906; Parma Herald, April 27, 1907.
34 Omaha Daily Bee, September 4, 1918.
35 His employment data is incomplete. His 1942 World War II registration card still shows his employment with the Justice Department.
36 Theoharis et al, The FBI, 4; Sanford J. Ungar, FBI: An Uncensored Look Behind the Walls (New York: Atlantic-Little, Brown, 1975), 40.
37 Finch to Poulin, May 2, July 6, 16, 1910; Finch to Kennoch, June 9, 1910; Finch to Brennan, September 26, 1910, CE.
38 Lewiston Evening Teller, November 23, 1908.
39 Topeka State Journal, December 30, 1909.
40 Finch to Schmid, July 19, 1910, CE.
41 Waterbury Evening Democrat, February 28, 1908.
42 Tacoma Times, December 11, 1909.
43 New York Sun, November 11, 1909.
44 New York Sun, November 11, 1909.
45 New York Sun, November 11, 1909.
46 Theoharis et al., The FBI, 3, 6.
47 Finch to Vann, November 5, 1910; Finch to Lancaster, November 8, 1910, CE.

48 Finch to Bielaski, June 9, 1908, CE.
49 Finch to Bielaski, April 17, 1908; Finch to Sherwood, April 17, 1908, CE.
50 Finch to Donnelle, May 9, 1910, CE.
51 Finch to Munson, July 20, 1910, CE.
52 Finch to Schmid, June 18, 1910, CE.
53 Finch to Schmid, October 12, 1910, CE.
54 Finch to Herrington, October 21, 1910, CE.
55 Finch to All Examiners, October 14, 1908, CE.
56 Watkins report, November 18, 1911; Betjeman reports, November 21, December 11, 1911; Grgurevich report, January 3, 1912, BI, roll 851; Theoharis et al., The FBI, 4.
57 Betjeman report, November 23, 1911, BI, roll 851.
58 See, for instance, the file of local white slave officer Charles B. Brown, Waco, Texas, FRC-FW.
59 Colin M. MacLachlan, *Anarchism and the Mexican Revolution: The Political Trials of Ricardo Flores Magón in the United States* (Berkeley, Los Angeles, Oxford: University of California Press, 1991), 13.
60 See Claudio Lomnitz-Adler, *The Return of Comrade Ricardo Flores Magón* (New York: Zone Books, 2014).
61 James D. Cockcroft, *Intellectual Precursors of the Mexican Revolution, 1900-1913* (Austin: University of Texas Press, 1968), 88.
62 Lowell L. Blaisdell, *The Desert Revolution: Baja California, 1911* (Madison: University of Wisconsin Press, 1962), 7.
63 Charles H. Harris III and Louis R. Sadler, *The Secret War in El Paso: Mexican Revolutionary Intrigue, 1906-1920* (Albuquerque: University of New Mexico Press, 2009), 19-21; W. Dirk Raat, *Revoltosos: Mexico's Rebels in the United States, 1903-1923* (College Station: Texas A & M University Press, 1981), 122.
64 Dorothy Pierson Kerig, *Luther T. Ellsworth: U. S. Consul on the Border During the Mexican Revolution* (El Paso: Texas Western Press, 1975), 11.
65 NMF, file no. 5028, microcopy M-862, RDS.
66 Michael M. Smith, "The Mexican Secret Service in the United States, 1910-1920," *The Americas*, 59, no. 1 (July 2002): 66-67.
67 Raat, *Revoltosos*, 124.
68 Thomas Furlong, *Fifty Years a Detective* (St. Louis: C. E. Barnett, 1912), 137-146.
69 MacLachlan, *Anarchism*, 29; Raat, *Revoltosos*, 165-166.
70 Ward S. Albro, *Always a Rebel: Ricardo Flores Magón and the Mexican Revolution* (Fort Worth: Texas Christian University Press, 1992), 109.
71 U. S. Commissioner, El Paso, nos. 88, 100, 101, 117, 156, and U. S. District Court, El Paso, nos. 1359, 1362-69, 1371-74, 1376, and San Antonio 2006, 2007, FRC-FW.
72 US Attorney to Attorney General, July 20, 1908, CE; Kerig, *Luther Ellsworth*, 15-16.
73 Kerig, *Luther Ellsworth*, 16-17.
74 Kerig, *Luther Ellsworth*, 18.
75 Priest to Secretary of State, September 20, 1909; Ellsworth to Assistant Secretary of State, September 30, 1909, 90755-158, Department of Justice, RG 60, NARA.
76 Finch to Lancaster, June 14, 1910, CE.

77 Kerig, Luther Ellsworth, 25.
78 Kerig, Luther Ellsworth, 26-27.
79 Priest to Secretary of State, September 20, 1909, 90755-158, Department of Justice, RG 60, NARA.
80 Mexican revolutionists habitually carried incriminating papers. Thus, hundreds of documents seized by the authorities are in United States archives.
81 Raat, Revoltosos, 167.
82 Owosso Times, May 4, 1906
83 Santa Fe New Mexican, August 3, 1903.
84 Elizabeth Cole succumbed to her illness in El Paso within days after the outbreak of the Mexican Revolution in November 1910 (Detroit Times, November 19, 1910).
85 Steven Devitt, The Pen that Set Mexico on Fire: The Betrayal of Ricardo Flores Magón During the Mexican Revolution (Amissville: Henselstone Verlag, 2017), 94-95.
86 Devitt, The Pen that Set Mexico on Fire, 106.
87 Case 232, April 2, 14, 16, 23, 1910, BI, roll 851. For 1910 and 1911, most reports are designated as "Case 232," with summaries rather than agent reports. The citations are: Case 232, date of summary, BI, roll ___. Agent reports are cited by name, date, BI, and roll of microfilm.
88 Devitt, The Pen that Set Mexico on Fire, 108.
89 Scarborough report, June 30, 1910, BI, roll 851; see also Finch to Cole, May 2, 1910, CE.
90 Guthrie Daily Leader, December 8, 1909.
91 Geck report, January 25-27, 1910, BI, roll 851.
92 Geck report, January 12, 1910, BI, roll 851.
93 Vann report, February 15, 1910, BI, roll 851.
94 El Paso Daily Herald, July 10, 1900.
95 Brownsville Daily Herald, May 31, 1906.
96 Palestine Daily Herald, December 19, 1908; Brownsville Daily Herald, March 17, 1909.
97 Lancaster reports, February 18, 19, March 7, 10, 11, April 30, 1910, BI, roll 851.
98 For a complete biography, see Henry Jay Case, Guy Hamilton Scull: Soldier Writer, Explorer and War Correspondent (New York: Duffield and Company, 1922).
99 US Census 1880 and 1900 "Marshall Eberstein.".
100 Producers News, January 2, 1925.
101 Scull reports, February 8, 11, 12, 14, 21, 1910, BI, roll 851.
102 See, for example, Finch to DeWoody, November 21, 1910, CE, and Royce report, November 27, 1911, BI, roll 851.
103 Hebert reports, February 21, 24, March 2, 3, 1910, BI, roll 851.
104 Thibodaux Sentinel, June 19, 1908; St. Landry Clarion, March 27, 1909.
105 Geck reports, May 5, 9, 13, 1910, BI, roll 851.
106 Lancaster reports, March 18, 30, April 1, 2, 15, 1910, BI, roll 851.
107 Cole reports, March 16, 22, May 23, 1910, BI, roll 851.
108 Cole report, April 11, 1910, BI, roll 851.
109 Cole report, March 22, 1910, BI, roll 851.
110 Cole report, April 20, 1910, BI, roll 851.

111 Geck report, June 24, 1910, BI, roll 851.
112 Cole report, March 29, 1910, BI, roll 851.
113 Cole reports, May 14, 1910, June 10, BI, roll 851.
114 [Santos] Coy reports, June 23, August 5, 11, 1910, BI, roll 851.
115 Finch to Lancaster, July 23, 1910, CE.
116 Finch to Geck, July 16, 1910, CE.
117 Surprisingly, the bureau had known back in January that the state prison was in Florence, not Yuma.
118 Geck reports, August 1, 4, 5, 10, 11, 12, 1910, BI, roll 851.
119 Simmons reports, August 13, 17, 18, 24, 1910, BI, roll 851.
120 Priest reports, August 5, 31, 1910, roll 851.
121 Vann reports, August 4, 9, 1910, BI, roll 851.
122 Vann report, September 1, 1910, BI, roll 851.
123 Simmons reports, September 8, 12, 19, 20, 22, 30, October 7, 1910, BI, roll 851.
124 Geck report, September 15, 1910, BI, roll 851.
125 Finch to Geck, July 25, 1910, CE.
126 Finch to Lancaster, September 13, 1910, CE.
127 Finch to Simmons, October 11, 1910, CE.
128 Charles C. Cumberland, "Mexican Revolutionary Movements from Texas, 1906-1912," *Southwestern Historical Quarterly*, 52 (January 1949): 306-313.
129 Harris and Sadler, *Secret War*, 28-29.
130 The Mexican government's case against Madero was summarized by Roberto A. Esteva Ruiz for the Foreign Secretary, January 4, 1911, DHRM, 5:141-146.
131 Finch to Simmons, November 3, 1910, and to Cole, November 8, 1910, CE.
132 The best study of maderista activities in San Antonio is David N. Johnson, "Exiles and Intrigue: Francisco I. Madero and the Mexican Revolutionary Junta in San Antonio, 1910-1911," M. A. Thesis, Trinity University, 1975.
133 Case 232, March 29, 1911, BI, roll 851; Berta Ulloa, *Revolución mexicana, 1910-1920. Archivo histórico diplomático mexicano. Guía para la historia diplomática de Mexico*, No. 3 (Mexico, DF: Secretaría de Relaciones Exteriores, 1985): 73, 78, 79, 83, 96.
134 Heribert von Feilitzsch, *In Plain Sight: Felix A. Sommerfeld, Spymaster in Mexico, 1908-1914* (Amissville: Henselstone Verlag, 2012), 121-122.
135 *The Evening Bulletin* (Maysville, KY), November 5, 1887.
136 *The Washington Times*, October 10, 1898.
137 Official program, Admiral Dewey Reception, October 2 and 3, Washington, 1899.
138 Memorandum for Lt. Col. Dunn, September 25, 1920, NARA, RG 165, MID, file 2338-997.
139 The "Banana Wars" are referring to multiple US interventions in Central America in the first decades of the 20th century to reinforce US commercial interests in the region.
140 von Feilitzsch, *In Plain Sight*, 100-101.
141 Mitchell report, February 24, 1911, BI, roll 851.
142 Case 232, October 20, 21, 24, 27, 1910, BI, roll 851.
143 Case 232, February 14, 1911, BI, roll 851.
144 Harris and Sadler, *Secret War*, 32.

145 US Senate, *Revolutions in Mexico: Hearing before a Subcommittee of the Committee on Foreign Relations*. 62nd Cong. 2nd sess. (Washington, DC: Government Printing Office, 1913), 124.

146 Francisco R. Almada, *Diccionario de Historia, Geografía, y Biografía Chihuahuenses*, 2nd ed. (Chihuahua: Universidad de Chihuahua, 1968), 229.

147 Several of Thiel's agents, Hy A. Thompson, Henry C. Kramp and Louis E. Ross, were to play important roles in El Paso: Kramp as future manager of the local Thiel branch office, Thompson as agent in charge of the San Antonio BI office, and L. E. Ross as a future BI agent in El Paso.

148 Beckham report, December 5, 1914, BI, roll 855.

149 Harris and Sadler, *Secret War*, 35, 82.

150 Scully report, February 7, 1911, BI, roll 851.

151 Scully report, February 10, 1911, BI, roll 851.

152 Harris and Sadler, *Secret War*, 33, 87; Scully report, April 24, 1912, BI, roll 851.

153 Scully report, February 18, 1911, BI, roll 851.

154 George T. Díaz, *Border Contraband: A History of Smuggling Across the Rio Grande* (Austin: University of Texas Press, 2015) leaves much to be desired since he avoids discussing the most important part of his subject. El Paso was the principal center of smuggling, not just on the Rio Grande, but on the entire Mexican border, especially during the decade of the Mexican Revolution. Díaz makes scant reference to El Paso, and to the crucial revolutionary decade in that city he devotes two references to an article and one footnote (197, note 55) from a book. Díaz's book might more accurately be entitled, *Border Contraband: A History of Smuggling Across Part of the Rio Grande Some of the Time*.

155 Cole report, February 23, April 15, 1911, BI, roll 851.

156 Wilbur report, February 11, 13, 14, March 21, 1911, BI, roll 851.

157 Wilbur report, March 6, 1911, BI, roll 851.

158 Scull report, March 7-9, 1911, BI, roll 851.

159 Eberstein report, March 21, 1911, BI, roll 851.

160 Eberstein report, March 28, 1911, BI, roll 851.

161 Case 232, March 12, 1911, BI, roll 851.

162 "Translations of Letters, Telegrams, Bills, etc. Made from Fragments of Papers Obtained by Informant Wilbur," in Eberstein to Boynton, Case 232, undated but received at bureau headquarters on April 4, 1911, BI, roll 852.

163 Case 232, April 1, 4, 5, 1911, BI, roll 851; Nos. 69, 70, 71, US Commissioner, Del Rio, no. 2033, US District Court, San Antonio, FRC-FW.

164 Statement of John C. Wilbur, March 30, 1911; see also Case 232, February 28, March 2, 1911, BI, roll 851; Agent 19 report, June 16, 1911 (for a time in 1911, agents reported using their badge number); Wilbur reports, June 14, July 3, 1911, BI roll 852.

165 Wilbur reports, April 13, 15, May 8, 14-16, 18, 19, 1911, BI, roll 851; Barnes reports, February 19, 20, 21, 1912, BI, roll 852.

166 Thompson report, January 13, 1913, BI, roll 853.

167 *New York Sun*, April 30, 1911.

168 Ibid.; *San Francisco Call*, July 16, 1911; *Arizona Republican*, October 8, 1908.

169 Guy H. Scull, *Lassoing Wild Animals in Africa* (New York: Frederick A. Stokes Company, 1911).

170 Henry Jay Case, *Guy Hamilton Scull: Soldier, Writer, Explorer and Correspondent* (New York: Duffield and Company, 1922), 209-216. He returned in 1914, moved to New York, and married. There, he served as Deputy Police Commissioner and hunted German saboteurs. In 1917, he joined the war effort as a military intelligence agent in Washington, DC and New York rounding up "slackers," as suspected draft-dodgers were then called. (*Breckenridge News*, September 1, 1915; *New York Evening World*, November 2, 1920; Harvard's Military Record in the World War). He achieved the rank of major during the war. Scull died in New York in 1920 from blood poisoning caused by a carbuncle in his nose. (www.ancestry.com. Guy Hamilton Scull family tree).

171 Case, *Guy Hamilton Scull*, 206.

172 William H. Beezley, *Insurgent Governor: Abraham González and the Mexican Revolution in Chihuahua* (Lincoln: University of Nebraska Press, 1973), 34.

173 Lomelí to Foreign Secretary, February 14, 1911, DHRM, 5:244-245; no. 771, US Commissioner, El Paso, FRC-FW.

174 The bureau had filed a criminal complaint against Madero, González, Martín Casillas and Gabino Cano. Madero and González escaped, and in April the federal grand jury found "no bill" against Casillas and Cano. Case 232, April 18, 1911, BI, roll 851.

175 Friedrich Katz, *The Life and Times of Pancho Villa* (Stanford: Stanford University Press, 1998), 93.

176 See for example Friedrich Katz, *The Secret War in Mexico: Europe, the United States, and the Mexican Revolution* (Chicago: University of Chicago Press, 1981), 333-337; Katz, *Life and Times*, 554-555; Michael C. Meyer, "Villa, Sommerfeld, Columbus y los alemanes," *Historia Mexicana* (Vol. 28, No. 4, April to June 1979), 546-567; Alan Knight, *The Mexican Revolution: Volume 2, Counter-Revolution and Reconstruction* (Lincoln: University of Nebraska Press, 1986), 346; Clarence C. Clendenen, *The United States and Pancho Villa: A Study in Unconventional Diplomacy* (Ithaca: Cornell University Press, 1961), 56-57.

177 von Feilitzsch, *In Plain Sight*, 95.

178 Case 232, April 10, 12, 1911, BI, roll 851.

179 Case 232, April 6, June 1, 2, 1911, BI, roll 851; see also Lawrence D. Taylor, *La gran aventura en Mexico: El papel de los voluntarios extranjeros en los ejércitos revolucionarios, 1910-1915*, 2 vols. (Mexico, D.F.: Consejo Nacional Para la Cultura y las Artes, 1993).

180 Case 232, April 25, May 1, 1911, BI, roll 851.

181 Vann report, May 8, 1911, BI, roll 851.

182 Case 232, April 18, 22, May 2-6, 1911, BI, roll 851.

183 Harris and Sadler, *Secret War*, 51-52.

184 Eberstein report, May 15, 1911; Agent 71 [Cole] reports, May 16, 18, 1911, BI, roll 851.

185 Finch to Eberstein, May 15, 20, 1911, BI, roll 851.

186 Eberstein reports, May 20, 23, 1911, BI, roll 851.

187 Finch to Eberstein, May 25, 1911, BI, roll 851.

188 *National Guard Registers*, vol. 72, Unattached Companies 2nd and 3rd Brigades Enlisted Men, 1880 – 1894.

189 *Daily Yellowstone Journal*, March 25, 1887.

190 *Wheeling Daily Intelligencer*, Jan. 23, 1889.

191 *Guthrie Daily Leader*, January 27, 1906; *Tulsa Daily World*, August 7, 1906; *Vinita Daily Chieftain*, January 23, 1907; *Omaha Daily Bee*, August 16, 1907.
192 *Parma Herald*, April 27, 1907.
193 *Bisbee Daily Review*, March 18, 1911.
194 Eberstein headed the BI field office in Omaha until 1918, when he became Omaha's Chief of Police. He was forced to resign in 1921 amid several scandals and political upheaval. A police shooting resulting in the death of an inmate, and violent race riots in the city that had to be quelled by the military caused his downfall. After a "long vacation," lasting the better part of a year, he re-joined the BI in 1922 as agent in charge of the Kansas City field office. His next assignments took him to Seattle, Washington, Portland, Oregon, and Minneapolis, Minnesota before retiring in 1929. His son, Russell, became one of the youngest members of the BI, joining the bureau's Omaha office in 1918 at the age of 22 (*Audubon Republican*, October 9, 1919; *Omaha Daily Bee*, September 4, 1918, May 14, October 21, 1921, July 11, 1922; US City Directory, Seattle Washington, 1925).
195 Case 232, May 18, 22, 1911, BI, roll 851.
196 Simmons report, May 22, 1911, BI, roll 851; for the IWW, see William Preston, Jr., *Aliens and Dissenters: Federal Suppression of Radicals, 1903-1933* (New York: Harper & Row, 1963).
197 Simmons reports, April 4, 1911, BI, roll 851.
198 Agent 90 reports, June 14, 15, 1911; Herrington reports, June 14, 15, 18, 1911, BI, roll 852. US Senate, *Revolutions in Mexico: Hearing before a Subcommittee of the Committee on Foreign Relations*. 62nd Cong. 2nd sess. (Washington, DC: Government Printing Office, 1913), 136-137; Wickersham to McCormick, June 16, 1911; Agent 66 reports, June 25, 26, 1911, BI, roll 851.
199 1880 Census; *Catalogue of Iowa College, 1877-1888* (Grinnell: Herald Job Printing Office, 1877), 8.
200 *San Francisco Call*, May 4, 1911; *Maryland Suffrage News*, April 27, 1912.
201 Herrington reports, March 2, 10, 15, 20, 28, 1911, BI, roll 851.
202 Baker reports, June 23, 24, July 3, 1911; Irvine Mitchell memorandum, June 24, 1911; Bagley report, June 28, 1911; Mitchell report, July 2, 1911, BI, roll 852.
203 Colin M. MacLachlan, *Anarchism*, 35-36.
204 Ganor reports, March 30, April 7, 1911, BI, roll 851.
205 Agent 98 reports, June 16, 18, 1911, BI, roll 852.
206 Agent 66 report, June 21, 1911, BI, roll 851.
207 Agent 66 report, June 22, July 1, 1911, BI, roll 851; Thompson report, July 6, 1911, BI, roll 852.
208 Finch to Secretary of State, May 2, 1913, RDS 812.00/7383.
209 Agent 98 reports, July 9, 14, 16, 20, 21, 1911; Agent 66 report, July 10, 1911, BI, roll 851.
210 MacLachlan, *Anarchism*, 24.
211 Ganor report, March 22, 1912, BI, roll 851.
212 Ganor report, February 27, 1912, BI, roll 852.
213 See Prieto to Sub-Prefecto, May 2, 1911, BI, roll 851.
214 Ganor report, May 31, 1911, BI, roll 851.

215 Lowell L. Blaisdell, *The Desert Revolution: Baja California, 1911* (Madison: University of Wisconsin Press, 1962), 136-137; Wickersham to McCormick, June 16, 1911; Agent 66 reports, June 25, 26, 1911, BI, roll 851.
216 Case 232, April 25, 27, May 1, 1911, BI, roll 851; Agent 98 reports, June 23, 25, 1911, BI roll 852.
217 The War Department subsequently released 95 of the prisoners; Case 232, June 23, 1911; Agent 98 report, June 25, 1911, BI, roll 852.
218 Agent 66 reports, June 17-19, 1911, BI, roll 852, June 19-21, 1911, BI, roll 851.
219 Agent 66 report, June 21, 1911; Case 232, June 24, 1911, BI, roll 851.
220 Ganor reports, March 3,1 May 25, 26, 1912, BI, roll 851.
221 Harris reports, July 22, 31, August 1, 1911; Case 232, July 29, August 5, 1911, BI, roll 851.
222 Agent 96 reports, August 25, 26, 30, September 1, 3, 4, 6, October 4, 5, 1911, BI, roll 851 and October 6, 9, 1911, BI, roll 852.
223 Harris report, October 20, 1911, BI, roll 851.
224 Dorey to Chief, March 4, 1911, BI, roll 854, enclosing a chronological list of events pertaining to the case of the vessel *Hornet*—US vs. Manuel Bonilla, Lee Christmas et al.
225 He and his entourage left the next day.
226 See E. V. Niemeyer, Jr., *El General Bernardo Reyes* (Monterrey: Universidad de Nuevo León, 1966), 188-205, and his "Frustrated Invasion: The Revolutionary Attempt of General Bernardo Reyes from San Antonio in 1911," *Southwestern Historical Quarterly*, 67, no. 2 (1963): 213-225.
227 Wilbur report, October 9, 1911, BI, roll 852.
228 This was how Colonel Edward M. House, President Woodrow Wilson's closest advisor, became a [lieutenant] colonel.
229 Wilbur reports, October 11, 1911, BI, roll 852 and October 12, 1911, BI, roll 851; Thompson report, October 13, 1911, BI, roll 851.
230 Case 232, October 13, 1911; Lancaster report, October 15, 1911, BI, roll 851.
231 Lancaster report, October 16, 1911, BI, roll 851.
232 *A Twentieth Century History of Southwest Texas*, 3 vols. (Chicago, New York, Los Angeles: Lewis Publishing Company, 1907), II, 94.
233 Thompson to Finch, October 19, 1911, BI, roll 852.
234 Wilbur report, October 17, 1911; Lancaster report, October 20, 1911, BI, roll 851.
235 Wilbur reports, October 18, 1911, BI, roll 852; October 24, 1911, BI, roll 851.
236 Lancaster report, October 17, 1911, BI, roll 852.
237 Lancaster report, October 18, 1911, BI, roll 852.
238 Charles H. Harris III and Louis R. Sadler, "The 1911 Reyes Conspiracy: The Texas Side," *Southwestern Historical Quarterly*, 83, No. 4 (April 1980): 332-333.
239 Lancaster report, October 19, 1911, BI, roll 851.
240 Lancaster reports, October 17, 18, 1911, BI, roll 852.
241 Lancaster reports, October 24, 26, 1911; see also Thompson report, October 26, 1911, BI, roll 851.
242 Wilbur report, October 19, 1911, BI roll 851; October 22, 1911, BI, roll 852.
243 Wilbur report, October 31, 1911, BI, roll 852.

[244] Thompson to Finch, October 19, 1911; Thompson report, October 22, 1911, BI, roll 852.
[245] Lancaster report, October 28, 1911, with pamphlet enclosed, BI, roll 851, and November 3, 1911, BI, roll 852.
[246] Thompson to Finch, October 30, 1911, roll 851.
[247] *Los Angeles Times*, March 29, 1913.
[248] *White Pine News Weekly Mining Review*, June 9, 1912; *Evening Standard*, September 10, 1912.
[249] Ancestry.com, Lamoreaux family tree, viewed March 2022.
[250] Lamoreaux reports, November 29, 1911, BI, roll 852 and November 30, December 2, 1911, BI, roll 853.
[251] Thompson report, October 28, 1911, BI, roll 851.
[252] Ellsworth to Secretary of State, February 2, 1912, RDS 812.00/2756.
[253] Thompson report, October 29, 1911, BI, roll 852.
[254] Thompson to Finch, October 30, 1911, BI, roll 851.
[255] Anthony Templeton Bryan, "Mexican Politics in Transition, 1900-1913: The Role of General Bernardo Reyes," (Ph.D. dissertation, University of Nebraska, 1970), 314-315.
[256] Lancaster report, October 31, 1911, BI, roll 851.
[257] Hebert report, October 31, 1911, BI, roll 851.
[258] Chamberlain reports, November 2, 4, 8, 14, 1911, BI, roll 852; November 19, 22-28, 1911, BI, roll 853.
[259] Hebert report, November 16, 1911, BI, roll 852.
[260] Thompson report, November 16, 1911, BI, roll 852.
[261] Matthews to Nolte, November 14, 1911; Warren to Nolte, November 15, 1911, attached to Thompson report, November 16, 1911; Hebert reports, November 19, 22, 1911, BI, roll 852; Hebert reports, November 20, 21, 1911, BI, roll 853.
[262] No. 93, US Commissioner, San Antonio; nos. 552, 893, US District Court, Laredo, no. 2060, US District Court, Brownsville, FRC-FW.
[263] Lancaster report, November 20, 1911, BI, roll 852 and November 25, 1911, BI, roll 853.
[264] *San Antonio Express*, November 19, 1911.
[265] Thompson report, November 28, 1911, BI, roll 853.
[266] Thompson report, November 21, 1911, BI, roll 852.
[267] *Revolutions in Mexico*, Testimony of Felix A. Sommerfeld, 389.
[268] *Revolutions in Mexico*, Testimony of C. D. Hebert, 531.
[269] *Revolutions in Mexico*, Testimony of F. A. Sommerfeld, 387 ff.
[270] *Revolutions in Mexico*, Testimony of Felix A. Sommerfeld, 419.
[271] Statement of F. A. Sommerfeld, June 21-24, 1918, file 9-16-12, Department of Justice, RG 60, NARA.
[272] *Revolutions in Mexico*, Testimony of C. D. Hebert, 531.
[273] Thompson report, November 29, 1911; Lancaster report, November 27, 1911, BI, roll 853.
[274] Thompson reports, November 22, 24, 1911, BI, roll 852 and November 28, 1911, BI, roll 853, enclosing the translation of Reyes's manifesto.
[275] Thompson report, December 8, 1911, BI, roll 853.

276 Thompson report, November 25, 1911; Lancaster report, November 25, 1911, BI, roll 853 lists the witnesses being held in the guardhouse at Fort McIntosh.
277 Lancaster reports, November 28-30, 1911, BI, roll 853.
278 Lancaster report, November 30, 1911, BI, roll 853, enclosing a copy of the notebook, and December 2, 1911; Thompson report, December 2, 1911, BI, roll 853.
279 Lamoreaux report, December 24, 1911, BI, roll 853.
280 Thompson report, November 29, 1911, BI, roll 852.
281 Case 232, December 1, 2, 9, 1911; Thompson report, December 9, 1911, BI, roll 853.
282 Chamberlain reports, December 4, 6, 1911, BI, roll 853.
283 Hebert reports, September 15, 19-22, 26-30, October 1, 1911, BI, roll 851, and October 5, 1911, BI, roll 852.
284 Hebert reports, October 6, 7, 1911, BI, roll 852.
285 Chamberlain reports, November 29, 30, December 2-4, 1911, BI, roll 853.
286 No. 983, US Commissioner, El Paso, and no. 1564, District Court, El Paso, FRC-FW; Harris and Sadler, *Secret War*, 63-66.
287 Thompson report, December 5, 1911, BI, roll 853.
288 Chamberlain reports, December 5, 6, 1911, BI, roll 853.
289 Chamberlain report, December 16, 1911, BI, roll 853.
290 Statement of F. A. Sommerfeld, June 24, 1918, file 9-16-12, Department of Justice, RG 60, NARA.
291 Lancaster report, December 12, 1911, BI, roll 853, lists their names and specifies violations of Section 37, Chapter 4 and Sections 10 and 13, Chapter 2 of the Federal Criminal Code.
292 Chamberlain report, December 22, 1911, BI, roll 853.
293 Chamberlain report, December 27, 1911; Lamoreaux report, December 28, 1911, BI, roll 853.
294 Lamoreaux report, December 30, 1911, BI, roll 852; Thompson report, December 30, 1911, BI, roll 853.
295 Unless otherwise indicated, this account is based on Harris and Sadler, "The Reyes Conspiracy," 335-348.
296 Lancaster report, January 4, 1912, BI, roll 853.
297 Chamberlain report, January 3, 1912, roll 852.
298 Ellsworth to Secretary of State, January 10, 1912, RDS 812.00/2694.
299 Thompson report, January 12, 1912, BI, roll 852; Waller Thomas Burns was District Judge for the Southern District of Texas from 1902-1917.
300 Hebert report, January 11, 12, 1912, BI, roll 852.
301 Thompson report, December 9, 1912, BI, roll 853; for a list of fines imposed, see the final report of Major Charles B. Hagadorn, January 13, 1912, 49682F/W40260, Records of United States Army Continental Commands, 1821-1920, General Correspondence, Department of Texas, 1870-1913, RG 393, NARA.
302 Thompson report, January 21, 1912, BI, roll 852.
303 See Thompson report, January 15, 1912, roll 852.
304 Thompson report, February 6, 1912, BI, roll 852.

305 McDaniel to Attorney General, July 16, 1912, US Department of State, File 312.11/752, RG 59, NARA.
306 Sommerfeld statement, June 24, 1918, Department of Justice, RG 60, NARA.
307 Charles Ghequiere Fenwick, *The Neutrality Laws of the United States* (Washington, DC: Carnegie Endowment for International Peace, 1913), 57.
308 Thompson report, June 8, 1912, BI, roll 852.
309 Charles H. Harris and Louis R. Sadler, The Border and the Revolution: Clandestine Activities of the Mexican Revolution, 1910-1920 (Silver City: High Lonesome Books, 1988), 44.
310 Thompson to Finch, January 15, 1912, BI, roll 852.
311 https://www.fbi.gov/history/directors/stanley-w-finch, viewed July 1, 2023.
312 Theoharis, The FBI, 326; Special Commissioner to all local white slave officers, Dec. 30, 1913, Agent Braun file FRC-FW. Chief Finch left the Department of Justice in 1914 (not 1913 as stated in Theoharis, see Braun letter, Dec. 30, 1913), and pursued a career in private law practice and as an inventor of toys with over 100 patents to his name. He briefly returned as an assistant to the Attorney General in 1922. Finch asked for an appointment with J. Edgar Hoover in 1934. Largely forgotten for his service as Chief of the BI, he felt that he had to introduce himself to as the "'Grand-Daddy' of the Division of Investigation." Whether Director Hoover ever received the former chief remains unknown. For a more detailed description of Finch's career subsequent to his service at the Department of Justice, see Theoharis, The FBI.
313 Bielaski has been dismissed and denigrated. For example, Theoharis et al., The FBI, 316, devotes three sentences to Bielaski's tenure as Chief of the agency (1912-1919). And Jeffreys-Jones, The FBI, 61, highlights Bielaski's athleticism and love of gardening, characterizing on 57 the whole period from 1909 to 1924 as "Loss of Mission." Details of his career are contained in his personnel file, 062-HQ-2817_Bielaski A B_001-050. For his cultural background see also James S. Pula, "Bruce Bielaski and the Origin of the FBI," *Polish American Studies*, Vol. 68, No. 1 (Spring 2011), 43-57; New York Times, Feb. 20, 1964, Obituaries: "The Lithuanian FBI Boss."
314 *Washington Evening Star*, August 20, 1905.
315 https://gwsports.com/honors/hall-of-fame/alexander-bielaski/13, viewed March 3, 2022.
316 *Washington Evening Star*, July 2, 1907.
317 His height is sometimes quoted as 5' 7." His 1919 passport lists his height as 5'11", which sounds more likely.
318 *Washington Evening star*, June 20, 1909. Bielaski's sister, Ruth B. Shipley, also had a distinguished career in government. Starting in 1908 in the Patent and Trademark Office, she joined the State Department in 1914. She headed the Passport Division of the Department for 27 years and retired at age 70. She received a Distinguished Service Medal upon retirement.
319 *Washington Evening Star*, October 26, 1909.
320 Theoharis et al., The FBI, 316.
321 Don Whitehead, *The FBI Story: A Report to the People* (New York: Random House, 1956).
322 The position of Chief turned into Director after 1924.
323 Eli Murray Blanford, born in 1883 in Kentucky, graduated from Georgetown University Law School in 1910. He joined the BI on December 27, 1913, as a Special Agent in El Paso, Texas,

with a salary of $1,400 per annum. He resigned in December 1921 and joined A. Bruce Bielaski as an investigator in the National Board of Fire Underwriters. He died in San Francisco, California in 1966. Blanford Personnel File, National Personnel Records Center, St. Louis, MO; Bynum/Hardaway Family Tree.

324 Chief to Blanford, November 12, 1915, BI, roll 856.
325 Thompson report, March 4, 1912, BI, roll 851.
326 *San Antonio Express*, November 23, 1911; Hebert report, March 2, 1912, BI, roll 851.
327 Lancaster report, July 24, 1912, BI, roll 853; see also his report of August 17, 1912, BI, roll 852.
328 Lancaster report, April 10, 1912, BI, roll 851.
329 The treaty allowed the Mexican government to request the arrest of Mexican subjects in the US and file evidence for extradition within forty days. If no evidence was forthcoming (which happened in many cases) the US authorities had to release the arrestees.
330 Chamberlain reports, December 7, 8, 9, 15, 1911, BI, roll 853; Thompson reports, February 26, 27, 1912, BI, roll 852; Barnes reports, February 27, 1912, BI roll 852 and March 5, 1912, BI, roll 851.
331 Finch to Durell, November 21, 1910, CE; *El Paso Herald*, December 17, 1913.
332 Barnes report, March 6, 1912, roll 851.
333 Hebert testimony, *Revolutions in Mexico*, 528.
334 Hebert report, March 31, 1912, BI, roll 851.
335 Hebert report, March 31, 1912, BI, roll 851.
336 Thompson reports, March 7, 9, 20, 1912; Thompson to Finch, March 9, 1912, BI, roll 851.
337 Thompson report, February 28, 1912, BI, roll 852; Hebert reports, February 29, March 5, 8, 1912, BI, roll 851.
338 Thompson report, March 12, 1912, BI, roll 851.
339 Barnes reports, September 9, 11, 12, 17, 19, 29, 1912; Buckholtz reports, September 23-26, 1912; Thompson report, October 3, 1912, BI, roll 852.
340 Lancaster report, April 16, 1912, BI, roll 851.
341 Lancaster reports, April 7, 8, 1912, BI, roll 851.
342 Thompson report, February 28, 1912, BI, roll 852; see also his reports of March 2, 3, 31, 1912, BI, roll 851.
343 Thompson reports, March 7, 9, 12, 28, 1912, BI, roll 851.
344 Ellsworth to Secretary of State, April 1, 1912, RDS, 812.00/3511.
345 Barnes reports, October 31, November 6, 1912; Thompson report, November 29, 1912, BI, roll 853.
346 Thompson report, March 10, 1912, BI, roll 851.
347 Thompson report, March 29, 1912, with enclosures, BI, roll 851.
348 Barnes reports, March 11, 12, 1912, BI, roll 851.
349 Today Ciudad Acuña.
350 Thompson reports, March 12, 15, 16, 18, 1912, BI, roll 851.
351 Barnes reports, April 23, 24, 26, 1912, BI, roll 851 and May 9, 1912, BI, roll 852; Lancaster report, May 3, 1912; Thompson report, May 4, 1912, BI, roll 852.
352 Hebert reports, March 24-27, 29, 30, 1912, BI, roll 851.

353 Thompson report, March 30, 1912, BI, roll 851.
354 Hebert reports, April 16, 17, 1912, BI, roll 851.
355 Hebert report, April 11, 1912, BI, roll 851.
356 Thompson report, May 7, 1912, BI, roll 852.
357 Barnes report, April 27, 1914, BI, roll 854.
358 Thompson report, May 11, 1912, BI, roll 852.
359 Thompson reports, May 10, 12, 1912; Barnes report, May 18, 1912, BI, roll 852.
360 Ross report, September 21, 1912, BI, roll 853.
361 Ross report, April 10, 1912, BI, roll 851.
362 Thompson to Finch, April 21, 1912, BI, roll 851.
363 Kramp to Lancaster, April 22, 25, 1912, BI, roll 851.
364 Thompson report, March 10, 1912, BI, roll 851.
365 Nicanor Valdez was the former mayor of Piedras Negras under Porfirio Díaz.
366 Thompson report, March 20, 1912, BI, roll 851.
367 Kerig, *Luther T. Ellsworth*, 54-56.
368 Thompson report, April 8, 1912, BI, roll 851.
369 Thompson report, October 14, 1912; Vann report, October 17, 1912, BI, roll 852.
370 Thompson to Finch, April 21, 1912, BI, roll 851.
371 Lancaster report, May 15, 1912, BI, roll 852.
372 Palmer report, November 20, 1912, BI, roll 853.
373 Elton Atwater, *American Regulation of Arms Exports* (Washington, DC: Carnegie Endowment for International Peace, 1941), 51-55, 58-59.
374 von Feilitzsch, *In Plain Sight*, 170-173.
375 Thompson report, August 15, 1912, BI, roll 852.
376 Thompson report, May 4, 1912; Ross report, May 4, 1912, BI, roll 852.
377 Hebert report, May 5, 1912, BI, roll 852.
378 Thompson report, May 11, 1912, BI, roll 852.
379 Thompson report, May 14, 1912, BI, roll 852; Lancaster report, July 19, 1912, BI, roll 853.
380 Ross report, July 9, 1912; Lancaster reports, July 11, 18, 1912, BI, roll 853; Ross report, August 8, 1912, BI, roll 854.
381 Thompson reports, April 22, 1912, BI, roll 851 and May 10, 12, 1912, BI, roll 852.
382 Ross report, July 9, 1912, BI, roll 853.
383 Thompson report, July 18, 1912, BI, roll 854.
384 Lancaster reports, March 31, April 4, 1912, BI, roll 851.
385 Thompson reports, July 22, 1912, BI, roll 854 and July 30, 1912, BI, roll 853.
386 Thompson report, September 19, 1912, BI, roll 852.
387 Barnes report, September 20, 1912; Thompson report, September 20, 1912, BI, roll 852.
388 Barnes reports, September 21, 22, November 5, 8, 1912, BI, roll 853 and September 24, 25, BI, roll 852; no. 121, US Commissioner, San Antonio, no. 2069, US District Court, San Antonio—FRC-FW.
389 Thompson reports July 22, 1912, BI, roll 854 and July 26, 1912, BI, roll 853; Lancaster reports, July 23, 1912, BI, roll 852 and July 24, 1912, BI, roll 853; Ross reports, July 24, 1912, BI, rolls 852 and 853 and July 30, 1912, BI, roll 854.

390 Ross report, September 3, 1912, BI, roll 853.
391 Thompson reports, August 12, September 1, 1912; Hawkins reports, August 10, 12, 1912, BI, roll 852.
392 Thompson report, August 9, 1912, BI, roll 853.
393 Hawkins report, August 12, 1912; Thompson reports, August 12, 13, 19, 1912, BI, roll 852; the code is found under August 12, BI, roll 857.
394 Thompson reports, August 12, 13, 16, 1912; Lancaster report, August 14, 1912, BI, roll 852; Hawkins report, August 12, 1912, BI, roll 853.
395 Thompson report, September 3, 1912; Ross report, September 7, 1912, BI, roll 853.
396 Gómez Robelo to Steever, September 10, 1912; Gómez Robelo to Smith, September 12, 1912, BI, roll 853.
397 Thompson report, September 20, 1912, BI, roll 852.
398 Thompson report, September 7, 1912, BI, roll 853.
399 Didapp letter, September 8, 1912; Thompson report, September 13, 1912, BI, roll 853.
400 Ross report, September 24, 1912; Thompson report, September 27, 1912, BI, roll 853; Barnes report, September 25, 1912, BI, roll 852.
401 Barnes reports, July 27, 30, 1912; Hebert reports, July 27- 29, 1912, BI, roll 854; Thompson reports, July 30, 31, 1912, BI, roll 853.
402 Barnes report, August 1, 1912, BI, roll 854.
403 Blanford report, March 26, 1913, BI, roll 853.
404 Thompson reports, January 10, March 12, 1913, BI, roll 853; Nos. 117, 125, US Commissioner, San Antonio; no. 2080, US District Court, San Antonio, FRC- FW; Notably, those indicted included Emiliano Zapata, in addition to Paulino Martínez alias Luis González, Dr. Policarpo Rueda alias F. P. Rice alias J. P. Weel, Francisco I. Guzmán, Felipe Fortuño Miramón, Manuel L. Márquez, Dr. Luis (Ludwig) J. Snowball alias L. J. Stone alias Luis J. Straight, Manuel Garza Aldape, Miguel Garza Aldape, J. A. Fernández, Ramón Vázquez, Teodoro G. Rodríguez alias Francisco Rodríguez, Antonio M. Franco, Candelario Inzuñza, José Villa, Joaquín Esquer y Barbecho, Belisario García, Camilo Gastélum, Teodoro Valenzuela alias Francisco Valenzuela, Porfirio Gómez, Manuel Mascarenas, Jr., Juan Reyes, J. García, Dr. José S. Saenz, David de la Fuente, Ricardo Gómez Robelo, Delio Moreno Cantón, Juan Pedro Didapp alias José Hackim, J. Cantú Cárdenas, Emilio L. Llanes, José Cavazos Echeverría, Felipe L. López, Luis Martínez, Herminio R. Ramírez, Francisco M. Herrera, Francisco R. Pradillo, Alberto Salas, and Melchor Camacho.
405 Ellsworth to Secretary of State, January 11, 1913, RDS, 812.00/5863.
406 Blanford report, January 13, 1913; Thompson reports, January 13, 19, 20, February 21, 1913, BI, roll 853.
407 This case was dismissed on May 16, 1917.
408 Barnes report, July 20, 1912, BI, roll 854.
409 Thompson report, May 16, 1912, BI, roll 852.
410 Thompson report, April 8, 1912; Kramp to Lancaster, April 10, 1912; Hawkins report, April 24, 1912, BI, roll 851.
411 Nos. C-181, C-182, US Commissioner, Douglas, FRC-LN; Hawkins report, April 17, 1912, BI, roll 851.

412 Barnes report, July 19, 1912, BI, roll 854.
413 McDaniel to Attorney General, March 9, 1912, 90755-1384, DOJ.
414 Hebert reports, June 29, 30, July 3, 1912, BI, roll 852.
415 No. C-213, US Commissioner, Douglas, FRC-LN.
416 Hebert report, June 16, 1912, BI, roll 852.
417 Dye to Secretary of State, April 25, 1912, RDS, 812.00/1506.
418 Hebert report, July 17, 1912, BI, roll 853.
419 Hebert report, July 26, 1912, BI, roll 853; see also his report on August 2, 1912, BI, roll 852.
420 Barnes report, July 25, 1912, BI, roll 853.
421 Thompson report, June 21, 1912; Thompson to Bielaski, June 21, 1912, BI, roll 852; Hebert report August 4, 1912, BI, roll 854.
422 Hebert report, July 19, 1912, BI, roll 853.
423 Thomas Sheldon Maxey was born in Mississippi in 1846. He served in the Confederate Army. After the Civil War he received his law degree from the University of Virginia in 1869. After a private practice career in Mississippi and Texas, he served as District Judge in the Southern District of Texas from 1888 until 1916. He died at age 75 in 1921 in Austin, Texas.
424 No. 1081, US Commissioner, and no. 1590, US District Court, El Paso, FRC-FW.
425 Thompson report, June 28, 1912, BI, roll 852.
426 Thompson report, July 6, 1912; Hebert reports, July 4-6, 9, 18, 1912, BI, roll 853.
427 Hebert report, July 20, 1912, BI, roll 853.
428 Barnes reports, July 21, 1912, BI, roll 854 and July 31, 1912, BI, roll 853.
429 Barnes report, August 14, 1912, BI, roll 852.
430 Thompson report, August 19, 1912, BI, roll 852.
431 Thompson report, September 7, 1912, BI, roll 853.
432 Blanford report, February 21, 1913, BI, roll 853.
433 Thompson to Bielaski, September 13, 1912, BI, roll 853.
434 Thompson report, September 21, 1912, BI, roll 853; Hebert report, September 25, 1912, BI, roll 852.
435 Hebert testimony, *Revolutions in Mexico*, 530; Thompson report, September 27, 1912, BI, roll 853.
436 Hebert report, May 5, 1912, BI, roll 852; Barnes report, July 18, 1912, BI, roll 854.
437 Blanford report, April 14, 1912, BI, roll 851.
438 Thompson report, June 21, 1912, BI, roll 852.
439 Blanford report, March 9, 1913; see also his report of March 10, 1913, BI, roll 853.
440 Blanford reports, April 7, 14, May 31, 1913; Barnes to Blanford, April 17, 1913, BI, roll 853.
441 Cuesta affidavit, July 26, 1913, BI, roll 853.
442 Guy report, January 24, 1915, BI, roll 863.
443 Breniman reports, September 10-12, 1912; Ross report, September 11, 1912, BI, roll 853.
444 Hebert report, September 12, 1912, BI, roll 853; Ross report, September 13, 1912, BI, roll 852.
445 Breniman report, September 20, 1912, BI, roll 853.
446 Breniman reports, September 27, 1912, BI, roll 853 and September 28, 1912, BI, roll 852.

447 Breniman reports, September 30, October 1, 3, 1912, BI, roll 852; *Daily Missoulian*, October 2, 1912; *Guthrie Daily Leader*, October 2, 1912.
448 Blanford report, February 21, 1913; see also his report of February 22, 1913, BI, roll 853.
449 Hebert remained on the border and engaged in import/export business. As he had alleged, both Agents Thompson and Ross indeed worked with and for the Mexican Secret Service under Felix A. Sommerfeld. Shortly after Hebert resigned, both federal agents left the bureau and worked officially as agents of the Mexican Secret Service for a short time. Hebert died of pulmonary tuberculosis in Douglas, Arizona in 1915; Arizona State Board of Health, Death Certificate of S. D. Hebert, April 26, 1915.
450 Hebert report, February 28, 1912, with enclosures; Thompson report, March 7, 1912; see also Barnes report, March 22, 1912, BI, roll 851.
451 Ganor reports, April 3, 5, 6, 1912; Herrington reports, April 6, 18, 1912, BI, roll 851.
452 Ganor report, March 22, 1912, BI, roll 851.
453 Herrington reports, August 14, 21, 1911; Case 232, September 22, October 5, 1911, BI, roll 851. Clayton Herrington took charge of the San Francisco field office in April 1912. He rose to become Assistant Attorney General until June 1913, when Chief Bielaski suspended him under significant political pressure. Herrington had written a letter to President Wilson, demanding the resignation of Attorney General James Clark McReynolds over firing the local US attorney and delaying several cases involving prominent Americans. The letter and resulting firing of Herrington touched off a nationwide scandal. After his government service, Herrington worked as a lawyer in San Francisco, catering to a Hispanic customer base. He died in December 1920 in San Francisco, *Valdez Daily Prospector*, June 24, 1913; *Pensacola Journal*, June 26, 1913; *Commoner*, July 4, 1913; *Manning Times*, July 2, 1913; *La Crónica*, October 15, 1916; *La Crónica*, November 12, 1916; *San Francisco Examiner*, December 30, 1920.
454 Harris and Sadler, *Secret War*, 70-71.
455 Vázquez Gómez to Orozco, March 21, 1912, BI, roll 853.
456 Barnes report, April 27, 1914, BI, roll 854.
457 Zapata to Martínez, May 12, 1912, BI, roll 853.
458 von Feilitzsch, *In Plain Sight*, 186; Ross report, July 5, 1912, BI, roll 852.
459 Woodrow Wilson, Proclamation 1263—Concerning the Shipment of Arms into Mexico Online by Gerhard Peters and John T. Woolley, *The American Presidency Project* (https://www.presidency.ucsb.edu/node/317582, viewed June 2022); Von Feilitzsch, *In Plain Sight*, 175; also *Walsenburg World*, 26, no. 6, February 5, 1914.
460 Michael C. Meyer, *Mexican Rebel: Pascual Orozco and the Mexican Revolution, 1910-1915* (Lincoln: University of Nebraska Press, 1967), 45n30; see also 70-71, 74.
461 Krakauer to Fall, July 25, 1912, A. B. Fall Family Papers, Ms8, Box 8, Rio Grande Historical Collections, New Mexico State University, Las Cruces, NM.
462 Breniman reports, September 25, 26, 1912, BI, roll 852.
463 Harris and Sadler, *Secret War*, 100-101, 105.
464 Lancaster to Finch, "Personal and Confidential," March 23, 1912, BI, roll 851.
465 Geck reports, April 1, 2, 1912.
466 Ross reports, April 1, 4, 1912, BI, roll 851.

[467] See no. 1630, US District Court, El Paso, FRC-FW.
[468] Harris and Sadler, *Secret War*, 74.
[469] Ross report, June 13, 1912, BI, roll 852.
[470] Harris and Sadler, *Secret War*, 84-85.
[471] Barnes report, July 17, 1912, BI, roll 854.
[472] Thompson to Chief, April 21, 1912, BI, roll 851.
[473] Harris and Sadler, *Secret War*, 90-91; No. 1161, US Commissioner, District of New Mexico, and no. 85, US District Court, Santa Fe, FRC-D.
[474] See the extensive file on Lee Christmas in BI, roll 851; see also Harris reports, January 1, 1912, BI, roll 852 and April 5, 1912, BI, roll 851.
[475] Matthews report, May 9, 1913, BI, roll 853.
[476] Harris report, January 19, 1912, BI, roll 852; April 7, 8, 1912, BI, roll 851.
[477] Unless otherwise indicated, this account is based on Charles H. Harris III and Louis R. Sadler, "The Underside of the Mexican Revolution: El Paso, 1912," *The Americas*, 39, No. 1, (July 1982), 69-83.
[478] Thompson report, October 3, 1912, BI, roll 852.
[479] Pendleton to Thompson, November 8, 1913, BI, roll 854.
[480] Harris reports, May 5, 6, 8, 10-14, BI, roll 852.
[481] Harris report, May 24, 1912; see also Harris reports, May 25, 27, June 4, 6, 1912, BI, roll 852.
[482] Harris report, May 28, 1912, BI, roll 852.
[483] Blanford report, October 3, 1913; Pendleton report, October 7, 1913, BI, roll 854.
[484] Ross reports, May 18, 19, 21, 22, 1912; Thompson reports, May 12, 19, 21, 22, 23, October 18, 1912; Hebert report, May 22, 1912; Harris reports, June 6, 7, November 4, 1912, BI, roll 852; Breniman report, February 6, 1913, BI, roll 853.
[485] Harris reports, July 25, 31, October 13, November 3, 1912, BI, roll 853.
[486] Harris report, November 6, 1912; Breniman reports, November 9, 11, 13, 1912, BI, roll 853.
[487] Diccionario Porrúa de historia, biografía y geografía de Mexico, 2nd ed. (México, DF: Editorial Porrúa, 1965), 1470.
[488] Harris report, January 23, 1913, BI, roll 853.
[489] Harris reports, July 25, 31, August 2, 1912; Thompson report, February 4, 1913, BI, roll 853.
[490] Harris reports, August 4, 7, 9, 1912, BI, roll 853, August 26, 1912, BI, roll 852.
[491] Harris reports, September 19, 21, 23, 28, 1912, BI, roll 852 and September 3, 14, 24, 1912, BI, roll 853.
[492] Harris reports, October 25, 1912, BI, roll 852 and October 29, 1912, BI, roll 853.
[493] Harris report, November 29, 1912, BI, roll 853.
[494] Barnes report, September 28, 1912, BI, roll 852.
[495] See, for example, Thompson report, May 27, 1912, BI, roll 852.
[496] No. 162, US Commissioner, Marfa; no. 1559, US District Court, El Paso; see also no. 1307, US District Court, Austin, FRC-FW.
[497] Thompson report, October 21, 1912, BI, roll 852.
[498] Harris and Sadler, *Secret War*, 123-125; Ellsworth to Secretary of State, February 7, 1913, RDS, 812.00/6073.

499 Thompson report, August 19, 1912, BI, roll 852.
500 Thompson report, August 28, 1912, RDS, 812.00/4915.
501 Assistant Attorney General to Camp, July 8, 1913, BI, roll 854; Blanford reports, June 6, 22, 1913; Breniman report, June 10, 1913, BI roll 853.
502 Memorandum for the Pardon Attorney, April 8, 1914, BI, roll 859. After becoming a whistleblower and testifying against his colleagues, Hebert left the BI in 1912 and became a tobacco merchant in Douglas. He died at his house there on April 26, 1915, of tuberculosis (Arizona State Board of Health, Death Certificate #340, C. D. Hebert).
503 Blanford report, April 9, 1914, BI, roll 855; Harris and Sadler, *Secret War*, 119-120.
504 Harris and Sadler, *Secret War*, 121-122; *El Paso Morning Times*, January 18, 1913.
505 See, for example, the "Confidential" letter from Ernest Knaebel at the Department of Justice to the Secretary of State, May 15, 1912, 90755-1557, Records of the Department of Justice, RG 60, NARA, hereafter cited as DOJ; Wickersham to Boynton, May 16, 1912, 90755-1562, DOJ; Wickersham to United States Attorney, May 20, 1912, 90755-1565, DOJ; Boynton to Attorney General, June 8, 1912, 90755-1590, DOJ; Attorney General to Secretary of State, June 13, 1912, 90755-1590, DOJ.
506 Madero to Llorente, May 30, 1912, Isidro Fabela et al., *Documentos históricos de la Revolución Mexicana*, 28 vols. (Mexico, DF: Editorial Jus, 1960-1976), 7:422. Hereafter cited as DHRM.
507 Ross report, June 13, 1912, RDS, 812.00/4220.
508 Secretary of State [Knox] to American Ambassador [Wilson], referring to messages from Wickersham to Secretary of State, June 13, 19, 1912, RDS, 812.00/4246.
509 Secretary of State [Knox] to American Ambassador [Wilson], June 28, 1912, RDS, 812.00/4246.
510 No. 1607, US District Court, El Paso, FRC-FW; Thompson report, February 6, 1913, BI, roll 853.
511 Harris and Sadler, *Secret War*, 117-118, 132-133, 177-178.
512 Thompson report, May 7, 1912, BI, roll 852.
513 Lancaster reports, July 2, 1912, BI, roll 852; July 6, 1912, BI, roll 853.
514 Lancaster report, August 20, 1912; Thompson report, August 21, 1912, BI, roll 852.
515 *El Paso Herald*, September 13, 1912.
516 Thompson report, October 14, 1912; see also his report of October 11, 1912, BI, roll 852.
517 https://www.ancestry.com, Bynum/Hardaway Family Tree, viewed March 2022; Blanford resigned from the BI on December 6, 1921. Blanford file, NPRC.
518 Palmer report, October 27, 1912; Blanford report, October 27, 1912, BI, roll 853; Thompson reports, October 24, 1912, BI, roll 852 and October 29, 1912, BI, roll 853.
519 Lancaster reports, April 16, 17, 20, 1912, BI, roll 851.
520 Scully report, April 25, 1912; see also Offley to Chief, April 24, 1912, BI, roll 851; Offley report, May 1, 1912; Offley to Chief, May 11, 1912, BI, roll 852.
521 A. G. Adams, C. J. Scully, Harry J. Jentzer, Henry Dotzert, J. O. Tucker, P. Pigniuolo, George M. Royce, W. C. Dannenberg, and an Agent Poulin.
522 Scully report, April 12, 1912, Offley report, April 12, 1912; Dannenberg report, April 17, 1912, BI, roll 851.
523 See above agents' reports for April 1912, BI, roll 851.

[524] Almada, *Diccionario*, 249; Dannenberg report April 17, 1912, BI, roll 851.
[525] Hopkins memorandum, April 13, 1912; Ambrose report, April 13, 1912; Offley report, April 14, 1912, BI, roll 851.
[526] Hebert report, April 25, 1912; [Kramp] to [Lancaster], April 25, 1912; Craft report, May 2, 1912, BI, roll 851; Thompson report, April 10, 1913, BI, roll 853.
[527] McCormick to Attorney General, March 30, 1912, 90755-1473; [Attorney General] to McCormick, April 11, 1912, 90755-1473, DOJ.
[528] Ganor reports, March 14, 16, 22, April 3, 5, 6, 7, 20, 1912; Herrington reports, April 6, 18, 1912, BI, roll 851.
[529] Ganor report, April 3, 1912, BI, roll 851.
[530] Ganor report, May 5, 1912, BI, roll 852.
[531] Ganor report, May 25, 1912, BI, roll 852.
[532] Ganor reports, June 7, 13, 23, 27, 1912, BI, roll 852; July 11, 1912, BI, roll 853.
[533] Ganor reports, August 12, 14, 1912, BI, roll 852; for an account of the Díaz-Taft meeting and the attempted assassinations see Harris and Sadler, *Secret War*, 1-16.
[534] Ganor report, September 12, 1912, BI, roll 853.
[535] Ganor report, September 25, 1912, roll 852.
[536] Ganor report, October 1, 1912, BI, roll 852.
[537] Ganor report, September 25, 1912, BI, roll 852.
[538] Ganor reports, September 30, October 7, 1912, BI, roll 852.
[539] Ganor report, October 18, 1912, BI, roll 852.
[540] Ganor report, October 23, 1912, BI, roll 852.
[541] Ganor report, October 31, 1912, BI, roll 853.
[542] Luis Liceaga, *Félix Díaz* (Mexico DF: Editorial Jus, 1958), 63-89.
[543] *New York Tribune*, August 2, 1915.
[544] Harry Berliner to John Embleton, February 16, 1913, courtesy of Kirstin Keller Rounds, private collection.
[545] Liceaga, *Félix Díaz*, 151-226; Michael C. Meyer, *Huerta: A Political Portrait* (Lincoln: University of Nebraska Press, 1972), 45-63.
[546] Harry Berliner to John Embleton, February 10, 1913, courtesy of Kirstin Keller Rounds, private collection.
[547] Barnes report, November 9, 1914, BI, roll 856.
[548] Berliner may have been more than a messenger. In an unpublished manuscript of Henry Lane Wilson, William F. Buckley, Jr. to whom Wilson had sent the manuscript states: "True to Mexican character, no plan had been made as an alternative to the surrender of the palace and Félix Díaz and Mondragón did not know what to do. It was the general belief in Mexico City that at this juncture our old friend Harry Berliner rushed up and advised Félix Díaz to take the 'ciudadela'." W. Dirk Raat and William H. Beezley, eds. *Twentieth-Century Mexico* (Lincoln and London: University of Nebraska Press, 1986), 113.
[549] *Buffalo Evening News*, October 9, 1915.
[550] Wilson to Secretary of State, February 21, 1913, RDS, 812.00/6288.
[551] Huerta to Taft, February 18, 1913, RDS, 812.00/6250.
[552] Wilson to Secretary of State, February 20, 1913, RDS, 812.00/6271.

553 *San Antonio Light*, October 31, 1915; Bielaski to Canova, November 5, 1915, BI, roll 858.
554 De la Barra announcement, February 23, 1913, RDS, 812.00/7239; Wilson to Secretary of State, February 23, 1913, RDS, 812.00/6321.
555 Thompson report, February 17, 1913; Blanford report, February 20, 1913; Breniman reports, February 18, April 2, 1913, BI, roll 853.
556 Kerig, *Luther T. Ellsworth*, 56-57.
557 Raymond Caballero, *Orozco: The Life and Death of a Mexican Revolutionary* (Norman: University of Oklahoma Press, 2017), 231.
558 Holland to Secretary of State, February 20, 1913, RDS, 812.00/6272 and February 21, 1913, RDS, 812.00/6302; Carranza to President, February 26, 1913, RDS, 812.00/6425.
559 Breniman report, December 24, 1913, BI, roll 854.
560 Thompson reports, January 24, March 18, 1913, BI, roll 853.
561 Curtis to Secretary of State, February 17, 1913, RDS, 812.00/6238.
562 Barnes reports, April 5, 6, 1913, BI, roll 853.
563 Barnes reports June 26, July 16, 21, 1913, BI, roll 853.
564 Barnes report, April 8, 1913; see also Thompson report, May 22, 1913, BI, roll 853.
565 Velasco was annexed by Freeport in 1957. https://en.wikipedia.org/wiki/Velasco,_Texas, viewed March 2022.
566 Scully report, May 21, 1913; Thompson report, May 22, 1913, BI, roll 853.
567 Thompson reports, May 30, 31, 1913, BI, roll 853.
568 Johnson to Secretary of State, June 4, 1913, RDS, 812.00/7694; Charles C. Cumberland, *The Mexican Revolution: Constitutionalist Years* (Austin and London: University of Texas Press, 1992), 39-40.
569 Barnes report, August 6, 1913, BI, roll 853.
570 Executive Order, June 9, 1914; McAdoo to Attorney General, June 12, 1914, BI, roll 855; Barnes report, December 27, 1915; Barnes to Bielaski, June 2, 1916, BI, roll 859. *Sunshine* on May 20, 1914, with 2,050 cases (usually 1,000 rounds per case) of ammunition, and on June 25, 1914 with 1,950 cases; *Grampus* on June 25, 1914 with 1,113 cases of ammunition; *Emily P. Wright* on July 10, 1914 with 375 cases of rifles and 1,999 cases of ammunition, and on August 18, 1914 with 293 cases of rifles and 2,250 cases of ammunition; *Hatteras* on July 21, 1914 with 1,602 cases of ammunition; *Spectre* on August 15, 1914 with 94 cases of rifles and 113 cases of ammunition.
571 findagrave.com/memorial/196058980/herbert-janvrin-browne.
572 *Billings Gazette*, December 18, 1908.
573 Webb report, May 1, 1916, BI, roll 859.
574 Kelly to Gregory, November 29, 1915; Webb reports, December 22, 1915, February 20, 1916, May 1, 1916; Barnes to Bielaski, June 2, 1916; Barnes report, June 10, 1916, BI, roll 859.
575 Barnes to Bielaski, June 2, 1916, BI, roll 859.
576 Barnes report, December 27, 1915; Barnes to Webb, June 12, 1916, BI, roll 859.
577 Phillips to Anderson, October 23, 1914; Anderson to Leckie, October 23, November 3, 1914; Austin to Fidelity & Deposit Company, July 24, 1914; Statement of Salvatoris Calando [sic],

October 7, 1914; Webb report, December 29, 1915; Weakley report, June 10, 1916, BI, roll 859; Guy report, September 14, 1914, BI, roll 857.
578. Barnes to McGee, June 3, 1916, BI, roll 859.
579. Lillard report, June 13, 1916, BI, roll 859; Browne was listed as a lawyer in the 1916 Washington city directory. That same year, he arrived in New Orleans from a trip to Honduras, Guatemala, and Belize, intimating to the Collector of Customs that he had been in South America on a confidential mission for the president. His passport application in 1919 listed him as a capitalist, who was going to Cuba, Central and South America. In 1934, the Washington directory listed him as a meteorologist. Herbert J. Browne died on January 21, 1936, in Washington and was buried in Rock Creek Cemetery.
580. McGee report, June 4, 1916; Barnes to Webb, October 18, 1915; Seagraves to unknown, October 30, 1915, BI, roll 859; Webb reports, October 20, 1915, BI roll 858 and November 3, 10, 11, 15, 1915, BI, roll 859.
581. Webb reports, July 26, 27, November 15, 1915, BI, roll 859.
582. Barnes to Bielaski, June 2, 1916; Barnes to McGee, June 3, 1916; Barnes report, June 10, 1916; Barnes to Webb, June 12, 1916; Leckie to Bielaski, June 22, 1916, BI, roll 859.
583. Barnes reports, June 5-7, July 10, 1913, BI, roll 853.
584. Barnes report, June 19, 1913, BI, roll 853.
585. Barnes reports, July 24-26, 28, 1913, BI, roll 853. The guardsman in question was later arrested for stealing government property.
586. Charles H. Harris and Louis R. Sadler, *The Great Call-Up: The Guard, the Border, and the Mexican Revolution* (Norman: University of Oklahoma Press, 2015), 38-39.
587. Barnes reports, August 16, 18, 22, 28, 1913; Thompson report, August 16, 1913, BI, roll 854.
588. Barnes reports, June 15, 21, 25, 26, 1913; Thompson report, June 21, 1913, BI, roll 853.
589. US v. Lucio Blanco, Vicente Segura, Charles More, Macedonio J. García, Amado Stevens et al. Barnes report, August 5, 1913; Barnes to McDaniel, October 29, 1913, BI, roll 854, BI, roll 853.
590. Thompson report, June 19, 1913, BI, roll 853.
591. Barnes report, June 17, 1913, BI, roll 853.
592. Barnes reports, June 20, 29, August 5, 1913, BI, roll 853.
593. Barnes report, June 20, 1913, BI, roll 853.
594. Barnes report, June 28, 1913, BI, roll 853.
595. Barnes report, August 3, 1913, BI, roll 853. The policy had been enacted on July 21 as a pressure tactic for negotiations between US emissary John Lind and President Huerta. The president announced the policy change publicly on August 28, 1913, after talks with Huerta had failed.
596. Barnes report, August 12, 1913, BI, roll 853.
597. Barnes report, August 31, 1913, BI, roll 854.
598. Harris reports, January 3-5, 8, 10, 15-17, 19, 1913, BI, roll 853.
599. Ibid.
600. Ibid.
601. Harris report, February 8, 1913, BI, roll 853.
602. Harris report, February 12, 1913, BI, roll 853.

603 Matthews reports, March 28, April 20, 1913, BI, roll 853.
604 Matthews report, March 28, 1913, BI, roll 853.
605 Matthews report, April 17, 1913; Barnes report, April 18, 1913, roll 853.
606 Matthews report, April 19, 1913, BI, roll 853.
607 Matthews report, April 19, 1913, BI, roll 853.
608 Matthews report, May 20, 1913, BI, roll 853.
609 Matthews report, April 20, 1913, BI, roll 853.
610 Farmer report, April 27, BI, roll 853.
611 Farmer reports, April 27, 29, 1913, BI, roll 853.
612 Farmer report, April 30, 1913, BI, roll 853.
613 Matthews report, May 4, 1913, BI, roll 853.
614 Matthews report, May 8, 1913, BI, 853.
615 Matthews report, May 12, 1913, BI, roll 853.
616 Matthews report, May 15, 1913, BI, roll 853.
617 Matthews report, July 8, 1913; see also his July 3, 1913, report, BI, roll 853.
618 Diccionario Porrúa, 118-119.
619 Matthews report, May 26, 1913, BI, roll 853.
620 Matthews reports, May 29, 30, 1913, BI, roll 853.
621 Matthews reports, June 4, 5, 9, 24, 1913, BI, roll 853.
622 Barnes report, August 5, 1913; Matthews reports, July 12, 13, 1913; Thompson report, July 4, 1913, BI, roll 853.
623 Matthews report, July 28, 29, 1913, BI, roll 853.
624 Matthews report, July 10, 1913, BI, roll 853.
625 Thompson to Bielaski, August 16, 1913, BI, roll 854.
626 www.ancestry.com, Official Register of the United States, 1905, government employees Washington, DC.
627 *Evening Star*, July 6, 1908.
628 *Washington Herald*, April 9, 1911.
629 Kansas City, Missouri, City Directory, 1912.
630 Pendleton report, April 19, 1912, BI, roll 851; Harris reports, August 15, 20, 1913, BI, roll 854; http://www.facebook.com/pages/Pendleton-Security/134736833362649.
631 Ancestry.com, sourced Pendleton family tree, viewed March 2022.
632 Pendleton report, August 16, 1913, BI, roll 854.
633 Assistant Attorney General to Perkins, April 30, 1914, BI, roll 859.
634 Pendleton reports, August 18-20, 25, 1913, BI, roll 854.
635 By July 1913, Vicente Segura resided in Matamoros. He had cast his lot with the Constitutionalists and became a colonel in their army. (Agent report, Brownsville, July 27, 1913, RDS, 812.00/8266.) In 1915, Venustiano Carranza promoted him general. He fought in Morelos and Puebla against *zapatistas* until his retirement in 1921. He died in Cuernavaca, Morelos, in 1953 (Francisco Naranjo, *Diccionario biográfico Revolucionario* (Mexico, DF: Imprenta Editorial "Cosmos," 1935).
636 Pendleton reports, August 28, 29, 1913, BI, roll 854.
637 Pendleton reports, September 7-10, October 8, 1913, BI, roll 854.

638 Pendleton reports, November 11, 13, 1913, BI, roll 854.
639 Pendleton reports, December 11, 12, 1913, BI, roll 854.
640 Pendleton reports, December 27, 28, 30, 31, 1913, BI, roll 854.
641 Offley report, May 26, 1913, BI, roll 853; Harris and Sadler, *Secret War*, 193.
642 Adams reports, July 31, August 2, 1913, BI, roll 853 and August 28, 1913, BI, roll 854; Offley reports, July 31, August 1, 2, 1913; Bielaski to Offley, July 31, 1913; BI, roll 853; RDS, 812.113/2508.
643 Scully report, April 12, 1912, Offley report, April 12, 1912; Dannenberg report, April 17, 1912, BI, roll 851.
644 Matthews report, July 8, 1913, BI, roll 853.
645 Blocker to Secretary of State, August 9, 1913, RDS, 812.00/8351.
646 Thompson report, February 8, 1913, BI, roll 853.
647 Barnes report, February 17, 1913, BI, roll 853.
648 Thompson report, February 18, 1913; Barnes reports, February 17, 21, March 3, 1913, BI, roll 853. Indalecio Ballesteros, by the way, would subsequently change sides and operate with Constitutionalists in Calexico, California, going under the surname of Sifuentes. Barnes report, January 1, 1914, BI, roll 854.
649 Garrett to Secretary of State, February 15, 1913, RDS, 812.00/6197.
650 Thompson report, February 17, 1913; Barnes reports, February 15, 17, 19, 23, 26, March 3, 1913, BI, roll 853.
651 Barnes reports, February 18, 19, April 1, 2, 9, May 17, 1913; Thompson report, May 23, 1913; Spates report, August 3, 1913, BI, roll 853.
652 Thompson reports, February 20, 21, 1913; Barnes report, February 20, 1913, BI, roll 853.
653 Barnes report, May 15, 1913; Thompson reports, June 13, 17, 19, 1913, BI, roll 853; No 538, District Court, Laredo, FRC-FW.
654 Spates file, NPRC.
655 Spates report, August 9, 1913; see also his August 2, 10, 1913, reports, BI, roll 853.
656 Spates report, September 7, 1913; see also his September 7, 1913, report, BI, roll 854.
657 Spates report, August 28, 1913, BI, roll 854.
658 Spates reports, August 3, 5, 6, 8, 10, 1913, BI, roll 853, August 15, 17, 22, 23, 28, September 7, 1913, BI, roll 854; Thompson reports, August 8, 9, 1913, BI, roll 853; Flores to Attorney General, August 15, 1913; Assistant Attorney General to Legarde, September 5, 1913, BI, roll 854.
659 Spates report, September 18, 1913; see also his reports for September 15, 24, 1913, BI, roll 854.
660 Spates report, November 13, 1913; Barnes report, November 13, 1913, BI, roll 854.
661 Chief to Spates, November 15, 1913, BI, roll 854.
662 Thompson report, April 7, 1913; Breniman reports, April 18, 1913, BI, roll 854 and April 20, May 9, 1913, BI, roll 853; Barnes report, August 6, 1913, BI, roll 853.
663 Thompson report, April 7, 1913; Breniman reports May 17, 22, 1913, BI, roll 853.
664 Barnes reports, January 13, April 21, May 13, 15, 17, 19, 23, 1913; Thompson report, May 23, 1913, BI, roll 853. Fred Thompson may have been H. A. Thompson's son. H. A. Thompson headed the San Antonio field office.

665 Barnes to Daniel, December 26, 1913, BI, roll 854.
666 Daniel reports, December 18, 19, 21, 26, 30, 31, 1913; Barnes report, December 22, 1913; Barnes to Daniel, December 31, 1913, BI, roll 854.
667 Daniel report, December 17, 1913, BI, roll 854.
668 Cumberland, Constitutionalist Years, 30.
669 Ellsworth to Secretary of State, March 27, 1913, RDS, 812.00/6966 and March 31, 1913, RDS, 812.00/6995.
670 Ellsworth to Secretary of State, April 8, 1913, RDS, 812.00/7048.
671 Barnes report, April 16, 1913, BI, roll 853.
672 www.ancestry.com, viewed March 2022; Family Tree of Charles Edward Breniman (public).
673 Breniman report, May 4, 1913, BI, roll 853.
674 Beltrán to Bryan, April 6, 1913, RDS, 812.00/7031; Assistant Attorney General to Secretary of State, June 4, 1913, RDS, 812.00/7716.
675 Army report of border conditions for week ending May 17, 1913, RDS, 812.00/7748.
676 Breniman report, July 5, 1913, BI, roll 853.
677 Breniman report, April 29, 1913, BI, roll 853.
678 Breniman reports, May 2, 4, 17, 20, 1913; Barnes report, May 14, 1913; Ellsworth list, June 1, 1913, BI, roll 853.
679 Carr to Ellsworth, May 8, 1913, RDS, 812.00/7331.
680 Ellsworth to Secretary of State, May 27, 1913, RDS, 812.00/7669.
681 Reynolds to Bryan, June 18, 1913, RDS, 812.00/7813.
682 Breniman reports, May 30, July 19, 1913, BI, roll 853.
683 For a history of the firm, see Edward Andrew Peden, *Peden - 1965* (Houston: Premier Printing Company, 1965).
684 DeBelle report, June 20, 1913, BI, roll 853.
685 Thompson reports, April 9, May 30, 31, 1913; Breniman reports, May 2, 4, 30, 31, June 6, 1913, BI, roll 853.
686 Breniman reports, June 18-20, 25, 1913, BI, roll 853; interestingly, the Chamber of Commerce in San Antonio contacted their congressman, who inquired of the DOJ whether anything could be done to release the uniforms, which had been purchased in San Antonio. Adkins to Breniman, June 24, BI, roll 853.
687 Breniman report, June 17, 1913, BI, roll 853.
688 Breniman reports, July 3, 5, 1913, BI, roll 853.
689 Thompson report, July 20, 1913, BI, roll 853.
690 Breniman reports, May 13, July 12, 1913, BI, roll 853.
691 Breniman reports, July 23, August 4, 1913, BI, roll 853.
692 Thompson report, August 29, 1913, BI, roll 854.
693 Thompson reports, June 24, August 8, 19, 1913, BI, roll 853.
694 Thompson reports, September 5, 11, 22, 29, 1913; Swigelson report, September 6, 1913; Barnes reports, September 24, 25, 1913; Chief to Thompson, October 7, 1913, BI, roll 854.
695 Spates report, October 24, 1913; Daniel reports, December 5, 7, 10, 11, 1913; Thompson report, December 11, 1913, BI, roll 854.
696 Thompson reports, February 22, March 26, 28, April 30, May 1, 2, 3, 8, 9, 1913, BI, roll 853.

697 Barnes reports, April 18, May 16, 1913, BI, roll 853.
698 Thompson report, May 9, 1913, BI, roll 853.
699 Barnes report, May 16, 1913, BI, roll 853.
700 Thompson report, June 13, 1913, BI, roll 853.
701 A native of Columbia, Arkansas, Daniel was born on December 17, 1880. He had the distinction of being one of the original hires of the bureau, joining on January 23, 1908.
702 Daniel report, August 14, 1913, BI, roll 853.
703 Thompson reports, June 13, 30, 1913, BI, roll 853.
704 Thompson report, August 7, 1913, BI, roll 853.
705 Daniel reports, August 9, 11, 14, 1913, BI, roll 853.
706 Thompson report, August 16, 1913, BI, roll 854.
707 Sanders reports, August 25, 27, 913, BI, roll 854.
708 Thompson reports, August 28, September 1, 1913, BI, roll 854.
709 Barnes report, October 6, 1913, BI, roll 854.
710 Stevens report, August 31, 1913; Yelvington reports, September 12, 13, 1913, BI, roll 854.
711 Thompson report, August 28, 1913, BI, roll 854.
712 Thompson reports, September 11, 13, 1913, BI, roll 854.
713 Thompson report, October 8, 1913, BI, roll 854.
714 Thompson report, August 28, 1913, BI, roll 854.
715 Thompson report, September 11, 1913, BI, roll 854.
716 Thompson report, September 17, 1913; McNeel report, September 17, 1913, BI, roll 854.
717 Thompson report, September 22, 1913; Barnes reports, September 25, 30, 1913; Barnes to Spates, October 24, 1913, BI, roll 854.
718 Barnes report, October 25, 1913; see also his report for October 22, 1913, BI, roll 854.
719 Thompson reports, October 3, 4, 9, 1913; Barnes reports, October 4, December 25, 1913; Spates report, October 8, 1913, BI, roll 854.
720 Palmer report, January 7, 1913; Blanford reports, January 3, 7, 23, 1913; Breniman report, February 1, 1913, BI, roll 853. El Paso Herald, March 22, 1912. Hall became captain in the El Paso police department in 1914 and kept that position until he received a commission as captain in the 64th US Infantry in France during World War I. El Paso Herald, June 28, 1919.
721 Breniman report, March 8, 13, 1913, BI, roll 853.
722 Blanford reports, March 5, 12, 1913, BI, roll 853.
723 McAdoo to Secretary of State, RDS, 812.00/6683.
724 Breniman report, March 9, 1913, BI, roll 853.
725 Katz, *Life and Times*, 206; El Paso Herald, February 19, 20, 1913.
726 Blanford reports, February 20, 21, 28, 1913; Thompson report, March 11, 1913, BI, roll 853. Katz, *Life and Times*, 206.
727 No. 1626, US District Court, El Paso, FRC-FW.
728 Harris and Sadler, *Secret War*, 132.
729 Diebold to Foreign Secretary, May 14, 1913, L-E 766 (24), exps. 1-8, AREM.
730 Huerta operatives sometimes managed to intercept Hopkins's mail, and in June 1914, somebody broke into his office and stole his files. The *New York Herald* published a

sensational—and most embarrassing—selection of his correspondence. Harris and Sadler, *Secret War*, 140-141; von Feilitzsch, *In Plain Sight*, 373ff;

731 Harris and Sadler, *Secret War*, 148.
732 Harris and Sadler, *Secret War*, 145-146; Blanford reports, July 26, 1913, BI, roll 853, and October 21, 1913, BI, roll 854; nos. 1227, 1229, US Commissioner and nos. 1680, 1681, US District Court, El Paso, FRC-FW.
733 Blanford report, September 24, 1913, BI, roll 854.
734 David Grann, *Killers of the Flower Moon: The Osage Murders and the Birth of the FBI* (New York: Doubleday, 2017), 125-127; El Paso Herald, November 19, 1912; Blanford reports, November 3, 27, December 23, 1913; Wren reports, November 2-4, 1913, BI, roll 854.
735 Blanford report, November 10, 1913, BI, roll 854.
736 Harris and Sadler, *Secret War*, 144-145.
737 Blanford report, March 3, 1913, BI, roll 853.
738 Blanford report, March 6, 1913; see also his report for March 5, 1913, BI, roll 853.
739 Blanford reports, March 5, 10, 27, 1913, BI, roll 853.
740 Sage to Commanding General, May 6, 1913, BI, roll 857.
741 Blanford report, March 9, 1913, BI, roll 853.
742 Blanford report, March 7, 13, 1913, BI, roll 853.
743 Blanford reports, March 14, 16, 1913, BI, roll 853.
744 Blanford report, March 30, 1913, BI, roll 853.
745 Thompson reports, February 3, March 4, 1913; Breniman report, February 27, 1913; Blanford reports March 5, 6, 1913, BI, roll 853.
746 Blanford reports, March 8, 10, 11, 13, 14, 15, 1913, BI, roll 853.
747 Theoharis, *The FBI*, 338; *Diccionario Porrúa*, 860-861; Cornelius C. Smith, Jr., *Emilio Kosterlitzky: Eagle of Sonora and the Southwest Border* (Glendale: Arthur H. Clark, 1970).
748 Simpich to Secretary of State, March 13, 1913, RDS, 812.00/6677; Blanford reports, March 14, 16, 23, 1913, BI, roll 853.
749 Blanford report, March 16, 1913, BI, roll 853.
750 Blanford report, June 11, 1913, BI, roll 853.
751 Blanford report, June 22, 1913, BI, roll 853.
752 No. C-705, US District Court, Tucson, FRC-LN.
753 Evans to [Blanford], June 28, 1913; Breniman reports, August 8, 10, 1913, BI, roll 853.
754 Dan Hagedorn, *Conquistadors of the Sky: A History of Aviation in Latin America* (Gainesville: University Press of Florida: 2008), 75; a photograph of the airplane is on 76; Lawrence Douglas Taylor Hansen, "Los orígenes de la Fuerza Aerea Mexicana, 1913-1915," *Historia Mexicana*, 56, no. 1 (July-September 2006), 181-183; Breniman report, February 5, 1914, BI, roll 854.
755 Taylor, "Los orígenes," 183; Hagedorn, *Conquistadors*, 549, n111.
756 Johnson statement, September 2, 1913, BI, roll 854; see also Blanford report, May 8, 1913, BI, roll 853.
757 Blanford report, June 1, 1913, BI, roll 853.
758 Johnson statement, September 2, 1913, BI, roll 854.

759 Overlock to Attorney General, September 3, 1913; also see Assistant Attorney General to Overlock, August 21, 1913, BI, roll 854.
760 Breniman report, August 10, 1913, BI, roll 853.
761 In 1916-1917, Noonan was a customs inspector in Arizona. Neunhoffer report, August 5, 1916; Barnes report, August 12, 1916, BI roll 865; Hopkins report, March 15, 1917, Old German Files, 1909-21, case no. 8000-2633, microfilm publication no. M1085, Investigative Records, 1908-1922, FBI, RG 65, NARA.
762 Taylor, "Los orígenes," 184.
763 Simpich to Secretary of State, May 28, 1913, RDS, 812.00/7625; see also Hostetter to Secretary of State, May 28, 1913, RDS, 812.00/7685 and Hunt to Secretary of State, May 29, 1913, RDS, 812.00/7639.
764 Breniman reports, August 11, 20, 22, 1913, BI, roll 854.
765 Breniman report, August 15, 1913, BI, roll 854.
766 Thompson report, July 27, 1913, BI, roll 853; Webster report, September 5, 1914, BI, roll 857.
767 Breniman report, October 5, 1913, BI, roll 854; Thompson report, July 27, 1913, BI, roll 853.
768 Bowen report, August 19, 1913, BI, roll 854.
769 One source says the driver was James McDean [sic], Masson's mechanic, who accompanied Masson to Mexico. Hagedorn, *Conquistadors*, 549, n111.
770 Chief to Offley, July 18, 1913, BI, roll 853; Bowen reports, August 16, 22, October 13, 18, December 14, 1913, BI, roll 854.
771 Bowen reports, August 28, 30, 1913, BI, roll 854.
772 Bowen report, December 14, 1913, BI, roll 854.
773 Bowen report, October 31, 1913, BI, roll 854.
774 Hagedorn, *Conquistadors*, 76: the "'bombs' consisted of eighteen-inch lengths of iron pipe three inches in diameter with screw caps on each end. In the center of the nose cap a hole was drilled to fix a rod, which stopped short of the detonator attached to the tail cap. The explosive charge consisted of dynamite packed in with steel rivets; crude tail fins were also mounted." Ibid., 549, n113; Taylor, "Los orígenes," 185, states that Masson and Dean attacked the gunboats on June 21.
775 Bowen report, September 20, 1913, BI, roll 854.
776 Lamoreaux reports, March 25, 26, 1913, BI, roll 853. Agent Arthur M. Allen at San Francisco reported no arms trafficking; Allen report, August 28, 1913, BI, roll 854.
777 Bowen reports, August 28, 1913, BI, roll 854.
778 Bowen report, August 29, 1913, BI, roll 854; *Imperial Valley Press*, November 17, 1913.
779 *Audubon Republican*, November 2, 1899, June 11, 1903.
780 *Audubon Republican*, April 20, 1905.
781 *Audubon County Journal*, December 3, 1908.
782 El Paso, Texas, City Directory, 1913. Breniman is listed as a Special Agent for the Department of Justice.
783 *Saratoga Sun*, June 1, 1916.
784 *Omaha Daily Bee*, December 3, 1920.
785 Breniman reports, August 29, 30, 1913, BI, roll 854.

786 Assistant Secretary of the Treasury to Secretary of State, August 2, 1913, RDS, 812.00/8236.
787 Harris and Sadler, *Secret War*, 148-149; nos. C-698, C-699, C-700, C-701, C-705, US District Court, Phoenix, FRC- LN; Thompson report, August 8, 1913, BI, roll 853; Breniman reports, September 28, October 9, 10, 15, 25, November 1, 10, 16, 23, December 24, 1913, BI, roll 854.
788 Nos. C-525, C-676, C-677, C-679, US District Court, Phoenix, FRC- LN.
789 Breniman reports, December 5-7, 11, 12, 1913; BI, roll 854; Bielaski to Barnes, January 12, 1914; Assistant Attorney General to Morrison, January 13, 1914, BI, roll 859.
790 Thompson report, December 13, 1913, BI, roll 854; see also Bielaski to Barnes, January 12, 1914, BI, roll 859.
791 Webster reports, September 21, 22, 1914, BI, roll 857.
792 Blanford report, March 2, 1917, BI, roll 857.
793 Barnes reports, October 6, 8, 1914; Blanford reports, October 7, 8, 12, November 10, 1914, BI, roll 856.
794 Bielaski to Barnes, January 10, 1915, BI, roll 854.
795 Webster report, September 4, 1914; see also Bowen report, September 16, 1914, BI, roll 857.
796 Webster reports, September 5, 7, 1914, BI, roll 857.
797 Gershon reports, February 18, 19, 22, 1917, BI, roll 857.
798 Hall to Honeyman, May 13, 1915, BI, roll 858.
799 Born in 1879 in Brooklyn, Hall came from a wealthy background. The 1900 Census shows the 21-year-old living with his parents and three servants in Park Avenue, Orange, New Jersey. He settled in Los Angeles in the early 1900s and worked in his father's arms trading company, H. H. Hall and Sons (reincorporated as R. L. Hall, Incorporated after his father's passing). Hall became a prominent arms dealer in the Mexican Revolution. He cultivated commercial relationships in Japan, where he sourced arms for the Carranza faction in 1915. The international arms dealer served in the US Army during World War I, after which he returned to Los Angeles. He died in 1936.
800 Webster report, September 5, 1914, BI, roll 857.
801 Blanford to Bielaski, March 6, 1916, BI, roll 857.
802 *San Bernardino County Sun*, September 24, 1944; *Fresno Bee*, September 23, 1944.
803 Blanford report, February 16, 1915, BI, roll 857.
804 Bowen report, September 10, 1914, BI, roll 857; see also Bowen report, June 2, 1914, BI, roll 863.
805 Webster report, September 11, 1914, BI, roll 857.
806 Bowen report, September 14, 1914, BI, roll 857.
807 Bowen report, September 14, 1914; Webster report, September 21, 1914, BI, roll 857.
808 Webster reports, September 23, 24, 1914, BI, roll 857; Bowen report, September 26, 1914, BI, roll 856.
809 Bowen report, December 5, 1914, BI, roll 855.
810 Webster reports, January 12, 13, 1915, BI, roll 857.
811 Blanford report, January 18, 1915, BI, roll 857.
812 Blanford report, January 19, 1915, BI, roll 857.
813 Webster report, February 2, 1915, BI, roll 857.

[814] Webster report, February 3, 1915; Blanford report, February 6, 1915, BI, roll 857.
[815] Blanford report, February 5, 1915; Webster report, February 8, 1915, BI, roll 857.
[816] Blanford report, February 6, 1915, BI, roll 858.
[817] Blanford reports, February 13, 19, 1915, BI, roll 857.
[818] Webster reports, February 9-11, 1915, BI, roll 857.
[819] Webster reports, February 6, 13, 15, 1915; Blanford report, February 13, 1915, BI, roll 857.
[820] Blanford report, February 16, 1915, BI, roll 857.
[821] Translations of Avilés's extensive personal correspondence file are in Webster reports, February 18, March 13, 1915, BI, roll 857.
[822] Webster reports, February 18, March 13, 1915, BI, roll 857.
[823] Blanford report, February 16, 1915, BI, roll 857.
[824] Blanford reports, February 19, 26, 1915; see also Webster reports, February 24, March 11, 1915, BI, roll 857.
[825] Valdez Daily Prospector, February 20, 1915; Richmond Virginian, March 27, 1915.
[826] Blanford to Bielaski, April 1, 1915, BI, roll 857.
[827] Blanford report, March 25, 1915, BI, roll 857.
[828] Blanford report, February 19, 1915, BI, roll 857.
[829] Chief to Blanford, March 1, 1915, BI, roll 854; Blanford report, March 24, 1915, BI, roll 857; Chief to Danziger, March 30, 1915, BI, roll 858; see also Webster report, April 15, 1915, BI, roll 857.
[830] Assistant Attorney General to Danziger, March 14, 1915; Assistant Attorney General to Schoonover, March 24, 1915, BI, roll 857.
[831] Webster report, March 11, 1915, BI, roll 857.
[832] Kosterlitzky report, January 31, 1920, BI, roll 862.
[833] These three letters are among the many translations attached to Webster reports, March 13, 17, 1915, BI, roll 857.
[834] Blanford reports, March 31, April 1, 2, 30, 1915; Webster reports, April 6, 7, 9, 10, 12, 13, 19, 20, 27, 29, 1915, BI, roll 857.
[835] Webster report, April 14, 1915, BI, roll 857.
[836] Blanford reports, May 12, 13, 18, 1915, BI, roll 857.
[837] Blanford report, July 16, 1915, BI, roll 859.
[838] Another witness, Díaz de León, received the same instructions after he claimed he had been offered $200 and asked to sign a receipt; Blanford report, July 19, 1915, BI, roll 857.
[839] Bowen personnel file, Acceptance of Resignation letter by Attorney General Gregory, December 7, 1914, NPRC.
[840] Webster report, July 22, 1915; see also Webster report, August 13, 1915, BI, roll 857.
[841] Blanford to Breniman, October 13, 1915, BI, roll 857.
[842] Blanford report, June 2, 1915, BI, roll 857.
[843] Blanford report, June 7, 1915; see also Blanford reports, June 21, July 23, 1915, BI, roll 857 and June 24, 1915, BI, roll 859; Webster report, June 7, 1915, BI, roll 857; Chief to Blanford, June 16, 1915, BI, roll 854.
[844] Blanford report, May 25, 1915, BI, roll 857.
[845] Webster report, July 28, 1915, BI, roll 858.

846 Boden report, August 18, 1915, BI, roll 858.
847 Webster report, June 17, 1915, BI, roll 859; Blanford reports, June 22, July 12, 1915; Webster reports, July 30, August 6, September 27, 29, 1915, BI, roll 857.
848 Webster report, August 11, 1915; see also Webster report, August 24, 1915, BI, roll 857.
849 Webster report, August 14, 1915, BI, roll 857.
850 Chief to Webster, September 13, 1915; Blanford report, September 28, 1915, BI, roll 859; Webster reports, September 30, October 2, 4, 5, 1915, BI, roll 857 and October 11, 1915, BI, roll 858.
851 Webster report, November 8, 1915, BI, roll 858.
852 Webster reports, August 17, 26, 1915, BI, roll 857.
853 Webster reports, August 20, September 27, 1915, BI, roll 857.
854 Webster reports, September 18, October 11, 1915; Blanford to Brassell, October 11, November 6, 1915; Guy report, November 8, 1915; Blanford report, November 15, 1915, BI, roll 857.
855 Webster report, October 6, 1915, BI, roll 857.
856 Webster report, October 13, 1915, BI, roll 858.
857 Webster report, November 10, 1915, BI, roll 858.
858 Blanford reports, November 10, 1915, BI, roll 857 and November 11, 1915, BI, roll 858; Webster report, January 14, 1916, BI, roll 857.
859 Webster report, January 12, 1916, BI, roll 857.
860 Blanford to Gallaher, February 14, 1916, BI, roll 857.
861 Blanford reports, January 15, February 2, 1916, BI, roll 857.
862 Blanford to Bielaski, March 7, 1916, BI, roll 857.
863 Blanford report, March 11, 1916, BI, roll 857.
864 Blanford to Brassell, March 11, 1916, BI, roll 857.
865 Blanford report, April 11, 1916, BI, roll 857.
866 Blanford report, May 24, 1916; see also Chief to Blanford, July 3, 1916, BI, roll 857.
867 Breniman report, July 5, 1916, BI, roll 857. Breniman refers to his reports for June 28-30.
868 "Pedro Badillo—Tijuana; Luis Rivas Isais—San Diego; Pedro Martínez—San Diego; W. Herman Bacon—San Diego; Frank J. Kiessig—1211 5th St., San Diego; Archie Aldrich—1211 5th St., San Diego; J. M. Hood—San Diego Hardware Co., 658 6th St., San Diego; F. A. Bennett, Western Union Telegraph Office, San Diego—subpoena duces tecum for telegrams mentioned in Agent's report of November 9, 1915: telegrams between Avilés, G. Guzmán, C. M. Sandoval, Brassell, and Fernández, B. J. Viljoen, Manuel Brassell, W. K. Bowker, José F. Costillo, Adolph Danziger, their dates, sender, and cities sent from are listed; B. F. Moss—San Diego (deceased); E. J. Irwin—Central Meat Market, El Centro; Ramón Sánchez—El Centro J. M. Julian—J. M. Julian Grocery Store, El Centro; Frank Núñez—El Centro; Count Wilhelm Von Hardenberg—Crown Hill Apartments, Los Angeles; William Tufts—c/o Tufts Lyon Company, Los Angeles; Adolph Danziger—Higgins Building, Los Angeles; Manuel G. Brassell, 107 Utah St., Los Angeles (now said to be in Arizona); Juan N. Fernández—435 North Figueroa (now said to be in the interior of Mexico); Ignacio Díaz de León—whereabouts unknown, fugitive from justice, Los Angeles County; Juan and Timoteo Córdova—619 North Alameda St. or 746 New High St., Los Angeles; Pedro Delgado—704

½ West 3rd St., Los Angeles (said to have left Los Angeles, whereabouts unknown); Ed V. Vega—319 Stockton St., Los Angeles (He being at this address at present is doubtful); José Salinas—San Fernando St., Los Angeles; Eduardo García—address unknown; José F. Costillo—last address known, county jail (Has not been seen by Agent for past six months.); Arnaldo Basurto—Date St. near Brooklyn Ave., Los Angeles (He being at this address at present is doubtful); Justino Mendieta—last address known, Havana (This office has recently been informed by Col. Emilio Kosterlitzky that Mendieta has recently gone to the State of Oaxaca.); José M. Maytorena—Hotel McAlpin, New York City." Webster report, August 9, 1916, BI, roll 857.

[869] Blanford report, August 9, 1916, BI, roll 857.
[870] Webster to Gershon, August 11, 1916, BI, roll 857.
[871] "Manuel G. Brassell—715 Temple St. Order dated July 4, 1916. J. N. Fernández—Hesta Hotel, 506 Temple St. Order dated Nov. 30, 1915. Eduardo García—152 West 22nd St. Ignacio Díaz de León, Juan Córdova, Timoteo Córdova, José Salinas, José F. Costillo, Arnaldo Basurto."
[872] Webster report, August 14, 1916, BI, roll 867.
[873] Webster report, August 17, 1916, BI, roll 857.
[874] Gershon reports, August 21, 22, 1916, BI, roll 857.
[875] Blanford to Gershon, August 23, 1916, BI, roll 857.
[876] Webster report, August 23, 1916, BI, roll 857.
[877] Webster report, August 23, 1916, BI, roll 857.
[878] Webster report, August 25, 1915, BI, roll 857.
[879] Gershon reports, August 27, 31, 1916, BI, roll 857.
[880] Gershon report, August 30, 1916, BI, roll 857.
[881] Gershon report, September 5, 1916, BI, roll 857.
[882] Webster report, September 1, 1916; Blanford to Gershon, August 31, 1916, BI, roll 857.
[883] Gershon report, September 5, 1916, BI, roll 857.
[884] Gershon report, September 5, 1916; Webster report, September 7, 1916, BI, roll 857.
[885] Gershon report, September 8, 1916, BI, roll 857.
[886] Webster to Warden, August 31, 1916; September 1, 1916, BI, roll 857; Webster reports, September 1, 7, 1916, BI, roll 857.
[887] Webster to Fernández, August 31, 1916; Webster to Stone, August 31, 1916; Webster report, September 1, 1916, BI, roll 857.
[888] Blanford report, September 1, 1916, BI, roll 857.
[889] Blanford report, September 8, 1916, BI, roll 857.
[890] Campbell report, September 4, 1916; Blanford reports, September 11, 12, 1916, BI, roll 857.
[891] Blanford report, July 5, 1916, BI, roll 857.
[892] Blanford reports, September 5, 8, 1916, BI, roll 857.
[893] Blanford reports, September 12, 14, 19, 1916; Stone report, September 20, 1916; Blanford to Fernández, October 13, 1916, BI, roll 857.
[894] Blanford report, September 11, 1916, BI, roll 857.
[895] Blanford reports, September 14, 19, 1916, BI, roll 857.
[896] Blanford report, September 14, 1916, BI, roll 857.

[897] Blanford reports, September 14, October 9, 1916; Blanford to US Marshal, September 25, 1916, BI, roll 857.
[898] Blanford report, September 19, 1916, BI, roll 857.
[899] Blanford reports, September 16, November 2, 1916; Blanford to Gershon, September 23, 1916, BI, roll 857.
[900] Gershon reports, September 27, 29, 1916, BI, roll 857.
[901] Boden report, August 14, 1915, BI, roll 858.
[902] Blanford report, November 2, 1916, BI, roll 857.
[903] Gershon report, December 23, 1916, BI, roll 857.
[904] Blanford report, November 2, 1916, BI, roll 857.
[905] Blanford report, November 15, 1916, BI, roll 857.
[906] Blanford reports, November 18, 21, December 21, 1916, BI, roll 857.
[907] Blanford report, December 18, 1916, BI, roll 857.
[908] Chief to Blanford, November 2, 1916, BI, roll 857.
[909] Blanford reports, July 19, 1916, BI, roll 855 and November 15, 1916, BI, roll 857; C. G. Varcos in July 1916 interviewed the manager of W. Stokes Kirk Army and Navy Goods store in Los Angeles about ammunition; Blanford reports, July 19, 29, 1916, BI, roll 855.
[910] Varcos reports, November 21, 27, 1916, BI, roll 857.
[911] Varcos report, December 1, 1916, BI, roll 857.
[912] Blanford report, January 6, 1917, BI, roll 857.
[913] Varcos reports, January 13, February 1, 8, 18, 1917, BI, roll 857. He listed their names, their political affiliation, and clubs to which they belonged, starting with Harry Chandler (Republican, Director, Los Angeles Athletic Club, Jonathan Club, owner of *Los Angeles Times*); attorney Oscar Lawler (Republican, Los Angeles Athletic Club, California Club); attorney R. W. Hunsaker (Republican, Los Angeles Athletic Club, California Club, Jonathan Club); W. B. [?] Britt (Republican, California Club); J. Deghan (Republican). A summary of the information concerning the venire was: 45 Republicans, 7 Democrats, 4 Progressives, 6 not stated, 13 not registered; 23 were members of the Los Angeles Club, 40 were members of the California Club, 9 were members of the Jonathan Club, 37 were known to be advertisers in the *Los Angeles Times*. Detailed information concerning men on the jury list was: 75 men were listed alphabetically with their addresses and occupations and whether Republican, Democrat, Progressive, Not registered, Not stated, member of Los Angeles Athletic Club, California Club, Jonathan Club, and/or *Los Angeles Times* advertiser. At the request of US Attorney Schoonover, Varcos interviewed several men to determine whether one of the veniremen, Ernest A. Wallenberg, had any connection with the Los Angeles Investment Company. To their knowledge he had none.
[914] Jones report, December 6, 1916, BI, roll 857.
[915] Stone to Barnes, January 11, 1917, BI, roll 857.
[916] Stone to Blanford, January 13, 1917, BI, roll 857.
[917] Blanford report, January 18, 1917, BI, roll 857.
[918] Blanford report, May 15, 1917, BI, roll 857.
[919] Webster report, January 29, 1917; Blanford reports, January 23, 29, February 28, 1917, BI, roll 857.

920 Blanford reports, January 29, February 14, 1917, BI, roll 857.
921 The summary is in Blanford report, March 2, 1917, BI, roll 857.
922 Blanford reports, February 1, 5, 8, 10, 23, March 7, 1917; Allen report, February 9, 1917; Gershon report, February 20, 1917, BI, roll 857.
923 Ramón Sánchez, E. J. Irwin, J. M. Julian, José F. Costillo, F. A. Bennett, Luis Rivas Isais, Pedro Martínez, Archie Aldrich, J. M. Wood, Ed. V. Vega, Eduardo García, William Tufts, Manuel G. Brassell, W. A. Lawrence, Adolph Danziger, W. Sherman Bacon, Pedro Delgado, (Blanford noted that Pedro Delgado was said to be under subpoena, he having come from New York when the case was set for trial the last time. He was now said to be stopping at the Atlas Hotel on South Figueroa St.) For the following, subpoenas had been issued but no return had been made: Wilhelm von Hardenberg, Juan N. Fernández, Pedro Badillo, Ignacio Díaz de León. These parties should be served with no trouble before the trial. For the following, subpoenas had been issued but were not able to be served: Frank Kiessig, said to be in Mexico; Timoteo Cordova, in the Arizona State Penitentiary, Florence, Arizona; Juan Córdova, unable to locate; José Salinas, unable to locate; Arnaldo ___ no surname listed. A subpoena duces tecum had been issued for the Western Union manager at Calexico to produce telegrams sent to Baltasar Avilés, 1274 Julian St., San Diego, dated Dec. 27, 1914, signed Bowker, but no subpoena nor praecipe had been issued for the Western Union manager at Calexico for this trial. Justino Mendieta would be notified to appear in Los Angeles after it was determined whether or not this trial would be heard on March 19.
924 Webster report, March 9, 1917, BI, roll 857.
925 Blanford report, March 12, 1917; Blanford to Brassell March 12, 1917, BI, roll 857.
926 Wren report, March 14, 1917, BI, roll 857.
927 Assistant Attorney General to Schoonover, April 23, 1917, BI, roll 857.
928 Blanford report, April 30, 1917, BI, roll 857.
929 Bielaski to Blanford, May 3, 1917, BI, roll 857.
930 Lillard report, May 5, 1917; Blanford reports, May 14, 15, 1917, BI, roll 857.
931 Webster report, May 11, 1917; Blanford reports, May 15, 17, 1917, BI, roll 857.
932 Blanford report, May 14, 1917, BI, roll 857.
933 Keep report, May 12, 1917, BI, roll 857.
934 Blanford reports, May 8, 12, 14, 15, 1917, BI, roll 857.
935 Blanford report, May 31, 1917, BI, roll 857.
936 Gershon report, May 16, 1917; see also Blanford report, May 31, 1917, BI, roll 857.
937 Blanford report, May 15, 1917, BI, roll 857.
938 Gershon report, May 23, 1917, BI, roll 857.
939 Webster report, May 23, 1917, BI, roll 857.
940 Kosterlitzky report, May 21, 1917, BI, roll 857.
941 Blanford report, February 20, 1915, BI, roll 857.
942 Blanford reports, March 30, April 30, 1915; Webster report, June 12, 1915, BI, roll 857.
943 Blanford report, June 14, 1915; see also Webster reports, June 12, July 30, 1915, BI, roll 857.
944 Blanford report, May 25, 1917, BI, roll 857.
945 Blanford report, May 31, 1917, BI, roll 857.

946 Lowell L. Blaisdell, "Harry Chandler and Mexican Border Intrigue, 1914-1917," *Pacific Historical Review*, 35, no. 4 (November 1966), 385-393.
947 Barnes reports, January 1, 1914, BI, roll 854 and May 12, 1914, BI, roll 859.
948 A collection of de la Garza's work with Villa is contained in 9 boxes at the Benson Latin American Library at the University of Texas at Austin. The papers cover the period 1913 to 1917. See for example, Papers of Lázaro de la Garza, Box 9, Folder A, Financials of the División del Norte 1915.
949 Cobb to Davis, April 16, 1915, RDS, 812.00/ 15118 and May 31, 1915, RDS, 812.00/15099; John F. Chalkley, *Zach Lamar Cobb: El Paso Collector of Customs and Intelligence During the Mexican Revolution* (El Paso: Texas Western Press, 1998), 21. De la Garza moved to New York in 1915 and started his own trading company. In October 1915, he stole a $65,000 down payment for munitions from Villa and the Madero Bros. agency. Pursued by Villa and the Maderos, he "retired" from the Revolution in 1916 and moved to Los Angeles, where he bought a large mansion. Villa's brother Hipólito and Alberto Madero sued him into the 1930s, until, despite his guilt, the Mexican Supreme Court cleared him in 1933. Disgraced as a swindler and traitor to the Mexican Revolution, he died in the city of Torreón in August 1939. See von Feilitzsch, Felix A. *Sommerfeld and the Mexican Front in the Great War* (Amissville: Henselstone Verlag, 2015), 119-121.
950 Harris and Sadler, *Secret War*, 163-164.
951 Madero Bros. were slain president Francisco Madero's uncles Ernesto, Alberto, and Alfredo Madero.
952 Papers of Lázaro de la Garza, Box 5, Folder A, correspondence of F. Stallforth with A. Madero, February 10, 1914.
953 Papers of Lázaro de la Garza, Box 2, Folder J, June 26, 1914 to July 26, 1914, correspondence of Felix Sommerfeld with C. R. Flint, payment of $40,000 commissions to Sommerfeld.
954 Papers of Lázaro de la Garza, Box 5, Folder A, Tauscher correspondence with L. de la Garza, February 9 to February 27, 1914. The British sea blockade starting in August 1914 made shipments of arms from Germany to Villa impossible.
955 Papers of Lázaro de la Garza, Box 5, Folder E, Correspondence with Western Cartridge Company.
956 Blanford report, January 9, 1914; Daniel report, January 13, 1914, BI, roll 854.
957 Martín Luis Guzmán, *Memorias de Pancho Villa* (Mexico, DF: Compañía General de Ediciones, 1951), 130; von Feilitzsch, *In Plain Sight*, 312-313; Cumberland, *Constitutionalist Years*, 133.
958 Von Feilitzsch, *In Plain Sight*, 313; The US Army interned 3,352 soldiers and 1,607 women in Fort Bliss.
959 Wren report, January 15, 1914, BI, roll 859.
960 Blanford report, February 1, 1914, BI, roll 855.
961 Harris and Sadler, *Secret War*, 169-170; Blanford report, February 23, 1914; Bielaski to Blanford, March 3, 1914, BI, roll 859.
962 Harris and Sadler, *Secret War*, 179; see also Blanford report, April 18, 1915, BI, roll 855.
963 Harris and Sadler, *Secret War*, 161-162; Blanford report, April 7, 1914, BI, roll 859.
964 Blanford report, February 1, 1914, BI, roll 855; see also Blanford report January 20, 1914, roll 854.

965 Blanford reports, January 17, 1914, BI roll 859, and March 10-12, 14, 16, 1914, BI, roll 855; Wren reports, January 21, 27, 1914, BI, roll 859.
966 Barnes report, April 9, 1914, BI, roll 855.
967 Blanford report, February 19, 1914, BI, roll 855; see also Blanford report, January 20, 1914, BI, roll 854; Blanford to Bielaski, February 9, 1914, BI, roll 859 and February 17, 1914, BI, roll 855.
968 Diebold to Blanford, February 11, 1914; Bielaski to Diebold, February 26, 1914, BI, roll 855.
969 Harris and Sadler, *Secret War*, 168-171.
970 Harris and Sadler, *Secret War*, 172; New York Times, March 10, 1914.
971 Blanford report, October 23, 1914, BI, roll 857.
972 Harris and Sadler, *Secret War*, 173-175, 178.
973 Blanford reports, October 17, 1914, BI, roll 855 and October 23, 1914, BI, roll 857.
974 McCluer report, July 29, 1914, BI, roll 859; see also Blanford report, October 22, 1914, BI, roll 857.
975 McCluer report, October 30, 1914, BI, roll 857.
976 Blanford to McCluer, October 30, 1914; McCluer report, November 3, 1914, BI, roll 857.
977 Barnes report, January 21, 1915, BI, roll 855.
978 Harris and Sadler, *Secret War*, 183.
979 Harris and Sadler, *Secret War*, 181-184.
980 WDT case, 1816
981 "Orozco on October 22, 1914, had caused to be purchased from Fred J. Feldman and Co. a large amount of munitions, rifles, etc., and on same day did cause same to be shipped to Tandy Sanford [at] Hermanas, NM." Offley report, August 14, 1915, BI, roll 855.
982 Barnes to Pinckney, April 14, 1914, BI, roll 855.
983 Pinckney reports, April 29, May 1, 1915, BI, roll 855; Harris and Sadler, *Secret War*, 189-190.
984 Breniman report, March 25, 1915, BI, roll 855.
985 No. 1816, US District Court, El Paso, FRC-FW.
986 Barnes to Breniman, March 29, 1915, BI, roll 855.
987 Pinckney report, November 13, 1915, BI, roll 855. Pinckney was born in Austin. He received his law degree in 1912 from the University of Texas at Austin. The Bureau hired him in January 1915 as a special agent for the Atlanta field office. A short time later he was transferred back to his home state and assigned to the Houston field office. He worked for the BI until the First World War then joined the MID as an intelligence officer. In the 1920s he became engaged in Texas politics as a Democrat. He fought the resurgence of the Ku-Klux-Klan. Pinckney lived in Houston until his death in 1949.
988 Holmdahl Papers, C-B-921, Bancroft Library, University of California at Berkley.
989 Harris and Sadler, *Secret War*, 242, 285-287.
990 Pinckney report, April 18, 1915, BI, roll 855.
991 Barnes report, September 7, 1914, BI, roll 858; Barnes to Wright, May 18, 1915, BI, roll 855.
992 Pinckney report, December 10, 1915; Chief to Barnes, December 10, 1915; Barnes to Pinckney, December 11, 1915, BI, roll 855.

993 Bielaski to Beckham, January 21, 1915; see also Barnes to Bielaski, February 18, 1915; Barnes report, April 22, 1915, BI, roll 855.
994 Blanford report, December 22, 1914; Guy report, February 2, 1915; notarized statement by Ofelia Ortega de Otero, February 2, 1915; Barnes reports, February 8, May 13, 18, 1915; Geck voucher, February 7, 1915; Beckham reports, November 27, December 2, 4, 7, 29, 1914, January 4, February 9, 11, 13, 15-17, March 23, May 11, 29, June 6, September 11, 1915; Beckham to Geck, March 23, 1915; Bielaski to Beckham, January 21, March 25, 1915; Wright report, May 26, 1915; Pinckney reports, August 4, September 3, 4, 6, 9-11, 14, 16, 18, October 19, November 17, December 2, 3, 10, 15, 21, 1915; Stone report, September 11, 1915; Beckham to Pickney, November 13, 1915; Barnes report, December 11, 1915; Beckham to Williams, February 3, 1915, Gregory to US Attorney, February 4, 1915; Barnes to Guy, February 9, 1915, BI, roll 855.
995 Barnes reports, April 22, December 11, 1915, BI, roll 855; *Albuquerque Morning Journal*, April 11, 1915.
996 Pinckney report, June 4, 1915, BI roll 855.
997 Harris and Sadler, *Secret War*, 157-160, 308-309; Ralph H. Vigil, "Revolution and Confusion: The Peculiar Case of José Inés Salazar," *New Mexico Historical Review*, 53, no. 2 (1978), 145-170.
998 Burkhart to Barnes, December 21, 1915; see also Barnes to Burkhart, December 27, 1915; Chief to Barnes, December 10, 1915, BI, roll 855.
999 Barnes reports, January 5, 9, 14, 17, 22, February 1, 17, 19, 27, 1914; Daniel reports, February 11, 21, 1914; Daniel to Barnes, February 13, 1914; Blanford to Barnes, February 20, 1914, BI, roll 854.
1000 Caballero, *Orozco*, 183.
1001 Pendleton report, February 26, 1914, BI, roll 854.
1002 Barnes reports, January 8, 14, May 8, 1914, BI, roll 854 and February 12, 1914, BI, roll 859.
1003 Barnes report, January 14, 1914, BI, roll 854.
1004 See, for example, Wren report, January 13, 1914, BI, roll 859.
1005 Barnes report, January 14, 1914, BI, roll 854.
1006 Barnes reports, January 8, February 9, 1914, BI, roll 854 and February 4, 1914, BI, roll 855; Bielaski to Barnes, February 9, 1914, BI, roll 855.
1007 Barnes to Blanford, March 27, 1914; Blanford reports, March 25, April 3, 1914; Barnes reports, April 9, May 20, June 6, 1914, BI, roll 854. The government did collect some money from the bonds that several prominent *vazquistas* had forfeited: $1,000 and costs for Miguel Garza Aldape and $500 and costs for Juan Pedro Didapp.
1008 Barnes reports, April 27, 28, 1914, BI, roll 856 and April 29, 1914, BI, roll 855 and April 30, 1914, BI, roll 859; Guy reports, April 26, 1914, BI, roll 862 and April 28, 1914, BI, roll 857; Stevens reports, April 28, 30, 1914, BI, roll 857 and April 28, 1914, BI, roll 862.
1009 Stevens report, May 2, 1914, BI, roll 857.
1010 Barnes report, May 28, 1914, BI, roll 857.
1011 Cumberland, *Constitutionalist Years*, 112-113.
1012 US Census 1900 and 1910.
1013 Barnes report, January 2, 1914; Barnes to Englesby, January 16, 1914, BI roll 859; Barnes to Walker, January 2, 1914, BI, roll 854.

[1014] Englesby report, January 15, 1914, BI, roll 859.
[1015] Englesby report, January 19, 1914, BI, roll 859.
[1016] Englesby report, January 16, 1914, BI, roll 859.
[1017] Englesby report, January 16, 1914; Assistant Attorney General to Secretary of State, January 16, 1914, BI, roll 859.
[1018] Englesby report, January 29, 1914, BI, roll 859.
[1019] Englesby report, January 7, 1914, BI, roll 859.
[1020] Englesby report, January 14, 1914, BI, roll 859; see also Barnes to Englesby, January 16, 1914, BI, roll 859; Englesby report, January 20, 1914, BI, roll 855.
[1021] Englesby report, January 23, 1914, BI, roll 855.
[1022] Englesby report, January 20, 1914, BI, roll 859.
[1023] Englesby report, January 22, 1914, BI, roll 859.
[1024] Englesby report, January 26, 1914, BI, roll 859.
[1025] Englesby report, January 30, 1914; Barnes to Englesby, February 5, 1914, BI, roll 859.
[1026] Theo Emery, *Hellfire Boys: The Birth of the U.S. Chemical Warfare* (New York: Little, Brown and Company, 2017), 456.
[1027] Ancestry.com, Englesby family tree, viewed March 2022.
[1028] Daniel reports, January 1-4, 6, 8, 10, 1914, BI, roll 854.
[1029] Daniel report, January 12, 1914, BI, roll 859.
[1030] Daniel reports, January 12-14, 16, 1914, BI, roll 859.
[1031] Daniel report, January 22, 1914, BI, roll 859.
[1032] Barnes reports, February 19, March 5, 1914; Breniman report, April 7, 1914, BI, roll 854.
[1033] Barnes report, January 1, 1914, BI, roll 854.
[1034] Barnes reports, January 1, 8, 1914; Barnes to Collector of Customs January 2, 1914, BI, roll 854.
[1035] Barnes report, January 30, 114, BI, roll 855.
[1036] Spates report, February 1, 1914, BI, roll 855.
[1037] Assistant Attorney General to Sheppard, February 2, 1914, BI, roll 859.
[1038] Spates report, February 4, 1914, BI, roll 855.
[1039] Blanford report, January 1, 1914, BI, roll 854.
[1040] Barnes report, January 7, 1914; Pendleton reports, January 7, 8, 11, 1914, BI, roll 855.
[1041] Harris and Sadler, *Secret War*, 155-156; *Mexico: A Weekly*, December 20, 1913, BI, roll 854; Pendleton reports, January 14, 1914, BI, roll 855 and February 1, 1914, BI, roll 859.
[1042] Pendleton report, January 4, 1914; see also Pendleton report, January 9, 1914, BI, roll 855.
[1043] Pendleton reports, July 4, 6, 1914; Pendleton to Bielaski, July 29, 1914, BI, roll 855.
[1044] Pendleton reports, January 30, 31, 1914, BI, roll 855; Darling report, March 6, 1914, BI, roll 856; Darling to Bielaski, May 12, 1914; Bielaski to Offley, May 14, 1914; Offley report, May 16, 1914, BI, roll 859.
[1045] Blanford report, June 23, 1914; Bielaski to Barnes, June 8, 1914, BI, roll 855.
[1046] Pendleton reports, January 2, 3, 21, 1914, BI, roll 859.
[1047] Pendleton report, January 29, 1914, BI, roll 859.
[1048] Pendleton report, January 21, 1914, BI, roll 859.
[1049] Breniman reports, January 18, 1914, BI, roll 856 and January 20, 23, 1914, BI, roll 855.

[1050] Breniman report, January 17, 1914, BI, roll 859.
[1051] Breniman report, January 22, 1914, BI, roll 859.
[1052] Breniman report, January 25, 1914, BI, roll 859.
[1053] Breniman reports, January 7, 1914, BI, roll 859 and January 9, 1914, BI, roll 855.
[1054] Bielaski to Breniman, January 17, 1914, BI, roll 859.
[1055] Gardner report, January 31, 1914; Breniman reports, January 26, February 13, 1914, BI, roll 859.
[1056] Breniman report, January 30, 1914, BI, roll 859.
[1057] Breniman report, March 22, 1914, BI, roll 858; Simpich to Secretary of State, March 28, 1914; Assistant Attorney General to Secretary of State, March 31, 1914; Gardner report, February 25, 1914, BI, roll 859.
[1058] Bowen reports, January 3, February 9, 1914; Breniman report, January 2, 1914, BI, roll 854; Bowen report, February 6, 1914, BI, roll 859.
[1059] Bowen report, January 16, 1914, BI, roll 854.
[1060] Barnes reports, January 2, 5, 1914; Bowen reports, January 3, 7, 1914, BI, roll 854 and January 29, 1914, BI, roll 859; Breniman reports, January 4, 6, 1914, BI, roll 854.
[1061] Bowen reports, January 8, 1914, BI, roll 859 and January 12, 22, 1914, BI, roll 854.
[1062] Bowen reports, January 28, 31, 1914, BI, roll 854 and January 29, 1914, BI, roll 859.
[1063] Breniman reports, February 4, 5, 1914, BI, roll 854.
[1064] Assistant Attorney General to Camp, February 13, 1914, BI, roll 859; see also Bielaski to Webster, September 15, 1914, and Bowen report, October 3, 1914, BI, roll 857.
[1065] McCluer report, September 10, 1914; Blanford reports December 14, 17, 1914, BI, roll 858.
[1066] Assistant Attorney General to Flynn, October 12, 1914; Bielaski to Barnes, October 30, 1914, BI, roll 857.
[1067] Breniman reports, November 5, 8, 11-13, 18, 1914; Breniman to Bielaski, November 6, 10, 12, 1914; Attorney General to Secretary of State, November 19, 1914; Bowen reports, December 1, 7, 8, 1914, BI, roll 857.
[1068] Breniman reports, November 21, December 2, 1914, BI, roll 857.
[1069] Barnes report, December 14, 1914; Wren report, December 19, 1914; Barnes to Guy, December 22, 1914, January 11, 1915; Guy reports, December 30, 1914, January 3, 5, 14, 1915, BI, roll 855.
[1070] Barnes report, January 5, 1915, BI, roll 855.
[1071] Orme report, January 6, 1915, BI, roll 857.
[1072] Bielaski letters, January 23, 1914; Bielaski to Barnes, January 29, 1914, BI, roll 859.
[1073] Bowen report, June 22, 1914; Allen reports, June 22, July 23, 1914, BI, roll 856; Rathbun reports, June 29, 1914, BI, roll 856 and July 8, 1914, BI, roll 859.
[1074] Bowen report, July 7, 1914; Webster reports, July 10, 13, 1914, BI, roll 856.
[1075] Allen report, January 14, 1914; Rathbun report, February 5, 1914, BI, roll 856.
[1076] Bowen to Rathbun, July 7, 1914; Rathbun report, July 9, 1914; Bowen report, July 9, 1914; Allen reports, July 9, 16, 1914, BI, roll 857.
[1077] Bowen report, February 9, 1914, BI, roll 854.
[1078] Bowen to Bielaski, October 2, 1914, BI, roll 859; Bielaski to Barnes, September 23, 1914, BI, roll 857.

[1079] Bowen reports, May 6, 11, 14, July 2, 3, 1914, BI, roll 855 and May 18, 1914, BI, roll 859.
[1080] Bowen reports, June 2, 4, 26, 1914, BI, roll 863 and June 5, 1914, BI, roll 859; Freston report, June 5, 1914, BI, roll 857.
[1081] Michael C. Meyer, "The Arms of the Ypiranga," *Hispanic American Historical Review*, 50, no. 3 (August 1970), 543-556. The article is based on the copies of BI agent reports sent to the State Department; see also Michael C. Meyer, *Huerta: A Political Portrait* (Lincoln: University of Nebraska Press, 1972), 197 ff.; a more recent account of the arms of the Ypiranga is Heribert von Feilitzsch, *In Plain Sight*, 340-363.
[1082] Ancestry.com, FHL Database, roll 2234441, file 86252, page 24.
[1083] *Jersey City News*, March 13, 1896; *Bismark Daily Tribune*, March 16, 1896.
[1084] *Trenton Evening Times*, April 6, 1896.
[1085] *Boletín Oficial de la Secretaría de Relaciones Exteriores*, Tomo VII, noviembre de 1898 a abril de 1899 (México: Salvador Gutiérrez, 1898), 193-194; The closest estimate available online is for the year 1902: 20,000 Swiss francs in 1902 was equivalent to 5,806 grams of gold, worth $278,525 as of this writing.
[1086] Victor Castillo et al., *Revista de Legislación y jurisprudencia, El Delito de Quiebra* (Mexico, DF: Imprenta del Gobierno Federal, 1898), 529-535.
[1087] www.in2013dollars.com; 50,000 Marks in 1896 were worth approximately 1.7 million US dollars in 2022.
[1088] *El Derecho, Quinta Época, Sección de jurisprudencia*, Tomo II (Mexico, DF: Talleres de la Ciencia Jurídica, 1898), 50-52.
[1089] Ibid., 53.
[1090] *El Paso Daily Herald*, January 6, 1899
[1091] Ibid.
[1092] Andrew Paxman, "The Rise and Fall of Leon Rasst, the Jewish-Russian Merchant of Puebla," unpublished paper, May 1, 2017.
[1093] Death Registrations for Zaragoza, Puebla Mexico, page 159, April 18, 1899; The mother's name is listed as Dacia Luro.
[1094] Leticia Gamboa, *Los empresarios de ayer: El grupo dominante en la industria textil de Puebla, 1906-1929* (Puebla: UAP, 1985), 65.
[1095] Birth Registrations, Zaragoza, Puebla Mexico, December 11, 1907.
[1096] Paxman, "Rise and Fall," 4.
[1097] Paxman, "Rise and Fall," 4.
[1098] Paxman, "Rise and Fall," 2.
[1099] Paxman, "Rise and Fall," 5.
[1100] Paxman, "Rise and Fall," 5. Paxman cites correspondence between Stalewski and Foreign Minister Enrique Creel, as well as between Creel and Martínez in October and November 1910.
[1101] *Arizona Oasis*, November 26, 1910.
[1102] Doyas to Department, September 25, 1918, file 9140-1754-39, RG 165, MID, NARA.
[1103] Berliner to Department, August 3, 1918, file 9140-1754-40, RG 165, MID, NARA.

1104 Passenger and Crew Lists of Vessels, New York arrivals 1913, microfilm series T715, roll 26, page 2, RG 85, NARA.
1105 Scully report, December 17, 1913, BI, roll 854.
1106 Chief to Offley, April 21, 1914, enclosing a "Private and Confidential" letter from Bowring & Co., Ship Brokers, Steamship Agents, and Commission Merchants at New York to E. H. Duff, April 21, 1914, BI, roll 856.
1107 Scully reports, April 29, 30, 1914, BI, roll 856.
1108 Thomas Baecker, "The Arms of the Ypiranga: The German Side," *The Americas*, 30, no. 1 (July 1973), 5.
1109 Baecker, "The Arms of the Ypiranga," 7.
1110 Ibid.
1111 Hintze to Auswärtiges Amt, April 18, 1914, AA Politisches Archiv Berlin, Mexiko V, Paket 33.
1112 Wilson to Köhler, August 25, 1914, Albert Papers, Box 32, RG 65, NARA.
1113 The Ypiranga alone carried 17,899 cases, 1,000 cases filling one railcar. "The arms and ammunition, he [Consul Canada] continued, would immediately be loaded aboard three trains of ten cars each and rushed to Mexico City." Meyer, "The Arms of the Ypiranga," 551.
1114 United States Senate, *Investigation of Mexican Affairs*. 2 vols. Senate doc. no. 285. 66th Cong, 2nd sess. (Washington, DC: Government Printing Office, 1920), 782.
1115 *New York Times*, May 31, 1914.
1116 Baecker, "The Arms of the Ypiranga," 15.
1117 Papen to War Department, May 28, 1914, Albert Papers, Box 27, RG 65, NARA.
1118 *New York Times*, May 31, 1914.
1119 Barbara Tuchman, *The Zimmermann Telegram* (New York: MacMillan, 1958), 52.
1120 Bielaski to Offley, April 28, 1914, BI, roll 859.
1121 Lázaro de la Garza papers, Box 1, Folder E, de la Garza to Villa, May 3, 1914.
1122 Scully reports, May 4, 20, 1914, BI, roll 856.
1123 Baker reports, July 21, 24, 28, 31, 1914; Barnes to Guy, September 6, 1914, BI, roll 856.
1124 Lázaro de la Garza papers, Box 1, Folders C, D, E.
1125 Baker reports, May 18, 22, June 4, 6, 13, 23, 26, 27, July 7, 1914; Offley reports, May 20, August 7, 1914; Clabaugh reports, June 25, August 3, 1914, BI, roll 856.
1126 Barnes report, August 3, 1914, BI, roll 856; *New York Times*, March 8, 1915.

Bibliography

Archives

Ancestry.com, various online archives.

National Archives and Records Administration, Washington, DC and College Park, Maryland.

RG 59 Records of the Department of State.

    Decimal Files, Internal Affairs of Mexico, 1910-1929, Microcopy no. 274.

    Numerical and Minor Files, 1906-1910, Microcopy M-862.

RG 60 Records of the Department of Justice.

RG 65 Records of the Federal Bureau of Investigation: Investigative Case Files of the Bureau of Investigation, 1908-1922

    Old Mex 232 Files, Microcopy.
    Old German Files, 1909-21, Microfilm Publication No. M1085.
    Miscellaneous Files, 1909-21, Microcopy.
    Papers of Heinrich F. Albert.

RG 76 Records of Boundary and Claims Commissions and Arbitrations

    Mixed Claims Commission.

RG 85 Department of the Immigration and Naturalization Service.

    Passenger and Crew Lists of Vessels.

    Selected Indices to naturalization Records of the U.S. Circuit and District Courts, Northern District of California.

RG 87 Records of the United States Secret Service.

    Daily Reports of Agents, 1875 Thru 1936, Microcopy.

RG 92 Records of the Office of the Quartermaster General.

RG 131 Records of the Alien Property Custodian.

RG 165 Records of the War Department General and Special Staffs.

    Army War College, General Correspondence

    Military Intelligence Division.

RG 242 Collection of Foreign Records

Captured German Documents.

RG 393 Records of United States Army

    Continental Commands, 1821-1920

        General Correspondence, Department of Texas, 1870-1913.

National Personnel Records Center, Civilian Personnel Records, St. Louis, Missouri.

Federal Records Center, Fort Worth, Texas.

    US Commissioner, Del Rio, El Paso, Marfa.

US District Court, San Antonio, Austin, Brownsville, El Paso, Laredo.
Federal Records Center, Denver, Colorado.
    US Commissioner, District of New Mexico.
    US District Court, Santa Fe.
Federal Records Center, Laguna Niguel, California.
    US Commissioner, Douglas.
    US District Court, Phoenix, Tucson.
Library of Congress, Washington, D.C.
    Lansing Private Memoranda, 1915-1917.
Archivo Histórico Diplomático Mexicano de la Secretaría de Relaciones Exteriores, Mexico, DF.
Auswärtiges Amt, Politisches Archiv Berlin, Mexiko V.
National Guard Registers, vol. 72, Unattached Companies 2nd and 3rd Brigades Enlisted Men, 1880 – 1894.
Private Collections and Personal Papers.
Albert Bacon Fall Family Papers, Rio Grande Historical Collections, New Mexico State University, Las Cruces, NM.
Berliner, Harry, Letters to John Embleton, courtesy of Kirstin Keller Rounds, private collection.
Papers of Lázaro De La Garza, Nettie Lee Benson Latin American Collection, University of Texas at Austin.
Papers of Enrique Llorente, New York Public Library.
Papers of Emil Holmdahl, Bancroft Library, University of California at Berkley.

Government Documents

Annual Report of the Attorney General of the United States for the Year 1907, 2 vols. Washington, D.C.: Government Printing Office, 1907.

Annual Report of the Attorney General of the United States for the Year 1908. Washington, D.C.: Government Printing Office, 1908.

Lansing Papers, 1914-1920. 2 vols. Washington D.C.: Government Printing Office, 1939.

Birth Registrations, Zaragoza, Puebla Mexico, December 11, 1907.

Boletín Oficial de la Secretaria de Relaciones Exteriores, Tomo VII, noviembre de 1898 a abril de 1899. México: Salvador Gutiérrez, 1898.

Death Registrations for Zaragoza, Puebla Mexico, April 18, 1899.

Deutschland und Österreich, Verzeichnisse von Militär- und Marineoffizieren, 1600-1918. Provo: Ancestry.com Operations, Inc., 2015.

El Derecho, Quinta época, sección de Jurisprudencia, Tomo II. México: Talleres de la Ciencia jurídica, 1898.

Kansas City, Missouri, City Directory, 1912.

Maryland Appellate Court, Morris v Rasst, 1918.
Maryland Circuit Court, Morris v Rasst, 1916.
Maryland Supreme Court, Morris v. Rasst, 1922.
Reports of the International Arbitral Awards, Mixed Claims Commission. Vol. 8 New York: United Nations, 2006.
US Census 1880 to 1960.
US City Directories, 1880-1942.
US Senate, *Investigation of Mexican Affairs*. 2 vols. Senate doc. no. 285, 66th Cong., 2nd sess. Washington D.C.: Government Printing Office, 1920.
US Senate, Revolutions in Mexico: Hearing before a Subcommittee of the Committee on Foreign Relations. 62nd Cong. 2nd sess. Washington, D. C.: Government Printing Office, 1913.

Books

A Twentieth Century History of Southwest Texas. 3 vols. Chicago, New York, Los Angeles: Lewis Publishing Company, 1907.

Albro, Ward S., *Always a Rebel: Ricardo Flores Magon and the Mexican Revolution*. Fort Worth: Texas Christian University Press, 1992.

Almada, Francisco R., *Diccionario de historia, geografía, y biografía Chihuahuenses*. 2nd ed. Chihuahua: Universidad de Chihuahua, 1968.

Atwater, Elton, *American Regulation of Arms Exports*. Washington, D.C.: Carnegie Endowment for International Peace, 1941.

Batvinis, Raymond J., *The Origins of FBI Counterintelligence*. Lawrence: University Press of Kansas, 2007.

Beezley William H., *Insurgent Governor: Abraham Gonzalez and the Mexican Revolution in Chihuahua*. Lincoln: University of Nebraska Press, 1973.

Bisher, Jamie, *The Intelligence War in Latin America, 1914-1922*. Jefferson: McFarland, 2016.

Blaisdell, Lowell L., *The Desert Revolution: Baja California, 1911*. Madison: University of Wisconsin Press, 1962.

Boghardt, Thomas, *The Zimmermann Telegram: Intelligence, Diplomacy, and America's Entry into World War I*. Annapolis: Naval Institute Press, 2012.

Brands, H. W., *T. R. The Last Romantic*. New York: Basic Books, 1997.

Bryan, Anthony Templeton, "Mexican Politics in Transition, 1900-1913: The Role of General Bernardo Reyes." Ph.D. dissertation, University of Nebraska, 1970.

Byrne, Gary J., *Secrets of the Secret Service: The History and Uncertain Future of the US Secret Service*. New York: Hachette Book Group, 2018.

Caballero, Raymond, *Orozco: The Life and Death of a Mexican Revolutionary*. Norman: University of Oklahoma Press, 2017.

Case, Henry Jay, *Guy Hamilton Scull: Soldier Writer, Explorer and War Correspondent*. New York: Duffield, 1922).

Castillo, Víctor et al., *Revista de legislación y jurisprudencia, El delito de quiebra*. México, D.F.: Imprenta del Gobierno Federal, 1898.

Chalkley, John F., *Zach Lamar Cobb: El Paso Collector of Customs and Intelligence During the Mexican Revolution*. El Paso: Texas Western Press, 1998.

Clendenen, Clarence C., *The United States and Pancho Villa: A Study in Unconventional Diplomacy*. Ithaca: Cornell University Press, 1961.

Cockcroft, James D., *Intellectual Precursors of the Mexican Revolution, 1900-1913*. Austin: University of Texas Press, 1968.

Devitt, Steven, *The Pen that Set Mexico on Fire: The Betrayal of Ricardo Flores Magón During the Mexican Revolution*. Amissville, Va.: Henselstone Verlag, 2017.

Diaz, George T., *Border Contraband: A History of Smuggling Across the Rio Grande*. Austin: University of Texas Press, 2015.

Diccionario Porrúa de historia, biografía y geografía de México. 2nd ed. México, D.F.: Editorial Porrúa, 1965.

Doerries, Reinhard, *Imperial Challenge: Ambassador Count Bernstorff and German-American Relations, 1908-1917*. Chapel Hill: University of North Carolina Press, 1989.

Dosal, Paul J., *Doing Business with the Dictators: A Political History of United Fruit in Guatemala, 1899-1944*. Oxford: Rowan and Littlefield, 2005.

Eisenhower, John, S. D., *Intervention! The United States and the Mexican Revolution, 1913-1917*. New York: W. W. Norton and Company, 1993.

Emery, Theo, *Hellfire Boys: The Birth of the U.S. Chemical Warfare*. New York: Little, Brown, 2017.

Fabela, Isidro et al., *Documentos históricos de la revolución mexicana*, 28 vols. México, DF: Editorial Jus, 1960-1976.

Federation of American Scientists, Intelligence Resource Program, *A Counterintelligence Reader*, Vol. 1, Chapter 3, 2005. https://irp.fas.org/ops/ci/docs/ci1/chap3.pdf, 27.

Fenwick, Charles Ghequiere, *The Neutrality Laws of the United States*. Washington, DC: Carnegie Endowment for International Peace, 1913.

Fulwider, Chad R., *German Propaganda and U.S. Neutrality in World War I*. Columbia: University of Missouri Press, 2017.

Furlong, Thomas, *Fifty Years a Detective*. St. Louis: C. E. Barnett, 1912.

Gamboa, Leticia, *Los empresarios de ayer: El grupo dominante en la industria textil de Puebla, 1906-1929*. Puebla: UAP, 1985.

Graff, Garrett M., *Watergate: A New History*. New York: Simon and Schuster, 2022.

Grann, David, *Killers of the Flower Moon: The Osage Murders and the Birth of the FBI*. New York: Doubleday, 2017.

Grayson, Robert, *The FBI and National Security*. Broomall: Mason Crest, 2010.

Guzman, Martin Luis, *Memorias de Pancho Villa*. Mexico D.F.: Compañía General de Ediciones, 1951.

Hagedorn, Dan, *Conquistadors of the Sky: A History of Aviation in Latin America*. Gainesville: University Press of Florida, 2008.

Haley, Edward P., *Revolution and Intervention: The Diplomacy of Taft and Wilson with Mexico, 1910-1917*. Cambridge: MIT University Press, 1970.

Harris, Charles H. III and Louis R. Sadler, *The Great Call-Up: The Guard, the Border, and the Mexican Revolution*. Norman: University of Oklahoma Press, 2015.

_____, *The Secret War in El Paso: Mexican Revolutionary Intrigue, 1906-1920*. Albuquerque: University of New Mexico Press, 2009.

_____, *The Archaeologist Was a Spy: Sylvanus G. Morley and the Office of Naval Intelligence*. Albuquerque: University of New Mexico Press, 2003.

_____, *The Border and the Revolution: Clandestine Activities of the Mexican Revolution: 1910-1920*. Silver City, NM: High-Lonesome Books, 1988.

_____, *The Plan de San Diego: Tejano Rebellion, Mexican Intrigue*. Lincoln: University of Nebraska Press, 2013.

Hawkins, Richard A., *Progressive Politics in the Democratic Party: Samuel Untermeyr and the Jewish Anti-Nazi Boycott Campaign*. New York, I.B. Tauris, 2022.

Henderson, Peter V. N., *Felix Diaz, the Porfirians, and the Mexican Revolution*. Lincoln: University of Nebraska Press, 1981.

Hill, Kathleen and Gerald N. Hill, *Encyclopedia of Federal Agencies and Commissions*. New York: Facts on File, 2014.

History of the Bureau of Diplomatic Security of the United States. Washington D.C.: Global Publishing Solutions, 2011.

Hurst, James W., *The Villista Prisoners of 1916-1917*. Las Cruces, NM: Yucca Tree Press, 2000.

Jacoby, Carl, *The Strange Career of William Ellis: The Texas Slave Who Became a Mexican Millionaire*. New York: Norton, 2016.

Jeffreys-Jones, Rhodri, *The FBI: A History*. New Haven: Yale University Press, 2007.

Jensen, Joan M., *The Price of Vigilance*. New York: Rand McNally, 1968.

Johnson, David N., "Exiles and Intrigue: Francisco I. Madero and the Mexican Revolutionary Junta in San Antonio, 1910-1911," M. A. thesis, Trinity University, 1975.

Jones, Charles and Eugene Jones, *Double Trouble: The Autobiography of the Jones Twins, Cameramen – Correspondents*. Boston: Little Brown, 1952.

Jones, John Price and Paul Merrick Hollister, *The German Secret Service in America, 1914-1918*. Boston: Small, Maynard, 1918.

Kahn, David, *The Reader of Gentlemen's Mail: Herbert O. Yardley and the Birth of American Codebreaking*. New Haven: Yale University Press, 2004.

_____, *The Codebreakers: The Story of Secret Writing*. New York: Macmillan, 1967.

Katz, Friedrich, *Deutschland, Diaz und die Mexikanische Revolution: Die Deutsche Politik in Mexiko, 1870-1920*. Berlin: VEB Deutscher Verlag der Wissenschaften, 1964.

_____, *The Life and Times of Pancho Villa*. Stanford: Stanford University Press, 1998.

———, *The Secret War in Mexico: Europe, the United States, and the Mexican Revolution*. Chicago: University of Chicago Press, 1981.

Kerig, Dorothy Pierson, *Luther T. Ellsworth: U. S. Consul on the Border During the Mexican Revolution*. El Paso: Texas Western Press, 1975.

Kessler, Ronald, *The Bureau: The Secret History of the FBI*. New York: St. Martin's Press, 2002.

Knight, Alan, *The Mexican Revolution*, 2 vols. Lincoln: University of Nebraska Press, 1986.

Landau, Henry, *The Enemy Within: The Inside Story of German Sabotage in America*. New York: G. P. Putnam's Sons, 1937.

Lansing, Robert, *War Memoirs of Robert Lansing, Secretary of State*. New York: Bobbs-Merrill, 1935.

Liceaga, Luis, *Felix Diaz*. Mexico DF: Editorial Jus, 1958.

Link, Arthur S., *Papers of Woodrow Wilson*. 69 vols. Princeton: Princeton University Press, 1966-1994.

———, *Wilson: The Struggle for Neutrality, 1914-1915*. Princeton: Princeton University Press, 1960.

Logan, Keith Gregory, *Homeland Security and Intelligence*. Santa Barbara, CA: Praeger Security International Textbook, 2017.

Lomnitz-Adler, Claudio, *The Return of Comrade Ricardo Flores Magon*. New York: Zone Books, 2014.

MacLachlan, Colin M., *Anarchism and the Mexican Revolution: The Political Trials of Ricardo Flores Magon in the United States*. Berkeley, Los Angeles, Oxford: University of California Press, 1991.

Mason, Herbert Molloy, Jr., *The Great Pursuit: Pershing's Expedition to Destroy Pancho Villa*. New York: Smithmark Publishers Inc, 1970.

Messimer, Dwight R., *The Baltimore Sabotage Cell: German Agents, American Traitors, and the U-Boat Deutschland During World War I*. Annapolis: Naval Institute Press, 2015.

Meyer, Michael C., *Huerta: A Political Portrait*. Lincoln: University of Nebraska Press, 1972.

———, *Mexican Rebel: Pascual Orozco and the Mexican Revolution, 1910-1915*. Lincoln: University of Nebraska Press 1967.

Mickolus, Edward, *The Counterintelligence Chronology: Spying By and Against*. Jefferson: McFarland, 2015.

Millman, Chad, *The Detonators: The Secret Plot to Destroy America and an Epic Hunt for Justice*. New York: Little, Brown, 2006.

Naranjo, Francisco, *Diccionario biográfico Revolucionario*. Mexico, D.F.: Imprenta Editorial "Cosmos" edición, 1935.

Niemeyer E. V., Jr., *El General Bernardo Reyes*. Monterrey: Universidad de Nuevo León, 1966.

Obregón, Álvaro, *Ocho mil kilómetros en campaña*. Mexico, D.F.: Fondo de Cultura Económica, 1959.

Oliver, Willard M., *The Birth of the FBI: Teddy Roosevelt, the Secret Service, and the Fight Over America's Premier Law Enforcement Agency*. Lanham: Roman & Littlefield, 2019.

Peden, Edward Andrew, *Peden – 1965*. Houston: Premier Printing Company, 1965.

Preston, William, Jr., *Aliens and Dissenters: Federal Suppression of Radicals, 1903-1933*. New York: Harper & Row, 1963.

Quirk, Robert E., *The Mexican Revolution and the Catholic Church, 1910-1929*. Bloomington: Indiana University Press, 1973.

Raat, W. Dirk and William H. Beezley, eds. *Twentieth-Century Mexico*. Lincoln and London: University of Nebraska Press, 1986.

Raat, W. Dirk, *Revoltosos: Mexico's Rebels in the United States, 1903-1923*. College Station: Texas A & M University Press, 1981.

Rausch, George Jay, Jr., "Victoriano Huerta: A Political Biography," Ph.D dissertation, University of Illinois, 1960.

Reiling, Johannes, *Deutschland, Safe for Democracy?* Stuttgart: Franz Steiner Verlag, 1997.

Rintelen von Kleist, Franz, *The Dark Invader: Wartime Reminiscences of a German Naval Intelligence Officer*. London: Lovat Dickson Ltd, 1933.

_____, *The Return of the Dark Invader*. London: Peter Davies Ltd, 1935.

Robenault, James D., *The Harding Affair: Love and Espionage during the Great War*. New York: St. Martin's Press, 2009.

Roberts, Marcia, *Moments in History: Department of Treasury United States Secret Service*. Washington D.C.: PU Books, 1990.

Salinas Carranza, Umberto, *La Expedición Punitiva*. Mexico D.F.: Ediciones Botas, 1936.

Scott, Hugh L., *Some Memories of a Soldier*. New York: Century Company, 1928.

Scull Guy H., *Lassoing Wild Animals in Africa*. New York: Frederick A. Stokes, 1911.

Seymour, Charles, ed., *The Intimate Papers of Colonel House*. 2 vols. Boston, New York: Houghton Mifflin, 1926-1928.

Smith, Cornelius C., Jr., *Emilio Kosterlitzky: Eagle of Sonora and the Southwest Border*. Glendale, CA: Arthur H. Clark, 1970.

Soto Hall, Maximo et al., *El "Libro Azul" de Guatemala*. New Orleans: Searcy & Pfaff, 1915.

Stout, Joseph A., Jr., *Border Conflict: Villistas, Carrancistas, and the Punitive Expedition, 1915-1920*. Ft. Worth: Texas Christian University Press, 1999.

Taylor, Lawrence D., *La gran aventura en México: El papél de los voluntarios extranjeros en los ejércitos revolucionarios, 1910-1915*. 2 vols. México, D.F.: Consejo Nacional Para la Cultura y las Artes, 1993.

Theoharis, Athan G. with Tony G. Poveda, Susan Rosenfeld and Richard Gid Powers, *The FBI: A Comprehensive Reference Guide From J. Edgar Hoover to The X-Files*. New York: Checkmark Books, 2000.

The Story of the FBI: The Official Picture History of the Federal Bureau of Investigation, by the Editors of Look, New York: E.P. Dutton and Co., 1947.

Tompkins, Frank, *Chasing Villa: The Last Campaign of the U.S. Cavalry*. 2nd ed. Silver City, NM: High-Lonesome Books, 1996.

_____, *Chasing Villa: The Story behind the Story of Pershing's Expedition into Mexico.* Harrisburg: The Military Service Publishing Company, 1934.

Tuchman, Barbara, *The Zimmermann Telegram.* New York: MacMillan, 1958.

Tunney, Thomas J. and Paul M. Hollister, *Throttled! The Detection of the German and Anarchist Bomb Plotters.* Boston: Small, Maynard, 1919.

Ulloa, Berta, *Revolución mexicana, 1910-1920.* Archivo histórico diplomático mexicano. Guía para la historia diplomática de México, No. 3. México, DF: Secretaria de Relaciones Exteriores, 1985.

Ungar, Sanford J., *FBI: An Uncensored Look Behind the Walls.* New York: Atlantic-Little, Brown, 1975.

von der Goltz, Horst, *My Adventures as a German Secret Agent.* New York: McBride, 1917.

von Feilitzsch, Heribert, *In Plain Sight: Felix A. Sommerfeld, Spymaster in Mexico, 1908-1914.* Amissville VA: Henselstone Verlag, 2012.

_____, *The Secret War Council: The German Fight Against the Entente in America in 1914.* Amissville, VA: Henselstone Verlag, 2015.

_____, *The Secret War on the United States in 1915: A Tale of Sabotage, Labor Unrest, and Border Troubles.* Amissville, VA: Henselstone Verlag, 2015.

_____, *Felix A. Sommerfeld and the Mexican Front in the Great War.* Amissville, VA: Henselstone Verlag, 2015.

Voska, Emanuel, *Spy and Counter-Spy.* London: George G. Harrap, 1941.

Welsome, Eileen, *The General and the Jaguar: Pershing's Hunt for Pancho Villa, a True Story of Revolution and Revenge.* Lincoln: University of Nebraska Press, 2006.

Whitcover, Jules, *Sabotage at Black Tom Island.* Chapel Hill: Algonquin Books, 1989.

Whitehead, Don, *The FBI Story: A Report to the People.* New York: Random House, 1956.

ARTICLES

Baecker, Thomas "The Arms of the *Ypiranga*: The German Side," *The Americas,* 30, no. 1 (July 1973), 1-17.

Blaisdell, Lowell L., "Harry Chandler and Mexican Border Intrigue, 1914-1917," *Pacific Historical Review,* 35, no. 4 (November 1966), 385-393.

Briscoe, Edward Eugene, "Pershing's Chinese Refugees in Texas," *Southwestern Historical Quarterly,* 62, no. 4 (April 1959), 467-488.

Cumberland, Charles C., "Mexican Revolutionary Movements from Texas, 1906-1912," *Southwestern Historical Quarterly,* 52 (January 1949), 301-324.

Curtis, Roy Emerson, "The Law of Hostile Military Expeditions as Applied by the United States," *The American Journal of International Law,* 8, (January 1914), 1-37.

Fox, John R. Jr., "The Birth of the Federal Bureau of Investigation," Federal Bureau of Investigation website, July 2003 (www.fbi.gov/ history/history-publications-reports/ the-birth-of-the-federal-bureau-of-investigation.)

Grams, Grant W., "Karl Respa and German Espionage in Canada during World War One," Journal of Military and Strategic Studies, 8, no. 1 (Fall 2005), 1-17.

Harris, Charles H. III and Louis R. Sadler., "The 1911 Reyes Conspiracy: The Texas Side," Southwestern Historical Quarterly, 83, no. 4 (April 1980), 325-348.

_____, "Pancho Villa and the Columbus Raid: The Missing Documents," New Mexico Historical Review, 50, no. 4 (October 1975), 335-346.

_____ "The Underside of the Mexican Revolution: El Paso 1912," The Americas, 39, No. 1 (July 1982), 69-83.

Kahle, Louis G., "Robert Lansing and the Recognition of Venustiano Carranza," Hispanic American Historical Review, 38, no. 3 (August 1958), 353-372.

Katz, Friedrich, "Pancho Villa and the Attack on Columbus, New Mexico," American Historical Review, 83, no. 1 (February 1978), 101-130.

Meyer, Michael C., "The Mexican-German Conspiracy of 1915," The Americas, 23, no. 1 (July 1966), 76-89.

_____, "The Arms of the Ypiranga," Hispanic American Historical Review, 50, no. 3 (August 1970), 543-556.

_____, "Villa, Sommerfeld, Columbus y los Alemanes," Historia Mexicana, Vol. 28, No. 4 (April – June 1979), 546-566.

Munch, Francis J., "Villa's Columbus Raid: Practical Politics or German Design?" New Mexico Historical Review, 44 (July 1969), 189-214.

Niemeyer E. V., Jr., "Frustrated Invasion: The Revolutionary Attempt of General Bernardo Reyes from San Antonio in 1911," Southwestern Historical Quarterly, 67, no. 2 (1963), 213-225.

Paxman, Andrew, "The Rise and Fall of Leon Rasst, the Jewish-Russian Merchant of Puebla," unpublished paper, May 1, 2017.

Peters, Gerhard and John T. Woolley, Woodrow Wilson, Proclamation 1263—Concerning the Shipment of Arms into Mexico Online by, The American Presidency Project (https://www.presidency.ucsb.edu/node/317582, viewed June 2022).

Rausch, George J., Jr., "The Exile and Death of Victoriano Huerta," Hispanic American Historical Review, 42, no. 2 (May 1962), 133-151.

Smith, Michael M., "The Mexican Secret Service in the United States, 1910-1920," The Americas, 59, no. 1 (July 2002), 65-85.

Stone, Michael, "The Fall Committee and Double Agent Jones," Southern New Mexico Historical Review, 6, no. 1 (January 1999), 45-49.

Taylor Hansen, Lawrence Douglas, "Los orígenes de la Fuerza Aérea Mexicana, 1913-1915," Historia Mexicana, 56, no. 1 (July-September 2006), 175-230.

Vigil, Ralph H., "Revolution and Confusion: The Peculiar Case of Jose Ines Salazar," *New Mexico Historical Review*, 53, no. 2 (April 1978), 145-170.

von Feilitzsch, Heribert, "Prelude to the Columbus Raid of 1916: The Battle of Naco," *Journal of the Southwest*, 64, no. 3 (Fall 2022), 473-494.

⸻, "The Real Wolf of Wall Street," *FCH Annals*, 23 (June 2016), 25-38.

⸻, "Leon J. Canova and Pancho Villa's Columbus Raid of 1916," *FCH Annals*, 25 (June 2019), 9-22.

⸻, "The German Sabotage Campaign of 1915/16 revisited," *FCH Annals*, 26 (June 2020), 1-16.

⸻, "Questionable Loyalty: Frederico Stallforth and the Mixed Claims Commission," *FCH Annals*, 27 (January 2021), 17-26.

⸻, "The Canadian Parliament Fire of 1916: A Severely Flawed Investigation," *FCH Annals*, 28 (January 2022), 61-74.

NEWSPAPERS

Albuquerque Morning Journal.
Arizona Oasis.
Arizona Republican.
Atlanta Georgian.
Audubon County Journal.
Baltimore Evening Star.
Baltimore Sun.
Billings Gazette.
Bisbee Daily Review.
Bismarck Daily Tribune.
Breckenridge News.
Brownsville Daily Herald.
Buffalo Evening News.
Commoner.
Crónica.
Daily Missoulian.
Daily Press.
Daily Sentinel.
Day Book.
Daily Yellowstone Journal
Der Deutsche Korrespondent.
Detroit Times.
Detroiter Abend-Post.
East Oregonian.
El Paso Daily Herald.
El Paso Herald.
El Paso Morning Times.
Evening Independent.
Evening Standard.
Fresno Bee.
Garland Globe.
Guthrie Daily Leader.
Honolulu Star-Bulletin.
Hopkinsville Kentuckian.
Imperial Valley Press.
Jersey City News.
La Prensa.
Lewiston Evening Teller.
Maryland Suffrage News.
Minneapolis Journal.
New Britain Herald.
New York Evening Sun.
New York Evening Telegram.
New York Evening World.
New York Sun.
New York Times.
New York Tribune.
New York World.
Nogales Daily Herald.
Olean Evening Herald.

Omaha Daily Bee.
Owosso Times.
Palestine Daily Herald.
Parma Herald.
Pensacola Journal.
Pine Bluff Daily Graphic.
Producers News.
Richmond Virginian.
Sacramento Daily Union.
San Antonio Light.
San Bernardino County Sun.
San Francisco Call.
San Francisco Examiner.
San Miguel Examiner.
Santa Fe New Mexican.
Saratoga Sun.
Seattle Star.
South Bend News-Times.
St. Landry Clarion.
Syracuse Herald.
Tabor Independent.
Tacoma Times.
The Copper Era and Morenci Leader.
Topeka State Journal.
Trenton Evening Times.
Tulsa Daily World.
Valdez Daily Prospector.
Vinita Daily Chieftain.
Walsenburg World.
Washington Evening Star.
Washington Herald.
Washington Post.
Washington Times.
Waterbury Evening Democrat.
Weekly Journal-Miner.
Wheeling Daily Intelligencer.
White Pine News Weekly Mining Review.

INDEX

1

13th US Cavalry, 304
1912 Joint Resolution, 235

A

A. Baldwin & Co., 147, 148, 149, 150, 151, 152, 153, 184, 190, 193, 197, 198
Agis, S. T., 32, 34
Agua Prieta, 18, 87, 126, 127, 128, 129, 130, 131, 133, 136, 224, 229, 230, 324, 329
Aguirre, Amelia, 269, 272, 282
Aguirre, Lauro, 17
Ainslie, Alejandro, 227, 228
Alamo Safe and Lock Company, 111, 212
Albert Steinfeld & Company, 225
Albert, Heinrich, 298, 342, 391
Aldape, Manuel Garza, 108, 109, 110, 111, 113, 161, 365
Allen, J. J., 42
Ambrose, C. R., 162, 370
American Chicle, 44
American Ice Company, 7
Anaya, Enrique V., 228, 230, 238, 239, 240, 241, 242, 243, 253, 264, 265, 267, 292, 325, 326
Arriaga, Camilo, 192, 193
Arriola, Jesús María, 54
Arriola, José María, 57
Astor Hotel, 45
Avilés, Baltazar, 237, 244, 245, 246, 247, 248, 249, 250, 251, 252, 253, 254, 255, 256, 257, 258, 259, 260, 261, 262, 263, 264, 265, 266, 267, 271, 273, 274, 275, 276, 277, 278, 279, 280, 281, 282, 284, 285, 286, 287, 289, 291, 292, 293, 294, 380, 381, 384
Ayón, Francisco, 247, 248, 249, 250, 255, 256, 261, 287

B

Baca, Elfego, 307, 308, 309, 310
Badillo, Pedro, 262, 263, 264, 265, 267, 268, 275, 276, 381, 384
Bailey, Joseph Weldon, 97
Baker, J. A., 63
Baldwin & Co., 185, 196, 197
Baldwin, Albert, 184, 185, 186, 187, 188, 189, 192, 196
Ballesteros, Jr., Indalecio, 109, 110, 115, 200, 201, 202, 374
Banana Wars, 45
Bannerman, Francis, 47, 76, 199, 213, 343, 344
Barnes, Robert Lee, 106, 107, 108, 110, 111, 116, 117, 118, 121, 124, 125, 128, 130, 131, 132, 133, 135, 178, 180, 182, 183, 184, 200, 201, 202, 205, 208, 213, 215, 217, 267, 269, 272, 274, 300, 305, 308, 311, 313, 314, 316, 318, 330, 363, 364, 365, 366, 367, 370, 371, 372, 373, 374, 375, 376, 378, 379, 383, 385, 386, 387, 388, 389, 391
Bauche Alcalde, Joaquín, 226, 229, 230, 231, 232, 324, 325, 326
Bauche Alcalde, Manuel, 226, 325
Belden, Samuel, 73, 80, 311
Beltrán, Teódulo R., 110, 111, 139, 205, 207, 208, 212, 313, 375
Benson, Amelia, 101
Berliner, Harry, 172, 173, 338, 339, 370, 390
Berthold, Simon, 61

405

Betjeman, Daniel Clinton, 11, 353
Bielaski, Alexander Bruce, viii, x, 3, 9, 98, 101, 102, 103, 104, 120, 124, 132, 133, 158, 182, 187, 195, 197, 206, 209, 212, 213, 215, 216, 218, 238, 244, 250, 251, 252, 257, 261, 264, 265, 280, 285, 301, 309, 319, 323, 330, 343, 344, 347, 351, 352, 353, 366, 367, 371, 372, 373, 374, 379, 380, 381, 384, 385, 386, 387, 388, 389, 391
Blanco, Lucio, 179, 182, 183, 193, 214, 372
Blanford, Eli Murray, 133, 134, 135, 161, 222, 223, 225, 242, 246, 247, 248, 250, 251, 252, 256, 257, 258, 259, 260, 261, 262, 264, 265, 266, 267, 268, 270, 271, 272, 273, 274, 275, 276, 277, 278, 279, 280, 282, 283, 284, 285, 286, 287, 288, 289, 291, 292, 299, 300, 301, 302, 303, 304, 307, 308, 309, 319, 321, 365, 366, 367, 368, 369, 376, 377, 379, 380, 381, 382, 383, 384, 385, 386, 387, 388, 389
Blanquet, Aureliano, 174
Boden, Fred C., 260, 286, 381, 383
Bonales Sandoval, José, 93
Bonaparte, Charles J., viii, 1, 2, 3, 4, 8, 17, 21, 22, 101
Border Hardware Company, 209
Bowen, John M., 242, 243, 244, 245, 257, 258, 259, 262, 264, 265, 289, 324, 325, 331, 332, 333, 334, 379, 380, 389, 390
Bowker, Walter K., 238, 239, 241, 242, 243, 247, 248, 250, 251, 255, 256, 257, 260, 264, 265, 289, 292, 381, 384
Bowman, John T., 92
Boy-Ed, Karl, 345
Boynton, Charles A., 20, 21, 22, 49, 356, 369
Brassell, Manuel G., 246, 247, 249, 252, 253, 255, 256, 257, 258, 259, 260, 261, 262, 264, 265, 266, 267, 268, 269, 271, 272, 273, 275, 276, 277, 278, 279, 281, 282, 283, 284, 287, 289, 381, 382, 384
Brassell, Porfirio, 282
Breceda, Alfredo, 207
Breniman, Charles Edward, 205, 206, 207, 208, 209, 210, 216, 218, 229, 230, 233, 234, 259, 267, 305, 322, 323, 324, 325, 326, 327, 328, 329, 374, 375, 376, 377, 378, 379, 380, 381, 386, 388, 389
Brinkburn, 340
Browne, Herbert Janvrin, 179, 180, 181, 182, 372
Bruchhausen, Peter, 56
Bryan, William Jennings, 180
Buckholtz, H. C., 108, 363
Buckley, William F., 342
Buffalo Jones African Expedition, 53
Burns Detective Agency, 42, 153
Burns, Waller T., 92, 93, 94, 95, 96, 97, 98, 99, 153, 159
Bush Terminal Company, 48
Butcher, Byron S., 136, 222

C

Cafferelli Brothers, 318, 319
California-Mexico Land and Cattle Company, 238, 240, 243, 263, See C-M Land and Cattle Company
Calles, Plutarco Elías, 224, 225, 351
Cano, Frank F., 33, 34
Cantú Cárdenas, Joaquín, 202, 206
Cantú, Esteban, 237, 238, 239
Caracristi, C. F. Z., 54, 200, 201
Cárdenas, Francisco, 174, 365
Carothers, George, 297
Carranza, Jesús, 206
Carranza, Julio, 327, 329
Carranza, Venustiano, xii, 42, 58, 175, 176, 181, 192, 200, 202, 205, 206, 208, 211, 212, 214, 218, 220, 226,

237, 238, 239, 243, 244, 245, 246, 254, 259, 260, 267, 295, 304, 305, 306, 312, 315, 327, 328, 345, 346, 371, 373, 379
Carroway, Thomas W., 327, 328
Cartagena scandal, 6
Casas Grandes, Battle of, 56
Castillo Brito, Manuel, 320
Castro, Juan, 24
Chamberlain, William Chapman, 73, 74, 75, 76, 78, 79, 80, 81, 86, 88, 91, 92, 360, 361
Chandler, Harry, 241, 242, 243, 249, 250, 251, 252, 253, 255, 256, 257, 258, 260, 261, 263, 264, 265, 269, 273, 274, 275, 279, 280, 281, 284, 285, 286, 290, 291, 292, 293, 294, 383, 385
Chapa, F. A., 69, 72, 74, 75, 81, 82, 84, 85, 86, 91, 92, 93, 97, 98, 100, 107, 108, 112, 161, 212, 213, 214
Charles R. Flint & Co.. *See* Flint, Charles Ranlett
Charpentier, Emile, 159
Christmas, Lee, 67, 147, 368
Científico Party, 137, 152
Ciudad Porfirio Díaz, 23, 113, 115, 208
C-M Land and Cattle Company, 238, 239, 241, 242, 245, 247, 248, 249, 250, 252, 253, 257, 275
C-M Ranch. *See* California-Mexico Land and Cattle Company
Coahuila Mining and Smelting Company, 110
Cobb, Zach Lamar, 297, 385
Cole, Elizabeth, 354
Cole, Jay Herbert, 24, 25, 26, 27, 28, 30, 31, 32, 39, 46, 49, 54, 57, 354, 355, 356, 357
Colliers Magazine, 53
Colquitt, Oscar, 72, 74, 75, 82, 87, 91, 92, 97, 98, 99
Columbian College. *See* George Washington University

Computing Tabulating Recording Company. *See* IBM
Conners, Maurice D., 150, 152, 153, 154, 185, 186, 187, 188, 190, 191, 193, 194, 195, 197, 198
Conrad, C. H., 20
Constitutionalist Army, 176
Correo Mexicano, 261
Costillo, José F., 247, 249, 252, 253, 267, 268, 269, 270, 271, 283, 284, 287, 288, 289, 381, 382, 384
Creel, Enrique, 19, 72, 338, 390
Crum, Jack R. "Big Dude", 57
Cuerpos Rurales, 13, 57
Cuesta, Manuel, 119, 126, 131, 132, 133, 134, 135, 136, 137, 138, 223, 366
Culberson, Charles A., 99
Cunningham, Ed B., 47
Cunningham, Thomas Branham, 47, 126, 135

D

Daniel, Thomas "Todd" Monroe, 205, 206, 213, 214, 311, 316, 317, 375, 376, 385, 387, 388
Dantzler, 153, 185, 193, 194, 196, 197, 198, 321
Danziger, Adolph, 248, 249, 250, 251, 252, 256, 262, 263, 275, 276, 285, 292, 380, 381, 384
de la Fuente, David, 113, 118, 122, 365
de la Garza, Lázaro, 296, 297, 298, 344, 385, 391
de la Garza, Vidal, 296
de la Sierra, Enrique, 244, 260
Decena Trágica, 172
del Rio, Carlos, 72
Díaz de León, Ignacio, 247, 250, 261, 283, 380, 382, 384
Díaz Guerra, Encarnación, 19, 20, 22, 23

Díaz, Félix, xii, 152, 171, 172, 173, 174, 178, 188, 191, 192, 201, 312, 335, 349, 370
Díaz, Ignacio, 381
Díaz, Porfirio, 13, 14, 15, 16, 17, 18, 19, 20, 31, 37, 38, 39, 40, 41, 42, 45, 49, 54, 55, 57, 58, 59, 60, 65, 68, 69, 71, 72, 73, 74, 104, 105, 106, 110, 113, 115, 127, 137, 142, 162, 166, 175, 237, 253, 356, 364, 370
Didapp, Juan Pedro, 110, 123, 124, 365
Diebold, Miguel E., 218, 219, 300, 301, 302, 303, 376, 386
División del Norte. See Division of the North
Division of the North, 221
Donnelly Anti-Monopoly Act, 7
Dorey, Brett H., 67, 359
Douglas Daily Dispatch, 131, 137, 222
Douglas, Charles A., 181
Dowe, Robert W., 20, 41
Dreben, Sam, 142, 143, 154, 212, 311, 320, 345
Duncan, J. W., 79, 85

E

Eberstein, Marshall Frank, 28, 29, 50, 51, 52, 53, 58, 59, 60, 354, 356, 357, 358
Echegaray, Carlos H., 301, 302, 303
El Imparcial de Texas, 85, 92
El Mundo, 344
El Obrero, 32
El Paso Daily Herald, 336, 390
El Porvenir, 74
El Progreso, 202
El Sol, 344
Elías, Arturo M., 64, 65, 194, 195, 205, 313
Elías, Francisco, 234
Ellsworth, Luther T., 20, 21, 22, 23, 26, 30, 32, 33, 39, 40, 46, 49, 110, 115, 116, 117, 174, 206, 208, 209, 212, 353, 354, 363, 364, 365, 371, 375

Emily P. Wright, 181, 182, 371
Englesby, Leverett Francis, 314, 315, 316, 387, 388
Enrile, Gonzalo, 147
Escobosa, José, 228, 229, 230, 240, 325, 326
Espinosa de los Monteros, Samuel, 72, 74, 85
Espinoza y Rondero, Francisco, 108
Esteva, Manuel A., 41, 76, 80, 83, 84, 105, 112, 117, 119, 160, 355
Excelsior, 68
Exclusion Act, 11

F

Fall, Albert B., 123, 143, 200, 367
Falomir, Julio, 73
Farmer, J. P., 188, 190, 194, 373
Fernández y Arteaga, Ernesto, 192, 193
Fernández, Juan N., 246, 247, 249, 255, 256, 257, 258, 259, 260, 265, 271, 274, 279, 282, 287, 381, 382, 384
Ferris, Dick, 62, 63, 66
Figueroa, Anselmo L., 64, 103, 165
Finch, Stanley Wellington, viii, 2, 3, 4, 5, 7, 8, 9, 10, 11, 22, 28, 34, 78, 80, 88, 101, 102, 347, 351, 352, 353, 354, 355, 359, 360, 362
Fitzpatrick, William, 185, 186, 187, 188, 190, 193, 195
Flint, Charles Ranlett, 44, 45, 48, 298, 344, 385
Flores Magón, Enrique, 14, 20, 64, 103, 165
Flores Magón, Jesús, 14
Flores Magón, Ricardo, xii, 14, 15, 16, 17, 18, 19, 20, 25, 31, 32, 33, 34, 38, 64, 139, 163, 165, 166, 266, 348, 354
Flores, Emeterio, 112, 113
Fort Rosecrans, 66
Foster, J. Ellen, 5
French Intervention, 13

Frisco Railroad System, 60
Frost National Bank, 81, 86
Furlong Detective Agency, 19, 21
Furlong, Thomas, 18, 19, 353

G

Gadsden Hotel, 127, 128, 131, 134, 136, 138
Gallaher, M. G., 265, 266, 273, 277, 284, 381
Ganor, James, 63, 64, 65, 66, 139, 163, 164, 165, 166, 167, 168, 169, 312, 358, 359, 367, 370
Garibaldi, Giuseppe, 57, 58, 158
Garner, John Nance, 99
Garza Aldape, Manuel, 108
Garza Galán, Andrés, 73, 74, 106, 108, 109, 110, 111, 114, 115, 116, 200, 202
Garza, Juan, 202
Geck, Samuel L., 26, 30, 31, 32, 33, 34, 39, 54, 144, 309, 354, 355, 367, 387
Geneva, 331
George Washington University, 3, 101
Gershon, Dave, 241, 267, 268, 269, 270, 271, 277, 278, 284, 288, 289, 379, 382, 383, 384
Goldman, Emma, 25
González, Abraham, 46, 55, 56, 114, 144, 162, 176, 357
González, Pablo, 295, 314, 316, 345, 346
Grampus, 181, 182, 371
Gray, Henry N., 126
Guerra, Calixto, 21, 23
Guerrero, Práxedis G., 15, 19, 20, 26, 27, 28, 30, 31, 32, 34
Guzmán, Francisco I., 108, 120, 121, 365

H

H. M. Marquardt & Co., 199
Hagadorn, Charles B., 82, 85, 86

Hall, Robert Lincoln, 241, 242, 243, 244, 245, 247, 257, 259, 379
Hamlin, C. S., 180
Hanson, William Martin, 41, 51
HAPAG, 341, 342
Hardenberg, Wilhelm von, 247, 268, 381, 384
Hare, Jimmy, 53
Harriman, Job, 25
Harris, Billups, 67, 68, 147, 148, 149, 150, 151, 152, 153, 154, 185, 186, 187, 188, 190, 194, 195, 355, 356, 357, 359, 367, 368, 372, 373
Harris, Mary. *See* Mother Jones
Hartup, Charles W., 210
Harvard Club, 53
Hearst, William Randolph, 242
Hebert, Curley D., 29, 81, 84, 87, 107, 112, 113, 119, 124, 127, 128, 129, 130, 131, 132, 133, 135, 136, 137, 138, 139, 156, 158, 354, 360, 361, 363, 364, 365, 366, 367, 368, 369, 370
Heinze, Augustus F., 6
Herminio Echegaray, Carlos, 222
Herrera, Cástulo, 146, 163, 167, 168, 219
Herrington, Clayton E., 62, 63, 358
Heynen, Carl, 342
Hicks, Marshall, 86, 91, 92, 98, 107
Hill, Benjamín, 305
Hintze, Paul von, 341, 391
Holmdahl, Emil, 305, 306, 307, 386
Hoover, J. Edgar, vii, viii, ix, xi, 4, 102, 351, 352
Hopkins, Arthur A., 126, 128, 133, 134, 135, 136, 222, 323
Hopkins, Sherburne Gillette, 42, 43, 44, 45, 48, 56, 96, 117, 118, 123, 162, 220, 228, 229, 230, 234, 295, 298, 345, 370, 376, 378
Hopkins, Thomas Snell, 44
Hotel Astor. *See* Astor Hotel
House Judiciary Committee, 3
Houston, Sam, 3, 78, 79, 91, 99, 313

409

Huerta, Victoriano, xii, 154, 173, 174, 175, 176, 177, 178, 183, 184, 188, 189, 190, 194, 196, 197, 199, 200, 201, 202, 204, 205, 206, 207, 211, 212, 213, 215, 216, 217, 218, 219, 220, 221, 222, 223, 224, 225, 227, 228, 231, 233, 295, 296, 298, 299, 300, 307, 308, 311, 312, 313, 314, 315, 316, 317, 320, 321, 325, 332, 333, 334, 339, 340, 342, 343, 345, 346, 349, 370, 372, 376, 390
Human Intelligence. *See* HUMINT
HUMINT, xi, 348
Hutchings, Henry, 82

I

IBM, 44
Imperial Valley Hardware Company, 240
Importers' Warehouse, 190, 191, 192, 193, 194, 196
Industrial Workers of the World. *See* IWW
insurrectos, 40, 46, 48, 50, 54, 55, 56, 57, 58, 63
Isais, Luis Rivas, 247, 267, 269, 270, 271, 381, 384
IWW, 61, 62, 348, 358

J

Jentzer, Harry John, 5
Johnson, L. D., 227, 228, 230, 269, 326, 355, 371, 377
Jones, Gus T. "Buster", 281, 383
Juárez, Battle of, 1911, 17, 19, 57, 58, 59, 118, 141, 142, 143, 144, 154, 158, 218, 221, 222, 226, 296
junta liberal, 16, 17, 25

K

King of Ice. *See* Morse, Charles W.
King, Richard, 73
Knickerbocker Trust Company, 6

Knox, Philander C., 42, 44, 96, 117, 159, 369
Kosterlitzky, Emilio, 224, 225, 244, 253, 265, 273, 275, 276, 280, 290, 377, 380, 382
Krakauer, Adolph, 46, 219
Krakauer, Julius, 143, 156, 219, 367
Krakauer, Robert, 219
Krakauer, Zork & Moye, 46, 115, 143, 156, 219, 221, 234, 299
Kramp, Henry C., 144, 299, 370

L

L. Frank Saddlery Company, 86, 111
La Libertad, 260
La Prensa, 252, 253
La Voz de Nuevo León, 78
Lamoreaux, Isaac F., 79, 83, 86, 91, 360, 361
Lancaster, Fred Hill, 22, 26, 27, 28, 30, 31, 32, 33, 34, 40, 46, 54, 55, 56, 57, 58, 61, 73, 75, 76, 78, 82, 84, 85, 86, 91, 105, 108, 109, 117, 119, 120, 122, 124, 160, 161, 353, 354, 355, 359, 360, 361, 363, 364, 365, 367, 369, 370
Las Antillas, 213
Lascuráin, Pedro, 174
Leavenworth Penitentiary, 64
Leckie, Cox, and Kratz, 181
León de la Barra, Francisco, 42, 59, 80, 83, 213
Lillard, George W., 180, 181, 372
Limantour, José Yves, 42
Lind, John, 180
Llorente, Enrique C., 83, 144, 145, 156, 158, 159, 218, 219, 226, 304, 345, 369
Lomelí, Antonio, 34, 54
Lomelí, Victor, 139
Longoria, Jesús M., 26, 30
López, Horacio E., 65
Los Angeles Examiner, 285

Los Angeles Times, 207, 242, 269, 280, 285, 383
Lozano, Antonio, 65

M

Macías, José, 329, 330
Madero, Alfonso, 49, 50, 51
Madero, Emilio, 296
Madero, Ernesto, 297
Madero, Francisco I., xii, 37, 38, 39, 40, 41, 42, 45, 46, 47, 48, 49, 50, 51, 55, 56, 57, 58, 59, 61, 68, 69, 71, 72, 73, 79, 80, 81, 82, 83, 85, 86, 87, 89, 91, 96, 98, 104, 105, 106, 107, 108, 110, 111, 112, 113, 115, 116, 117, 118, 119, 121, 123, 126, 127, 129, 130, 132, 133, 139, 141, 142, 143, 144, 145, 146, 147, 150, 151, 152, 154, 155, 157, 158, 162, 164, 165, 171, 173, 174, 175, 176, 192, 199, 200, 212, 213, 217, 218, 219, 220, 223, 226, 296, 297, 298, 312, 339, 345, 355, 357, 369, 385
Madero, Julio, 49, 51, 192
Madero, Raúl, 86, 192
Madison, John M. "Dynamite Slim", 57, 359
Magnón, Antonio, 76, 78, 84, 86, 94, 107, 202
magonistas, 33, 34
Mahan, John J., 160
Mahoney, D. J., 159
Mann Act, ix, xi, 11, 52, 195, 258, 259, 314, 315, 347
Manoil, James, 298
Marlin Arms Co., 209
Marquard & Co., 339, 340
Martin Pusher Airplane Company, 226
Martínez Baca, Francisco, 164
Martínez, Manuel, 27
Martínez, Paulino, 34
Mascarenas, Jr., Manuel, 127, 167, 168, 365

Mason, Paul, 57, 69
Masson, Didier, 226
Mata, Filomeno, 14
Matthews, G. Raymond, 188, 189, 190, 191, 192, 193, 194, 195, 200, 373, 374
Maurer, Ed, 47, 48, 199
Maxy, Thomas Sheldon, 129, 157, 177, 212, 219
Maxy, Thomas Sheldon, 129, 130
Mayflower, 45
Maytorena, José María, 176, 219, 226, 228, 232, 237, 255, 284, 329, 330, 345, 382
Maza, Antonio, 18
McCloskey, James Henry, 50
McCluer, L. M., 304, 305, 327, 386, 389
McDaniel, Lock, 96
McDonald, R. H. G., 159, 304
McInerny, J. R., 328
McTeague, Josefina B. de, 111
Mendieta, Justino, 246, 249, 252, 262, 263, 265, 273, 275, 276, 284, 382, 384
Mendoza, Carlos V., 65
Menger Hotel, 111, 212
Mexican Crude Rubber Company, 110
Mexican Liberal Party. See PLM
Mexican Revolution, x, xi, xii, xiii, 13, 37, 38, 49, 55, 58, 60, 66, 103, 106, 117, 147, 178, 212, 214, 238, 243, 343, 344, 346, 347, 353, 354, 395, 396, 397, 398, 399, 401
Mexico Northwestern Railway, 47
Miramón, Felipe Fortuño, 120, 121
Miranda, Manuel M., 148, 149, 150, 151, 318
Mitchell, Senator John H., 1
Moctezuma Copper Company, 126
Molina, Abraham, 87, 110, 114, 115, 118, 143, 144, 145, 156, 219
Molina, Rafael Limón, 87
Monahan, A.. See Noonan, J. H. "Jack"
Mondragón, Manuel, 172, 370
Morgan Line, 196, 197, 213, 344

411

Morgan, John Pierpont, 6
Morín, José, 105
Morín, Juan, 30
Morse, Charles W., 6, 7, 8
Mother Jones, 25
Mott, J. L., 191, 194, 195, 196, 197, 321
Munson, Lyn G., 10, 352, 353
Murray, John, 22, 25

N

Nacozari Railroad, 126
National Arms Company, 181
National Dictograph Company, 4, 352
National University Law School. See George Washington University
Navarro, Juan, 58
New York American, 63
New York Journal, 179
New York Sun, 7, 352
New York Times, 63, 342, 343, 391
Nolte, Eugene, 20, 49
Noonan, J. H. "Jack", 159, 238, 239, 240, 241, 242, 264, 265, 292
Northey, Pablo. See Northey, Paul
Northey, Paul, 189, 190, 191, 192, 193, 194, 196, 197
Núñez, Francisco, 269, 270, 278, 283, 284, 381

O

Obregón, Álvaro, 175, 295, 345, 346
Ochoa, Victor Leaton, 57, 122, 143, 144, 218, 219, 304, 305, 306, 307
Offley, William, 161, 162, 340, 343, 344, 369, 370, 386, 388, 391
Ojeda, Pedro, 224
Ojinaga, Battle of, 1914, 154, 295, 298, 308, 317
Oliver Typewriter Company, 172
Oliver, George B., 55
Ornelas, Enrique, 26, 33, 50, 51

Orozco, Jorge, 305, 306
Orozco, José, 304, 305, 306, 307
Orozco, Pascual, xii, 81, 85, 111, 119, 137, 138, 141, 142, 143, 144, 146, 148, 150, 151, 154, 155, 157, 158, 162, 163, 165, 166, 167, 168, 169, 171, 175, 200, 201, 202, 217, 218, 226, 298, 310, 311, 339, 367, 371, 386
Orozco, Sr., Pascual, 155, 163
Otis, Harrison Gray, 242, 263, 269, 275, 285, 290, 291
Otis, Marian, 242

P

Papen, Franz von, 298, 342, 391
Parker, James, 172, 179
Parker, Walter C., 110
Partido Liberal Mexicano. See PLM
Pearce Forwarding Company, 179, 181
Peden Iron & Steel Co., 209, 214
Pendleton, Forrest Currier, 195, 196, 197, 198, 311, 319, 320, 321, 373, 374, 387, 388
Pesqueira, Ignacio, 220, 226, 229
Pesqueira, Roberto, 223
Phelps-Dodge Company, 126, 128, 235
Phillips, Harvey J., 48, 123, 124, 200
Pinckney, Stephen L., 306, 310, 386, 387
Pino Suárez, José María, 173
Pío Araujo, Antonio de, 20, 23, 64
Plan de Guadalupe, 176, 226
Plan de San Antonio, 40
Plan de San Luis Potosí, 40, 48
PLM, 15, 16, 17, 19, 20, 22, 25, 29, 33, 165
Praeger Hardware Co., 211
Priest, Joseph, 21, 22, 33, 353, 354, 355
Proclamation of 1912, 326
Pryce, Caryl Rhys, 62, 63
Puebla, 67

Q

Quiroga, Miguel, 72, 74, 84, 86, 88, 93

R

Ramírez, Basilio, 30
Ramírez, José María, 23, 30
Ramos, Hector, 299, 300, 303, 304, 306, 330
Rangel, José M., 24, 26
Rasst, Leon, 334, 335, 336, 337, 338, 339, 340, 390
Rathbun, Don S., 331, 389
Ratner, Abraham, 199, 339
Ratner, José B., 199
Regeneración, 14, 15, 33, 34, 103
Reichin, Leon Moses. See Rasst, Leon
Rellano, Battle of, 146
Remington Arms Co., 191, 213, 343, 344
Republic of Baja California, 62, 63
Retana, David Reyes, 69, 84, 86, 88, 108
Revolución, 17
Reyes, Adolfo, 86
Reyes, Bernardo, 71, 72, 73, 74, 75, 76, 77, 78, 79, 80, 81, 82, 84, 85, 86, 87, 88, 89, 91, 92, 93, 95, 96, 97, 98, 99, 100, 105, 106, 107, 108, 141, 171, 173, 188, 200, 202, 219, 312, 349, 359, 360, 361, 365
Reyes, Ismael, 108
Reyes, Rodolfo, 88
Rich, John Treadway, 24
Richardson, Tracy, 142
Riley, Daniel, 21
Riley, Edward J., 185, 186, 187, 188, 190, 194, 197
Rivera, Librado, 15, 19, 25, 31, 33, 34, 165
Robelo, Ricardo Gómez, 122, 123, 365
Roberts, Powell, 129, 136, 137, 145, 220, 299
Rockefeller, John D., 6
Rodarte, María, 26, 30
Rojas Vertíz, Salvador, 148, 149, 150, 151
Roosevelt, Theodore, 1, 7, 8, 53

Root, Elihu, 17
Ross, Louis E., 84, 87, 114, 115, 118, 119, 120, 123, 124, 132, 143, 144, 145, 146, 156, 157, 158, 167, 219, 364, 365, 366, 367, 368, 369
Rough Riders, 53
Russo-Japanese war, 53

S

Salazar, José Inés, 307, 308, 309, 310, 387
San Antonio Daily Light, 120
San Jacinto, Battle of, 99
Sánchez, Amador, 75, 78, 81, 84, 85, 86, 92, 94, 97, 98, 99, 200, 315, 332
Sánchez, José R., 84, 94
Sánchez, Amador, 92, 99
Sandoval, Gerónimo, 247, 248, 249, 250, 251, 252, 256, 259, 260, 261, 287, 381
Santos Coy, Andrés, 26, 31, 33, 160
Sarabia, Juan, 15, 25, 31, 32
Sarabia, Manuel, 18, 31
Sarabia, Tomás, 24
Sawtelle, William Henry, 234, 326
Schoonover, Albert, 242, 245, 257, 258, 264, 266, 267, 269, 271, 273, 274, 277, 278, 280, 281, 282, 283, 284, 285, 288, 380, 383, 384
Scull, Guy Hamilton, 28, 29, 50, 51, 52, 53, 54, 354, 356, 357
Scully, Charles Joseph, 45, 47, 48, 340, 343, 344, 356, 391
Secret Service. See US Secret Service
Segura y Martínez, Vicente, 151, 152, 153, 154, 184, 185, 186, 187, 188, 189, 190, 191, 192, 193, 196, 197, 372, 373
Sheldon Hotel, 56
Shelton-Payne, 46, 48, 143, 151, 178, 205, 219, 220, 221, 234, 235, 299, 305, 319, 344
Silva, Benjamín G., 23, 30
Silva, Priciliano G., 23

413

Simmons, F. D., 39, 61, 64, 65, 66, 355, 358
SMS Dresden, 341, 345
Snyder, Virgil L., 144, 156, 157
Solomon, T. M., 320, 321
Sommerfeld, Felix A., 55, 56, 82, 83, 84, 85, 87, 89, 91, 95, 96, 97, 118, 131, 132, 142, 144, 158, 168, 201, 212, 215, 298, 299, 313, 317, 320, 345, 355, 357, 360, 361, 362, 385
Sonora, 67, 175, 176, 181, 190
Spanish-American War, 47, 53
Spates, Webster, 203, 204, 215, 374, 375, 376
SS Dunkeld, 67
Stallforth, Frederico, 298, 385
Stauffer, Eshleman & Co., 67, 148, 149, 197
Staver, W. C., 183, 318
Stevens, Charles, 79
Stone, Edward B., 271, 272, 274, 279, 281, 282, 382, 383
Stratton, William P. "Red", 56
Sunmount Sanitorium, 24

T

Taft, William Howard, 7, 8, 27, 96, 97, 98, 99, 117, 137, 142, 166, 173, 370
Tailhook scandal, 6
Tampico News Company, 199
Tauscher, Hans, 298
Terrazas, Alberto, 165
Terrazas, Luis, 165
Texas National Guard, 72, 182
Texas Rangers, 41, 46
The FBI Story, 102, 362
The Posse Comitatus Act, 49
The Union Metallic Cartridge Company. See Remington Arms Co.
Theoharis, Athan, 102, 362
Thiel Detective Agency, 46, 60, 114, 115, 126, 135, 136, 144, 356

Thompson, Fred D., 205
Thompson, Hy A., 58, 59, 60, 64, 72, 73, 77, 78, 79, 80, 81, 82, 83, 84, 85, 86, 88, 91, 92, 95, 97, 98, 100, 104, 106, 107, 109, 110, 111, 112, 113, 114, 115, 116, 117, 118, 119, 120, 122, 123, 124, 125, 130, 131, 132, 133, 134, 138, 146, 155, 156, 159, 160, 161, 163, 174, 183, 195, 200, 202, 212, 213, 214, 215, 216, 217, 233, 234, 235, 312, 317, 345, 356, 358, 359, 360, 361, 362, 363, 364, 365, 366, 367, 368, 369, 370, 371, 372, 373, 374, 375, 376, 377, 378, 379
Times-Democrat, 311
Tinker, Edward Laroque, 42, 45
Treasury Department, 1, 5
Treviño, Gerónimo, 77
Treviño, Juan García, xiii
Treviño, Leocadio B., 23, 85
Trippet, Oscar, 264, 292
Trowbridge, Elizabeth D., 31
Tufts-Lyons Sporting Goods House, 246
Turner, John Kenneth, 25, 33, 34

U

U.S. Rubber Corporation, 44
Ullman, Stern and Krause, 178
US Secret Service, xi, 1, 2, 3, 4, 5, 6, 8, 21, 28, 29, 56, 60, 115, 180, 206, 217, 332, 349, 351, 353, 367

V

Vann, John W., 27, 33, 34, 144, 354, 355
Varcoe, Charles George, 280
Vasconcelos, José, 42
Vázquez Gómez, Emilio, 104, 105, 106, 108, 109, 110, 111, 112, 113, 118, 119, 120, 122, 124, 125, 127, 138, 141, 142, 143, 166, 171, 174, 189, 200, 312, 367
Vázquez Gómez, Francisco, 42
Vázquez, Ildefonso, 72

Veracruz, Occupation of, 1914, 14, 76, 171, 295, 313, 330, 334, 336, 341, 342, 343
Viljoen, Benjamin Johannis, 57, 237, 241, 243, 248, 249, 250, 251, 252, 253, 254, 255, 256, 260, 263, 266, 274, 275, 280, 381
Villa, Francisco "Pancho", xii, 218, 221, 222, 237, 243, 244, 245, 246, 254, 255, 260, 278, 286, 295, 296, 297, 298, 299, 300, 303, 305, 306, 308, 314, 317, 320, 329, 330, 344, 345, 346, 385, 391
Villa, Hipólito, 296
Villar, Lauro, 81
Villarreal González, Andrea, 31
Villarreal, Antonio I., 15, 17, 19, 20, 25, 31, 32, 33, 34
Villarreal, Severo, 84
Villarreal, Teresa, 32
Villavicencio, Francisco, 80
Villavicencio, Francisco R., 200, 211, 217, 311, 312

W

Warmbold, Beatrice, 108, 109
Washington Evening Star, 102, 362
Washington Post, 110
Webster, F. P., 238, 239, 240, 241, 243, 244, 245, 246, 247, 248, 249, 253, 256, 258, 260, 261, 262, 263, 264, 265, 266, 267, 268, 269, 271, 278, 279, 282, 283, 284, 286, 289, 290, 379, 380, 381, 382, 383, 384
Wells Fargo Express, 227
Western Cartridge Company, 298
Western Detective Agency, 144, 156
White Slave Traffic Act. *See* Mann Act
Whiting, Alice, 84, 91
Wickersham, George W., viii, 8, 9, 22, 33, 97, 98, 99, 102, 158, 369

Wilbur, John C., 49, 50, 51, 52, 59, 72, 73, 74, 77, 78, 356, 359
Williamson, John N., 1
Wilson, Henry Lane, 173, 174, 180, 197, 370, 371
Wilson, Woodrow, 98, 99, 295, 297, 319, 326, 339, 342, 346, 391
Winchester Repeating Arms Co., 162, 196
Winkleman, J. H.. *See* Zogg, Nicolas Senn
Wolters, Jacob F. "Jake", 91, 93
Womack, J. D., 51
Wood, Leonard, 53
Wren, John Killian, 221, 299, 321, 377, 385, 386, 387, 389

Y

Ypiranga, 295, 334, 340, 341, 342, 390, 391

Z

Zaldívar Cervantes, Viviano, 105
Zapata, Emiliano, xii, 41, 105, 124, 141, 142, 171, 175, 295, 312, 345, 365, 367
Zaragoza, 311, 390
Zogg, Nicolas Senn, 289, 290, 291